The Psychology of Contemporary Art

While recent studies in neuroscience and psychology have shed light on our sensory and perceptual experiences of art, they have yet to explain how contemporary art downplays perceptual responses and, instead, encourages conceptual thought. *The Psychology of Contemporary Art* brings together the most important developments in recent scientific research on visual perception and cognition and applies the results of empirical experiments to analyses of contemporary artworks not normally addressed by psychological studies. The author explains, in simple terms, how neuroaesthetics, embodiment, metaphor, conceptual blending, situated cognition and extended mind offer fresh perspectives on specific contemporary artworks – including those of Marina Abramović, Francis Alÿs, Martin Creed, Tracy Emin, Felix Gonzales-Torres, Marcus Harvey, Mona Hatoum, Thomas Hirschorn, Gabriel Orozco, Marc Quinn and Cindy Sherman. This book will appeal to psychologists, cognitive scientists, artists and art historians, as well as those interested in a deeper understanding of contemporary art.

Gregory Minissale is a Senior Lecturer in the Department of Art History at the University of Auckland where he teaches contemporary art and theory. He is the author of *Framing Consciousness in Art* (2009) and *Images of Thought* (2006).

The Psychology of Contemporary Art

Gregory Minissale

CAMBRIDGE
UNIVERSITY PRESS

CAMBRIDGE
UNIVERSITY PRESS

University Printing House, Cambridge CB2 8BS, United Kingdom

Published in the United States of America by Cambridge University Press, New York

Cambridge University Press is part of the University of Cambridge.

It furthers the University's mission by disseminating knowledge in the pursuit of education, learning, and research at the highest international levels of excellence.

www.cambridge.org
Information on this title: www.cambridge.org/9781107019324

First published 2013

Printing in the United Kingdom by TJ International Ltd. Padstow Cornwall

A catalogue record for this publication is available from the British Library

ISBN 978-1-107-01932-4 Hardback

Cambridge University Press has no responsibility for the persistence or accuracy of URLs for external or third-party internet websites referred to in this publication, and does not guarantee that any content on such websites is, or will remain, accurate or appropriate.

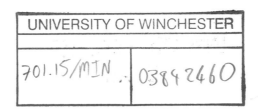

For my mother, Pat Bird, kind above all others

Contents

Contents

Figures

Preface

Contemporary art can be absorbing, challenging and sometimes infuriating. *The Psychology of Contemporary Art* examines the cognitive psychology of these responses and shows how artworks trigger them. The approach taken here brings together domains of knowledge that rarely meet: cognitive psychology and contemporary art history and theory. It steers through polar extremes in psychology: on the one hand, strong embodiment theories that imply that all knowledge is derived from sensory perceptions and, on the other, the cognitive psychology of abstract concepts implying the 'disembodied' logic of cognition. It aims to do this by showing how contemporary artworks provide situations where emotions, sensory perceptions and concepts combine in unique ways to structure meaning.

The Psychology of Contemporary Art looks at a broad range of contemporary artworks in order to show how meaning creation involves a dynamic complexity of different thoughts and feelings. This, in effect, means relying on a variety of explanatory models and theories about cognition, embodiment and situatedness, sometimes integrating or moderating these, not because the synthesis of approaches is in itself an aim but because this pragmatic and open approach seems best suited to account for the power of contemporary artworks to absorb us in many variable ways. The book shows how this absorption is arranged by ad hoc combinations of concepts, accompanied by sensory and emotional processes – an improvisation that an artwork's complex system of signs helps to sustain.

Artists, art historians and lovers of art might ask why they should be concerned with psychology. The short answer is that psychology has developed sophisticated approaches to understanding how we group concepts together in order to create different kinds of relational knowledge. However, these approaches have not yet been applied to the study of contemporary art. A contemporary artist will bring together a body of work over a period of time, or a group of works in an exhibition. Many of these works will reference other artists' works. We also often read books that bring together collections of artworks. While we regard an artwork as a stand-alone object with unique features, these features can point to this web of artworks creating a system of relational knowledge that elaborates perceptions, concepts, emotions and memories quickly and automatically. Equipped with the systematicity of psychological approaches, this book analyses relational knowledge of this kind and makes its sensory and conceptual structures explicit, providing fresh perspectives on how art encourages creative thought, problem solving and metacognition.

The intricate and rapidly deployed association of concepts involved in creative thought and problem solving exercises the imagination both for artists producing works of art and for viewers interpreting them. While it is true that, as individuals, we can create very different concepts about the same works of art, to do so we must recall concepts we are already familiar with, take the time to explore them, and sometimes reorder them and adjust them in the light of new experience. If we stop to think about it, we are being creative in these situations, and art often encourages this. If only we knew how to become more aware of our concepts and how we combine them, we might be able to appreciate exactly how creative we are when we experience art; we might also use this creativity at will for many other situations in life. This creativity in viewing demonstrates that we are never just passive consumers of images.

From the point of view of psychology, this book provides an evaluation of well-known models of conceptual integration used to explain how relational knowledge is built up, and suggests that such knowledge is supported by the cooperation of a wide range of resources distributed across the brain and body as well as situations in the world. A work of art is a situation that applies various constraints on the emergence of thoughts, actions, feelings and sensations; it can also encourage us to reflect on these constraints. The psychology involved in the production and reception of contemporary art represents an important opportunity to understand how we construct new knowledge about ourselves and the world we live in today.

There are many examples in art where we 'see' concepts intended by the artist even though they are not, in fact, visible. These concepts are pieced together by the viewer from various perceptual cues in the artwork. Whether it is the interlocking colours and forms of the Sistine Chapel ceiling that suggest an intricate dance through history, the harsh lighting and broken glass of Picasso's *Guernica* assaulting beauty, or Damien Hirst's disquieting cows in formaldehyde that transform art's aesthetic tryst with death into a laboratory, slaughterhouse or freak show, works of art may arouse our wonder or ire. They can also command our rapt attention and commitment. This kind of engagement is sustained by a rapidly multiplying network of concepts, the intricate emergence of which goes largely unnoticed by us as we lose ourselves in the intensity of the moment. Somewhat surprisingly, the elaborate substructure of concepts involved in the simulations that artworks provide remains largely unmapped by science and art.

Art history and aesthetics have helped us understand our emotional attachment to the textures, colours, stories and myths of art and the characters they depict, and they have sensitised us to the social and political settings these artworks appear to reflect. These disciplines have also shown us how we form ethical responses to art. Meanwhile, neuroscience and the psychology of art have shed some light on how our brains process the colour, form, rhythm and tactile qualities of art, and they have explained the role of evolutionary processes in our responses to faces, gestures and bodies. These scientific investigations have elucidated many other sensory and perceptual responses involved in viewing art, yet they have not shown us how the process of becoming absorbed by art is premised on the creative and dynamic integration of concepts in complex networks.

This book is not about measuring the beauty of art by examining and comparing its colours and forms and our responses to them, or about defining the variety of its functions or laws, as is the case with more traditional art history, aesthetics and science. At no point does this book suggest that individuals in different periods and cultures interpret art in the same way. However, it does attempt to explain how our responses to art can be variable and psychologically complex. This book looks at the number of ways in which we connect memories, sensations, concepts and emotions – connections that are often inspired by the perceptual cues of the artwork. This complexity of response can be relatively orderly and measured, or passionate and even chaotic. Sometimes we take a particular kind of pleasure from producing concepts and relations between concepts, which may bring to rest our effort after meaning. Alternatively, we might enjoy concepts that inflame us or move and enthral us in a struggle for meaning that we do not seem to win. Other works leave us cold or annoyed either through a lack of familiarity or an over-familiarity with their themes. While recent studies in neuroscience and psychology have shed light on our sensory and perceptual responses to art, they have not shown how our engagement with an artwork, both in contextualising it within our broader knowledge of art and in the novel thoughts and feelings that can arise from this encounter, draws upon our abilities to creatively integrate concepts and to upload them into larger wholes.

Because neuroscientific approaches are intent at looking at the formal and perceptible qualities found in traditional and modernist art, from

Michelangelo to Mondrian, contemporary artworks that emphasise references to a conceptually rich prior knowledge rather than the immediate rewards of perceptual exploration are often overlooked.[1] Such art has frequently been misunderstood as the acquired taste of an educated elite. Even if largely neglected by science, such art presents an important opportunity for us to understand the nature of our conceptual thought as it engages with many different kinds of art. Cognitive science and psychology need to be informed by trends in contemporary art that provide an emphasis on conceptual production rather than the formalism of traditional aesthetics that serves as the basis for most empirical studies. Artworks in all periods, cultures and forms reference prior knowledge. An artwork is able to facilitate the interplay of emotional chords with various knowledge structures, often causing us to repay the artwork with judgements about how well they are able to do this. There are a great many reasons why people become fully engaged by artworks and this book examines some of the psychological mechanisms that typically support different kinds of absorption in art. Such an experience of absorption will undoubtedly depend on integrating some or all of the following: conceptual blending, long-term memory and relational knowledge, rational induction, analogical reasoning, proprioceptive and embodied experience, and emotional and sensory integration. This book focuses on how particular contemporary artworks situate and constrain these different kinds of integration.

While this book helps to map the manner in which concepts emerge in our encounters with contemporary art, I will also show how this analysis allows us to look again at some key examples of art from different periods, demonstrating the wide applicability of this approach. Although conceptual networks underlie the experience of all kinds of art, it is contemporary art, particularly conceptual art, which treats conceptual production and categorisation as explicit themes.

---

[1] This is so even in the work of Cupchik et al. (2009) and Leder et al. (2004, 2006), whose work on contemporary art, mainly painting, is framed by notions of traditional aesthetics, style and the appearance of artworks rather than specific processes of conceptual combinations involved in art interpretation, which I attempt here. There has been some treatment of Duchamp's L. H. O. O. Q. by Solso (2003) in terms of how we form a cognitive set to be able to read art, which Solso calls schemata. This excellent introduction to art, however, mainly deals with perception, not conceptual production. Among a plethora of examples from pre-twentieth century art, Stafford (2007) occasionally turns to some contemporary artworks while ignoring many important themes of such art, particularly the anti-formalism of conceptualism, readymades and other aspects of Duchamp's legacy. The cognitive psychology of conceptual production, which is well placed to address many of these themes, is also ignored.

Conceptual art is a loosely historical term referring to the works of artists, musicians, filmmakers and writers in the 1960s and 1970s, often directly or indirectly referencing Duchamp's work. Themes identified with conceptual art may be found before and after this period, running through Dada, Pop and Neo-Dada to contemporary art. At the risk of simplification, it brings together non-art objects ('readymades') that appear to have no author, purpose or artistic process behind them. Conceptual themes challenge traditional notions of beauty and formal design, artistic dexterity, aesthetic composition, and technique and authorship – the qualities that neuroaesthetics and psychology examine in detail in order to understand the brain and its interactions with art.

One might object that many of these examples are 'anti-art' even though they continue to be celebrated as art in the history books and galleries, and are considered as such by artists and philosophers.[2] It has been argued that conceptual and contemporary art stimulates us, that it has cognitive or metacognitive value: it allows us to reflect on our cogitations (Carroll, 2006; Gaut, 2006); some find such art to be thought provoking, entertaining or puzzling, and still others find the stripping down of perceptible qualities in conceptual artworks witty, challenging or perverse. It has been ventured that the aesthetic content of such art can be compared to the elegance of a mathematical proof (Goldie and Schellekens, 2010, p. 102). It is also possible that art of this type presents us with 'thought experiments': counterfactuals that rely on imaginative simulations that add cognitive as well as aesthetic value to our lives (Currie, 2006; Gaut, 2006). Yet others, such as Larmarque (2006), question whether cognitive value (when construed as a truth–value) is an essential feature of art. It is not the case that contemporary art *must* have cognitive value or reveal the truth for it to be art. It is true, however, that contemporary art often does provide cognitive value, and I am interested in exploring how this cognition is structured psychologically and how we read the signs to arrive at these judgements. It is possible to argue that this structuring creates artistic, pleasurable, beautiful or cognitive values but it is not the primary purpose of this book to argue that these processes help us to distinguish art from non-art.

It is hoped that a consideration of contemporary art, instead of the traditional art forms usually studied by science, will encourage neuroaesthetics and psychology to take into account large-scale neural events such as conceptual integration and relational knowledge that cooperate with perceptions in visual experience. By providing this wider cognitive

---

[2] See various scholars supporting this view in Goldie and Schellekens (2007).

Figure 1. Mona Hatoum, *Keffiyeh*, 1993–1999 (human hair on cotton fabric, 120 x 120 cm). Courtesy of the artist. Photograph by Agostino Osio. Courtesy of Fondazione Querini Stampalia, Venice.

context, which contemporary art clearly demands, we stand a much better chance of understanding our varied and subtle experiences of art. Keeping this wider context in mind, this book offers multiple levels of explanation, incorporating studies of perceptual processes in art foregrounded by the sciences, which suggest a partial view of aesthetic experience, and balances this with research into concrete and abstract concepts constrained by the 'external marks' of art. Such an integrated and pluralistic approach promises to give us insights into how neurological events, embodied action and social and cultural situations cooperate in producing different kinds of conceptual content.

In this book, I will interpret artworks using the following four approaches:

A Formal and technical approaches: the analysis of composition including details of facture
B Psychological and phenomenological approaches: how we come to understand an artwork's import
C Social context, along with biographical, political and cultural specificities that surround the artwork or can otherwise be associated with it
D Relational knowledge: how an artwork references other artworks and art historical traditions and theories

These approaches can overlap.[3] For example, the following description of an artwork uses the four approaches listed. Mona Hatoum's *Keffiyeh*, 1993–1999, is a white cloth embroidered with human hair in the pattern associated with the Palestinian struggle and dealing with her own diaspora identity. It appears delicate and fragile. The fact that it is human hair creates an affect, as does its soft, tactile quality. The laborious sewing technique requires patience and determination, the hair has to grow to be sewn in. We construct anthropomorphisms (this analysis draws upon approaches A, B and C). The work activates a series of related concepts (scripts or schemata) to do with cloth or wearing cloth. It is also a strange kind of pun that the *keffiyeh* is a male headdress; Hatoum's version suggests a wig to be worn on the head. In thinking about the idea of woven cloth, we imagine some of the sensorimotor actions needed to weave it. There is also a set of ideas associated with hair: strength, beauty, sacrifice, washing feet with hair, Samson and Delilah, knotted hair, tearing out hair, producing feelings of anxiety (B, D). This work, and many other works by the artist, uses the grid form. This reminds us of the modernist grid popular in the art of the 1960s, which was often used to question the artwork as a personal gesture by substituting dehumanising, repetitive work, also emptying the work of content in the pursuit of the high modernist ideals of formalism. The work is thus ironic as it balances formalist concerns with affect and political content, here also linked to women's work: sewing and quilt making that became symbols of feminist art in the 1970s and 1980s. The latter move was meant as a foil to the 'masculine' gaze of high art, where women's bodies are seen as objects from which to derive pleasure (A, C, D); in Hatoum's work, a woman's body is signified by the use of her hair in the artwork and as a vehicle for political protest. Many of these concepts and approaches are integrated in the artist's statement about this work: 'I imagined women pulling their hair out in anger and controlling that anger through the patient act of transcribing those same strands of hair into an everyday item of clothing that has become a potent symbol of the Palestinian resistance movement. The act of embroidering can be seen in this case as another language, a kind of quiet protest.'[4]

---

[3] It might also be said that phenomenology, which seeks to understand the human mind across times and cultures, is at odds with historical specificity. Yet these different disciplines can be brought to bear on an interpretation of an artwork as mutually constraining, contrasting views, or by positing the historical specificity of certain phenomenal, third-person accounts or by showing that certain historical periodisations are driven by phenomenal and affective perspectives.

[4] Interview with Mark Francis for the brochure accompanying *Images from Elsewhere* exhibition at Fig-1 (50 Projects in 50 weeks), London, 2000.

It must be noted that all of these approaches and the way they overlap may be analysed from cognitive psychological perspectives, especially if part of this analysis includes social and emotional psychology as well as aspects of situated cognition. This book is informed by these four different approaches and explains how we often apply them tacitly in our encounters with art.

Recent studies in psychology on 'situated cognition', the study of how social and cultural contexts affect psychology, either have largely neglected the context of art or have little detail to offer us as to how, exactly, we integrate concepts in conjunction with the perceptual experience of the artwork. This is an important mapping process to which I will turn my attention in later pages. Studies of situated cognition employ mainly social and lexical examples that contextualise psychological events.[5]

The pluralistic approach of this book represents an attempt to drive a course through two warring factions. On the one hand are those sympathetic to aesthetic empiricism (Kieran, 2004), which emphasises the perceptible details of artworks (intrinsic properties of the artwork) that are conceived of as its contents (accessed largely through 'direct perception'). On the other hand is the contextualist approach (Danto, 1964; Dickie, 1984/1997), much favoured by conceptual and contemporary art, which emphasises knowledge strictly extrinsic to the artwork, allowing such perceptible features to be seen as clues to other nonpresent artworks or to aspects of cultural tradition. These factors can influence how direct perception unfolds and, indeed, what is actually perceived. The aim here is to show how a synthesis of art historical and psychological approaches can reveal the important role context plays in the processing of the perceptible details of contemporary art, and also how perceptual details of the artwork activate conceptual relations and categories. Importantly, such a hybrid strategy can also show how these details guide, constrain and help to order contextual knowledge assembled for particular encounters with artworks.

This is not to say that it is not important to enjoy the sensuous details of art, but it is clearly not the case that an artwork's perceptible details always have to be treated thematically *qua* perceptible qualities rather than as aids

---

[5] See, for example, Mesquita et al. (2010). Myin and Veldman (2011) and Pepperell (2011) deal generally with the principles of what a situated aesthetics might entail but fail to provide details of how conceptual, attentional, affective or semantic complexity come together in the processing of external cues in specific artworks. What is missing is the kind of detailed matching exercise between internal resources and the specific details of artworks that conceptual blending and structure mapping can provide, and which I attempt to show in later pages.

in thinking about other things. In fact, with many contemporary artworks, as we shall see, we are encouraged to switch from thematic perceptual processing to perceptual processing as a function of a larger conceptual task; either use of perceptible properties may be pleasurable and co-present. The ability to balance sensations with complex conceptual systems possibly may turn out to be an important way to ascertain the aesthetic status of an artwork, but this is an argument best left for the philosophy of art.

Normally, we are not even conscious of how we process line and colour and, indeed, most people are not aware of this processing unless the work of art is abstract, where lines and colours are all that seem to fill the visual field. Interestingly, while we naturally suppress knowledge of our processes of shape recognition and colour identification, especially while we attend to other aspects of a work of art, for example when trying to interpret the story it might convey, we also tend to ignore the unfolding story of our conceptual production. Contemporary art consistently encourages us to combine concepts not normally brought together in everyday life, as we have seen with Hatoum's *Keffiyeh*. As thought experiments or counterfactuals, contemporary artworks give us the time to reflect on these unusual encounters rather than relegating them to the realm of idle or random thought rarely held in the memory. We often credit the artwork for making these new conceptual combinations, although we are the agents that actually experience the connections, but this transference from our interpretative faculties to the artwork raises its value in our eyes.

This book attempts to provide ways of raising awareness of the underlying psychology of our often tacitly exercised system of values and relational knowledge, which is definitive of the art experience for many artists and viewers, but which may otherwise remain implicit. I try to do this, firstly, by evaluating various models of conceptual combination in cognitive psychology and, secondly, by examining in depth processes of conceptual and perceptual integration guided by the coded details of contemporary artworks that we can learn to read. The aim is to show how the perceptual cues found in art provide lines of flight, a joining of the dotted lines suggesting how seemingly incongruous concepts might come together. This focus can also help us, consciously, to report on this process.

We remember the general opinions we have of certain kinds of art, but often we fail to consider how we come to acquire them. We remain ignorant of how different combinations of concepts, different routes on the conceptual map, lead us to seeing works of art from a rich variety of perspectives. While this is how art historians should, and most often do, proceed, this process tends to be automatic. This book aims to make explicit the conceptual production involved in thinking about art. What makes the large and densely patterned edifice of conceptual thought invisible to us and to art history is the fact that it is often constituted not so much from visible, perceptible 'things' depicted in works of art but from the relations between them. We can easily understand this if, for example, we take a painting that depicts furniture in a room, objects on a table, or a collection of books on the shelf. These objects may come together to describe an individual's personality, her interests, or her social standing, and even though she is not visible, we can build up a picture of her identity, or an event (she sat here, she read a book, she ate her food, she left). Such a picture is structured as a system of relations of perceptual cues.

The relations between objects (either lexical or visual) need not be based on a network of single, discrete objects. Sometimes in art, even in one work, we map a series of relations premised on several collections of things, each collection containing a number of smaller objects. In other words, if we go back to the example of a painting, it is possible to build up a picture of several identities or events from the relations of *groups* of things rather than simple objects; the Sistine Chapel and its marshalling together of bodies and forces in groups and areas again springs to mind. In many kinds of art, this is not only commonplace but also definitive of the richness of the experience of being deeply engaged in a work of art, an experience that has a large part to play in our feelings about how art is powerful or transformative. Yet the density of the visual field is not necessary for the complexity of a conceptual network attending it. The apparent simplicity of a Brancusi sculpture of a soaring bird, the fluent lines of a Japanese watercolour of a mountain pass, or the lightly carved handle of a Mughal jade cup in the form of a sinuous, leafy stem can trigger cascades of concepts that seem to vibrate and flow along the lines suggested by the works themselves, trailing off beyond them.

Acknowledgements

Many thanks are due to the University of Auckland, Faculty of the Arts, for providing funds for a research assistant, image copyright and reproduction fees and travel abroad to the Venice Biennale and other research trips where many ideas contained in this book were hatched. I would also like to thank all my colleagues in the Art History department, Professor Elizabeth Rankin, Associate Professor Ian Buchanan, Associate Professor Len Bell, Dr Erin Griffey, Dr Robin Woodward, Dr Ngarino Ellis, Dr Donald Bassett, Lyn Oppenheim, Lloma Yong, Sonya Tuimaseve and Jane Percival, who have gone out of their way to make me feel at home in New Zealand. Dr Caroline Vercoe deserves special mention for being a visionary, creative and inspiring leader and mentor; I would like to thank her for her expert guidance in teaching, supervising and research, important aspects of which have found their way into the pages of this book.

I am extremely grateful to Distinguished Professor Stephen Davies, University of Auckland, Professor Emeritus John Onians, University of East Anglia and Professor Gerry Cupchik, University of Toronto – all have been very generous and supportive in reading and commenting on earlier drafts. Thanks also to Associate Professor of Psychology Tony Lambert, University of Auckland, Associate Professor Bob Wicks and Dr David Angluin for many interesting and useful conversations on perceptual psychology and philosophy. I would like to thank Cambridge University Press, in particular Hetty Marx, Commissioning Editor for Psychology and Carrie Parkinson, Editor, Politics, Sociology and Psychology, Sarah Payne, Production Editor and Jeanette Mitchell, copy-editor, who have been extremely helpful and supportive in editing and preparing the manuscript.

For proofreading the manuscript, my deepest thanks to Firuza Pastakia, a gifted writer, professional editor and friend who has enriched my life in many ways since we met in Karachi in 1990. A special thanks, also, to Victoria Wynne-Jones, my research assistant, who has helped enormously with the copyright enquiries, image lists and indexes.

I would like to thank many artists, foundations and galleries that have supported me in this project by providing images: Sir Anthony Caro,

Annie Cattrell, Tracey Emin, Marcus Harvey, Mona Hatoum, Norma Jeane, Brian Jungen, Alain Kahn-Sriber, Dane Mitchell, Yasumasa Morimora, Kate Newby, Gabriel Orozco, Jenny Saville, Cindy Sherman, Francis Upritchard, Joana Vasconcelos, The Carnegie Museum of Art, The Collection Mony Vibescu, The Gagosian Gallery, The Felix Gonzales-Torres Foundation, Manchester City Galleries, The Gallery Max Hetzler, The Museum of Modern Art, New York, The Saatchi Collection, White Cube, Tate Britain and, most of all, Zanele Muholi who gave me permission to use her moving and inspiring work for the book cover.

The work would never have seen the light of day without the help and support of Malcolm Sired. I would like to thank him for his faith in me, and not least, for producing many of the book's elegant line drawings and illustrations.

Eight major trends in contemporary art

If philosophers were ever inclined to agree on a definition of contemporary art, I have no doubt that some of the trends introduced here would count towards that definition, and some, perhaps, might be discarded. My aim is not to provide a definition of contemporary art. For the purposes of this book, I shall deal only with recognised artists and artworks that are treated as such by authors in journal essays, monographs, encyclopaedia entries, galleries and museums. This is not to say that I subscribe to the theory of an institutional definition of art, but this is a necessary way of delimiting the material. Nevertheless, given the nature of how the contemporary is in constant flux, many of the trends listed here may be ephemeral while some are likely to endure: trends in the 'contemporary' art of tomorrow are bound to be different. Perhaps one way to avoid the essentialism of attributing features and properties to art or, more particularly, contemporary art is to compare it to the 'Ship of Theseus'. Theseus' ship, embarking on a journey from its home port after several years and after many repairs, was eventually replaced, plank by plank, and was no longer physically the same ship that returned to its port of origin, although for all intents and purposes, it was still the 'Ship of Theseus'.

People generally understand that contemporary art is produced 'today', anywhere in the world, including 'recent' work of the last thirty years or so. One of the reasons why the period is imprecise is that, if a work of art produced decades ago still seems to be 'relevant', fresh and important, a Richard Serra work for example, it can generally be referred to as 'contemporary'. This is obviously arbitrary and some might say that only work produced in the last ten years should be counted as 'contemporary', yet this may also be equally arbitrary. This theme of 'newness' is, of course, a tangled web that contemporary art often addresses, and may be related to what the philosopher Badiou insists is one of contemporary art's main functions: to create new possibilities which, presumably, also includes the possibility of thinking a new art, beyond the novelty of forms

(Badiou, 2004). The underlying ways in which this newness is conceptualised by different artists, and implied by contemporary art's appropriation of traditional art, will be examined in later pages.

The following is a list of trends in contemporary art that I will address in later chapters. It is not an exhaustive list and the trends identified are dealt with in some artworks and absent in others; some of them are not even exclusive to the category of contemporary art. The list is meant as an open-ended, flexible list that I hope will make prominent a few key areas consistently distinguished from the general visual world by studies of contemporary art.

1 Much of contemporary art is surprising or has shock value, exploring taboo subjects (Gilbert and George, Marcus Harvey, Damien Hirst, Robert Mapplethorpe, Paul McCarthy, Chris Offili, Mark Quinn, Andres Serrano) and deliberately offending aesthetic convictions based on pleasure and reward, unity and coherence, morality and beauty. Yet sometimes it reconfigures these conventions in unconventional ways. Contemporary art need not be functional or beautiful; in fact, it often seems senseless, ugly or neurotic. It is up to the viewer to find value from contemporary art's rupture of traditional art categories, rationalism and aesthetic emotions. The freedom of the imagination is valorised,[1] as is the ability to shock us out of our comfort zone, and to test what is permissible in terms of social mores.

2 Contemporary art often has an ambiguous relationship to the art market because of the tension between the need to be avant-garde (Burger, 1984) or to reinvent formal and aesthetic qualities. Some contemporary artists see art as shackled to 'trends': the underlying principle of capitalist production and advertising where products embrace novelty, gimmicks or sensationalism in the pursuit of profit. It is thus seen as being parasitic upon yet critical of corporate culture, mass icons, brands, and the news and entertainment. It often makes us aware of our acculturated responses to these things. Contemporary art often critiques yet is also complicit with art as corporate business, where the status of the art object as a commodity and the artist as celebrity become subjects of art most often with irony, frequently employing the notion of kitsch (see Jeff Koon's *Michael Jackson with Bubbles*, porcelain with gold lustre, 2001, or his many large public sculptures that ape cheap, brightly coloured balloons twisted into animal shapes). Such work, indebted to Pop Art, places

---

[1] Badiou speaks of a kind of poetic liberty of contemporary art beyond the rational democratic kind of liberty.

value on creating problems for instant recognition, suggesting simulacra, stimulating reality checking and raising questions about aesthetic relevance, sometimes oddly, succeeding in reinstating this in unexpected or uncanny ways (Cai Guo-Qiang, Damien Hirst, Yayoi Kushama).

3 In contrast to the previous trend, contemporary art may be site specific, deliberately placed outside of the gallery's domain. Some 'happenings' or works of performance art may consist of one-off events (Marina Abramović, Vito Acconci, Banksy, Joseph Beuys, Marcel Broodthaers, Fluxus events, Hans Haacke) that are subsequently known to us through photographs, continuing the theme of the 'dematerialization of the art object' (Lippard, 1973). Other such works involve amateur volunteers or the general public in long-term projects that involve no tangible artworks but only acts or social interactions (Spencer Tunick), but also self-documentation, role-play, simulation (Sophie Calle, Oleg Kulik); artworks that seem intangible, ephemeral, vanishing into the ether (Robert Barry, Martin Creed, Santiago Sierra). This continues with land and environment art (Francis Alÿs, Richard Long, Robert Smithson) where the artist's trace and the structures built to dissolve into nature's processes or into the landscape (Ana Mendieta) convey concepts to do with transience and entropy. Meanwhile, the Belgian artist, Wim Delvoye, set up an 'Art Farm' in Beijing where he raised pigs and tattooed them, turning animals into live art outside the white cube of the gallery space.

4 It is an important aspect of many contemporary artworks that they are social, providing a place or time for discursive and intersubjective exchanges, allowing viewers to take up a variety of roles and to communicate and negotiate difference (Francis Alÿs, Jacob Dahlgren, Rirkrit Tiravanija). Some contemporary art attempts to facilitate a sense of agency for the viewer in creating meaning as a social communication, parodies this or attempts meaninglessness (in order to show the importance of agency). Some artists have assistants (Damien Hirst) and relinquish control in terms of letting viewers rearrange or compose the artwork from material provided by the artist (Norma Jeane, Allan Kaprow). There are many 'situations' designed by artists that involve viewer participation that becomes the 'material' of the artwork. Many of the examples in this tendency challenge traditional notions that it is the brain, primarily, that is the causal aspect of art: indeed, art that enhances complex social engagements with the world shows that cognition is supported, affected and even extended by aspects of the environment. This kind of art has been dubbed 'participative' art (Bishop, 2006) and is related to the theorist Nicholas Bourriaud's 'relational aesthetics' (1998).

5 Some examples or aspects of contemporary art stimulate or explore themes related to the body. This involves staging situations centred on

the body of the performer in collusion with the audience, in works that explore abjection, pain and fear, as well as forms of ritual masochism and sadism (Marina Abramović, Ron Athey, Gina Pane). In sculpture and photography this means focusing on bodily functions and processes using blood (Zanele Muholi, Mark Quinn), faeces (Wim Delvoye, Piero Manzoni, Andres Serrano), seminal fluid (Marcel Duchamp), and/or juxtaposing these with questions of purpose, functionality or meaningfulness. Contemporary artworks employ irony, parody or absurdity to displace gut feelings and reactions, fears about the body and disease (Hannah Wilke), and they sometimes function as a kind of therapy (Bob Flanagan). Contemporary art often explores automatic emotional, sensory and perceptual responses to the body and its natural processes, sometimes using human tissue in the facture of the artwork (Mona Hatoum, Orlan, Mark Quinn). Related to this, artworks engage with contemporary science such as robotics, biotechnology, cloning, genetics, environmental engineering, biochemistry, Internet and computer technology (Jake and Dinos Chapman, Wim Delvoye, Critical Art Ensemble, Eduardo Kac, Patricia Piccinini, Stelarc, Victoria Vesna). Responses to science range from technophilia to technophobia.

6 Contemporary art often engages political, ethical and epistemological themes in the exploration of cultural memory, diaspora memory, war, rituals of death, love, mourning and history (Christian Boltanski, Peter Eisenman, Alfredo Jaar, Doris Salcedo, Kara Walker, Rachel Whiteread, Peter Witkin). Some contemporary artworks have retrospective tendencies where art reinstates traditional notions of contemplation and spiritual issues tied in with cultural memory and ritual (Sugiyama Sugimoto, Bill Viola); traditional processes of skill in painting, and materials and cultural memory (Gerard Richter); or religion, myth, faith and value (Matthew Barney, Anish Kapoor, Anselm Kiefer).

7 Another consistent thread running through many artworks is the conceptualist tradition of producing images that employ linguistic and our capacities for word games and puzzles, as well as parodying advertising conventions or public messaging (Martin Creed, Tracey Emin, Cerith Wynn Evans, Jasper Johns, Joseph Kosuth, Barbara Kruger, Bruce Nauman).

8 Many contemporary artworks valorise themes of multiplicity, hybridity and pluralism,[2] as opposed to notions of purity, essentialism and the univocal. The heterogeneity of media in an artwork may often be

---

[2] For a recent defence of pluralism, see Kieran (2004) who argues that many kinds of contemporary art provide the opportunity to negotiate, explore or rethink beliefs rather than stick to absolute values and universal claims.

interwoven with a multiplicity of cultural and subjective viewpoints, and thus there is a mutual reinforcing strategy of theme and facture. Many contemporary artworks employ unusual combinations of techniques and media, allowing this hybridity to stand for ideological and cultural multiplicity (Mona Hatoum, Yinka Shonibare). This continues with assisted (or altered) readymades consisting of contemporary, traditional and/or synthetic materials and processes used to signify mélange/hybridity (Brian Jungen, Wangechi Mutu, Francis Upritchard); flux, rootlessness (Ana Mendieta, Do Ho Su); globalised commercial processes and detritus (Thomas Hirschorn); erosion or renovation of tradition and identity (Song Dong, Sooja Kim, Michael Parekowhai, Do-Ho Suh, Michael Tuffery, Ai Wei Wei); or gender and LGBT (lesbian, gay, bisexual and transgender) stereotypes (Shigeyuki Kihara, Yasumasa Morimora, Catherine Opie, Cindy Sherman). At the core of many of these practices is a profound questioning of identity and the self. I examine these topics from a psychological point of view in conjunction with art in later chapters.

Many of these trends in contemporary art are often combined, or remain 'open' or unresolved. This raises questions and doubts in novel and unusual ways. This phenomenon in relation to literature has been characterised by the Russian critical theorist Mikhail Bakhtin as 'polyphony' (1984), the notion that a novel (and, in my extension, a visual work of art or group of artworks) can present situations where different voices or subjectivities come into negotiation. This kind of interaction between qualitative differences causes the artwork to have a certain structure, heterogeneity and character. A variation on this is Berys Gaut's idea that '[i]n creating a character, a novelist in effect creates a new concept, which bundles together a set of characteristics' (2006, p. 123).[3] Thus, even one 'character' can represent a group of concepts the precise contents of which change through the different contexts presented in the literary work. In the domain of interpretation, this notion of a set of concepts grouped together may be seen with Carroll's notion that the artwork is an ensemble of choices intended to realise the point of an artwork (2006, p. 78). This multiplicity may often take on political and tactical purposes understood to resist grand claims to truth, univocal narratives that speak from positions of authority, institutional power or commerce. This tendency is reflected by the continuing influence on contemporary art and theory exercised by French philosophy, in particular, the work of Alain Badiou,

---

[3] Stephen Davies (2004) has argued that this kind of cluster theory of art is to be associated with disjunctive theories of art. I will not argue the philosophical point here; suffice it to say that for the purposes of this book, these trends in contemporary art are a practical way of limiting the field of inquiry to manageable proportions.

Roland Barthes, George Bataille, Jean Baudrillard, Guy Debord, Michel de Certeau, Gilles Deleuze, Michel Foucault, and Jacques Rancière. For many, whether an artwork achieves resistance to traditional forms of authority and power by conveying content that conforms to aesthetic conventions or attacks them is a crucial difference.

The trends in contemporary art listed here can be combined or integrated in one work or exhibition, or may be spread over an artist's lifetime. How these combinations occur depends on the capabilities of the viewer and the configurations of perceptual cues provided by the artwork. This process of combination is often conceptual as it is material and technical (in terms of the medium, techniques and processes used by the artist), and it is the purpose of this book to use psychological and art historical methods to examine and suggest different ways in which this process of combining concepts with the perceptions of materials takes place. The phenomenal experience of this combination is often what we mean by the phrase: being 'absorbed' or 'immersed' in an artwork. Different events that is, exposure to the artwork at different times, and different contexts will provide different examples of absorption. Another way of describing the much vaunted 'non-retinal' aspect of conceptual art (a phrase coined by Duchamp that is quoted continually by contemporary artists and theorists) is 'conceptual integration', a process that takes time and is not immediately apparent. The materials of art might be instantly visible and recognisable but their significance and the thoughts they provoke may take some effort and time, fully involving the working memory of the spectator. Thus an artwork will have immediately visible details tied into early sensory stimulations and imperceptible aspects only revealed by later conceptual analysis. The latter process may be related to retrieving memories of artworks not present. If we saw a collection of clay sherds on the floor, we would understand them to be the remnants of a flower pot, not as incomprehensible shapes; they are sherds that 'belong' to the flower pot and are conceptualised rapidly with the scenario of how the breakage might have occurred, in conjunction with our sensory experience of them.[4] Many contemporary artists encourage us to see beyond the brute facts of the artwork and allow us to reflect on how we bring together conceptual wholes.

These trends affect us in four major ways that I explore in this book, providing some suggestions as to how cognitive psychology and neuro-aesthetics might approach new research in order to explain these important effects.

[4] An example taken from Talmy (1996, p. 254).

Firstly, much of conceptual and contemporary art has the power to stimulate us because it is witty or puzzling, as in a word game, and relies on the interplay between lexical and/or visual cues in order to ask philosophical questions concerning reality and appearance, abstraction and the concrete. It may well be that this 'effort after meaning' (Bartlett, 1932, p. 44) might be pleasurable, beautiful or artistic, but that does not mean that the end purpose of art *is* pleasure or beauty, or effort.[5] Some approaches in the cognitive psychology of problem solving and creativity can be used to shed some light on this aspect.

Secondly, and sometimes connected to the first area, art often stimulates the monitoring of internal states. We can look straightforwardly then reflexively (Husserl, 1983, p. 360) at art that achieves a 'narrativisation of one's gaze' (Joselit, *pace* Bois, 2003, p. 42), and which 'prompts a cognitive reorientation of the way my visual apprehension of objects is normally governed' (Vickery, 2003, p. 118).[6] These are the kinds of psychological responses contemporary artists are interested in achieving in the viewer. Providing opportunities to re-evaluate vision and subjectivity is the long-standing device of contrasting 'the visible and invisible': perceptible qualities played off against abstract concepts. It is also notable that attached to the play-off between perceptual visibility and abstract concepts are notions of art's materiality and its 'immaterial' aspect, respectively, both vying for the attention of the viewer. Many individuals find it refreshing that such art questions the traditional importance placed on the visible qualities of art; our perceptions of shape and form are less important here than the parody of them. This involves standing outside of our habitual emotional or perceptual responses in order to exercise metacognitive processes.

---

[5] One is struck by a great many contemporary artworks (those in the *Arte Povera* movement in particular) that seem to be effortlessly or possibly even incompletely put together to suggest and produce in the viewer a *lack* of effort. Some conceptual and contemporary artworks, for example, Martin Creed's Blu Tack or screwed up piece of paper, bring to mind the Italian concept of *sprezzatura*: an effortless display of grace either in the body's comportment or in the artistic execution of depicting that grace. What is assumed with this concept is that the viewer must, at least, be convinced that the execution of a graceful action is effortless, or not invested with earnestness; it seems as if effortlessness is integral to this aesthetic value and goes against the rather more utilitarian notion of 'effort after meaning'. An effortless puzzle or one arrived at with minimal means and without the need to be solved might best describe this aspect of contemporary art. However, such objects cannot be seen in isolation – we come to them with relational knowledge, expectations and schemata; they are situated in galleries; they reference other artworks and similar acts – these contextual factors may help both to solve or to sustain 'the problem' presented by the artwork.

[6] The passage is a generous interpretation of the art critic Michael Fried's approach; Vickery claims he was interested in the way art 'could reveal to us something in the nature of cognition itself' (2003, p. 118).

A third area of interest consists in how contemporary artworks represent a series of references to other artworks, a phenomenon that, for easy identification, I have called relational knowledge (adapted from psychology, see for example, Halford et al., 2010). In this process, viewers enjoy constructing complex conceptual relations between themes and artworks in short- and long-term memory, aided by perceptual cues in the artwork. These cues act as prompts to remember other artworks supported by the way in which an exhibition is organised. Thus, individual works, as well as the design of an exhibition, will have a significant bearing on the construction of this conceptual complexity.[7] How perceptual cues are configured in artworks in order to create a system of references is discussed in detail in later chapters. Relational knowledge of this kind questions the notion of a single moment, timeframe or object of attention. It is important that this relational knowledge is highly variable, both for artists producing works and viewers producing meanings in cooperation with them. We all have different knowledge bases, and artists and viewers can either knowingly or tacitly help to extend relational knowledge while interacting with artworks. Some references to artworks might be arbitrary and unintended. Yet relational knowledge assumes that it is extremely difficult, if not impossible, to isolate an artwork from the automatic system of contrasting and comparing with what we know and remember. Novel meaning emerges from the use one makes of relational knowledge, the way one connects things together in the situation provided by the artwork. In this sense, such knowledge resembles language, where words or phrases acquire a personal and unique meaning when combined in particular ways within certain contexts.

There are different ways to schematise this relational knowledge in order to see how it functions: conceptual blending (Fauconnier and Turner, 2002), analogical mapping processes (Gentner, 1983; Holyoak and Thagard, 1995) and psychological studies of metaphor (Gibbs, 2008).[8] As such, many of these processes come under the heading of conceptual combination and each of them attempts to show how we process features in the world, compare them and create categories out of

---

[7] Nevertheless, even here, I do not intend that this important feature of how artworks are intended and experienced is definitive of art, although it is one of the most consistent characteristics of contemporary artworks, but not all. To some extent this is anticipated by Jerrold Levinson, who comments: 'Artworks may be valuable to us artistically in ways that go beyond their value in experience to us, strictly speaking. Part of an artwork's value might reside in its art-historical relations to other artworks, e.g. ones of anticipation, or originality, or influence, independent of the value of experience of the work' (1996, p. 12).

[8] Conceptual blending is a form of integration comparable with 'analogy, recursion, mental modelling, conceptual categorisation and framing' (Fauconnier and Turner, 2002).

them. We are even at liberty to compare these categories (which are already a mass of relations), and we often do this effortlessly, in order to build up relational knowledge: a system of categories and concepts. This book is the first attempt to use such psychological studies to examine how we construct relational knowledge in the domain of art. Artworks help us to situate such systematicity, that is, they provide material anchors (Hutchins, 2005) for supporting and exploring this knowledge system.

Fourthly, many contemporary artworks can produce an immersive and absorbing experience, often accompanied by feelings of pleasure and reward, or sometimes feelings of being disturbed or depressed in ways that are similar to experiences of reading fiction or watching films. Sometimes this will be a somewhat inattentive process.[9] All of these different states could involve many of the trends listed earlier. This experience of widely varying intensities of involvement and attention may be characterised as feeling charmed, captivated or physically ensconced, or feeling mesmerised, moved or otherwise deeply affected. Immersion can occur in different ways: with the integration of different kinds of concepts and 'affects' in the domains of the political, imaginary, erotic, ethical or rational, for example. This is not to say that artworks that leave us cold, or that seem to be very simple, are not artworks. Many Minimalist artworks help to produce immersive experiences, yet the response they elicit can involve a heterogeneous complexity of different aspects of experience. This massive connectivity underlies immersive experience involving many aspects of our embodied mental life. At its most extreme, immersion may be premised on a complexity of different kinds of concepts: concrete, abstract, emotional, sensorimotor, lexical, logical, cultural, phenomenal and philosophical. These concepts will be integrated in a parallel fashion with ongoing 'affects', perceptions and sensations. This makes it a daunting task, teasing out the perceptual from the conceptual in this kind of experience. It is important to note that the artwork, with its complex configuration of perceptual cues, will constrain, stimulate, modulate and provide certain qualities to this immersion, lending it a particular character that is different, say, from being immersed in a cook book, a game of chess, or a Hollywood blockbuster. This immersion can consist of returning to an artwork for inspiration that can be rechanneled into other projects, a series of engagements that take place over many years.

I do not intend to analyse the exact differences between art, chess, cookery or sport. Each of these examples involves expert knowledge,

---

[9] This goes against the strong assertion that pleasure is a form of attentional absorption as defined by Ryle (1954, p. 60); it might also be somewhat capricious.

pleasure, aesthetics and relational knowledge; indeed, some might say that these are all different kinds of art. It is interesting that many contemporary artworks combine these domains of knowledge, as if to make the point that *sometimes* it is extremely difficult, if not impossible, to say that art is a special case. However, my aim is merely to show how, psychologically, we create special contexts for artworks; how we come to know that artworks reference other artworks, adopting a visual language and set of references that often appear peculiar to contemporary art. As part of this, I also attempt to examine how we understand that concepts can be 'shared' by different artworks. These commonalities between artworks usually are only implicitly acknowledged as 'dialogues', 'influences', 'themes' and 'tendencies' in art, and I believe that underlying these euphemisms are cognitively principled and systematic categorisations.

One is immersed in and attending to the artwork's qualities that help bring together emotional, conceptual and personal connections and particularities. Involved in this is a whole network of concepts constructed from a knowledge base to do with other artworks and *their* associated concepts. This network might not have come together in the particular way it has without the encounter with the artwork that causes a set of associations to be made. It is not hard to see how an encounter of this kind helps to enhance the pleasure and attraction of aesthetic experience, as well as giving us a sense of active participation in meaning creation. Yet there may be too much emphasis here on the encounter with the artwork as a 'new' experience. During an experience of an artwork that we have not encountered before, we may also be busy reconsidering artworks we have viewed in the past. In the sense of helping us to recall past conceptual complexities and creating fresh ones that can be used for new encounters with art, an artwork may be seen to present us with aspects of our past, present and future.

In visual art, the very notion of an exhibition of works is a multiplicity of conceptual systems, not single concepts. It is important that we view these conceptual systems not so much as self-contained brain events but as systems that are supported and constrained by the perceptual cues, feelings of embodiment or spatial settings of the artwork *and* social environments, contexts that we move in and around with others (and remember doing so with other artworks). This is also the case with books on art that bring together a number of illustrations we peruse, which help us to organise different artworks and the concepts they represent into groups and systems of thought. We commonly discuss these systems with others and alter them accordingly. This commonplace process of grouping artworks together is most often ignored by psychological studies. Artists are also curators of their own and others' works and they commonly think in groups of works rather than in terms of isolated cases. This means that we are continually reaching beyond the apparent detachment of an artwork. We frequently compare and contrast artworks, we make connections between them, we pick out themes and tendencies to create categories of style and period, and we attach emotional significance and meaning to such ordering privately and in social settings.

While often referencing the contemporary world around them, artworks help us to 'delay', spatialise and characterise these rapidly configured groupings of thoughts and sensations through books, exhibitions, installations and architectural works. Each of us has a collection of memories of artworks or places formed over several years that go to make up a relational knowledge system, aspects of which are brought to bear upon one's encounter with an individual artwork. However, rather than enclose all of this complexity in the head, which is automatically brought to bear on our experience, artworks, exhibitions, textbooks and discussions in the world are pivotal and, indeed, skilful in enabling us, creatively, to select and retrieve aspects of our relational knowledge. This improvisation for the task at hand might never happen again in quite the same way.

The Psychology of Contemporary Art is organised in four parts:

1 Introduction to processes of perception and cognition involved in art experience
2 Brain – neuroscientific and cognitive approaches to art and vision
3 Body – enactive, embodied and phenomenological approaches to art
4 World – situated cognition and extended mind approaches to art

The book progresses from basic perceptions, object recognition processes and scene recognition to categorisation and systems of relational knowledge in psychology and art, and then to embodiment and situating abstract concepts and processes of relational knowledge in the material and spatial environments presented by artworks.

Part I

Introduction

1.1 Processes of perception

In terms of neuroaesthetics, in particular, in relation to the visual arts, I will define visual perception in its simplest form as the detection of such features as line, colour, movement, luminance or texture in the visual field. The neurons responsible for the functioning of such perceptions are called feature detectors and these can work in large clusters in order to gain an overall sensory impression of an object in front of us, binding features together for object and scene identification, the mechanisms of which I examine later in relation to art. According to Marr (1982), low-level perception processes fine-grained local features before the inter-mediate level of perceptual binding into a percept (the thing identified); high-level perception produces categorical representations (but with the support of nonperceptual systems). According to Jackendoff (1987), con-sciousness arises on this intermediate level. Prinz (2009, p. 435) adds to this, that attention needs to be exercised here in order for conscious experience to arise. The process is complicated further by the fact that I am only dealing with the modality of sight, when perceptions will often depend on what the combined senses are telling it (we can imagine seeing, smelling, tasting and touching an apple). Yet it is also possible to have different perceptions about the same sensation, as we do when looking at pictures such as the rabbit/duck conundrum, where it is possible to switch perceptions from the same sensory signal.

The early stages of perception will proceed most often unconsciously, frequently called *bottom-up* processes, 'lower' perceptual processes that it is believed drive the goals of the organism in particular events or situations. However, if something is flagged as important, which can happen when certain memory areas are triggered, further processing of the visual field will be needed. Here, the prefrontal cortex will direct the sensory and motor systems to pay more attention to salient aspects of the environment. The prefrontal cortex, the role in relational knowledge of which I will return to often in this book, is an important executive frontal part of the brain that is largest in humans and is associated with the monitoring of internal states and for keeping long-term plans and objectives in mind, in connection with a hormone-based reward system. These kinds of processes are generally referred to as *top-down*, which may also include later analytical procedures that manipulate sensory information and perceptions. However, there is also nonconscious sampling of the environment complicating the simplistic stimulus–response model, suggesting that sometimes a response can turn into a stimulus, and that we are often sensitised to where or when stimuli will occur in the environment; we have expectations and nonconscious subliminal processes that prime us for a 'discovery' that we experience as a stimulus.[1]

Cognition can involve the interaction between bottom-up and top-down processes. This happens when the processing of stimuli cooperates with short-term memory that maintains information (representations) to be used later. For example, we may be making a salad. We have just sliced a tomato and we have put it aside while attending to the other ingredients in the recipe. Even though the tomato is no longer in our view and we are busy with something else, we have a representation of it in our minds so that we can return to it later. However, while it is not being viewed, we might think more purposefully about the taste of red tomatoes and what might complement it in a salad, and this will require other kinds of representation of stored knowledge in longer-term memory. Our knowledge of factual details will aid interpretation of an ongoing situation, which we must keep attending to lest we cut our fingers. At the same time, we can access episodic memories and semantic memory as a way to add value and further meaning to the ongoing situation or the object under examination. Memories of sensory episodes can trigger the emotions associated with the memory, and even give rise to self-reflection. Meanwhile, various glands and hormones in the bloodstream could be

---

[1] Indeed, some theorists believe that 'rather than a stimulus *causing* a response, it is the response which must occur *first* and then *act* on the incoming afferent signals to *produce* a stimulus' (Ellis, 1999, p. 267). The superior colliculus is an area in the brain responsible for changing the direction of saccades. Low-level conscious peripheral vision is strongly attracted to novel objects or movements appearing in the periphery of the visual field. Higher-level conscious awareness makes the discovery 'official'.

sending signals to the brain about the body's state, feeling tired, hungry or thirsty, for example. In sum, cognition and perception require a broad interconnectivity of brain areas *and* the contingencies and rich details of our bodies dynamically engaging with the world that will help us to 'personalise' or conceptualise the significance of perceptual experience. The relevance of this (admittedly extremely simplified) description of conscious attention is complicated when we are attending to another situation in the environment, a work of art: an oil painting on canvas, for example, which might depict a chef making a salad. The artwork may not only stimulate a rehearsal of this familiar activity in our minds, but we may also question the artwork's ability to do this, a kind of metacognitive activity involving the self-monitoring of cognitive states and judgements about how the artwork's perceptible ingredients are able to anticipate or challenge expectations and lead to complex conclusions. This self-monitoring induced by the artwork is a process I shall return to in later pages. As Martin O'Shea neatly observes, 'when we say the brain does x or y, the word "brain" is a shorthand for all of the interdependent interactive processes of a complex dynamical system consisting of the brain, the body and the outside world' (2005, p. 3).

Certain artworks puzzle, as is the case with Op Art, in order to make us conscious of our perceptions by exploiting effects, problems and paradoxes in the visual field. It is important to note that we do not need the object in front of us to stimulate our perceptual processes; we can imagine or recall such objects. Meanwhile, 'mirror neurons' (Rizzolati and Craighero, 2004) are neurons in our sensorimotor systems that we use when we watch people move (or imagine them moving), and these fire up in order to help us follow the movements and intentions of others, using the same sensorimotor areas of the brain that we would use when performing the actions themselves although, of course, not executing them. This 'offline' perceptual processing can occur watching a film, daydreaming or remembering objects or actions.

Perceptions are commonly understood as representations of line, colour, luminance and movement, with distinctions being made for sound, touch, taste and smell in the other senses. Traditional neuroscience identifies each of these senses or functions with particular brain areas. Perceptions and concepts are generally treated for the purposes of analysis as separate mental and physical operations even though, phenomenally, they appear to occur at the same time. There are many experiences of contemporary art where perceptions and concepts cooperate in interesting ways, and much of this book will analyse how this works. Traditional ways of making distinctions between or 'states' out of human thought denoted by the use of such terms as perceptions, percepts and concepts are most often arranged in various hierarchical models, with the sensations of objects then perceptions of their qualities placed at the bottom, and with percepts, the simplest form of identification, next. Then there are more complex concrete concepts that may be compounds (combine-harvester), followed by abstract concepts (equipment) at the top. The latter may utilise or abstract information from these lower levels. In sentences and in viewing art, we are quite adept at combining these different kinds of mental operations rapidly. Of course, this is a very simplified schema and is hotly debated, as is the amount of 'consciousness' to be apportioned to each of these states, and there is controversy over their underlying neural correlates and mechanisms. Perhaps more surprising is any rigorous application of these distinctions in contemporary art history, which is content to use 'concept' interchangeably with 'thought', 'idea', 'notion' and even 'the gaze' or 'the eye'.

1.2   Concepts

Because there are many different kinds of concepts and various ways of defining them, I shall restrict my introductory definition here to a broad consensus of views, although I shall provide further elaboration in later chapters as to how we combine concepts in larger systems of knowledge. A concept is a mental representation of a particular entity or category of entities that may be concrete or abstract. A standard psychological dictionary definition states that a concept is: 'acquired or learnt, usually from exposure to examples of items that belong to the concept category and items that do not belong to it. In general, it involves learning to distinguish and recognize the relevant attributes according to which items are classified and the rules governing the combination of relevant attributes, which may be disjunctive, as in the concept of a coin, which may be circular, polygonal, or annular' (Colman, 2009).[1]

An important distinction that continually arises in the psychological literature divides abstract from concrete concepts: 'Concrete concept nouns, such as *chair* and *book*, differ from abstract concept nouns, such as *freedom* and *language*. While the former refer to entities that are perceivable and spatially constrained, the latter refer to entities characterized by properties that are neither perceivable nor spatially constrained' (Setti and Caramelli, 2005, p. 1997).

In terms of art, this seems crucial, particularly because many artworks encourage us to shift from the processing of perceptible features as an end in itself, to using those perceptible features as symbols or tokens of abstract concepts, such as FREEDOM.[2] Arthur C. Danto suggests that much of art is conceptual, as it invites an 'enthymematic' phenomenon, whereby the viewer is responsible for supplying the 'missing' conceptual

---

[1] 'concept formation'.

[2] In many research studies in cognitive psychology, concrete and abstract concepts used as explicit examples are put into capital letters. I follow that convention throughout this book.

link, which the work itself suggests (Danto, 1981, p. 170). In a bold statement, Danto also writes: 'Whatever art is, it is no longer something primarily to be looked at' (Danto, 1997, p. 16). Directing his attention to Warhol's *Brillo Boxes*, 1964, a collection of wooden boxes printed to appear exactly like their commercial counterparts, Danto argued that to make a distinction between the ordinary and art required the relevant theory and cultural understanding, thereby emphasising not the physical appearance of artworks but the conceptual context. Carroll (2006, pp. 77–79) further suggests that the direct perception of an artwork is not necessary for aesthetic experience and that Duchamp's *Fountain* (a urinal turned on its side, signed in 1917 and entered for an exhibition) does not need to be visually inspected – clearly, embodied movement around many art objects is not essential for all artworks. Duchamp himself insisted: 'What art is in reality is this missing link, not the links which exist. It's not what you see that is art, art is the gap' (Schwarz, 1969, p. xxxii). While the visible, perceptual details of art are processed by the eye and the visual cortex, other areas of the brain are busy 'filling in' these gaps with conceptual information.

Perhaps one of the most often quoted remarks in contemporary art is when Duchamp referred to the 'non-retinal beauty of grey matter' that 'put art at the service of the mind' (Schwarz, 1969, pp. 18–19). Although this has been pursued with much alacrity in conceptual art and in many contemporary artworks, this does not mean, of course, that visual experience is totally irrelevant now. In fact, many of Duchamp's readymades remain visually interesting and suggestive. However, the way in which Duchamp placed the emphasis on the conceptual rather than the perceptual aspects of experiencing art has had a profound effect on contemporary art. The artwork can be viewed as one of many 'situations' that require the use and combination of both concrete and abstract concepts. Let us take the situation of thinking about a horse.

Nonconsciously and extremely rapidly, the sensory perceptions of a horse's shape, colour, surface texture, the sound it makes, its movements would be processed by feature detectors in the different senses to form a percept that binds the features together. A percept might be 'animal with four legs'; identifying it as an adult horse would be a concrete concept that stimulates processes of semantic and episodic memory. We might put the horse into a superordinate category of friendly domestic animals along with dogs, or with mythical animals such as unicorns. An abstract concept might associate the horse with a symbol of strength, speed and nobility, and we might associate a white horse with Pegasus.

According to a study undertaken by Crutch and Warrington (2005), superordinate categories are collections of concrete concepts, whereas abstract concepts can be organised into networks via association (not categorisation). The results suggest that there are at least two kinds of representation for concrete and abstract concepts, and that 'in the latter case, it is *unlikely* that this associative network is premised on perceptual or modal examples'. Furthermore, 'Experience of the perceptual features of objects via our five sensory channels appears to play a key role in the acquisition of concrete concepts ... Abstract concepts, however, may be acquired in the context of language without any direct perceptual input' (p. 623).

These are a few practical tasks where we might engage in combining such concepts:

1 In analyses of complex spatial events, such as puzzles, chess, the calculation of quantities and mathematical formulae using methodical procedures (rules) that have been learnt, applied to ad hoc situations using concrete exemplars.
2 Coordinating embodied action with reasoning: painting or drawing; re-enacting and retracing the steps of a thief; acting on the stage; playing the piano; looking for lost keys; coordinating embodied perceptual processes and conceptual analysis, for example when examining a modernist sculpture that requires us to walk around it, through it and under it.
3 Running through counterfactual or hypothetical scenarios and events (requiring a suspension of disbelief for the sake of a logical experiment). For example, art creates objects out of 'impossible events': see Meret Oppenheim's famous *Object (Le déjeuner en fourrure)*, 1936, often referred to as the Fur Cup, or Man Ray's *Gift*, 1921 (a clothes iron with a strip of nails on its smooth side sticking out like teeth). We can imagine impossible objects that do not resemble anything we have seen before. Yet, feeling that objects look familiar even though they are nonsensical is a bit like trying to scratch an itch without much success. We can imagine using these hybrid objects and they manage to put our habitual responses into conceptual focus. This may be accompanied by strong emotions, from pleasure to disgust, or we may conceptualise such emotions and how they seem to rise and fall in the encounter with the art object. Such hybrids of emotion and cognition are sometimes described as phenomenal concepts. When our 'normal' perceptual processes are at odds with our conceptual expectations in cases of art such as *Lunch in Fur*, it could be said, following Duchamp, that a kind of gap appears that is only really closed by the operations of relational knowledge drawing upon other artworks that employ similar strategies. A certain charm might be found in our *inability* to make sense of the *Lunch in Fur*. As with *Alice in Wonderland*, there is always a fleeting sensation that we have apprehended the conceptual logic of fantasy, yet we are often at a loss for words on how to report on it.

Figure 2. Meret Oppenheim, *Object (Le déjeuner en fourrure – Luncheon in Fur)*, 1936 (fur-covered cup, saucer and spoon; cup 10.9 cm diameter, saucer 23.7 cm diameter, spoon 20.2 cm long, overall height 7.3 cm). Digital image, The Museum of Modern Art (MoMA), New York and Scala, Florence. © DACS 2012.

4 Using and thinking about lexical concepts to do with comparison, contrast, quantity, size, characteristics, relying on context-sensitive information that might also require judgements about time: thinking about why this film seems longer that the other one you saw when, in fact, it is sixty minutes shorter in duration.

5 Performing a religious ritual that requires one to regulate one's movements and actions either with regard to objects or social situations (genuflecting, threading one's fingers together, adopting a particular gait at a funeral or wedding). The body is regulated by learnt traditions and social settings; it may be a subpersonal concept (one is going through the motions). These rituals, which are produced by traditions of conceptual thought, involve the regulation of the body in designated spaces (churches, hospitals, theatres, libraries, bars). They may also involve 'conceptual acts' of performing beliefs or social mores, and they may function as channels for emotion. Many performance artworks explore these kinds of 'conceptual acts' where the actual execution of kinaesthetic and embodied actions allow concepts to emerge which, in turn, affect such actions in a continuous feedback loop. This is less exploratory or ad hoc than 2.

In sum, concepts are used in specific situations for particular tasks and actions in the world, but they are also used and combined in order to communicate emotions, memories, imaginary scenarios, events or reasonable calculations for problem solving, education or pleasure. Artworks are special because they provide opportunities to exercise these different kinds of concepts imaginatively. In addition, artworks often provide unique circumstances in themselves and present us physically with social and public situations and spaces that constrain or encourage combinations of these different kinds of concepts, which otherwise might not come together in any other circumstance.

The cognitive psychology of concepts provides further details. According to Wiemer-Hastings and Xu (2005), 'Abstract concepts are anchored in situations and regularly involve subjective experiences, such as cognitive processes and emotion. Unlike concrete concepts, abstract concepts have fewer intrinsic and proportionally [more] relational properties' (p. 731). Importantly also, they state that many characteristics of abstract concepts are just as abstract as the concepts themselves. 'Thus, it is difficult to imagine how abstract concepts may be formed from purely perceptual sources' (p. 732).

Abstract concepts are distinct from concrete concepts such as HAMMER or CHAIR because, while the latter depend on real life, concrete situational examples or associated concrete concepts (NAILS, SOFA) and body references (to grip, to sit on), abstract concepts, such as TRUTH, rely more heavily on different kinds of situational examples that 'focus more on social aspects of situations, such as people, communication, and social institutions. Abstract concepts also focus more on introspections, especially beliefs and contingency/complex relations' (Barsalou and Wiemer-Hastings, 2005, p. 152).

However, it is not always the case that concrete or perceptual situations are needed to grasp abstract concepts. For example, 'the concept *comparison* requires (among other abstract constraints) the presence of two entities to be compared. The constraint does not dictate these entities to be of any particular nature, thus they could be people, essays, houses, laws, feelings' (Wiemer-Hastings et al., 2001, p. 1111).

Thus, one does not need to access or even to dwell upon ESSAY, HOUSE or LAW by rehearsing perceptual or sensory operations to demonstrate them. We may effortlessly combine them in sentence construction, leaving out the details. It is important to remember that purely logical examples may be contrasted with different kinds of concepts, such as those involving emotions, that require both concrete and abstract components and situations to communicate them.[3] It is interesting that

---

[3] Setti and Caramelli (2005) suggest four main domains of abstract concepts: cognitive processes (thought, idea), states of the self (childhood, identity), nominal kinds (error, plan) and emotions (fear). Note: 'There is an abstract *thinking*, just as there is abstract *feeling*, *sensation* and *intuition*. Abstract thinking singles out the rational, logical qualities...Abstract feeling does the same with...its feeling-values...I put abstract feelings on the same level as abstract thoughts...Abstract sensation would be aesthetic as opposed to sensuous *sensation*' (Jung, 1921/1971, p. 678).

many contemporary artworks function as situations, helping to constrain or elaborate concrete *and* abstract concepts, as I intend to show in later chapters, particularly with the use of metaphor.[4]

Concepts are not merely mental entities that are held in the memory as fixed representations; they are continually combined with incoming perceptual signals that help to provide such concepts with unprecedented detail and individuality. Choosing what we feel to be the right concept to describe a situation, which is itself full of groups of perceptions, sensations and imponderables, can be crucially important if we are to avoid putting ourselves into danger, for example, or when categorising a situation as pleasurable, giving us a sense of agency. Such ad hoc conceptualisations and generalisations of the details and events of an ongoing situation can draw us nearer to others in reading stories and watching films or listening to reports. Thus, it is not just incidental that concepts are mediated and constrained by social situations and the situations we find ourselves in while contemplating artworks or reading novels, for the way in which concepts are related to each other by the situation or task at hand allows us to get more involved in that situation. Concepts used to interact meaningfully with an artwork or performance will depend partly on our knowledge base and partly on the artwork that can provide the 'cognitive glue' – the catalyst that brings these concepts together in unusual combinations.

The question is how to find the right balance between stable or fixed aspects of concepts where, in order for them to shared, they need a certain invariability and identity (Fodor, 1998), and innovative ad hoc applications of them in conjunction with situations that may destabilise them.[5] A pragmatic approach that emphasises conceptual use and identification constrained by ongoing tasks and background knowledge shows how concepts are given an immediate if not absolute or universal coherence (as one would expect in a classical theory of concepts). For

---

[4] In addition, Barsalou and Wiemer-Hastings write: 'To our knowledge, no neuroscience research has assessed the processing of abstract concepts in situations. It would be interesting to see if situational processing shifted brain activation outside word generation areas.' (Barsalou and Wiemer-Hastings, 2005, p. 132). Artworks can provide such situational processing.

[5] Goldstone and Rogosky develop a theory of *correspondence* between concepts that they believe is 'sufficient to determine matching, and hence shared, concepts across systems' rather than strict identity matching. 'The advantage of accounting for shared concepts in terms of correspondence rather than identity is that one avoids the uncomfortable conclusion that people with demonstrably different knowledge associated with something have the identical concept of that thing. Although the notion of correspondence is less restrictive than identity, it is more constrained than similarity.' (2002, pp. 317–318).

the user and the social situation, concepts are interactional properties. Similarly, Wittgenstein in his *Philosophical Investigations* was loath to define concepts as absolute, reasonable and knowable across different minds, as they are lodged in immediate and contingent language use for the task at hand. Thus, he shows the impossibility of establishing an absolute definition for the concept GAME.[6] Relevant to how we might conceive of art, if for the sake of argument we define it as a compound or cluster concept, Murphy and Medin write: 'The interpretation of a compound concept may be thought of as a hypothesis generated by background theories' (1985, p. 306). These theory-building strategies are based on comparison and experience, and will provide concepts with constraints and coherence, especially if, to a certain extent, an artwork provides perceptual reference points to suggest particular juxtapositions of concepts. The conceptual task, which could be the examination of an artwork, will involve background knowledge (often of a specialist kind), questioning and hypotheses such as 'what could this artwork be about?' or 'it could be related to another piece of work which resembles it; how has the original concept been elaborated here?' These words will probably not be uttered, but they do indicate the kind of priming of conceptual processes involved in creative thought. The aim in this book is to show how we can explain this as a series of 'ad hoc concepts' and combinations in reference to the artwork, the features of which encourage these concepts to arise in association with each other.

According to Carson, ad hoc concepts 'are constructed pragmatically by a hearer in the process of utterance comprehension...they are not linguistically given, but are constructed on-line (on the fly) in response to specific expectations of relevance raised in specific contexts' (2002, p. 322). The key thing here is how this relevance between stored concepts and the situation presented by an artwork occurs so that new conceptual material arises. Fauconnier and Turner argue that their conceptual blending theory involves a mapping of one concept in one domain onto another from a different domain, so that new material emerges, rather than the basic material of each set of previous concepts (2002, p. 36). Thus, Duchamp mapped ART onto the concrete concept, urinal, to create *Fountain*. Concepts such as art can carry across different situational complexities, but this will entail new conceptual material (ad hoc concepts)

---

[6] 'Following Wittgenstein's example, consider four category exemplars with the features {A,B,C}, {A,B,D} and {A,C,D}, {B,C,D}. No single feature defines them as a single group but, instead, they form a group through partial, overlapping features...features extend across a variable range of concepts; features do not reliably co-occur with each other either over time or over examples' (Lambon-Ralph et al., 2010, pp. 2718–20).

and changes in categories. Psychological models such as analogical modification, structure mapping and metaphor, and conceptual blending come close to explaining some of the cognitively principled ways in which concepts change or remain the same. It is my argument here that the different contexts provided by contemporary artworks offer unique insights into how the balance between conceptual constancy and conceptual innovation is achieved.[7]

---

[7] This is in agreement with Mazzone and Lalumera, who believe that the context dependency of concepts (that is, how contexts change concepts) and their constancy across contexts, need not be a contradiction: 'It is true that in many cases category representations have no fixed sets of properties providing necessary and sufficient conditions for membership. This does not mean, however, that concepts cannot have a stable, although probabilistic, organization. And it is true that many aspects of category representations (order of accessibility, relations etc.) can be reorganized as a function of contexts. However, this does not mean that there is no structure unless contexts are given. Luckily for us, general information has the advantage of not changing from moment to moment.' (2010, p. 60).

1.3 The cooperation of perceptions with concepts

Lawrence Barsalou explains an important paradigm upon which traditional psychology has been founded: 'For more than 2,000 years, theorists viewed higher cognition as inherently perceptual. Since Aristotle and Epicurus, theorists saw the representations that underlie cognition as imagistic [and] had a strong perceptual character. After being widely accepted for two millennia, this view withered with mentalism in the early twentieth century' (Barsalou, 1999, p. 578).

Mentalism favours a view of the mind as a manipulator of complex symbols. Coding is achieved through word-like (and therefore not analogue) symbolic forms, called *amodal* symbols. Barsalou provides a useful summary of these: 'As amodal symbols become transduced from perceptual states, they enter into larger representational structures, such as feature lists, frames, schemata, semantic networks, and production systems. These structures in turn constitute a fully functional symbolic system with a combinatorial syntax and semantics...They are amodal because their internal structures bear no correspondence to the perceptual states that produced them' (1999, p. 578).

Those who support propositional (amodal) symbol representation, for example, Jerry Fodor (1975), famously suggest that thought is akin to language, a kind of 'mentalese' underlying and prefiguring language. Zenon Pylyshyn's (2006) work on mental imagery consistently supports a notion for propositions and amodal symbols in conceptual thought (see also Anderson, 1990; Newell, 1980; and Newell and Simon, 1976). Fodor and Pylyshyn are leading figures whose hypotheses concerning human thought are related to computational models of the human mind, requiring symbol manipulation. Fodor argues for an 'atomistic' theory of concepts, discrete units with precise, amodal kinds of connection, relationship or mutual exclusion. These kinds of connection or rules help to create syntactic-like structures that provide intelligible content for a mental representation or concept, not the unit or atomistic concept itself; it is the *relationship* to other units that provides meaning. Thus, Fodor's notion of 'mentalese' springs from his assertion that 'mental representation is a lot like language' (1975, p. 25), a series of logical relations between concepts which *govern* different kinds of modal and sensory experiences.

However, in recent years, 'embodied' approaches (Barsalou, 1999; Glenberg and Kashak, 2002; Johnson, 2008a; Lakoff and Johnson, 1980) seem to place much more importance on how perceptual experience supplies conceptual thought with substance, once again returning perception to prominence in cognition. This view is often called neo-empiricist.

These approaches either favour a reductive notion of direct perception of things in the world (without the need for elaborate representations) or a theory of representations that remain simple and have an analogue relation to stimuli being processed. In the latter case, *modal* areas of the brain responsible for sensory and motor functions process representations that have an image-like or sensory-like basis to their codification for later use. Associated with this perceptual bias are those who see art as a vehicle for perceptual, sensory, emotional and phenomenal exploration involving the body (Freedberg and Gallese, 2007; Gallagher and Cole, 1995; Johnson, 2008a; Krauss, 1981).

When we conceptualise, perceptions are normally co-present; when we perceive, our perceptions will be influenced or acted upon by various concepts. Rather than clearly creating a discrete binary between concepts and perceptions, Leonard Talmy (1996, p. 224) suggests that when viewing a scene, we use a cognitive range that extends from palpable perceptual details (the factual) to understanding less palpable concepts (the fictive). This range he calls 'ception'.[1] Meanwhile, Robert Goldstone et al., state: 'A sensory reductionist easily falls into the trap of claiming that Horse's meaning is given by its parts – hoof, mane, tail, etc. [but] Several of the associated concepts that imbue Horse with its meaning, such as Freedom, Domesticated, and Strength, are less concrete than Horse itself...these complementary aspects of meaning...are mutually reinforcing, not mutually exclusive' (2005, pp. 310–311). There are also supporting voices in social psychology where Lisa

---

[1] Talmy gives the example of perceiving a dent in a car. This will entail a conceptual understanding that this is a damaged surface and not its perfect form; the perfect form might be a schema, and we could also run a mental script of cause and effect, the reason why or how it could have happened; or we might estimate the angle or force of the impact, how expensive it might be to repair, etc. This would all be happening within the 'perceptual space', but many of the cogitations are abstract. In addition, there are also interesting temporal projections being processed while our sensory experience of visually attending to the dent continues. We have a grasp of the structural history or future of the object superimposed on the 'veridically seen static representation of the entity' (Talmy, 1996, p. 255).

Feldman Barrett et al., write: 'perception involves conception...categorization goals influence how sensory information is sampled and processed from a visual array...sensory based and memory-based processes probably run in parallel in the brain, constraining one another as they instantiate experience' (2007, p. 331).

We can fix upon the material details of a painting, the brushstrokes, the texture of the paint, or we pan over the details of an artwork to pick out the general composition, mood and gesture of the work in order to recognise it as a subordinate example of a category such as identifying a style. In viewing a painting, there is both perceptual attention to fine-grained detail, the overall concept of the composition that we hold in our minds, as well as our ability to formulate opinions about how the techniques support the meaning of the work. A good example of this process of 'ception' would be to look at the longstanding tradition in art of the equation of the viscosity of oil pigments and the patterns of the brush in the pigment (a fine-grained, local perceptual activity) with 'flesh' (a 'global' or coarse-grained perceptual activity that keeps in mind the figure to whom the fleshy colour 'belongs'). Referring to the Spanish artist, Jusepe de Ribera (1591–1652), art historians have written: 'He developed a technique in which the marks and lines traced by his coarse brushes in the wet paint create an exciting surface texture and intensify the naturalistic illusion...The topography of the human flesh was for Ribera the mirror of the human spirit, and by baring the nerves at the very surface of the skin he makes us acutely sensitive to the inner life of his heroes' (Held and Posner, n.d, p. 85).

The physicality of the body seems palpable, arising from the physicality of the paint, its creamy colour and sheen, the pattern of pockmarks left by the hairs of the brush suggesting the surface of the skin. It is an old trope and visual trick. These material factors and processes, often textured and random in their minute patterning, are part of the viewing process and invigorate narratives concerning the inanimate (paint) made animate (flesh). These techniques and the fleshy solidity they evoke may be said to constitute a sensuous narrative structure. However, note that in Ribera, the flesh is weak, his men old and struggling. His paintings make the flesh immanent but in such a way as to remind us of its inevitable disintegration; the fretful sensations of pain and suffering written on his faces transform our wonder at the appearance of skin to a quiet reverie of its frailty. This is also the fate of the pigment on canvas. Ribera's work brings together perceptual processing of 'skin' and the concept of 'the skin of the pigment', which involves understanding the skin as a metaphor. These metaphors can become even more complex. In a particularly striking painting, *Apollo Flaying Marsyas*, 1637, the artist paints the story of Marsyas who challenged Apollo to a competition of flute playing, judged by the Muses. As punishment for losing the contest, Marsyas was skinned alive. In both of Ribera's two versions of the scene, Marsyas is shown in agony while Apollo coldly and surgically detaches portions of his skin. This also serves as metaphor for two different aesthetic responses: the Apollonian, dispassionate and conceptual, and the Dionysian, sensual and visceral. Apollo's act of detaching skin is analogous with emotional detachment. While he subtracts skin, the painter adds flesh tones to the painting. The paintings have an immediate visceral effect, with the tactile qualities of fleshiness and the depiction of Marsyas' grimace of intense pain, yet this affect is 'detached' from our experience when examination of the handling of the paint is uppermost in our minds. The painting appeals to our openness to sensory perceptions and our ability to abstract away from them.

Interesting modern parallels with this are found in the works of Lucien Freud and Francis Bacon. One is also accustomed to speaking of Lucien Freud's treatment of impasto, thick layers of paint to suggest the atrophy of the skin doubled by the paint's stubborn resistance to gravity. Much has been written on Francis Bacon's paintings that distort the figure, suggesting spittle, gristle, wounds and trembling flesh. One can read across the canvas the artist's hand movement, twisting, quick or hesitant, erratic or tender, the brush loaded with a various spectrum of colours that the gesture blends when the hairs of the brush come together leaving the canvas. While this is a sensorimotor appreciation of art, a visceral, embodied response of affect and sensation, it is situated in a conceptual tradition that helps us to understand the equivocation of 'the flesh of the paint'. It is our ability to go from conceptual to perceptual thoughts in this way that falsifies both strong embodiment and extreme mentalism, balancing aspects of each or giving emphasis to one over the other, depending on the moment.

This is also true of the large-scale paintings of Jenny Saville. She painted *Plan*, 1993, in what I see as a kind of extension of a schematic conceptual organisation over the body. This picture is simply enormous (almost three metres tall) and shows us a woman cradled by her own arms with curious lines written all over her body. As the artist states about the picture: 'The lines on her body are the marks they make before you have liposuction done to you. They draw these things that look like targets. I like this idea of mapping of the body...like geographical contours on a map. I didn't draw on to the body. I wanted the idea of cutting into the paint. Like you would cut into the body. It evokes the idea of surgery. It has lots of connotations.'[2]

[2] *The Independent*, 20 January, 1994.

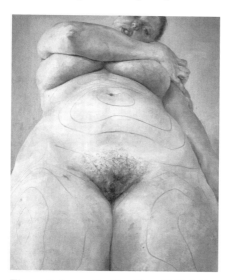

Figure 3. Jenny Saville, *Plan*, 1993 (oil on canvas, 274.3 × 213.4 cm). ©
2012 Jenny Saville. Courtesy of Gagosian Gallery.

Although the scale and fleshiness of the paint and the woman's size
come together to create a strong affective response to the painting, the
lines on the body are signs of society's standards of beauty, internalised by
the subject into her own self-image, that have territorialised the body. It is
a kind of contemporary Marsyas. In a sense, the marks on the body, which
indicate the incisions to be made to slice away folds of flesh, are the things
that distance us from the immediate effect of the naked. Feelings of
empathy might arise but the marks also indicate the cold, surgical stare,
where living flesh is transformed into a medium and a topology of aesthetic proportions. The marks on the flesh coincide with the marks of the
brush on the canvas; both are ways of mapping the skin with aesthetic
judgements, which the artist equates with invasive surgery. This interpretation echoes what I have ventured to write about Ribera and Bacon. It
helps to situate a system of relational knowledge based on conceptual
combinations that allows us to elaborate our experience of the painting.

We become accustomed to binding together large groups of perceptual
and conceptual processes; we learn how to fine-tune our perceptual habits
and responses, and to be alert to visual codes. We learn when to filter out
perceptual details as too much noise, or to turn our attention to them by
adding a conceptual frame to them. This top-down influence on perceptual processes, which we acquire when we become experts in certain tasks,

not only captures the variability of perceptual experience (allowing for bottom-up, fine-grained details to come through) but also shows how individuals have different groups of concepts that they use to interpret perception in domains such as art, sport or work.

These kinds of experiences of artworks can occur without much self-awareness or, when it comes to experts, with the distinct presence of such awareness. Different kinds and amounts of self-awareness must be premised on some ability to recognise codes as coding things, rather than just seeing through them to the things they are supposed to encode. This is very important for art, which deals with a great many codes and judgements about their efficacy. Visual codes remain invisible to the uninitiated but this does not mean that the initiated need only delight in how codes are structured; they can also see the things referred to and how these things referred to gain new significance as they are arrived at through different paths, depending on how the codes are structured and arranged. Many contemporary artworks may be seen as experimenting with different ways of coding the visual field that allow us not only to see familiar things differently but also to recall memories or use our imaginations accessing unaccustomed codes, configural spatial arrangements and fine-grained details provided by artworks and their perceptual cues acting as unexpected triggers.

How would the brain encode (or represent) this intertwining of perceptions with concepts? One suggestion is a pluralistic account of representation (de Bruin and Kästner, 2011; Dove, 2009; Kosslyn et al., 2006; Machery, 2007). One of the most interesting overviews of the modal and amodal approach is given by Machery (2007, p. 36), who refuses to characterise these different emphases as a divide, but rather sees them as a scale along which there are degrees of difference. Many of those who espouse amodal representation (propositions, equations, algorithms, rules) also accept that there are concepts that are grasped by situations using modal representations. Even Barsalou, who favours the perceptual grounding for concepts, accepts that there must be some important amodal mechanisms (2003, p. 87). Additionally misleading is the characterisation that the two sides of the argument cover all the important issues. Both approaches need to take into account context-dependent knowledge: social exchanges, artefacts and situations in the external world, which help to affect the encoding and retrieval of internal representations, concepts or categories (Minsky, 1975), and these situations also affect which concepts we choose to combine in order for new concepts to arise (Machery, 2007, p. 30).

'Sensorimotor chauvinists', a term coined by Clark (2001), fail to recognise that those who support a more amodal approach for conceptual combinations actually acknowledge the importance of how visual imagery is often used to solve conceptual tasks (see, for example, Fodor, 1975, pp. 174–194). Machery writes that what amodal theorists usually insist on is that '*not all* tasks are solved through imagery. In some situations, we retrieve from long-term memory and we manipulate some knowledge that is stored in a specific, non-modal representational system' (2007, p. 33). In addition, those who strongly support modal accounts claim that there is little or no evidence for amodal symbols. However, there is more than adequate behavioural and neuropsychological evidence that, for example, when estimating or approximating the cardinality of classes of entities such as objects, sounds and events, we depend on amodal symbols and analogical operations (Hauser and Spelke, 2004; Machery, 2007, p. 37; Piazza and Dehaene, 2004). Machery suggests that the interesting question is not 'Are concepts amodal or perceptual?' but rather 'To what extent do we use re-enacted perceptual representations in cognition and to what extent do we use amodal representations?' (2007, p. 42).

It is perhaps best not to think of the modal and perceptual or the amodal and conceptual distinction as an on-off switch but, rather, as a series of degrees along a continuum. It might even be possible to think of the transduction between higher-order amodal representations and bottom-up perceptual states as a process supported by examples of contemporary art that invite us to decouple/recouple with its perceptual cues. It seems that it would be wise to follow Dove (2009), de Bruin and Kästner (2011) and Machery (2007) in supposing that there are valid aspects of both amodal and modal arguments for concepts. The kind of approach that seems to get the right balance for describing the relationship between concepts and perceptions involved in our experience of contemporary art is Anjan Chatterjee's (2003) theoretical model of the cognitive and affective processes involved in visual aesthetic preference obtained from a meta-analysis of neuroimaging studies (2004–2006). The model posits the following stages:

1 The elementary visual attributes of an artwork are processed like any other visual object's (primary and secondary visual brain areas).
2 Attentional processes redirect information processing to prominent visual properties, such as colour, shape and composition (frontal–parietal networks).
3 Attentional networks modulate processing within the ventral visual stream that leads to attributional networks – the 'what pathway', i.e. experience of the stimulus, attributes and contents, such as faces and landscapes (temporal lobe).[3]

---

[3] In the dual visual systems (DVS) model (Milner and Goodale, 1995), it is the ventral stream involving temporal areas for semantic processing and recognition (this is capable of inferring allocentric perspectives), rather than the dorsal stream, including parietal areas

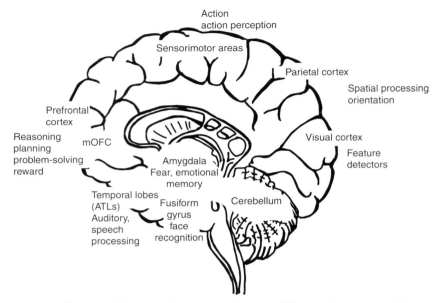

Figure 4. Diagram of the human brain. ATL: anterior temporal lobe; mOFC: medial orbitofrontal cortex.

4 Feed-back/feed-forward processes linking attentional and attributional circuits that enhance the experience of the visual object.
5 Emotional systems intervene in most cases (anterior medial temporal lobe, medial and orbitofrontal cortices and subcortical structures) (Chatterjee, 2003).

I would suggest that some of these processes are integrated or co-occurrent, and it is up to neuroscience and psychology to devise experiments that test the underlying hypothesis. Given that contemporary artworks stimulate a number of highly complex conceptual systems, as well as emotions, memories and sensations, it seems unlikely that this massive orchestration is dependent on sensorimotor processing, as the 'embodied' approach suggests, or that our experience of art can be encapsulated or exemplified by what happens in the visual cortex alone.

occupied with coordinating the position of the body and visuomotor actions (with predominantly egocentric frames of reference). Jeannerod and Jacob (2005) cast some doubt on the strict apportionment of functionality to this duality, and Gallese (2007) maintains that the dual system is actually more like a multiple system with various substreams. Whatever the truth about the shifting balance between the streams and the precise amount of consciousness that each entails, it is clear that overestimating the dorsal stream in visual experience in order to stress action in perception would not be the right approach.

This is a much-simplified diagram of the brain, reflecting how cognitive psychology localises the major cognitive, perceptual and motor functions, and I have highlighted those areas that play key roles in our experience of art. It does not, however, show various convergence zones and streams: how the brain continually integrates information requiring massive and dynamic interconnectivity and a multifunctionality of its parts, depending on the work of art being processed. I discuss this broader dynamic view of the brain's processes in later pages.

1.4   Scene and object recognition

Experiments indicate that, for some tasks, four to six items can be attended at the same time (Pylyshyn and Storm, 1988). In the visual field, these items can be four to six focal points of an object or scene that are bound or 'glued' together to form temporary object or scene recognition. Rensink (2000) suggests that attention may be seen as a hand that grasps the features of objects with four to six 'fingers': 'The release of focused attention is like the release of the items held by the hand, with these items returning to the "primal ooze", that is, the flux of constantly regenerating low-level structures' (Rensink, 2000, p. 26).[1]

Rensink goes on to suggest that the visual field can be characterised as a 'virtual representation'. Instead of holding all the objects in our surroundings in our short-term memory (which would be very wasteful as many of them would not be relevant to our purposes at any one moment), attention is coordinated so that a detailed representation of an object is formed whenever needed for the task. Rensink offers the metaphor of the Internet to explain how this works:

If we want to see the information at a particular site, our workstation checks to see if it is already in its memory. If so, nothing more needs to be done. Otherwise, it sends out a request to the appropriate site and has the requested information loaded in. If this transfer can be done sufficiently quickly, our workstation will appear to contain all the information in the network. But in reality, this information will have only a virtual representation: it is not all present simultaneously in the workstation, but is simply accessed whenever requested (2000, p. 30).

Thus, even though our conscious minds may have the impression that all the objects in front of us are simultaneously given a detailed, coherent representation somewhere in our brain, this need not be the case. Instead, this can result from a

---

[1] This bears close relation to FINST ('fingers of instantiation'), Pylyshyn and Storm (1998) theory, which Pylyshyn recently reasserted using the following explanation: 'If you imagine the cartoon character "Plastic Man" sticking long flexible fingers on a number of objects, and imagine that the fingers themselves cannot sense any properties of these objects directly but allow the individuated objects to be queried by attending to them, this captures the basic idea behind visual indexes' (2006, p. 206).

much sparser 'just in time' system that simply provides the right object representation at the right time (p. 32).

According to this theory, our peripheral vision will maintain a *global* or coarse-grained attention to more distant details (an abstract awareness of the general location or 'blurred' form of things), and this will provide the impression that all objects are represented in detail simultaneously before us. Meanwhile, we can attend to particular objects in a scene consecutively with fine-grained *local* detail, with the metaphorical 'fingers' of attention that will grasp each object, while relinquishing its hold on others in a continual and rapid shifting of attention from focal point to point. We may want to stop at certain objects or details in order to act upon them with higher-order semantic processes.

The key question for this attentional model is how the location of an object is discerned before attention is directed to it. One explanation invites us to change our assumption that attention is a 'spotlight' illuminating only one particular area of the visual field that our foveal vision settles on. For a start, we may be looking at something but not attending to it. However, as the *global* and *local* aspects of attention mentioned earlier indicate, there are different levels of attention: low-level attention in the first case, higher-definition attention in the second case and, in a third, a non-attentional subsystem that provides a *setting* that may alert the other two forms of attention (Rensink, 2000, p. 34). I believe that a good way to characterise this is to use terms we might use to describe a painting. We have a foreground (fine-grained and detailed and local), a mid-ground (rather more global but more blurred) and a background or out-of-the-frame kind of non-attentive 'setting'. We avail of a background setting outside of full conscious attention with the use of various possible schemata or sets of expectations, which might consist of layout information or 'scripts' (associated things we expect to find in situation types such as a wedding, a restaurant or in art, in a religious scene, still life or a history painting). We often know where to look next (yet this still surprises us).[2] Sometimes motion or an event in our environment will divert our attention to other schemata, or some events are strange and do not conform to our understanding and experience, eventualities that will all provide us with the feeling of discovery or surprise. If we are perplexed momentarily

---

[2] 'When perceptual learning occurs, what is learned can almost always be formulated in terms of what aspects of a scene the person learns to attend to (an extreme case of which is when people learn *where to look*, as in the chicken-sexing example)' where individuals in chicken factories are able quickly and expertly to discern differences between chicks in order to determine their sex, differences that remain imperceptible to most (Pylyshyn, 2006, p. 200).

by the next object we focus on, it only serves to show us the set of expectations, *scene schemas* or 'gists' that have been primed and held in standby mode until we settle on one interpretative frame that seems to fit, to make sense of it all.[3] Scene schemas are believed to include an inventory of objects *likely* to be present. Arguments persist as to how detailed or coded these are, but according to Henderson (1997), while objects in the visual field may be *detected*, a coherent representation of their structure need not be constructed. There also needs to be a system of representations as to where objects are *likely* to be present (imagine how we might go about finding a cup in someone else's house). The 'likely' aspect of these representations consists of probability scenarios. In art, there will be scene schemas for art objects, where we expect to find signatures or symbols; but art is mischievous and has always interested viewers by surprising us. Much of what we attend to is the result of our familiarity with the kinds of things that habitually interest us, yet the phenomenal qualities of novelty in these situations seem real, and this may be due more to familiarity within unexpected situations. The reverse, however, that unfamiliar objects in expected situations cause concern, is a strategy used quite often in Surrealism, and continues to influence contemporary art practice, as we shall see.

Often, in the context of contemporary art, the schemata and scripts we have available may not be of use, and we might be forced to rely on the fact that it is art or depend on an art gallery to decide that it is acceptable for something not to make sense in the ordinary way. Contemporary art seems to be able to provide a challenge to verification processes as a matter of course. Yet even here, schemata may be combined for the kind of novel situations that those familiar with contemporary art seem to relish, and those largely unfamiliar with it tend to dread or condemn. Psychologically, Rensink's useful study of the architecture of attention concerning object and scene recognition is relevant to our understanding of art. He writes: 'this architecture embodies a fundamental change of perspective: scene representations are no longer structures *built up* from eye movements and attentional shifts, but rather, are structures that *guide* such activities' (Rensink, 2000, p. 36).

---

[3] In addition, Martindale (1988) remarks that in visual art, as well as in literature and music, 'there seems to be a tendency to ignore or throw away details in favor of the gist or global form' (p. 24) – an abstracting process which relies on schemata. In addition, Bar (2004) reports visual false memory experiments, where participants 'remember' having seen, in a previously presented picture, objects that are contextually related to that scene that were not in fact depicted. 'Such memory distortions might be byproducts of an efficient mechanism for extracting and encoding the gist of a scene' (p. 618). In other words, the participants use schemata to complete scene retrieval and recognition.

1.5   Object recognition

We take for granted that identifying an object is a simple, basic process. Yet according to Martin (2007), such identification occurs over distributed areas of the brain (spatial, visual, sensorimotor and categorical): 'information about different types of object properties is stored in different brain regions...sensory and motor-based object properties are stored within sensory and motor systems, respectively [and the] occipitotemporal cortex that appears to be related to object category. [This suggests an] overlap between perceptual and conceptual neural processing systems' (p. 34).

The notion that an object is thus to be defined by its use and the sensorimotor actions to which we can put it ignores a vast store of encyclopaedic knowledge that we possess about objects and objects portrayed in the unusual and thought-provoking contexts provided by contemporary art. Objects that are retrieved from semantic memory are also often mediated in an emotional way (Damasio, 1995; Versace et al., 2009); and importantly, we sometimes respond to different *parts* of an object in qualitatively different ways. Art presents to us a number of partial objects, assisted readymades or hybrid objects, which engage the cognitive-emotional system in largely unaccustomed ways, encouraging us to focus on parts of objects and to assemble them into semantic wholes and make associations in novel ways. However, it is not only objects but also events that are deliberately fragmented into multisensory and subordinate parts, each of which might have a range of negative or positive emotional valences attached to them, or none at all. The principles of how categories as well as object identification are retrieved from long-term memory affecting ongoing perceptual tasks has been theorised by Versace et al. (2009). Various forms of knowledge are stored in long-term memory in various formats associated with different sensory modalities. We are able to associate quickly and blend such varying information in our memories as a creative process of remembering that meshes with unfolding present experience. Hence, memory is never a carbon copy; it is always contextualised to create extra dimensions of meaning. Emotional reactions to partial aspects of objects, whole objects, groups of objects and categories help to model complex emotional events and experiences. In addition, such emotional experiences can fragment or rearrange the significance of objects by shifting attentional focus to the constituent parts of objects with the help of the amygdala (fine tuning affect), fusiform gyrus (facial discrimination) and hippocampus (if emotional memory is involved), as well as the temporal lobes involved in semantic memory and interpretation (see Figure 4).

When object identification is not a given, reality testing sequences and evaluations come into play that may have a number of cognitive and emotional repercussions. In other words, particular complex objects such as assisted readymades found in modern and contemporary art that bring together unexpected constituent parts, often nonsensically, stimulate and re-sequence engrams and ongoing visual perceptions to do with object use (parietal and premotor areas), slow down and confuse automatic object recognition systems, along with destabilising emotional integration. One would expect immediate responses to *Lunch in Fur* for the first time to consist of bemusement or discomfort, perhaps eliciting a nervous laugh or even contempt; there may, however, be some curiosity or enchantment and, in a small number of cases, a feeling of arousal or nausea mixed in with these various other emotions. The point is that the identification based on anticipated use also helps to organise possible emotional responses, but we are unsure how to use *Lunch in Fur* and this creates a series of hybrid emotions, a number of mixed feelings based on scrambled processes normally dedicated to object identification as well as semantic construal.

However, one can also be emotionally motivated to solve the puzzle of meaning suggested by the work or to study the object as part of art history, in which case, the object becomes the pretext for creative processes of imagination and conceptual combination, often associated with poetry or word games. Both emotion and motivation signals may be integrated with perceptual and cognitive processes 'to effectively incorporate *value*' (Pessoa, 2010a, p. 440). Value may be shared by cognitive or emotional input or by the integration of each of these but, in art especially, where a visual item can be complex as well as unfamiliar and experimental, multiple brain areas will be involved in its evaluation. This suggests that it is counterproductive to separate out emotion and cognition when they are so intertwined and, importantly, when emotions are mixed and hybrid in any case.[1]

---

[1] 'the affective dimensions of a visual item are reflected at multiple processing stages, from early visual areas to prefrontal sites. In addition, visual cortical responses reflecting an

Episodic memory is selective, not encyclopaedic. It might store various multimodal properties of events or objects, but not all of them, perhaps only notable or salient features that seemed important in experience in terms of how they were processed by the semantic system. For example, I might not have remembered the plate on which the Madeleine cake was placed; I might add this detail to the event from my creative projections when retrieving this memory. Moreover, if I needed to think of the plate thematically, it would be for some present semantic need, as the constituent of another, larger task. The memory of an emotion attached to an object or event will work in a similar way; its features will be mapped differently each time to the context of present retrieval. The features of present experience, such as an encounter with an artwork, might emphasise or stimulate part of an original emotional event in a different sequence, creating a feeling of the uncanny, or *déjà vu*, creating a resonance and familiarity for the object without ever having seen it before. This is often at work in Surrealist art and many other kinds of art, where deliberately muddled automatic emotional responses make the encounter with art a complex and problematic experience, not easily identified. Thus integration, emotional and cognitive works on a number of levels: 'we should not speak in terms of an integration mechanism, but rather of various integration mechanisms, depending on the level of functioning, whether we are referring to the integration of the components of an object, the integration of the various objects forming a visual scene, or temporal integration' (Versace et al., 2009, p. 11).

I would like to mention here that, in art, this implies an embedded structure where the binding of an object's concrete features (a perceptual process) can occur within or alongside a conceptual process (object semantics) while attending to a scene. A scene can be attended to as the binding of a concrete concept BEACH, within a larger semantic structure (a landscape, a still life), within an even larger structure; Surrealist art, for example. Versace et al. (2009) do not refer to this embedding structure but they do come close to theorising this by admitting that memory, as a propagation of activations, is multimodal and intramodal and that these processes are not sequential so much as 'cascaded'. I take this to mean the synchronisation of co-occurent activations at different levels of fine-grainedness, as occurs with the production of a percept, concrete object and abstract concept. The prefrontal cortex is functional in helping to prioritise or integrate signals and to maintain the activation of several

item's significance will be a result of simultaneous top-down modulation from fronto-parietal attentional regions and emotional modulation from the amygdala, basal forebrain, orbitofrontal cortex, and other regions' (Pessoa, 2010a, p. 444).

signals for a long-term reward or goal. Creative problem solving is also associated with this area (Vartanian and Goel, 2004).

Simmons and Barsalou (2003) suggest that convergence zones – cooperative brain areas that integrate cascaded information – are hierarchically organised in order to process different levels of fine-grainedness (or abstraction) of an object, concept or, for that matter, an emotion. Take, for example, an apple: this can be attended to as an abstract or symbolic concept, or a concrete and ordinary concept, or we might absentmindedly just bite into it. Each kind of mental operation may converge, resulting in semantic and perceptual activity with rich thematic sensory experience or very little sensory input. Spreading activation can include not only attending to the apple as an object but also framing it as an abstract concept, such as TEMPTATION, as we would if we were engaged with a picture of Adam and Eve. To pick out one small part of this aesthetic experience, the sensorimotor processing of a scene or its objects and its emotional valence in terms of the depicted action, would be to trivialise how rapidly and cooperatively abstract symbolic processes can nuance sensory perceptions, especially in art where one is expected to think metaphorically and symbolically.

Semantic memory will have a role in retrieving multisensory episodes (the taste, feel, colour, sound of the experience of biting into an apple) and episodes with concrete and abstract concepts attached to them that may be used literally or symbolically depending on the task at hand. This task may be helped along by the tools available to working memory that can aid complex conceptual combinations, such as artworks. Many current theories regarding the organisation of conceptual knowledge are based on the assumption that a concept is composed of distinct types of information. However, there is much disagreement as to how different types of knowledge about the same object in the world are integrated (the binding problem). According to Caramazza and Shelton (1998, pp. 16–17), there are different kinds of functional and neural specialisation depending on types of knowledge, such as living animate or tools and various other basic categories, that bring together affective, spatial, visual and semantic processes, which are automatically activated when accessing that category. On this view, the identification of evolutionarily important objects (dangerous animals or ones that one could hunt, tools, faces, etc.) occurs quickly with different kinds of dedicated groups of brain areas that are accustomed to working in concert. A face will recruit a rapid connection of brain areas different from those processing a tool but these brain areas will be widely distributed in function (categorical, spatial, emotional), and sensorimotor areas will play only one part in this massive connectivity. It remains to be seen how contemporary art specialising in deliberately confusing or blending fundamental categorical knowledge and object domains affects neural areas specialised for discrete categories. Certainly, the brain will be working overtime trying to figure out how to use such automatic processes. It is in this light that the unsettling response we might have to the sculptures of Patricia Piccinini made out of synthetic polymers – half-animal, half-human – can be partly explained.

Another model concerning object recognition is that of Damasio (1995), who explains that this and some classification processes are emotionally driven, with more or less input from 'somatic markers': pulse rate, heartbeat, pains and aches, for example, which stimulate various reward or avoidance strategies. These somatic markers are thought to be held in the memory, triggering emotional and semantic associations. They are also closely associated with object properties and, more generally, the situations in which they are experienced. Features of a situation are marked by emotional or somatic complexes. On this view, the prefrontal cortex assigns these somatic markers to past emotional and situational experiences. Neurons in the prefrontal cortex can represent not just an object, but also the reward value it is associated with and the degree to which it is anticipated or worth pursuing in a given context that is purposefully processed for this reward. As a powerful association system, somatic markers are recognised intuitively in complex situations or examples of object identification as part of an overall habitual strategy in the pursuit of pleasure or the avoidance of danger. Despite various criticisms, Versace et al. suggest: 'somatic markers would make it possible to evaluate a given situation very rapidly, automatically and unconsciously. In contrast, when the emotional evaluation requires the integration of other characteristics, it would become less automatic, slower, more conscious, and would involve other nervous structures' (Versace et al., 2009, p. 17).

The general idea of somatic markers lends structure to the immediate question of risk assessment in various situations, the urgency of which, however, particularly in art, might not always seem compelling in a somatic sense. Art often allows us to abstract away from the immediacy of somatic markers, and even to become aware of them, allowing a kind of somatic markers testing. The emotional evaluation involved in the kind of experimental objects I have been discussing would lead to a range of emotional evaluations that are pleasurably ambiguous or tinged with traces of anxiety, urgency or pleasure. As always, psychological studies when applied to art need to process the dissociative effects of fiction that will often lose something in the translation from the cases usually studied in neuroscience and psychology. The point to salvage here, however, is that certain filtered or altered somatic markers probably bias object identification in art.

Object identification, and decision-making tasks directed towards them, involves an integration of neuropsychological processes and associations with episodic memory, emotional valence, reinforcement, risk assessment and the memory of visceral rewards and aversions. Notably, all of these can be sent into interesting and perhaps creative disarray and self-monitoring with the experimental objects I have been describing in art, such as Oppenheim's fur cup. Again, a sense of duration of a spreading semantic activation is useful here rather than thinking of this as an immediate or singular response frozen in time. A more relaxed timeframe involved in studying these experimental objects and counterfactuals in a gallery situation, or even leafing through an illustrated book, allows us to reflect on the automatic and conditioned nature of object identification in order to present new interpretative opportunities.

The object identification involved in these kinds of art objects is akin to the ways in which literature, philosophy, psychology or therapeutic strategies set up a number of counterfactuals or nonsensical examples and simulations in order to reason about mental states and behaviour using thought experiments (for example, what would happen if you walked to work backwards?). Although used in the service of explaining normal rational behaviour, momentarily we entertain nonsense scenarios. However, art often extends these episodes as ends in themselves and for a number of reasons, depending on the aims of the artist whose long-term strategies can best be discerned by adopting the art historical comparative method: a cross-examination of the artist's works and/or works by other artists.

According to Damasio, convergence zones (CZs) work as part of an underlying logic whereby neurons in a CZ reflect the similarity of the features they conjoin; the neurons are supposed to 'embody a binding code' for the object identified. However, what if we cannot identify an object because we have never seen it before? Art, particularly contemporary art, is constantly showing us objects we have never before experienced or seen; how does this affect our neurological plasticity? On the whole, in traditional figurative art, we are invited to make sense out of an already established coherence when it comes to object recognition. A recognisable body that stimulates familiar sensorimotor responses is usually supplied and, with the interpretation of actions depicted, we may intuit emotional states. Nevertheless, what do we do when such coherence is compromised by the hybrid assisted readymade or many other kinds of artworks, collage, words and images, or abstract painting, which cobble together unexpected parts of objects encouraging a number of sensorimotor responses that cannot latch on to the object of perception? This is so in even more complex scene recognition where singular object recognition is subordinate to an overall system of relations with other objects in a context. On this view, scene recognition does not seem to occur as discrete, consecutive or parallel processes but, instead, is a more interactive, variable process that integrates contextual information (Bartels, 2009; Bartels and Zeki, 2004).

1.6 Granularity in scene recognition

As we have seen in Rensink (2000), object recognition often depends on background information. As Moshe Bar explains: 'Our experience with the visual world dictates our predictions about what other objects to expect in a scene, and their spatial configuration. For example, seeing a steering wheel inside a car sets expectations about where the radio, ashtray and mirrors might be. These predictable properties of our environment can facilitate perception, and in particular object recognition' (Bar, 2004, p. 617).

Artworks will balance predictions about what to expect in a scene with some surprising incongruities, or they will attempt prototypicality (think, for example, of an Impressionist painting of a sunny afternoon gathering). The process of context or scene recognition (or prediction) makes the other process of object recognition easier, and yet, as indicated in earlier pages, objects (a bed or a hammer) will also activate types of scene or context associated with these objects, indicating 'a bidirectional exchange between the two processes' (Bar, 2004, p. 620).

Figure 5 is an indication of the kind of multiple processing of a scene's details (Saville's *Plan*) that will occur in a range of granularity from local to global.

Different brain regions in various cooperative relationships achieve a local to global, fine-grained to coarse-grained granularity, respectively. In the *Object Identification* box, an object's features would undergo perceptual binding in the occipital visual cortex and the fusiform gyrus where it would be put into basic-level categories in the inferior temporal cortex. There would also be sensorimotor processes involved in interpreting the pose of the figure. In *Situation/Scene*, contextual relations would be attempted in the parahippocampal cortex (PHC), where various aspects of episodic memory could be activated.[1] Here the 'scene' is established as a single entity (a library, royal court, zoo scene) and will need to cooperate with *Relational Knowledge*. In *Abstract Concepts*, semantic relations would be

---

[1] 'Structures in the medial temporal lobe...the hippocampus, PHC, and perirhinal and entorhinal cortices, are thought to be important in associative processing' (Bar, 2004, p. 621).

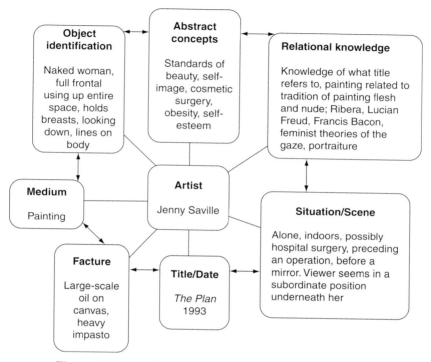

Figure 5. Various factors involved in understanding artworks (arrows show that these factors may influence each other and are non-sequential).

explored in the temporal lobes; along with *Relational Knowledge*, the prefrontal cortex and long-term memory would cooperate to build up representations of relational knowledge that might, for example, access category information to do with style or groups of works that deal with specific themes. Note that while *Abstract Concepts* can identify a theme, *Relational Knowledge* will furnish examples of artworks relevant to the theme, providing systematicity.

An additional complication is that *Artist, Title, Medium* are not perceptible properties in the scene itself but will have considerable influence on how the scene is interpreted. In these stages, abstract concepts in relational knowledge, what we know of the artist, her work and the title, will be accessed before local, thematic, fine-grained perceptions will take place.[2]

---

[2] For a psychological study of how titles affect interpretation, see Leder et al., 2006.

Importantly, such abstract concepts may be held in short-term memory while all the fine-grained processing continues. Yet a fine-grained focus will flow into a coarse-grained focus: the explicit intentional focus on a local detail could be a brushstroke on the surface of the canvas that is part of the handle of a jug held by a milkmaid in a kitchen scene; we may consider the overall composition to establish mood and time of day. Yet while we focus on the brushstroke, the general scene will fade into the background and become blurred 'global' cues, which for that moment are less actively attended. In a sense, the surrounding details are temporarily 'out of sight, out of mind' although, as we have seen with Rensink's theories, there may be non-attentional processing of these peripheral areas. Alternatively, it is important to note that it may be possible to skip stages where we can 'construct a coarse representation of a scene that bypasses object identities, where the scene is represented as a single entity. This rudimentary information can provide a shortcut for automatic activation of high-level semantic information by relatively low-level perceptual information' (Bar, 2004, p. 619).

It is interesting that this happens regularly with Impressionist artworks, which attempt to depict the simultaneous or global 'impression' of a scene rather than inviting distinct, fine-grained object perception, at least at first. In fact, when feature perception is activated, it will be at the level of facture where the shapes of painted daubs, pigment and brushstrokes will be discerned in *Medium*, yet which will work together with *Relational Knowledge* to build up a categorical judgement about style (a 'late Renoir' as opposed to an 'early Renoir', for example). Thus, it should be noted that all the different stages will not be consecutive. There will be parallel processing, overlap and, importantly, attentional priorities will allow any stage to be revisited more purposefully. Whereas scene recognition in *Situation/Scene* might be the result of a glance, *Relational Knowledge* might require considerable time to acquire where accrued information gathered from previous stages will be processed with ongoing perceptions. It is also the case that we may switch rapidly back from global to local, so that the patterned regularity of the brushstrokes are perceived as leaves on trees in the perceptual detail, or as part of a Renoir's late style. An interesting complication, however, is how the branches of some pine trees actually look like the grooved marks we associate with brushstrokes, and vice versa.[3]

---

[3] Church (2000, pp. 109–110) has argued that the process of 'seeing as', that is, seeing a painting as a landscape yet seeing it also as a painting, involves both conflict *and* convergence together. This obviously complicates categorisation. A similar attempt to disambiguate a scene into various kinds of granularity is the art historian Panofsky's

Abstract conceptual thought could be brought to bear on any level of granularity. It could include a fine-grained focus on one object, a horse for example: Pegasus, symbolising power, swift transport, energy, magic; or on the global scene associated with the theme as a whole: divine power, intervention, transcendence. Yet symbolisation is only one form of abstraction. Another is how, in art and music, we think of the way in which other artists in earlier periods have dealt with the same theme. The artwork attended to may also, as often happens, contain some clue or reference point to a previous treatment of the same scene by another artist. More generally, artworks can be grouped in terms of sharing the same period, cultural tradition or 'genre' (these could be 'situations' such as a still life, a portrait or a painting commemorating an important historical event); or artworks could share common features regarding artistic style and 'motifs' (consistent perceptual details), or the use of similar compositions (placing of objects, bodies in particular poses). They could use genre (or a particular mixture of genres), styles and motifs in order to help us grasp concepts such as TRUTH or POWER. In other words, many concepts, even quite abstract ones, can be grouped together into larger superordinate categories such as style, period or theme. Such categorisation requires a complex network of brain areas for its operation: the inferior temporal cortex encoding object identifications, the parahippocampal cortex providing contexts for them (keeping in mind that a context can also be a different artwork), while the prefrontal cortex will help to match these processes when multiple possibilities exist. It is assumed that the longer a picture is attended, involving a number of other sensory and emotional resources that I have not mentioned here, an even larger-scale network of interconnected brain areas and aspects of the nervous system will be required, and together will produce the experience of being absorbed by an artwork. Not all scenes or artworks can be resolved into coherent experiences, however. Many artworks specialise in providing incoherent juxtapositions of scene context and object identifications, as we shall see.

iconographical method that consists of three levels. At the first level of analysis, individual elements of an image are identified; at the second level, the ostensible topic of the image is determined; and at the third level, the underlying meaning is construed.

1.7   Object categorisation

Intricately involved with many aspects of scene recognition are categorisation processes. An important way that we act upon objects is to put them into categories or groups that temporarily change our conceptualisation (or even recognition). The situation, task or context will 'put objects in their place'. Yet the way in which we group objects will decide the level of attentional focus; for example, we may put various objects in a group such as breakfast things on a table, and not pay attention to them, or we may individuate an object such as a cup to discern its design. Categorisation will require that we pick out a common feature that is shared by these objects, filtering out other details. Alternatively, the situation itself which 'contains' the objects ('breakfast', for example) becomes the thing in common shared by each object, or it may itself become a situation with many others; for example, Victorian domestic scenes. In a more fine-grained manner, a bed, curtains, wardrobe and drawers may come together to make BEDROOM – a concept that does not require that, thematically, we attend to any of its component parts while discussing how many bedrooms there are in a house. Eleanor Rosch explains that there are good evolutionary reasons for categorisation: 'One purpose of categorization is to reduce the infinite differences among behaviourally and cognitively useable proportions. It is to the organism's advantage not to differentiate one stimulus from others when that differentiation is irrelevant to the purposes at hand' (1999, p. 190). There is thus no point in deciding whether the dangerous animal on the horizon is a panther, leopard, tiger or lion – running away works in fast cooperation with the category construction of a dangerous cat-like animal.

Categorisation is a form of abstraction in the sense that to abstract is to draw out some feature that is common to a number of entities (naming certain objects that all belong in a bedroom), ignoring other objects (washing machine, for example) for the sake of creating the category.[1]

---

[1]   Miller et al. (2002) note that, like objects, categories depend on the cooperation of many areas distributed in the brain and affected by the task at hand. They could be 'represented

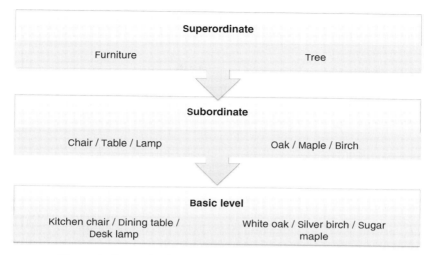

Figure 6. Categorisation: superordinate/subordinate/basic objects.

Thus, categorisation is also about exclusion. However, it is possible as well to make different kinds of categories out of the same finite members of a group, depending on the feature or features used for the purpose of categorisation. Thus, dishes, forks, plates, knives, bowls, wineglasses, tumblers, jug and spoons could all be grouped under dinnerware, or in different groups: cutlery, crockery, glassware, China, silver or junk. Eleanor Rosch (1999) suggests that there are different levels to categorisation.

The hypothesis is that basic level objects are the most *inclusive* level of classification at which objects have a number of attributes in common. There are fewer attributes for the superordinate category and more for the basic level.[2] Rosch writes: 'Objects may be first seen or recognised as

and stored in the same areas of the visual cortex that analyse form' (p. 1124). Or, such perceptual categories might be found in the prefrontal cortex, which receives the results of visual processing from the visual cortex. Both areas contain neurons specialised for processing complex stimuli 'such as tree, fishes, faces, brushes, etc.' It could be that both work in conjunction, the visual cortex selecting features and the prefrontal cortex activating categories in which to put them, but with different patterns of cooperation depending on the situation, goals, attention and the type of stimuli involved.

[2] This diagram could be represented differently in terms of a branched hierarchy – as a semantic network in the case of Collins and Quillian (1969) – rather than lists. The advantages of a network is that it suggests spreading activation and priming by association as models of encoding the relationality of subordinate terms to achieve relative automatic processes. Yet there are problems with how, exactly, this can be organised especially when there are more typical basic to higher-level thoughts: 'robin is a bird' is quicker to process

members of their basic category, and...only with the aid of additional processing can they be identified as members of their superordinate or subordinate category' (Rosch, 1999, p. 195).

Importantly, contexts and situations that constrain categorisation are also conceptual: 'both basic levels and prototypes are, in a sense, theories about context itself...it seems likely that, in the absence of a specified context, subjects assume what they consider the normal context or situation for occurrence of that object' (Rosch, 1999, p. 202). Thus, there is no absolute prototypicality or category membership (analysed in a laboratory). Context and situation influence categorisation and there are abstract concepts about typical contexts and situations (Rosch mentions 'events' that are associated with concrete objects).

Subtly and rapidly, even the mention of a concrete concept (a spoon) in a sentence or depicted in a painting can prime the situational context (or concept) in which that object is usually associated. Rosch asks: 'Could we use events as the basic unit from which to derive an understanding of objects? Could we view objects as props for the carrying out of events and have the functions, perceptual attributes, and levels of abstraction of objects fall out of their roles in such events?' (Rosch, 1999, p. 203). There are, thus, two mutually constraining processes that occur for effective categorisation to take place: an abstracting process of basic level or subordinate level objects where we pick out features generalisable across instances and, importantly for artworks, in cooperation with this, an abstracting of the situation or context as an organising set of parameters. In other words, 'abstraction' implies: 'a process of extracting and manipulating information from a context so that it can be deployed in new ones, or "projected". This process of abstraction is a form of generalization across time, place and individual instance, which crucially involves *selectively discarding* some information coming from the context' (Mazzone and Lalumera, 2010, p. 49; my emphasis). This process of discarding individual peculiarities of a specific instance 'can therefore be projected to other instances in different cognitive encounters' (p. 50).

This would mean that the situation we find ourselves in needs to be understood and conceptualised as a type in order for the details associated with it to come together as a coherent experience. These 'situational' concepts need to be stable across instances to a certain extent, yet they also need to be sensitive to contextual and perceptual peculiarities, often allowing ad hoc combinations of situations (a restaurant on a boat, for

---

than an atypical example 'chicken is a bird' (Rosch, 1973), suggesting various social and cultural contingencies intervening in a theoretically logical spreading activation structure: there seem to be short cuts in categorisation processes that depend on language and usage.

Figure 7. Man Ray, *The Enigma of Isidore Ducasse*, 1920 (reconstructed 1971) (object wrapped in felt and string, #8 from an edition of 10, 40.5 × 57.5 × 21.5). National Gallery of Australia, Canberra. Purchased 1973. © Man Ray Trust/ADAGP, Paris and DACS, London 2012.

example, with chairs fixed onto the floor, or a funeral in an unfamiliar cultural setting).

However, we also experiment regularly and imaginatively with our categorisation processes in games, stories, puzzles and contemporary art. By presenting us with fictional scenarios, artworks are able to disturb, in a creative manner, the tacit logic we employ in the formation of categories. Thus, in a Surrealist painting, for example, a bedroom can float on the sea or be found in a cave, while in a fairy story a lion can walk on its hind legs in a rose garden, and with Oppenheim's fur cup we are presented with the incongruous situation of tea with fur on the table. Many artworks complicate or destabilise this 'grammar' of logical construction, not only with the hybridity of a single object's features, but also by juxtaposing objects that we would not find together normally. This is a 'classic' principle behind the Surrealist facture of assisted readymades that continues to exercise an enormous influence on contemporary art practice.

This may be seen in a well-known work by Man Ray, *The Enigma of Isidore Ducasse* (1920). Ducasse was a nineteenth century writer admired by the Surrealists for the bizarre and potent dream imagery he experimented with in his nonlinear writings, *Les Chants de Maldoror* (1869). Ducasse adopted the pseudonym, the Comte de Lautréamont. The 'sculpture' features a cloth bound by a rope covering an object that cannot be seen underneath it, although this is known to be a sewing machine. This is a reference to Lautréamont's famous phrase 'Beautiful as the chance meeting, on a dissecting table, of a sewing machine and an umbrella'. Such an expression sparks several situational events that spring to mind in quick succession. The aesthetic feeling we derive from Man Ray's work is due not only to the enigmas of category inclusion (a dissecting table, a sewing machine and an umbrella) but also to the way in which a blanket is being used as an artistic medium that references the drapery of classical art, or the way in which the string seems twisted elegantly and efficiently around some kind of presence.

One could be forgiven for thinking that this is not a 'work of art' but something that *could be*, if it were uncovered. Like most of Ray's objects constructed up to the late 1940s, it was assembled to provide an unusual subject for a photograph and then discarded. This object was later reconstructed from the photograph as an 'edition' of ten, now in various collections around the world. This challenged the sacred aura of the original and of the artist in favour of the pure conceptual value of the art. Man Ray said: 'Is a book or a bronze an original? I leave such considerations to well intentioned collectors and amateurs of the rare.'[3]

The object is so well known that most people come to it with a prior knowledge of the references to Lautréamont and the themes involved. The blanket is an army sleeping blanket referencing sleep, and underneath is to be found the 'dream object', which can be seen in the cold light of day (signifying conscious awareness). Thus, the object and its layers index eidetic imagery, as well as low-level perceptions (rope, blanket, knots) and high-level abstraction in terms of category inclusion and verification problems: is it a 'real' blanket, an ordinary object or a fictional restaging of Lautréamont's verse? We tend to suspend our sensory commitment to the work because we are not sure what lies underneath the blanket. Yet the object beneath it *might* be a human body, a sculptural form with a flowing, sensuous finish. It is obvious that the enigma ignites lots of sensorimotor responses and categorical processes, only to leave them unsatisfied.

---

[3] *Man Ray*, Los Angeles County Museum of Art, 1966 (exhibition catalogue) **28–31**, 28.

The sculpture seems temporary and makeshift not only because it seems to be packed up as a parcel in transit but also because we cannot 'commit' to it in any naïve sensorimotor way or by settling on a final meaning because of its ambivalent status, elusive identity, use or *raison d'être*. It is as polysemous as it is awkward and disjunctive, a tear in the fabric of normal time. In an ordinary context, outside a gallery, one probably would not even notice it. Importantly, this very possibility allows one to think differently about the notion of reality itself, allowing us to think outside of our customary indifference to incidental details. It suggests a re-categorisation of objects in the real world. According to Surrealist theories, the artwork challenges us to apply a *verfremdungeffekt* (estrangement effect), a bracketing-out of the natural attitude to objects, to apply this frame of mind to any other object in ordinary reality and to endow it with a life of its own, either as a resource for our dreams, as a way to remember them or as a way to improvise an artistic creativity of seeing things differently. The Surrealist aim is to suggest that we might put objects that do not belong together into categories to see what happens. Rather than playing word games, the assisted readymade suggests that the things themselves are their own models, the objects by which we can construct irrational, dreamlike encounters or poetic scripts, where we engage in semantic displacements. The object encourages a critical awareness of the notions of skill, preciousness, craftsmanship and sensory and emotional response, as well as the unexpected association of ideas and feelings arising from 'irrational' syntactical arrangements. One of Man Ray's undoubted intentions was the transfiguration of the extraordinary: the hidden presence under the blanket can signify anything; imagining what it might be amounts to a form of concept production where illogical categorisation becomes an aesthetic process. Yet there is also the symbolism of the army blanket: the artwork was created two years after the trauma and displacement of the Second World War. The whiff of madness where the army blanket is imaginatively transformed into a hospital blanket is never far away.

The readymade depends on the systematic disruption of categorisation processes. Apart from the fact that the readymade allows ordinary objects and their combination to become the medium for aesthetic feeling based on the chance encounter, we find (basic level and subordinate level) objects taken out of their typical event structure in art intriguing and worrying. They also seem to suggest superordinate categories: bedroom, closet, sewing room or attic, by which we struggle to establish the concreteness and its typicality of the object (much of which is hidden). Lautréamont's text skews the 'normal' process of categorisation that allows objects to be identified with situations or events, and events to be

Figure 8. Thomas Hirschorn, *Crystal of Resistance*, 2011 (a view of the Venice Biennale installation). © ADAGP, Paris and DACS, London 2012.

triggered by associations with objects. The artwork is a kind of objectification of poetry. Rosch suggests that substituting object names at other than the basic level within superordinate categories (kinds of rooms, for example) results in obviously 'deviant descriptions'. On the other hand, the 'substitution of *subordinate* terms for basic level object names in scripts gives the effect of snobbery'. To illustrate this, she quotes the following from Leo Garis' *The Margaret Mead of Madison Avenue*: 'And so, after putting away my 10 year-old Royal 470 manual and lining up my Mongol number 3 pencils on my Goldsmith Brothers Formica imitation-wood desk, I slide into my oversize squirrel-skin L. L. Bean slippers and shuffle off to the kitchen. There, holding Decades in my trembling right hand, I drop it, plunk, into my new Sears 20-gallon, celadon-green Permanex trash can' (Garis, 1975, pp. 47–48, quoted in Rosch, 1999, p. 204).

Yet this is also a symptom of the inability to abstract all the detail in larger groups or general expressions, and the inability to detect errors efficiently.

Such a fastidiousness is reminiscent of an obsessive-compulsive disorder.[4] This is a deliberate strategy employed in many contemporary artworks, and is one of the mainstays of Thomas Hirschorn's work. His entry for the Swiss Pavilion at the Venice Biennial, 2010, *Crystal of Resistance*, was a bewildering collection of groups of objects: dozens of damaged television sets wrapped in brown packing tape, pallets and office furniture, magazine stands, kitchenware, many of which were wrapped in tin foil, with aisles of manufactured goods. There were also some rather eerie department store manikins with their midriffs torn out and replaced with quartz crystals, along with photographs of maimed victims of war and bombings placed on ropes winding their way throughout the display. It is an intricate perversion of categorisation on a mass scale, a Baroque elaboration of what we have seen in Surrealism. The contemporary version is an orchestration of plastic, detritus and accumulation within a broader post-apocalyptic vision we are familiar with from the darker examples of the science-fiction genre. The obsessive-compulsive disorder is externalised into a social problem on a massive scale, where rampant consumerism and heaps of detritus, the anonymity of mass production, seem coldly indifferent to human suffering and bloodshed. Yet the way in which Hirschorn organises his objects into groups suggests a system of categories, or a parody of one; an extreme anti-formalism that threatens to make visual judgement impossible, flooding the senses with too much information. Moreover, of course, this is a huge problem for neuroaesthetic and embodied approaches to art, which emphasise the visual and formal aspects of art.

---

[4] Obsessive-compulsive disorder has been associated with abnormal functioning of the anterior cingulated cortex (ACC) of the brain responsible for conflict resolution and reward (Radua and Mataix-Cols, 2009).

1.8 Schemata

Object categorisation and scene recognition suggest that we match objects to situations or contexts, and contexts spring to mind when we think about individual objects. In both cases, we seem to have already formed representations or structures of knowledge that we are ready to apply to ongoing experience. These structures are often referred to as 'schemata' (Bartlett, 1932; Neisser, 1967). Note that categories can act as schemata, as we have seen with the example of BEDROOM given earlier, but not all schemata are categorical. The underlying principle across many psychological theories, which differ over the exact mechanisms involved in encoding and retrieving schemata, is that such mechanisms consist of patterns of previous experience involving abstract or concrete examples or events. These are combined into specific episodic memories, often automatically retrieved, allowing us to impose them rapidly and flexibly onto present experience, thus helping us to categorise, organise, frame or attribute value to the wealth of incoming signals available to us. Schemata might also be stereotypes that colour our views of social situations, or they might act as formulae we use to help us adjust to a new understanding of what is going on in an unfamiliar cultural or artistic experience.

The vast number of social and cultural situations that it is possible to theorise about will involve previously coded and learnt abstracted lessons that would guide present experience, and so schemata may come in a similar broad variety of forms. One way of dealing with this variety is to consider that these schemata are more like situations, such as those of restaurants, holidays, museums or weddings, or a set of expectations that nevertheless can accommodate variables. It seems logical that there should be schemata for different levels of abstraction: for the more concrete situations just mentioned and for abstract concepts such as ART or RELIGION, or both at the same time as in a painting of the Virgin Mary and Child – thus, scripts may be combined.

In art, Ernst Gombrich (1966) supposed that paintings were not simply windows onto reality but scenes whose very framing (Minsky, 1975) and organisation were determined by longstanding schemata, which, in his use, were more like pictorial conventions through which we interpret art. Even Rudolf Arnheim's appeal to gestalt principles (1969), where we group together perceptual details into wholes, is premised on the encoding and storage of patterns or constants that we impose onto scene recognition. More recently, it has been suggested that we have a number of schemata or canonical representations (Solso, 2003, p. 240), impressions that are encoded in the brain and which help us to categorise and filter the large number of incoming details and stimuli we find in the world.[1] Empirical research into change blindness (where we are tested for what we notice in scene changes (Rensink, 2000)) allow us to understand that although it seems as if we see a visual scene in art in its entirety, only a small part of the scene falling on the fovea is in clear focus at any one time. With saccadic movements, we can sample details in the visual field in order to match them to schemata that 'complete' the scene, but we never examine every inch of a canvas. There is, for example, no need to look at every point in a line to see that it is a line.[2]

Something of this sort must occur with our interpretations of art where we understand that something has happened or is going to happen outside of the frame of the painting even though we do not see it; an interpretation triggered by the perceptual cues in the artwork. We 'complete' the scene using our schemata or conceptual knowledge.[3] However, artworks are not merely incoming signals that we fold effortlessly into preconceived categories, although this also happens. The way in which a scene is organised might bring together concepts that, for us, have never been combined before, and this can lead to new ideas that have the power to move us or to change our views. Art often creates a dissonance with the conceptual frames that we use to organise the great amounts of detail available in

---

[1] This encoding not only determines what is stored but what is stored determines which retrieval cues are effective (Tulving, 1983). This has particular relevance for the kind of expert encoding that is performed on artworks, creating differences in canonical representations, encoding and retrieval cues involved in art.

[2] Similarly, Turner writes: 'If we see a photograph of the middle of a bridge, we routinely and naturally conceive of the bridge as extending beyond the frame' (2003, p. 12); our knowledge of what a bridge looks like is mapped onto the gaps in the representation.

[3] Solso (2003, p. 260) calls these 'hidden units', which group input stimuli (perceptual cues). These hidden units are then further worked upon to create complex inferences (output). How these hidden units are coded as perceptual symbols or propositional networks is controversial, as is their relation to mental imagery, which we might experience from perceptual cues in an artwork and, importantly, *during* our perceptual processing of an artwork. It becomes extremely difficult to separate the mental image formation concurrent with direct perception if we insist that both processes are purely perceptual. Yet how far mental images may be classified as nonperceptual or perceptual is notoriously unresolved and drawn out (see Pylyshyn, 2006; for opposing views, Kosslyn et al. (2006), and Thomas (1997) for a meta-analysis).

the visual world, coaxing us to consider changing these frames and helping us to support new ones. At times like this, we often reflect on the
contingencies of vision, what we are allowed to see and understand
by means of the unusual perceptual cues configured by the artist. Thus,
it must be kept in mind that although all these different theories hold
that schemata tend to be relatively constant, they can also be changed
over time.

Many examples of conceptual and contemporary art challenge the
schemata by which we normally read or experience art. Duchamp's
Fountain does just this; it challenges us to extend our conceptual constants, the categories we use to define art, and to prime our expectations
for future scenarios by allowing the admission of a 'vulgar' object into that
very same superordinate category. We may do this by considering that
such a move adds cognitive value to art, or is something that introduces
humour and wit (or anti-aestheticism) into the traditional domain of
classical art. It shifts our attention to the nature of conceptual thought
away from aesthetic considerations based on the balance, colour, finish or
composition of the art object. These, and other lines of reasoning, help to
justify changing the settings of our conceptual filtering and categorisation
that can help us to be more or differently receptive to artworks in later
encounters.

It is important that these schemata in long-term memory are not viewed
as fixed entities with detailed representations but rather as framing devices
or categories that contain different contents when retrieved for the perceptual task at hand, which might have new perceptible properties not
experienced before.[4] These schemata may be rapidly and flexibly
deployed and blended with others. What most of these versions of schemata have trouble with is the way in which schemata combine in great
numbers when engaging with art, watching a film, having a conversation.
Most demonstrations of these schemata thus are often extremely
simplistic.[5]

Art stimulates innovative combinations of concepts more often than
simply appealing to what we already know, although this also happens. In
fact, much of conceptual and contemporary art is built on the premise that
art should be about making new links between concepts and creating new

[4] Bar (2004) suggests that schemata are stored in the semantic production areas of the brain;
for example, in the anterior temporal lobe, and the parahippocampal cortex where contextual information and associations are processed.
[5] See Fauconnier and Turner's analysis of time metaphors for an exception (2008), and also
Turner (2003, pp. 13–16) for an attempt at composing an imaginary scenario of Olga's
picture-world, consisting of blend after blend in linear narrative form, which reads
strangely like a dream. Turner calls this a double-scope conceptual integration network.

integrations, rather than simply repeating older ones, although it is true that many artists repeat the principles behind their works. Conceptual integration or combination can occur easily, fluently and intricately, just as listening to music, appearing to happen of its own accord when our thoughts wander.[6] In other situations, we will need to be more attentive in highly structured ways, perhaps involving less fluent passages, when we are problem solving and where logical procedures are required. The exertion of effort in conceptual production thus depends on the task at hand, which may be a novel learning experience. Motivation, reward, desire and emotional drives aid categorisation and conceptual integration at the low level of object integration as well as the higher level of abstract concepts, both for the artist in creating the work and the viewer retrieving it. Together, artist and viewer often form an 'expert system', the material of which is the artwork itself. What I would like to add to the general literature on schemata in relation to art, and what seems to strike the right kind of balance for many kinds of aesthetic experiences in the visual arts, is that schemata (however we would like to argue about their modal or amodal encoding) help us to structure object recognition, scene recognition, aesthetic experience and expertise. Thus, schemata must work at various levels of complexity and abstraction. A schema that we can bring to bear on any artwork can be style, theme, medium, cultural stereotype, movement, genre or, importantly for contemporary art, the eight major trends I have listed in the introduction. Importantly for both psychology and contemporary art, schemata also function as systems of relational knowledge that can be assembled ad hoc while attending to particular artworks. Depending on how the perceptual features of these artworks are configured, our retrieval of schemata or aspects of relational knowledge can be relatively straightforward ('it's a Picasso'; 'it's about hybridity'). However, often artworks outstrip the models or schemata available. In response, we may retrieve several partial areas of relational knowledge in order to deal with such a challenge that we try to fit to incoming information. We may be encouraged to blend or combine aspects from several knowledge systems to create new ones.

Barsalou's simulators and simulations (1999) are also a form of theorising about schemata, as are Lakoff and Johnson's image schemas (1980), which are recurring patterns of sensory experience that underpin our language use, helping us to order our world. Barsalou's theory of perceptual symbol systems (PSS) holds that perceptions are filtered into

---

[6] *Dolce far niente*, as the Italians say, is the pleasure of doing nothing in particular. Sometimes, enjoying purposelessness can inform art, involving the coupling and decoupling of concepts, or with procrastination, the imaginative elaboration of the present.

schematic (yet analogue) form, resembling their referents, and these are processed by the sensory modalities. This considerably upgrades psychology's view of the intelligent capabilities of our sensorimotor system, which are able to ground (others might say caricature) abstract kinds of concepts that are so crucial for the art experience and for learning categories by 'hearsay' through language (Harnad, 1990).

Perceptual symbols are distinct from the classical view of abstract, amodal symbols that do not resemble their referents and are immediately accessible to the sensorimotor system. They do not require an intervening level of processing responsible for manipulating abstract symbols in some other, non-sensorimotor brain areas that traditionally are thought to add a layer of intelligence to our sense perceptions. Instead, concepts that we usually associate with rational behaviour and intelligence are, for Barsalou, grounded in these perceptual symbols that we use to 'grasp' these concepts. On this view, conceptual schemata do not help us to grasp perceptual experience. Instead, perceptual schemata allow us to grasp abstract concepts.

One of the ways in which perceptual symbols remain mysterious is whether they contain any spatial or analogue information, as we might expect with picture-like symbols. Theorists such as Kosslyn (1999) maintain that mental imagery does have these properties, while Pylyshyn (2006) denies this, accepting only propositional content for such imagery. Barsalou attempts to sidestep this debate by asserting that perceptual symbols are unlike the qualities of *conscious* mental (eidetic) imagery.[7] Instead, perceptual symbols are schemata – filtered out or degraded perceptual properties such as scale or sharpness, fine-grained variability – that are nonconsciously assembled by the senses in order to grasp objects.

This can become quite complex in cross-modal experience, where several kinds of perceptual symbols are integrated, hence the phrase 'perceptual symbol systems'. It is still unclear, however, how any combination of these perceptual symbols could represent abstract concepts or categories such as SCIENCE, as it is simply understood in speech. If Barsalou claims the symbols for science are more abstract than for bicycles, this may simply amount to yet another amodal theory of symbols. For Barsalou, concepts can be demonstrated by a series of *simulations* assembled in working memory, yet these are combined with *simulators* that

---

[7] Pylyshyn and Kosslyn argue the qualities of mental imagery in what has been termed the analogue-propositional debate. Although many of their arguments for and against analogue coding are relevant to the analogue nature of Barsalou's perceptual symbols, and I will be examining Pylyshyn's theory of representation in later pages, I will not be discussing mental imagery per se.

offer more constant features from long-term memory. Gabora (1999) writes: 'As Barsalou considers increasingly abstract concepts, he increases the complexity of the perceptual symbol arrangements' (p. 617), a process that begins to sound rather unwieldy when we consider the complexity of certain examples of complex sentence construction on the fly. For Barsalou, the perceptual system is largely automatic, generative and flexible: symbols may be recombined in an infinite number of ways in frames and simulators; in effect, using parts of percepts to create meanings that are more complex. The problem is that some logical words or abstract concepts, such as 'therefore' or DIPLOMACY, regardless of whether they have core features that remain unchanged in different contexts and circumstances, do not need to be represented by sensorimotor situations. We know what they are without perceptual demonstrations; we can form abstractions without them, and more parsimoniously than by appealing to perceptual simulations.[8] What is clear, however, is that the PSS needs to be made systematic and highly complex in order to represent abstract concepts, and to put the entire burden of this systematicity on sensorimotor areas in order to preserve the analogue nature of perceptual symbols seems ambitious. Some of this organisation must be realised by other brain areas known to be specialised in rational thought and planning and in applying rules and goals (the prefrontal cortex, which also helps to create superordinate categories), and those responsible for processing complex linguistic concepts (the temporal lobes). The ways in which these areas cooperate with and help to organise sensorimotor knowledge involved in art is important,[9] and I intend to return to this topic in later pages.

As with the example of Machery (2007) discussed earlier, perhaps a step in the right direction is to question the modal/amodal divide as something that is clean-cut and, instead, consider that there are a range of hybrid convergences intervening between modal and amodal activities, where modal symbols become increasingly schematic and, therefore, easier to store and combine into groups and categories. This may mean reducing perceptual richness to abstract tokens denoting spatial positions or gross

---

[8] Opposing perceptual symbols, Ohlsson asserts rather strongly that it is a 'fundamental and remarkable fact that humans are capable of forming abstractions. The most natural explanation for this fact is that abstract concepts are exactly what they appear to be: internally generated patterns that are applied to perceptual experience to interpret the latter' (Ohlsson in Barsalou, 1999, p. 631).

[9] This is acknowledged by Barsalou: 'The evolution of the human frontal lobes provides one way to think about people's ability to construct multiple simulations simultaneously and to map between them' (Barsalou, 1999, p. 645). It is not clear how much this mapping between simulations depends on the use of perceptual symbols, if at all, or other kinds of representation ruled out by Barsalou.

features. This would also mean that fine-grained and rich modal simulations, which are being fully attended to, would become more schematic with shifts of attention away from such simulation. These simulations would, as it were, become more of a blur with only salient features remaining – a kind of series of degraded (parsed or partially represented) symbols that can be processed and further compressed and schematised when not thematically attended to (that is, put into patterns and made spatially distinct) by parietal and frontal areas.[10] Such a process would have to be reversible where abstract symbols assume a more sensory character. Rather than a simple cause and effect model from abstraction to concrete simulation, it could be that both processes can constrain each other in creative moments. At other times, one process would dominate the other depending on situatedness, circumstances and external events, the stimuli of cultural objects, emotional states and social interaction. One way to see how this might work would be to use a metaphor: we are attending a party; there are many conversations, perceptions, memories co-mingling and vying for attention. My organising capacities do not pay attention to each and every detail but I maintain a schematic and general attentiveness to many details, the buzz and excitement, mood and atmosphere of the event, as well as different degrees of detail; I could even ponder the nature of human interaction. This 'configural' rather than in-depth focus on the party is similar to the distinction between a fine-grained attentional focus and a coarser, more global one, and it seems important that we can switch fluently from one to the other.

---

[10] 'spatial location may be represented as a perceptual symbol (as a result of perception) and space provides organizing structure for perceptual symbol systems...Preserving spatial structure, different meaningful conceptualization levels can be achieved simply by "looking" more closely or less closely' (Freksa et al. in Barsalou, 1999, p. 616). The additional layer of symbolism that the spatial positioning of symbols allows can be supplemented in other ways. Nakayama and Shimojo (1992) have shown how the layout of *surfaces* in depth is encoded in the representation very early even before shapes have been detected. This suggests that there are many different ways to encode perceptual symbols beyond schematic relationships; perhaps perceptual symbols are made distinct from each other and yet are malleable enough to enter more complex combinations by virtue of their surfaces or textures. What is clear is that insisting on sensorimotor areas doing all this work, when parietal areas would aid in the efficient spatial manipulation of these symbols (and the prefrontal cortex could set goals and rules for this organisation), would be churlish. The involvement of amodal areas in the arrangement of perceptual symbols does, however, water down strong sensorimotor approaches, as well as the kind of neuroscience that makes a series of inferences from single cell experiments or matches particular brain areas to functions in a simplistic manner. Clearly for conceptual complexity, a massive cooperation and sequencing of brain areas and different kinds of representation are required.

1.9 Perceptual symbol systems and art

How does this psychological theory fare in situational examples provided by art? Many of Barsalou's examples deal with daily situations for everyday concepts (even 'Mary pounded the nail into the floor'). The ability to solve problems and imagine counterfactual and impossible situations often requires that we abort modal simulations for processes of logic. In trying to observe the component parts of how people grasp concepts, Barsalou's psychological experiments greatly slow down and simplify a densely coded and rapid process of conceptual production and categorisation that would only be hampered by modal experiences. The question remains: how do modal experiences become parsed or schematised so that we do not have to go through full sensory or perceptual experiences for each semantic unit of a complex sentence? Simply making a lot of this nonconscious does not solve the problem.

Presumably, such rapid, efficient and fluent mentalese responsible for the processing of abstract concepts also structures our experiences of art. When we encounter Gabriel Orozco's sculptural work consisting of several bicycles, do Barsalou's statements about situational examples for bicycles ring true? The sculpture is a composite of a number of bicycles and could even be said to be a 'Cubist sculpture' if we imagine that it is one bicycle seen through several different aspects, moments, perspectives. This challenges or makes us conscious of the normal way we come to recognise objects involving temporal, material and spatial binding. How are we to understand such a special object using modal simulations re-enacting the 'involvement of the conceptualizer?' Barsalou writes that thinking of a bicycle re-enacts various situations associated with riding a bicycle and is thus a 'situated conceptualization', which 'creates the experience of the conceptualizer being in the situation – the situation is not represented as detached and separate from the conceptualizer' (2009, p. 1283). Furthermore, '[a]s people describe an object, they situate it from their own perspective, simulating themselves in the situation as well. In other words, people construct the experience of being there with the object to generate its properties' (2009, p. 1286). This would obviously

Figure 9. Gabriel Orozco, *Four Bicycles (There is Always One Direction)*, 1984 (bicycles). Courtesy of the artist and Marian Goodman Gallery, New York.

be problematic in the abstract version of the concept BICYCLE intended by Orozco; how would people really be busy 'simulating themselves in the situation'?

The bicycles are 'impossible objects'; our sensorimotor knowledge is completely at odds with the conceptualisations that are normally associated with our sensorimotor capabilities, which here are disassociated. We need more than our sensorimotor capabilities to process the artwork. We need a system of relational knowledge. Orozco's sculpture may not require any of our skills or abilities (which are supposed to be concepts in Barsalou's psychology) to do with riding bicycles, or if it does, they are soon displaced by conceptual thought using a system of references to Duchamp's original readymade, a bicycle wheel fixed onto a stool (*Bicycle Wheel*, 1913/1951). Rather ambitiously, perhaps, the Museum of Modern Art, New York's website describes it as absurdist, but '[i]ts greatest power, however, is as a conceptual proposition'. Yet there is more to it than this. Duchamp was purported to have said, 'I enjoyed looking at it, just as I enjoy looking at the flames dancing in a fireplace.' This is probably a reference to how the spokes might catch the light, and the assisted readymade's ability to spark irrational and mischievous play.

There is also the contradiction that the bicycle seat has been transformed into a stool, confusing scripts: it is stationary and stable, we might find it in a kitchen, yet the wheel is part of an object for outdoor pursuits and is the embodiment of motion and repeat, momentum and spinning. The stool holds the wheel back, yet it 'takes to flight' with the wheel. This stop and go contradiction, which transforms the ordinariness of the objects into play, is what we see with Orozco's sculpture. Another reference active in the mind while contemplating Orozco's work is Picasso's bicycle seat and handlebars fashioned into a bull's head and horns, a bronze sculpture titled *Bull's Head (Tete de Toro)*, 1943. There is also Meret Oppenheim's *Untitled (Bee swarm)* photograph of 1977 showing a bicycle, its seat completely covered by a swarm of bees. Ai Wei Wei's *Freedom Bicycle* is remarkably similar to Orozco's, a group of bicycles twisted and fused together to form an abstract sculpture that speaks of the freedom to roam thwarted by contrary desires and the forces of rational organisation. The *Freedom Bicycle* is useless, a heap of junk, urban detritus, yet nevertheless acts as a kind of clarion call for the freedom of movement and the imagination.

Many of these artworks are premised on subverting the concept of sitting, where the seat (of rationality, perhaps) is turned into a hazardous proposition, threatening to sting us, or worse, gore us. Thus, while attending the Orozco sculpture, various processes of analogy and categorisation using references to these other sculptures may be more active than sensory experiences that play a part in a complex series of thoughts. Of course, it is no surprise psychologists such as Barsalou use the notion of simulation for real objects in the world, like bicycles. Yet, Orozco's sculpture is also a real object in the world and it could be stored as a series of counterfactuals of simulations that do not work. However, to understand its complexity art historically, one would need to reference Duchamp and Picasso; these are also 'simulations' that we run in order to grasp the Orozco sculpture. How are these complex conceptual simulations made to interact with each other? One theory, which I explore in later chapters, is that psychological work on analogical modification, conceptual blending and metaphors can show us how we map one kind of complex situation onto another. This, however, requires a massive neural interconnectivity beyond localised sensorimotor processes, and a situatedness provided by artworks that affects and engages with this mapping in coded ways.

The sculpture is a delectable 'problem'; it seems familiar and yet this familiarity is carved up and cobbled back together again illogically. The familiarity arises out of the impossibility or inappropriateness of applying our mental simulations of riding or sitting on the bicycles: they have no seats and only one set of handlebars. We are mentally rotating the bicycles that seem to be taking us for a ride. They seem to compete with each other for attention, each tugging in a different direction; the front wheel is difficult to distinguish from the back part. It not only appears like a logical problem of binocular rivalry, as it seems to be intending to go in all directions yet is going nowhere, but also, with the dazzling multiplicity of choices of directions, it could be construed as heading towards fragmentation; still it holds together.[1] The bicycles are cannibalised and grounded; symbols of freedom of movement are stuck in a modernist conundrum, a stammering resulting from too many intentions, a great exertion of effort all for nothing. The same motion/stasis is implied in the Chapman brothers' sculptures of clones fused together into one body, all set to walk in different directions on pain of death. Of course, our modal simulations arise in all of these examples but are useless to grasp the sculpture conceptually if we insist on giving them pre-eminence in our thoughts. Yet again, art takes aspects of the familiar and reassembles them into a different syntax, requiring a different order of thought that consists of making us aware of our automatic integration of impulses and sensory responses, making us laugh at them and at ourselves when this integration is made dysfunctional. The twisted bicycles give us the opportunity to experience how a sculpture's perceptual cues address the viewer, helping to make us aware of our organisation of concepts and sensations in novel and poetic relationships. Yet it is important to note that the work of art can run as a simulation providing a context and constraints for conceptual production, and providing a certain amount of stability across different minds.[2] A typical interpretation of the meaning of Orozco's sculpture shows clearly that we need to override, or consider as problematic, automatic sensorimotor impulses; to treat them metacognitively with conceptual knowledge. Far from providing exemplars for this knowledge, such sensorimotor simulation would amount to an inappropriate art historical interpretation although, viewed as a Surrealist object, the work invites us to entertain the nonsense of dreams, childhood regression and poetic, free association.

---

[1] Binocular rivalry where ambiguous shape forms (the rabbit-duck for example) need not be something that occurs on a local, perceptual level of feature detection but also involves higher-level processes in the temporal cortex and prefrontal cortex (for a review, see Tong et al., 2006).

[2] Similarly in cognitive linguistics: 'Rather than being mechanically derived from the meanings of its parts, an expression's meaning [and, by extension, the meaning found in art] is actively constructed, largely in top-down fashion, from the fragmentary clues provided by its constitutive elements. Its coherence derives from their reconciliation in a complex simulation that draws on all available resources (conceptual, linguistic, and contextual)' (Langacker, 1999, p. 625).

One of the lasting effects of Orozco's sculpture is a suggestion of its dynamic multi-directionality. On the one hand, the sculpture splices together bicycles, symbols of mechanical motion, seeming to throw them unceremoniously onto the scrap heap, robbing the bicycles of their functionality and *raison d'être*. On the other hand, they have a new life in the exploration of conceptual relations. There would also be rational inferences at work in a typical encounter with this sculpture. The fact that the bicycles can be seen configurally in a coarse-grained sense (rather than identified as concrete objects in fine-grained consecutive views) allows us to consider the sculpture in terms of an abstract composition of geometrical relationships (pentagons, circles, squares, triangles), which is part of its fascination. Yet the contraption also emerges as an auto-genesis of hybrid parts, or resembles the schematic for a kind of solar system; additionally, it brings to mind the concept of a mangled crash in a *Tour de France*, a robot spinning plates, and other comical aspects such as joke bicycles associated with circuses. None of these comic settings is used to *understand* the concept BICYCLE which, as a concept, has been stretched beyond recognition, its functionality rendered peculiarly purposeless. Moreover, although we might activate the appropriate neural mechanisms for interacting with bicycles when studying Orozco's sculpture, these mechanisms and predictions about use would lead only to dead ends.

What would be appropriate is to let these neural simulations subside in favour of other processes supporting linguistic processing, categorisation, analogy and logical inference, as I have demonstrated here, along with conceptual combination and metaphor. Barsalou states that '[i]n object perception...perceiving an object activates a background scene that can speed object categorisation' (Barsalou, 2009). Any background scene 'naturally' generated for this sculpture is apt to lead us to make mistakes in categorisation, and thus would be abandoned quite quickly in the art experience. What is happening here is an experience of the uncanny (*unheimlich*, in Freud's terms), where familiar and habitual object recognition processes, including situational examples, are destabilised and challenged: we feel we know the object but cannot integrate it with an appropriate event or context (Huppert and Piercy, 1976). The sculpture makes us aware of the futility of the sensorimotor simulations by which we might integrate the object and decide to act on it accordingly; it presents us with a kind of a narrative with missing words and failed or illogically assembled simulations. If there is any one defining tendency in contemporary art (which is doubtful), it would probably have to do with making us more aware of the contingencies of perception and how we come to imagine things by celebrating improvised and unlikely encounters between concepts. This awareness, matched to the cues and features of an artwork, seems to hold a fascination for us. On the one hand, the object seems to question our sense of order or gestalt and our integrative memory processes, gently suggesting the possibility of source amnesia (the feeling we know something but do not know why we do). On the other hand, it seems to offer new imaginative possibilities when we suspend 'logical' perceptual binding processes in order to enjoy the game. Thus, while gestalt psychology has been an important way in which to understand formalism and modernism, many avant-garde and contemporary artworks reveal the aesthetic bias involved in such psychology because such artworks encourage us to think beyond form and appearance.[3]

Contemporary art routinely transforms concrete concepts into abstract concepts by encouraging us to question or shed the normal situations connected to concrete concepts and to use them and combine them into abstract relations. The readymade, an ordinary object taken out of the normal background situations that we automatically rehearse while only glancing at it, is recontextualised or altered and fused with another object, challenging our notions of function and purpose associated with easy object identification. These readymades may be likened to lexical units in complex 'sentences'; their individual meanings are put into ad hoc categories. The relational knowledge acquired in experiences of art, which, for example, allows us to understand the history of the readymade and its continued presence in contemporary art, has a compositionality and systematicity. It helps us to re-edit, parse and 'chunk' the ordinary and to expect the extraordinary; it provides an imaginary apparatus by which gestalt design and concrete concepts and situations are not taken at face value but are used as building blocks for fantastical and poetic connections and ruptures.

The conclusion to this foray into Barsalou's grounded cognition is not to cast doubt upon its achievements. It has allowed us to focus our attention on how we process many everyday concepts, perceptions and objects using sensorimotor involvement, and this is impressive and influential. The question is how this work may be seen to be applicable to the

---

[3] Although this dualism between formalism and contextual knowledge may also be too strong; when we know more about the facts, background history and intentions of the artist, these factors can help us to appreciate the form of the artwork in ways that may be more sophisticated. A similar point is made by Davies (1991, pp. 199–200) about the composer Schonberg; the form of his twelve-tone compositions may be aesthetically appreciated by understanding its origins in tonal music. The synthesis involved in this kind of interpretation rejects pure (uninformed formalism), which privileges sensorimotor experience in favour of a contextualised formalism, where knowledge enhances such experience.

realm of art, which is not by definition ordinary but is rather a 'trans-figuration of the commonplace' (Danto, 1981). What is the psychological basis of this transfiguration that disassociates schemata or scripts from sensorimotor simulations?

If all we had in the world were the ability to process all things using our senses, the world would be a very dull and repetitive place. Contemporary art presents us with the ability to step outside of ordinary situations and 'appropriate' impulses and reactions by stimulating imaginative, some-times irrational, counterfactual situations in order to experiment with ideas, solve problems and puzzles, and to derive sensory pleasures from routes that avoid clichés. Orozco's bicycles allow us to reflect upon the distance between the ordinary and the extraordinary, how we are auto-matically primed to make sense of things, and it provides the opportunity to reconceptualise and use novel experiences, which need not make sense (at least not sensorimotor sense), as frames for other, fresh thought. It might be argued that examples of traditional art stimulate similar effects to do with narrativising the gaze and encouraging us to reflect upon how we process concepts, and this is true. Yet contemporary art seems to do this consistently and thematically, and in ways that are peculiar to it. Whereas in art history and neuroaesthetics the emphasis has been on how artists tacitly anticipate the problems of perceptual psychology, this is to the detriment of the relational knowledge system that contemporary artworks tap into in unusual ways – and this is much closer to experimenting with the complexities of cognitive psychology. Thus, cognitive psychology does not just help to explain what is going on in our experience and interpretation of contemporary artworks; in many cases, it has become part of an artwork's facture, and is tacitly explored by the artist whose 'words' are partial objects combined in novel situations.

1.10 'Illogical' hybrid objects

It is important to note how contemporary art is often experimental, creating objects where the binding of multisensory features is problematic, illogical and purely fantastical, creating hybrid, partial or 'anxious' objects that do not seem to come together or cohere. They seem to question normative psychological processes with counterfactuals that sometimes resemble laboratory experiments. Analytical Cubism was one of the earliest inversions of 'natural' psychological processes of binding. Whereas Analytical Cubism played with occluded contours, illogical transparencies and composites, pursuing the irrational with seemingly methodical and inductive steps (however improvised), the fragmented Surrealist object or the Dada-assisted readymade often assembled entities to produce a mélange of arousal, disgust, fear and sensuousness. Both Cubist and Surrealist strategies, however, aim at subverting automatic and logical sensorimotor responses, as well as rational explanations of embodiment arising from art.

The assisted readymade, the cobbling together of 'anxious' objects, continues to be a powerful strategy in contemporary art. New Zealand artist Francis Upritchard reworks a series of leather gloves, buttons and ceramic vessels into mangled fingers that seem to make themselves into heads, monkey faces or monsters, stuffed into ceramic jugs or flasks as trophies or strange flowers; objects that are awkward, yet their familiar details tug at the memory, at partially formed emotions and attachments. In such scenarios, our automatic binding processes are somehow halted, fragmented in series of binocular rivalries, which are also conceptual conflicts involving sensory stimulations that are unwelcome. These artworks stimulate the retrieval of memories of gloves, or patches of leather, buttons or fur, in the context of a grotesque hybridity that does not compute – a discordant contextualisation, a fractious kind of beauty. If the artwork succeeds at integration, it is a simulation that is off-kilter and disturbing, a flawed object or animal that limps its way to perfection; a desire that we regard, nevertheless, as tragic. Again, contemporary art aims not just to disturb the usual conventional triggers of aesthetic reward but also to

Figure 10. Francis Upritchard, *Bald Monkey Bottle*, 2011 (modelling material, foil, found buttons, ceramic, leather, 305 × 100 × 130 mm). Courtesy of the artist and Ivan Anthony Gallery.

rearrange perceptual subroutines in the service of unexpected conceptual alignments that seem, somehow, to be right.

There is a danger of overstating sensory content as indicative of a rich memory experience when, in fact, the sensory details are only being used to subserve a greater long-term task of conceptual exploration. In other words, Upritchard's cannibalised gloves can be recalled not so much as a well-known set of sensory features immediately bound into a manipulable tool with a familiar function, or an easy chiasm of hands touching skin, inserting themselves into soft, grey leather, but as a conceptual, perhaps even counterfactual, example of a particular kind of pathetic fallacy. We supply the conceptual unity upon a scarred body, torn engrams and desires. This is not only the trauma of object identification but also a glimpse of the fragmentation of identity itself.

These themes are explored by many contemporary artists. Brian Jungen is from British Columbia, and is of Swiss and Danezaa First Nations ancestry. He takes mass produced sports trainers or professional basket-ball shirts, icons of 'subcultural' or consumer identity, and reduces them methodically to their constituent parts (threads, strips, the tongue of a shoe, the arch of the sole). He then stitches them back together again to resemble Danezaa garments or blankets for ceremonial rituals or, in the case of sports shoes, he refigures them into faces that allude to traditional masks and fetish objects, or he piles sports bags upon each other to form totem poles. He thus not only creates an interesting hybrid: a handmade

Figure 11. Brian Jungen, *Golf Bags*, 2007 (installation view, Catriona Jeffries, Vancouver, 2007). Courtesy of Catriona Jeffries, Vancouver and the artist, Brian Jungen.

traditional art object that indexes his personal identity and references the Canadian First Nation reservations, where poor rubbish pickers routinely refashion discarded objects; but he also creates its opposite: a reconstituted machine-made, corporate, impersonal, commercial object, a brand, that has been creatively fragmented or, in the language of postmodernism, 'deconstructed'. One may be seen through the other, skill and process through a mechanised process, a personal statement through a marketing strategy, Adidas or Nike mass-produced sports shoes defaced, torn apart and reassembled into something unique.

The object identification here works on many levels and yet remains 'dislocated' allegorically, physically, mentally and emotionally. As I have mentioned, in terms of perceptual psychology, we attend to objects at the local level with a focus on fine-grained elements, or at the global one where we focus on coarse features; it is at this level that we might recognise a particular object in a scene. Again, artists are intuitively attracted by unusual optical effects; these global and local perceptual processes are exploited so that they are difficult to resolve. At the local level we identify Nike, at the global level we identify a ritual mask or a traditional shawl or blanket. Yet, attached to each of these different perceptual foci is a conceptual meaning.[1] At the local level the object reflects the modern, and at the global, the traditional, an interesting reversal of globalisation and local specificity. It is as if the artist has attached a conceptual process of symbolism onto the two kinds of perception. The rivalry between global and local also suggests nostalgia for traditional crafts in conflict with the banality of mass-produced sportswear. The emotion here is quite complex, a longing for or a grieving over lost traditional materials at the local level when the shawl is viewed as a basketball shirt, and an emergence of a Danezaa's artefact (with its skilful weaving) at the global level. As a whole, the object is a reinforcement of Danezaa design, a particular cultural and conceptual identity that emerges from a mass-produced, non-biodegradable, nylon substrate. One could say that the work is a triumph over materialism.

As some psychological studies have shown (Kober et al., 2008; Niedenthal, 1990, 2006), emotional experience is itself a strong binding mechanism that pulls together otherwise disparate sensory features and event fragments into the service of aversion or reward, yet in Jungen's and Upritchard's works these opposing forces struggle for ascendancy. There is also a struggle between fragmentation and integration: we recognise the functional and familiar units (a glove, a bit of fur, a dissected shoe, a sports bag) and we are tempted to apportion the correct sensorimotor use to each, yet there is also a kind of improvisation, an ad hoc *categorisation*, a convergence of objects or part objects to form a new intellectual entity with political, cultural and artistic identity. This is an example of the cooperation of sensory, emotional and higher-order relational knowledge. These hybrid objects are not only literally the result of the binding together of incongruous materials associated with different conceptual and sensory domains, but they also help create a new, expert system of looking that one acquires: that which enables us to compare Oppenheim's with Upritchard's or Jungen's works. Although the visceral response elicited from these artists' works would engage with how each object is rotated mentally and brought together by emotional drives, fears, desires and affects that make the art object identifiable in some way, a larger task might be the evaluation of facture and materials with semantics, and the patchwork of political and cultural signifiers, levels of engagement and commitment that these objects successfully sustain. Whereas Martin's

---

[1] Similarly in cognitive linguistics, Langacker argues that linguistic expressions can 'characterize a situation at any desired level of precision and detail ("granularity"), as seen in lexical hierarchies such as thing→creature→reptile→snake→rattlesnake→sidewinder. This progression from highly schematic to increasingly more specific expressions seems quite analogous to the visual experience of seeing something with progressively greater acuity while walking up to it from a distance' (Langacker in Barsalou, 1999, p. 625).

well-known study (2007) of how object identification takes place over a number of brain areas (spatial, sensorimotor, categorical), these assisted readymades allow us to become aware that there are also emotional, political and cultural ramifications involved in object identification: 'Beyond the perceptuomotor properties, the emotional value associated with objects is another property undoubtedly playing an important role in determining our behaviour. One might therefore imagine that emotional encoding occurs automatically and at an early stage in all forms of categorisation' (Versace et al., 2009, p. 20).

Hence hybrid objects, Upritchard's stitch-ups, Jungen's decoding of corporate branding, or a whole host of other artists' works, such as Piccinini's post-human genetic monstrosities, Mona Hatoum's clothes and objects woven with human hair or Yinka Shonibare's culturally hybrid objects, exacerbate emotional and multimodal contradictions and interactions so that they are thematised as binding problems or challenges, particularly because they are artworks *qua* artworks, which have an ambiguous ontological status as 'special' objects. Perceptual, conceptual and emotional associations and the ways in which we harmonise these to create meanings and categories are transformed into problems. It is as if a mundane kind of experience, such as failing to put a name to a face or recognising a face but not knowing why one does, a common disassociation phenomenon accompanied by feelings of confusion or amusement, is produced and sustained by the 'thought experiments' of these hybrid art objects, and with great success.

Such artworks eventually condition us to have appetites for even more bizarre, subtle and improbable combinations of partial objects, a new vocabulary that stutters on the edge of giving form to a new outline of practice. 'Stuttering' is key here, for whereas language, the act of labelling, can temporarily resolve ambiguity, Upritchard's glove puppet mutants or Jungen's scrambled syntax leave us tongue-tied, resisting object identification, fracturing the percept and our emotional cohesion. Such equivocal objects are composite and unresolved; we are unable to classify and constrain them in order for an appropriate or coherent emotional response to be formed. As with Cubism and Surrealism, this kind of art may be called 'the aesthetics of problem-making'. The rapid multiplication of possibilities, a kind of semantic strobe effect, which these objects encourage, prevents objectification and, to a certain extent, any settled kind of subjectivity in response to form. Fingers of gloves, the toes of shoes and soles tease out threads of a memory-based knowledge of emotions that struggle to come together. Attentional mechanisms become attuned to a new conceptual space reorganised on the basis of stimuli grouped together as a series of staccato interactions or

dissonances, of negotiations between words, known objects and functions, so that the dialogical process itself becomes the object of the
artwork. In such a scenario, it is not the concept behind the work that
is the art, as the saying goes, but the process of how concepts, brought to
the same place as the artwork, interact, combine or refuse to do so,
becoming objects of reflection.

We know that partial objects can become comfort blankets whose sleepy
intimacy may be verbalised and turned into protest banners in Tracey
Emin's quilted works. We know the logic of fetish objects may be seen in
the sore thumbs and phalluses of Louise Bourgeois' sculptures, or in the
punkish work of Sarah Lucas' fried eggs on breasts or the banana and
oranges she arranged on a mattress to suggest male genitalia – all cases of
displaced objects, 'experimental objects', assemblages that adopt a syntax
that is difficult to integrate into fluent speech, precisely in order to 'stut-
ter'. Rather than the seamless and easy fluency of perceptual binding and
habitual sensorimotor recognition, by which we identify a hammer or a
gymnast, these works point to interesting gaps and dislocations. As I have
mentioned, they also have consequences for our emotional identification
in response to these 'experiments'. Suffice it to say here that these two
important psychological processes of global, situational processing involving conceptual schemata and local, fine-grained perceptual analysis are
brought into imaginative dissonance in contemporary art. This dissonance does not merely produce metacognition but is also used as a way
to underpin conceptual dualisms: local culture-globalisation, identity-
fragmentation, aesthetic unity and problem-making. The conundrum in
contemporary art is intuitively exploited as both a visual and perceptual
fine- or coarse-grained focal processing, used as a metaphor for cultural
and aesthetic tensions.

1.11 Facial recognition

I have suggested that processes of object and scene recognition are mutually reinforcing, involving a complex and broad neural interconnectivity. Because artworks involve the depiction and often distortion of objects and scenes for artistic purposes, they frequently put these automatic processes into conflict, requiring us to purposefully reason or conceptualise the coherence of object and scene recognition. In a sense, these artworks are learning situations; we might have to work through a number of counterintuitive and counterfactual operations to interpret or engage with such artworks. In addition to object and scene recognition, an important psychological specialisation is facial recognition. Faces are special kinds of objects that will involve a particular network of pathways and brain areas that may cooperate with object and scene recognition, and classification systems, for the recognition of faces to occur. Artworks that depict faces will also complicate automatic facial recognition processes, especially if such faces are fantastical and irrational as they are in many Surrealist works, for example, and also provide unusual scenes and contexts that situate such faces. Here are some of the very complex processes that a facial recognition system needs to deal with efficiently:

1 Recognising a face in unexpected circumstances (someone you know at school bumps into you while you are away on holiday).
2 Recognising a face in different representational media (photography, film, painting, sculpture).
3 Recognising a face when the person is moving, is partially occluded, is in an emotional state that contorts the face, has changed her hairstyle, is wearing glasses, or has aged since you saw her last.
4 Recognising the emotion on the face recognised.
5 Recognising family resemblances ('seeing faces in faces').
6 Appending names to faces (obviously a notorious or celebrated attentional challenge).
7 Suppressing 'recognition' for people who look similar.
8 Various combinations of these examples.

The right fusiform area in the brain seems to be activated specifically for various processes of facial recognition. This area is yet more finely attuned. Faces and animals elicit stronger activation in the lateral fusiform gyrus, while houses and tools in the medial fusiform gyrus. The para-hippocampal/lingual gyri are responsive to buildings (Gorno-Tempini and Price, 2001). The fusiform areas regularly cooperate with many other areas outside of them, however, as discriminations about surface features (skin), contours, luminance and episodic memory would need to co-occur while discounting or compensating for a great many contingencies, only a few of which I have outlined. It seems important that facial recognition should proceed configurally (that is, looking globally at all the features of the face as a whole, rather than focusing on any one of its component parts), as well as dynamically. Yet we should be able to hold on to certain invariable features (facial schemata), which allow for recognition across instances and contingencies, such as with different lighting conditions or when we see faces in different media, paintings, films and photographs.

However, it has been suggested that the fusiform gyrus is not specifically devoted to facial recognition, and that this brain area can be trained to recognise new kinds of objects in the visual field (Xu, 2005). Gauthier and Tarr (1997) created 'greebles': images of characters that are assemblages of partial objects resistant to instant recognition. Activation of the right fusiform area increased when subjects became more expert in recognising greebles. Gauthier et al. (2000) also showed that people who become experts in differentiating between birds and cars (and I would warrant, recognition of style elements in art) use the same area of the brain involved in facial recognition. The implication is that the fusiform area is important for the differentiation and dynamic matching of expertly learnt recurrent patterns or configurations in the visual field.

This is interesting from the point of view of art because this psychological experiment suggests that many non-facial fantastical objects in art, as in abstract art, may recruit fusiform areas that might help provide us with a feeling of familiarity or even empathy for form, as we might feel for a house, for example. The fusiform area is coupled with emotional processing (the limbic system), to help process the composite situation in the visual field where a face is to be recognised, along with the emotional expression it is supposed to be wearing. It may be possible, then, that the feelings and perceptual and semantic associations that we recruit for processing faces and facial expressions could be activated by artworks that depict non-facial objects and that the artist is skilful in creating such ambiguities so that we 'feel' for the strange and unusual objects depicted. This still has to be tested empirically. It would be interesting to see how paintings by Roberto Matta or Sigmar Polke could evoke facial and emotional recognition systems for inanimate objects and fantastical scenes.

This is not quite the same as seeing faces in clouds in paradolia, as greebles are supposed to resist face recognition yet stimulate configural processes for non-facial features. This is in the hope of showing that so-called specific or specialised face processing areas can be trained to develop different kinds of expert systems that can configure or discriminate non-facial features, such as chessboard configurations. This seems important, as the visual language of art is also an acquired expert system that discriminates and configures features, and it seems that the fusiform area and other areas associated with facial and emotional recognition should be active in viewing art beyond recognising faces. What is clear is that 'facial recognition' can involve simple and relatively instant responses to stimuli or very complex conceptual processes. For example, the superior temporal sulcus will be involved in the detection of gaze direction and speech-related movements in observing others, limbic regions (the amygdala and insula) in facial expressions, the inferior frontal gyrus in semantic processing, and the orbitofrontal cortex where it is suggested that facial beauty and sexual discrimination are processed. Everhart et al. (2001) found gender-related differences in the underlying neurology of facial recognition, with men using the right and female subjects using the left hemisphere neural activation system in the processing of faces.

What I would like to suggest at this point is that the usefulness of the neuroscience of facial recognition for understanding art needs to go a long way to be able to come even close to providing a satisfying account for how we experience the facial aspects of contemporary artworks. Even in what might seem relatively straightforward cases of facial processing, in photography for example, photographers deliberately challenge what we regularly take for granted: that a face can be studied separately from our feelings and beliefs about people, as these laboratory experiments seem to suggest.

Contemporary photography is particularly adept at exploiting anomalies in facial recognition and adding conceptual complexity to such automatic processes. To get some idea of what neurocognitive studies will have to achieve to understand how art recruits facial recognition areas of the brain as part of a larger conceptual task, we can consider Cindy Sherman's photography. Sherman is well known for her series of photographs that simulate film stills, impersonations of actors and centrefolds. She has created a large body of work, different instances, roles and situations where her face is the only constant. Sherman's facial features form the schemata by which we identify a performance, a role. Sherman points to the face as a social performance enacted by internalising the 'gaze' of the camera, the intended audience for which visual cultural products featuring

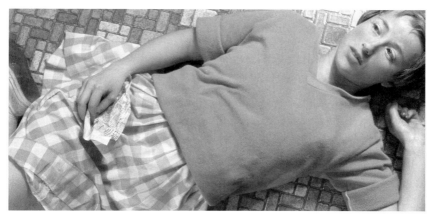

Figure 12. Cindy Sherman, *Untitled*, 1981 (colour photograph, 24 × 48 in). Edition of 10 (MP #96). Courtesy of the artist and Metro Pictures, New York.

women are produced, a gaze that is theorised as privileged and usually male (Mulvey, 1989). Sherman's 1981 *Centerfold* series attempts to make explicit the pivotal role facial recognition plays with scopic pleasure and objectification. In an interview, the artist stated, about *Centrefold #1* shown here: 'In content I wanted a man opening up the magazine, suddenly look at it with an expectation of something lascivious and then feel like the violator that they would be. Looking at this woman who is perhaps a victim. I didn't think of them as victims at the time. . .But I suppose. Obviously I'm trying to make someone feel bad for having a certain expectation'.[1]

Again and again, Sherman poses as different conventional types (with different kinds of contexts associated with them) meant to interest the male gaze: petulant model, nervous debutante, vamp, sporty woman, child-woman. These are roles that, through exposure to film photography and advertising, both men and women have learnt to identify expertly, automatically and configurally. We do not 'just' recognise the face in these works; such a process of recognition bleeds into a larger configuration of technical signs and visual vocabularies conventionalised by art, film and photography. She shows us how facial recognition is situated within a system of signs in order to produce pleasure or value judgements.

The conceptual processes extend the facial recognition system into a much larger conceptual network, transforming the face into an abstract

[1] This interview was filmed on the WN Network, dated 2009. www.wn.com/ Interview_Magazine__Cindy_Sherman

concept. In fact, one of the interesting effects of Sherman's photography is to question the very nature of recognition as a naïve construct. Facial recognition becomes the object of conceptual scrutiny rather than being simply activated, and yet this is what happens commonly when recognising faces; we bring a lot of conceptual material to the site of recognition. With Sherman's photographs, there are ethical reflections that do not allow facial recognition and conceptualisation to cohere. Art history students often misunderstand Sherman's project. One student I have taught in the past stated boldly that they disliked Sherman's self-portraits, believing her to be vain and self-obsessed. This illustrates a number of expectations regarding the function of the photograph. The photograph's popularly understood function is *to identify*. Facial recognition is often used to judge others' motives and personalities. Do we really recognise Sherman? Do we really know what she is about? As Krauss suggests: 'the play of stereotype in her work is a revelation of the artist herself as stereotypical. It functions as a refusal to understand the artist as a source of originality, a fount of subjective response...The inwardness of the artist as a reserve of consciousness that is fundamentally different from the world of appearances is a basic premise of Western art' (1981, p. 59).

Sherman's photographs are different. She succeeds in suggesting that there is no interiority, only schemata. Sherman's performances for the camera reveal that the 'natural' facial identification process is dependent on schemata, stereotypes, props, clues, poses and facial expressions that cue judgements and beliefs. This is made clear because we also know that these perceptual cues are fictions built into complex formulae we have become accustomed to using in our facial recognition systems when viewing films and magazines. When we become aware that Sherman is anticipating our desires to know, to objectify, to recognise, we might begin to reflect on systems of reward and desire that motivate the need to establish facial recognition and identity. We take great satisfaction from recognising a face. Sherman's photographs make this a pyrrhic victory. The way in which the photograph anticipates this desire thwarts the rewarding sense of agency also associated with discovery and recognition. Thus, although it is important for us to understand the underlying and complex cognitive apparatus of facial recognition, this is not a necessary and sufficient basis for the interpretation of faces in artworks of this kind. Far more important is to ponder the purpose for which the trigger mechanism of facial recognition is being used.[2]

---

[2] One could, of course, have taken the example of another artist, Chuck Close, who has prosopagnosia, the inability to fuse facial features into automatic recognition, usually attributed to faults in the fusiform gyrus. His portraits come across as faces composed of

There is no cheap reward in discovering the familiar in Sherman; she remains a phantom in dissimulation, thereby neatly stating the problem of photography and its claim to function neutrally as a tool for fixing identity. She does this by making 'photography' itself the abstract conceptual problem explored in her photographic works. In an almost tautological manner, Sherman seems to tell us 'this is what photographs do to us' – although the 'us' here is unclear, for it implies both the subject of the photograph and the viewer. There are at least three levels of absorption at work here: (1) the facial recognition system, (2) *becoming aware* of how this is not sufficient (and consequently the *desire* to know, as if identification scratches an itch), and (3) the manipulation of various relational knowledge structures to do with Sherman's works and feminist theories of the gaze.[3]

Sherman's photographs suggest that 'natural' phenomenal experiences of viewing photographs of women are, in fact, opportunities to construct stereotypes. They invite us to become aware of being the stereotyper. The works reveal the naïveties of phenomenological approaches to art, facial recognition and identification. Yet even the critical distance afforded by considering these three levels increases the power of the image. Sherman's photography is a conundrum of sorts sustained by the complex switch of attention from perceptual to conceptual processes through the three stages, looping back again. An important question is whether gaining knowledge into how photographs affect us on a number of levels primes us to look at things differently in the long term.

tiny, squarish, reflective pools in which pebbles have been dropped; each facial feature seems to ripple into the next and there is the impression of features continually beyond the grasp, overlapping and reverberating throughout the portrait. This is, indeed, an example of 'making problems' for easy vision or naïve notions of direct perception, problems in which contemporary art excels, yet one which seems devoted to perceptual rather than conceptual kinds of complications represented by Sherman, although both kinds of art, and mental processes, are complementary.

[3] The philosophers Deleuze and Guattari use the term 'faciality' to refer to a rather negative general dependency on routines that fix or anticipate meaning and meaning-making arising from new experiences and encounters where, alternatively, one might have tarried with polysemy and new discoveries. For them, a continual questioning of the habitual is desirable.

1.12 Expert objects

Pylyshyn (2006) suggests that postperceptual processes of judgement, memory and categorisation 'could result in the creation of different feature clusters' (p. 87); feature clusters defined as groups of perceptible details we learn to recognise in the visual field. All of this is relevant for the experience of viewing art, especially where an artist, well-informed viewer or researcher compares formal characteristics of art, motifs, details and themes across a large number of artworks and learns to look for and recognise certain patterns in the visual field. This may be so even in a variety of cases where artworks are meant to confuse perceptual experience. In other words, we become experts at dealing with perceptual confusion and extracting meaning from apparent nonsense, as we might when learning a new language. This may amount to sensitising feature clusters to certain configurations previously overlooked and through learning how to acquire selective attention 'on relevant objects, regions, properties of the visual field' (p. 88). Thus, Pylyshyn does accept that in perceptual learning, and expert learning in particular, top-down processes can become automatic, and absorbed into the visual system consisting of early stages of perception: 'the expert has learned where the critical distinguishing information is located within the stimulus pattern...the expert can direct focal attention to the critical locations...what the experts had tacitly learned, is how to bring the independent visual system to bear on the right spatial location and what types of patterns to encode into memory' (p. 86).

It is important to keep in mind that when psychological studies analyse our processing of the 'visual field', that art is part of this visual field yet it is a special case. The *representation* of a visual field within the visual field is an already parsed and coded conceptual view of what a visual field might contain, through the eyes of the artist. Thus the 'relevant objects, regions, properties of the visual field' that Pylyshyn speaks of are not simply perceptual details, but perceptual details that have been arranged by the artist to convey a particular conceptual, expert way of looking at the world, something that we can learn to see and which affects 'direct perception'.

An important part of expert systems, or indeed any particularly distinct kind of inspection of the visual field, is the allocation of attention given to perceptual cues, desires, objectives, planning, past experience, usually called top-down influences, that guide and influence searching the visual field for patterns that conform to these overarching directives: 'the allocation of focal attention also determines how visual perception carves up the world into distinct things – how the world is "parsed"...because of its key role as a gatekeeper between vision and the world, the allocation of attention is also one of the main loci of perceptual learning' (Pylyshyn, 2006, pp. 159–160).

It is not difficult to see that there are different kinds of parsing processes, day-to-day ones that might occur automatically or ones that allow us to step momentarily outside of these habitual responses. Art encourages us to parse the visual field in ways that may be unfamiliar to us, sometimes producing feelings of the uncanny, as Surrealism was often required to do, by producing unexpected poetic associations or by allowing us to look at how an artist has parsed the visual field that is also at the same time *part of our visual field*. This will occur more easily for those of us who are used to accepting that artists sometimes are intent on showing us not just things as they are in their visual field but often also how they feel about things in the visual field, and how they feel about the tools and techniques they are using while attending to these things. Of course, artists also paint from the imagination and there are abstract painters and artists who work with many different kinds of media. The point is, when looking at art we are continually parsing the already parsed.

When a chess player is studying a problem, she will probably not be contemplating the particular sheen of the chess pieces. One does not require an (offline) enactive understanding using sensorimotor processes to 'make a move' (that is, form a concept as to the next move), or project bodily involvement in that conceptual process, only a cursory sensorimotor process involved in actually moving the piece. When we visualise the next move and its consequences in a chess game, we do not need to calculate using sensorimotor skills; rather, 'much skilful performance requires counterfactual reasoning, where one is not letting the world be its own representation' (Grush and Mandik, 2002, p. 393). Conceptual thought may be even less dependent on sensorimotor engagements when one is studying algebraic chess notations.

Undoubtedly, there will be nonconscious perceptual processing but this will not play a significant role in making sense of the chess problem. The spatial coordinates of projected chess situations or models are held together in working memory; the chessboard will aid as a system of loci while rational procedures are rehearsed and mental models retrieved from long-term memory. In conjunction with this, various risk assessments and scenarios are rehearsed and sustained by representations in the prefrontal cortex. The complexity of these representations, compositional strategy, probabilistic reasoning and different kinds of memory cannot be integrated if we pay too much attention to the perceptible details. Yet we may be required to do so if the chess problem is represented in an artwork. When we are searching and looking for something, we will stop and look consecutively at the details of a painting or chess pieces in a game rather than standing back to see the whole composition or problem. However, to infer that the conceptual production required of art and chess *depend* on situational representations based on the brain's modality-specific systems would prevent us from understanding the significance of art, and such attention to detail would also probably lead us to losing a game of chess.

Chess masters' memory for chess positions makes their visual systems different from those of beginners because 'masters have a code for a large number of positions and…know where to look for significant chess-relevant patterns…what is special about experts' vision in this case is the system of classification they have learned that allows them to recognize and encode a large number of relevant patterns' (Pylyshyn, 2006, p. 85). This can be used to explain how the mechanism of relational knowledge works. Becoming habituated to this process can affect preperceptual processing through experiences of learning how to find particular distinctions in the visual field that have correspondences and relationships mirrored in other artworks that are not yet immediately perceptible. As Pylyshyn further explains: 'Another relevant aspect of the skill that is learned is contained in the inventory of pattern types that the observer assimilates (and perhaps stores in a special visual memory) and that helps in choosing the appropriate mnemonic encoding for a particular domain' (2006, p. 91).

The chess problem is identified using schemata or pattern types that non-experts will probably not have, and these are compared to others. The next moves are extrapolated through analogy and inference, with little or no processing of the texture and sheen of the chess pieces and other irrelevant details. The chess board becomes the material reference for a number of combinations of superordinate concepts (other chess problems emptied of their modal and perceptible aspects for ease of use). Hence, although we are unaccustomed to thinking of art in this way, viewing an artwork using analogical and rational processes may be more important than the sensory inspection of surfaces in many cases. Similarly, Stephen Pinker writes that visual thinking in chess, the kind we should assume is adopted when we study some artworks, 'is often driven more strongly by the conceptual knowledge we use to organize our images than by the contents of the images themselves' (1997, p. 291). Furthermore, 'Humans analyze the world using intuitive theories of objects, forces, paths, places, manners, states, substances, hidden bio-chemical essences, and, for other animals and people, beliefs and desires…People compose new knowledge and plans by mentally playing out combinatorial interactions among these laws in their mind's eye' (p. 188).

The following artwork gives us an indication of how even the most complex psychological processes involved in a game of chess can become thematic and given added political and aesthetic meaning by art. With the conceptual artwork *White Chess Set* (1966), Yoko Ono painted the black pieces white, as well as the black squares on the chessboard and added a brass plaque stating 'Chess Set for playing as long as you can remember where all your pieces are'. The work has been interpreted in the following way: 'the warring factions [are] indistinguishable from one another. This elegantly placed anti-war statement, particularly taken in the context of the Vietnam War [draws] attention to the deeply militaristic metaphors embedded in…games by conscientiously objecting to their implicit nar-ratives of combat and enmity' (Munroe, 2000, p. 138).

Not only do viewers familiar with the game of chess run a simulation to imagine how far it would be possible to continue with a game with all-white chess pieces, we are also somehow distanced from such logic, while nevertheless attempting it. The thwarting of sensorimotor knowledge and logical methods fills us with a sense of futility; it becomes implicated in the concept that it makes no sense to speak of sides in war where huge losses are borne by everyone and no one is a winner. The work also suggests that the mechanistic logic of chess, when associated with the strategies of warfare, as it often is, is an association that valorises reason over illogical human emotions, frailties and contingencies. Logical procedures and the values attached to them are also here, on trial, and displayed for us to consider in a conceptual rather than optical sense. Furthermore, there is an interesting encounter between the sensory appearance of the chess set and the logical inferences we use to understand its consequences. The notion of white playing itself, of using logic against itself, is a kind of suicide. *White Chess Set* is a thought experiment, a counterfactual that is typical of many contemporary artworks that attempt, in often humorous ways, to puzzle. Yet another kind of processing of meaning occurs with art historical relational knowledge. Duchamp's well-known quip that 'all chess players are artists' (and indeed he was known for being a serious chess player himself) was taken up by artists associated with the Fluxus group, with the 'Fluxchess' sets, variously altered chess sets that set out different ways to conceive of the rules of the game, isolated and maintained as a representation across different, often illogical circumstances. In the same period in the 1960s, a Japanese conceptual artist, Takako Saito, produced *Spice Chess* (1965), where players were supposed to remember chess pieces by the smell of the spices or herbs in each container standing for a chess piece. This encourages viewers to think of spatialising scent or using olfactory sensibilities for logical purposes. Like many examples of contemporary art, such work attempts to take us out of the ordinary, where sensory processes will have to be conceptualised differently because of the contexts they are required to work within that are highly unusual and thought provoking.

One of the things that these different kinds of works have in common is a deliberately ambiguous attitude to empirical experience and a priori knowledge. The art object plays a part in providing an experience where the viewer will need to respond creatively to the artwork. Thus, many of the more traditional cognitive processes studied by psychology, which are presumed to be 'ordinary', are deliberately subverted or questioned by such practices, as remarkably close to staging the kind of 'abnormal' cognitive processes we observe in lesion studies, with synaesthesia or in the 'language' of dreams. Visual agnosia, for example, results from damage to the 'binding' of sensory perceptions into a unified percept, and patients are not able to recognise the object but can detect its constituent parts; whereas apraxia is a condition where one is able to recognise an object but not use it or act upon it. In a sense, contemporary artworks often allow us to experience atypical mental operations such as these (or highly logical ones directed at atypical intentional objects) under controlled and often quite methodically engineered circumstances. Many studies on the psychology of art (Livingstone, 2002; Solso, 2003; Zeki, 2002) stress how many artists instinctively exploit properties of the perceptual system in order to provide viewers with an awareness, or at least the imagination of an awareness, of automatic (usually nonconscious) visual processes of perception. This has been theorised as the 'narrativization of one's gaze' (Joselit, 2003, p. 42, paraphrasing Yves Alain-Bois). Much less study has been devoted to how artists exploit properties of much higher cognitive and more complex conceptual thought processes, even though the examples of chess I have given here show that artists have been fascinated with providing situations that help us to grasp abstract concepts in relation to perceptual cues, and to reflect upon how we do so, for quite some time. Yoko Ono uses 'abnormal' psychological effects similar to apraxia to make us aware of the futility of taking action (in a game of chess and, by extension, war), although the *White Chess Set* also acts as a critique of our passive spectatorship of political events.

Part II

Brain

2.1   Neuroaesthetics

Neuroaesthetics is a relatively new discipline that focuses on material aspects of the brain, electrochemical activity and the activity of neurons during aesthetic experience. The basic assumption is that phenomenal aspects of experience can be matched to the activity of neurons or specific brain areas or their interactions, and that there is an underlying truth of functionality at the biological level, which can help us to understand how we process things like art, beauty or love. Many neuroaesthetic studies rely on data from functional magnetic resonance imaging (fMRI). This fairly recent technique measures increased blood flow to certain brain areas that are monitored while subjects are asked to complete a number of tasks. Increased blood flow is believed to indicate that a particular brain area is active.[1]

Semir Zeki (2009) and Margaret Livingstone (2002) are well-known scientists who have developed theories about our involvement with art from a series of experiments on brain cells or neurons or particular brain areas responsible for processing the basic features of art, such as line, colour and luminance, based on data from fMRI scans, lesion studies and optical illusion diagrams. Neurons responsible for the functioning of such perceptions are called feature detectors, and these can work in large groups in order to gain an overall impression of an object in front

---

[1] Positron emission tomography (PET) measures changes in cerebral blood flow (rCBF); fMRI measures blood oxygen level-dependent (BOLD) signals.

75

of us. The workings of these perceptions, often called the early stages of perception, are most often nonconscious although many kinds of art, for example Op Art or Minimalism, make us conscious of perceptions by exploiting effects, problems and paradoxes in the visual field that provide us with a rich fascination with visual material, often involving equivocation and multiple responses. These approaches have been particularly useful in explaining how our feature detectors process these aspects of the visual field, as well as pattern completion, facial recognition, binocular rivalry and other processes explored in the science of visual perception. For Zeki (2009), art is able to furnish us with rich feelings of ambiguity and beauty. These emotions (activated by various brain areas) bring into play perceptual constants, or ideals dependent on stored inner representations.

Ramachandran and Hirstein (1999) hold that certain homeostatic neural mechanisms of arousal and emotional regard, measured by galvanic skin response, are also involved in responses to art that are rooted in our evolutionary development. In other words, art is seen as the elaboration of caricatures of beauty or eroticism that trigger arousal or reward mechanisms.[2]

Criticisms of such approaches are wide ranging.[3] John Hyman (2008) questions Ramachandran and Hirstein's dependence on the erotic reflex or evolutionary sense of reward to explain our interest in art, mainly because there are many examples of art that are fascinating in other ways. The horrifying and repulsive black paintings by Goya, for example, do not fit easily into Hirstein and Ramachandran's model.[4] Art is not always a purposeful activity that promises reward. Irving Massey (2009, p. 137), citing Livingstone, observes the tendency to analyse vision and its neurological underpinnings as perfect laboratory models that ignore the differences in subjective experiences or attention spans. In other words, an increased knowledge of how the perceptual system works when analysing art provides us with a story of functionality in laboratory conditions but not motivation, neither does it account for top-down processes (conceptual categorisation, for example) that can direct or abstract the basic information gathering of perceptual processes. As a result, '[n]eurology is,

---

[2] For arguments against evolutionary explanations of art, see Davies (2006), pp. 103–118.

[3] (Amy Ione, 2000, 2003). For other criticisms of Ramachandran and Hirstein's kind of neuroscience, see numerous essays in 'Art and the Brain II', *Journal of Consciousness Studies*, 7(8–9), 2000, *passim*.

[4] Of Ramachandran and Hirstein and of Zeki, Hyman writes: 'Both authors propose extravagant generalisations about art – all art is caricature; all great art is ambiguous – and then discuss a small number of examples, which are chosen to illustrate the generalisation they favour and not to *test* it.' (2008, p. 260).

then, of great value in exploring the "how" of aesthetic processes, if not necessarily the "why" or the "what for", or in helping to decide whether one work of art is of greater value than another' (Massey, 2009, p. 18).

Meanwhile, Gregory Currie (2003) objects to treating the art experience from 'subpersonal' perspectives, as art is supremely personal and, therefore, there are aspects of one's brain and nervous system responsible for our personal traits, which provide particular qualities of experience we have of art over and above how we process line and colour in groups of neurons. From the perspective of both objections, we could use experiments on feature detectors and fMRI scans to analyse a subject's inspection of a painting by Monet, and this data would go some way to explaining *how* we inspect such a painting but not *why* we find it significant in our lives and why it might have an emotional resonance beyond optical stimulation. Alva Noë (2000) also points to this experiential quality of our lives, which necessarily involves contact with things outside our brain in order for us to experience them in the exact ways that we do. In other words, *the things themselves determine experience as much as the neurons processing aspects of experience.* For example, he writes: 'What is the causal substrate of the experience of the wine's flavor? Perhaps this substrate is only neural, but perhaps it is not'. Perhaps the only way to produce flavour sensations 'is by rolling a liquid across one's tongue. In that case, the liquid, the tongue, and the rolling action would be part of the physical substrate for the experience's occurrence' (2005, p. 220).

Brown and Dissanayake (2009) register another note of concern with how neuroaesthetics seems to focus on mainly European masterpieces and on notions of beautiful art: 'Aesthetic emotions are unquestionably an integral part of the arts, but they are neither necessary nor sufficient to characterize them. Thus, a narrow focus on aesthetic responses is ultimately a distraction from the larger picture of what the arts are about' (p. 54). Perhaps more forcibly, they state, 'presently conceived, neuroaesthetics has no way of distinguishing art from nonart' (p. 44).

Two major problems seem to emerge from the general criticism. The first problem has to do with how art and beauty are assumed to be synonymous in neuroaesthetics, that by finding the neural mechanisms of arousal, pleasure and reward, one gets closer to understanding art or 'great art'. This is a problem because there are many activities in the world that are pleasurable or rewarding, such as gardening, eating ice cream and taking the dog for a walk, but these activities do not qualify as art. Art itself has a number of features that have nothing to do with these feelings and sensations; the Goya paintings mentioned earlier seem to be the standard examples used to demonstrate this, although there is much in contemporary art that assiduously avoids easy pleasures, rewards and the feel-good factor.

The second problem is not particular to neuroscience and is something endemic to the broader psychology and philosophy of art. This is the belief that complex abstract concepts or ideals such as love, beauty or art either have great variability within cultures or, more broadly, possess no core set of features that allow these concepts to be measured. On this view, sensory perceptions do not define them but, in fact, provide particular instances of them that cannot capture their full complexity or our experiential richness that is closely attached to and determined by the phenomena themselves (Noë's wine tasting being a good example of this). In other words, measuring the 'early' processes of art experience to do with the activity of feature detectors or sensorimotor activity is merely a small part of that experience and will only provide a reduced schematic of its complexity: 'early brain activity associated with evaluative processes represents a fast impression formation which influences other processes related with attention, perception, response selection, and so on, but which may be crucial for decisions to continue or interrupt engagement with the stimulus' (Cela-Conde et al., 2011, p. 43).

Much of the later cognitive processes are concerned with contextual information, categories of style, what we know about the artist, how we assess culture and maintain ideals, how we are feeling at the time, whether the sun is shining and much more. In short, a great many 'later' cognitive processes, along with the contingencies of experience, are involved, which are not localised in particular brain areas in all cases but are the result of broad, distributed connectivity (Fairhall and Ishai, 2008) and *situatedness*. Semir Zeki himself admits: 'I have been vague about the precise neurological way through which ideals are constructed by the brain' (2009, p. 74). Zeki concedes that concepts that are used as standards by which to judge art are 'difficult to study at the level of brain cells; we just do not have the technology at present…we therefore have to limit ourselves to generalities and to hints…where the concept itself resides is problematic' (pp. 53–54).

Recently, some neuroscientific opinion has acknowledged these problems. Four arguments have been put forward to support the contention that neuroaesthetics cannot account for artistic behaviour: '(i) its strict focus on beauty, preference, liking, and so on; (ii) its search for general principles and neglect of particular aspects; (iii) its disregard for contextual features; (iv) its attempts to reduce art production and appreciation to general neurobiological mechanisms' (Cela-Conde et al., 2011, p. 46). Furthermore, art can intimidate, express sorrow or be used 'to extol a society's grandeur, to make us reflect on humanity's and our own existence, among many other functions. In fact, contemporary western art has seen many instances of works that are conceived as a reaction against beauty as an artistic concept' (p. 47).

The most interesting outcome of this sustained criticism of neuroaesthetics has been a retraction, of sorts, by its founder, Semir Zeki:

> many will today acknowledge that something considered to be a work of art need not be perceived as beautiful, good examples being some of the paintings of Francis Bacon, or the nudes of Lucian Freud, which is not to say that these works do not have considerable artistic merit both in their painterly style and in projecting truths, including truths about decay and ugliness. But any work, be it considered art or not, may be subjectively experienced as being beautiful by an individual. This leads us to divorce art from beauty in this discussion and concentrate on beauty alone (Ishizu and Zeki, 2011, p. 8).

It is quite clear from this that the authors seem not to be aware that truth or ethics may be considered a kind of beauty beyond their perceptible appearances. The rearguard action presents its own problems. Ishizu and Zeki's study of a brain-based theory of beauty (2011, an extension of work done by Kawabata and Zeki, 2004) claims to have discovered what they name the 'faculty of beauty' in the brain. This study required 21 subjects to look at 30 paintings and listen to 30 musical excerpts, rating each piece 'beautiful', 'indifferent' or 'ugly'. They found that many brain areas were active in the experience of inspecting artworks or listening to music but a small part of the medial orbitofrontal cortex (mOFC) was the only area that continued to be active across musical and visual experience, and the signal from this area was more intense when an artwork was rated 'beautiful'.

Perhaps their strongest statement is that this demonstrates that the mOFC, along with various sensory activations, determines beauty (2011, p. 9). However, this is a claim that is based on observing brain activity associated with pleasure, reward or value, which Ishizu and Zeki, along with other studies they mention (p. 7), assume is indicative of the experience of beauty. Ishizu and Zeki are aware of the fact that this area is associated primarily with pleasure and reward (p. 9) but this does not deter them from assuming that experiencing beauty is the same as experiencing reward and pleasure.

The OFC (in which the mOFC is situated) is one of the least understood regions of the brain but it has been suggested that this area tests certain mechanisms responsible for reinforcing 'affect', decision making and expectation (Kringelbach, 2005). It is also associated with planning with regard to reward and punishment. Thus, it is not a dedicated beauty faculty and can be used for various other tasks, judgements and activities that need not involve the evaluation of beauty. One wonders if the subjects might have returned similar results for food or games, advertisements or animals. It is interesting that subjects are more inclined to find something beautiful when the object under consideration has been clearly flagged as *art*, as other neurological studies confirm. Lacey et al. (2011) found an 'infusion' effect, an important priming effect where subjects responded more favourably to images that they were informed were art images, as opposed to other, non-art images, depicting the same or similar objects and scenes (p. 421). Leder et al. (2004, 2006) found positive responses to paintings stimulated by knowledge of their status as artworks, or by the consideration of the titles or gallery descriptions of artworks. Meanwhile, Cupchik et al. (2009) suggested that taking up an 'aesthetic attitude', possibly maintained by the prefrontal cortex (which is also associated with the self-monitoring of mental states), affects the evaluation of the artwork. Another study, by de Araujo et al. (2005), showed that word labels affected judgements about scents, while Plassmann et al. (2008) found that knowledge of the monetary value of wine affected preferences. In both cases, the mOFC was activated, suggesting that the mOFC is rather promiscuous in its response and that it is not particularly faithful to beauty. The mOFC seems more geared towards 'the subjective coding of hedonic valence' (Kirk et al., 2009, p. 1130), which can be applied to nearly anything. Yet even here, aesthetic philosophers have argued for centuries that aesthetic pleasure is distinguished from other kinds of pleasure because of its 'disinterested' dimension and this is also supported by traditional psychology: Martindale remarks that 'aesthetic experience is phenomenologically mild and subtle, and strong emotions and motives are not involved' (1988, p. 7).[5] It might thus be that subjects are translating their feelings of pleasure as 'beautiful' and that mOFC activity registers this kind of pleasure rather than the disinterested kind that psychologists and philosophers traditionally acknowledge.

Work on the reward system that is tied in with the experience of beauty is itself a complex process that complicates the over-simplistic notion of stimuli and response assumed in Ishizu and Zeki's (2011) study. Motivation affects 'attention': neuromodulatory areas responsible for the apportionment and regulation of mental effort, and vice versa (Pessoa, 2010a). Motivation will cooperate with the neurotransmitter dopamine, associated with pleasure, which helps to make salient certain stimuli in experience, enhancing visual inspection in the art context

---

[5] Whether one can have an entirely disinterested aesthetic experience, however, might be more of an ideal than an achievable state. Perhaps some kinds of Zen Buddhism envisage this experience of beauty without pleasure or reward. I will return to how contemporary art and art history have dealt with the issue of disinterestedness in later pages.

(Zaidel, 2010, p. 180). The role of valuation regions such as the OFC is part of a larger, more complex system of motivation, attention and reward. Chatterjee (2010a, p. 58) suggests the OFC may modulate the difference between 'liking' something and wanting it. We do not know how motivation affects the experience of beauty (and vice versa), or whether the mOFC indicated in the Ishizu and Zeki test evaluates the relevance of behaviour to motivation, which will be different for each artwork. After all, there are many different kinds of beauty and intensities of emotion associated with artworks and many different motivations for identifying artworks in different ways, often dependent on the priming context, by situatedness: laboratory test or art gallery, television or street performance, restaurant or living room or other public or private situation or categorisation. Should we classify the neural responses that process these contingent aspects as part of the experience of beauty? Semantic memory also modulates and cooperates with the mOFC (Kirk et al., 2009, p. 1131). In short, the mOFC spike might signal a brief and spontaneous surge of enthusiasm for an artwork or piece of music that the subject is primed to judge beautiful but in many other contexts might not.

There are other problems. One can understand beauty, and in so doing, one might not be particularly aroused or attracted to it. One does not have to like a work of art to acknowledge and understand that it is beautiful, especially when one tries to understand different cultures or time periods where ideas of beauty may be *appreciated* if not shared or felt. This might come close to the notion of disinterestedness. Thus, there is a difference between *analysing* beauty and instantly recognising it. The former has subtle gradations attached to it, arrived at through many different routes, the second is disposable and revisable more easily. A strong mOFC response may only signify the gross or vulgar aspects of such an experience of beauty, the gut reaction that may subside after several viewings or listening sessions. Importantly, Cupchik et al. (2009) showed that, in different viewing conditions, the same art object could elicit different neural responses associated with a range of experiences from subjective involvement to detachment. This could indicate variable conditions of beauty from immediate response associated with attractiveness or pleasure and later, meaningful engagement associated with a deeper understanding of beauty. The way in which time plays a role in the evaluation of beauty is important if we are to go beyond a snapshot of a partial mental process. The integration and patterning of concepts associated with beauty are likely to constitute subjectivity involved in judgements on beauty. We might be persuaded to call a snake or a picture of a snake beautiful, even though we are scared of them and do not experience any mOFC activity. For example, this might happen while recalling that something is beautiful. In other words, direct experience of the artwork is not always necessary to experience beauty or pleasure. Furthermore, pleasure is not necessary for something to be deemed beautiful (Carroll, 2006, p. 93). Muelder Eaton (2006) and Korsmeyer (2006) also argue that there are many different experiences of beauty that are not pleasurable so much as cognitive, dependent on understanding that something is beautiful; for example, learning how to appreciate wetland areas that sustain a variety of wildlife, which some might ordinarily think are ugly swamps (Muelder Eaton, 2006, p. 45). We learn to see beauty and can experience it without the mOFC spike.

One might feel relatively unmoved (or disinterested) by many examples of beauty. Muelder Eaton mentions attributing beauty to mathematics, science and legal systems (2006, p. 50). Architects learn to understand the beauty of a design by its efficiency and ingenuity, or in the way it improves people's lives, not primarily by its perceptible attractiveness. One wonders whether the mOFC spike would occur when considering an architectural plan or 'elegant mathematical equation'? (Goldie and Schellekens, 2010, p. 102). These evaluations of beauty depend on large resources of contextual knowledge. They are a 'difficult beauty' (Bosanquet, 1915/1963, p. 47). There are also longstanding theological traditions of disregarding 'outer appearances' for inner beauty, invisible to the eye. Of course, this ethical frame of mind valorises the truth as beautiful, even though it may not be particularly attractive or set off a strong mOFC response. When we hear of how people died, sometimes horribly, saving the lives of others, we are wont to think of the beauty of the human spirit, but it gives us no pleasure to do so in our sorrow. Beauty is often so moving, sad or engulfing that it is no longer 'attractive' or pleasurable. Moreover, we can fall out of love, even if we still think that the object of love is beautiful. It is interesting that Ishizu and Zeki state clearly (2011, p. 1) that notions of the sublime, which are very much associated with definitions of beauty, are not dealt with in their research, perhaps because this would show that beauty is a *range* of responses (and aesthetic levels) and is tremendously variable, not an on-off switch indicated by activation of the mOFC. The way in which the experience of beauty emerges with other states (empathy, sexual arousal, feelings allied with nurturing or being nurtured), and how the mOFC spike occurs within these other neurological contexts and motivations, changes the experience and significance of mOFC activity. Measuring the mOFC is akin to measuring the quantity of an aspect of the experience of beauty, not the quality of the whole experience of beauty, which is, in fact, durational and complex.

Context (as well as the object of contemplation itself) and timescale are important factors that change how much weight we should apportion to the mOFC spike. A strong mOFC spike for a fancy cake will not have the same lasting value for an individual as the same intensity measured for a mOFC spike associated with a Rembrandt. Again, the cognitive processes surrounding or working alongside the mOFC activation will change how that activation is used, interpreted, understood, filtered and weighted to produce very different phenomenal experiences of beauty. Yet feelings of pleasure or reward are themselves extremely variable in quality and, while we may understand such feelings to be innate and closely related to the English script *beauty*, they are not necessarily innate to some module or faculty of beauty. More generally, Feldman Barrett, a psychology of emotion expert, concludes that 'the available body of evidence suggests that there is no clear objective way to measure the experience of emotion' (2006, p. 24). Individuals who are low in emotional granularity report their experience in global terms such as 'beautiful', 'nice', 'awesome'. Furthermore, the verbal reports requested by Ishizu and Zeki in their test, 'beautiful', 'indifferent' and 'ugly' amount to a mistaken way of studying the experience of emotion: 'They are "shackles" from which scientists must be freed because they tell scientists more about emotion language than they do about the experience of emotion or the emotions from which those experiences are derived' (Feldman Barrett, 2006, p. 24).

Yet, despite the variable experience of beauty each of us have, Ishizu and Zeki claim that the 'subjective experience of beauty and ugliness can be objectively ascertained and measured' (2001, p. 9). We always knew that *some* forms of beauty provide satisfaction, reward, pleasure or evaluation, and that these feelings are biologically supported. However, what does locating a small part of this process tell us that we did not know already? What would we gain by adopting expressions such as 'the statue of David by Michelangelo stimulates my mOFC', instead of saying, 'it's beautiful', except to freeze-frame and locate a small aspect, and possibly even a superficial one, of a dynamic, temporally extended experience, one that perhaps better deserves the epithet of beauty?

Many experiences of contemporary art redefine beauty. A good example of how contemporary artists hold in contempt the traditional norms and values that lie behind the quest of neuroaesthetics to find beauty in the brain is Marina Abramović's filmed performance in the 1970s, where she repeated the phrase 'art must be beautiful, artist must be beautiful' while brushing her hair with a metal brush and comb until her hair and scalp were damaged, causing her pain and discomfort. I am pretty certain that my mOFC would not spike watching this film, although I do believe that there is a profound 'beauty' in Abramović's work, which consists in its deconstruction. The experience of beauty, at least of an acquired kind, is not to be 'found' in the brain; it is social and contextual, temporally extended and, most of all, it is contested.

2.2   Emotions in art: seeing is believing?

David Freedberg (2006, 2009, 2011) and Freedberg and Gallese (2007) believe that an important aspect of aesthetic experience is based on sensory and motor interpretations of figures, faces and body movements as depicted in art, details we interpret that provide a platform upon which it is possible to have richly emotional responses to art. Parts of our sensorimotor apparatus (areas responsible for our sensory exploration and bodily movements) are activated even if we do not act, smell or taste while we see others acting or moving (or smelling or tasting). This theory of the 'offline' appreciation of others' actions and movements is related to the discovery of 'mirror neurons' in the brain of the macaque monkey (Rizzolati and Craighero, 2004): 'Mirror neurons are sensorimotor neurons that fire when a monkey executes certain kinds of actions and when the monkey perceives the same action being perceived by another...The mirror system is the mechanism whereby an observer understands a perceived action by simulating, without executing, the agent's observed movements' (Jacob and Jeannerod, 2005, pp. 21, 24). Freedberg is the only notable art historian to date who seems to have used these neurological findings for a theory of art. The main thrust of his approach, which is to be commended, is to have reintroduced consideration of the body's facticity in art perception, which had waned somewhat after Merleau-Ponty's phenomenological interpretations of sculpture adapted with some skill and purpose by the likes of Rosalind Krauss (1981), an approach which I will analyse in some detail in later chapters. Freedberg, who is a specialist in more traditional art forms, employs the notion that we understand and interpret others' actions, positions of limbs and facial expressions in figurative art using sensorimotor areas of the brain to interpret mainly representational art, although there have been attempts to explain the gestural work of Pollock and Fontana's dramatic slashed canvas (Freedberg and Gallese, 2007), and the work of Richard Serra in term of scale, using standard phenomenological approaches (Freedberg, 2009). This 'offline' sensorimotor response to other people's 'online' sensorimotor actions is supposed to lay the basis for emotions such as empathy, anger and fear, which we read through people's facial features or body movements.

The link between reading or responding to the body's actions and emoting is controversial on several fronts. Imitating the sensorimotor acts of others using our own sensorimotor apparatus is not the same as understanding those actions. Understanding requires some knowledge of why people are acting the way they do in order to empathise. Indeed, given certain motives, watching someone's display of anger or fear might lead observers not to empathise at all, but actually to enjoy such displays, a spectacle we are used to seeing in much entertainment. The switch from sensorimotor mirroring to empathy is not guaranteed and needs to be mediated by conceptual interpretations of the social situation, cause and effect, and an evaluation of categories of depiction or aesthetics. We might consider whether the image is convincing, for example, or whether the sensorimotor actions are ironic or insincere. Our ability to interpret art and poetry undoubtedly will involve inferential reasoning about the beliefs and intentions of others (Goel, 1995) and the ability to understand sarcasm or irony, as well as inference and attribution. These are not sensorimotor processes, but are dominated by the role of the frontal areas of the brain (Stuss et al., 2001) and, in some cases, are premised on a theory of mind that will require metacognitive processes of self-monitoring (Christoff et al., 2009a).[1] From the perspective of psychology, there is much controversy in empirical studies concerning the classification of emotions and reading them through body language and expression, processes that are more unreliable than is commonly believed (Feldman Barrett, 2006, 2009 and Wilson-Mendenhall et al., 2011). There are also problems with categories: there are many different kinds of fear or anger, and the body and face often do not register these nuances, particularly because some people conceal their emotions more easily than others, even when strong emotions are involved. Thus, artworks will rely on a broad range of signifiers and conventions beyond body language to intimate emotional complexity, but this takes us away from the unfettered automatic response of empathy based on mirror neurons suggested by Freedberg and Gallese.

From the point of view of neuroscience, even the strongest emotions such as fear and anger are notoriously difficult to associate with particular

---

[1] A theory of mind is an awareness of the likely content of other people's minds or the minds of fictive characters. Such processes of inference and attribution are heavily dependent on the frontal regions of the brain. Lesions in the frontal lobes are associated with impaired perspective taking, and leads to the loss of 'the ability to associate social situations with personal affective markers' (Stuss et al., 2001, pp. 279–280).

brain areas (for a review, see Pessoa and Adolphs, 2010; Feldman Barrett, 2006), particularly because they occur with cognitive and linguistic processes before, during and after the emotion, indicating a massive interconnectivity of processes. Reading bodily actions and gestures, or even the shape and scale of abstract works depicted in art, could be said to amount to interpreting the artwork from the *sensus litteralis*, the crude idea of what the work is about, yet art history for many centuries has learnt to discard the husk of the self-evident. On this view, art can be misread as something that *primarily* functions as a physiognomic illustration of mirror neurons rather than as a phenomenon that involves a great many other functions.

A similar objection to this kind of interpretation of mirror neurons is levelled by scientists of visual perception, Jacob and Jeannerod (2005). Social cognition is thought to be based on the action of mirror neurons because these form the basis of our understanding of and empathy for others: 'The mirror system does not seem well designed for promoting fast responses to the perception of social actions...in response to the perception of a threat, it might be adaptive to flee, not to simulate the threatening agent's observed movements. Evidence from single cell recordings in the monkey shows that observing many actions...prompts purely perceptual responses *without* motor properties' (Jacob and Jeannerod, 2005, pp. 21, 24; my emphasis).

The authors are keen to stress that while we might have mirror responses to the actions of others observed in the environment, we need a lot more contextual information and cognition, which are not limited to sensorimotor processing, in order to discern the actor's intention or meaning (Mahon and Caramazza, 2008).[2] This is significant because it raises questions about whether sensorimotor processes, from which emotions and empathy spring, according to Freedberg's art theory, are interpretative and meaningful or whether interpretative and meaningful processes are brought to bear upon sensorimotor processes. It is, after all, reasonable to expect that empathy is not only an emotion but also a process of understanding that is more complex and socially mediated,

---

[2] 'There is a sense in which the sensory and motor information involved in using hammers is instrumental in determining what it means for something to be a hammer. But this fact about the world does not, in and of itself, license the inference that motor activation induced by merely looking at a hammer means that that motor information is critical – online – in retrieving the concept HAMMER...The question is whether the motor system is activated due to "leakage" of (or cascading) activation from an "abstract" conceptual level, or occurs in parallel to (or independently of) activation of the "abstract" conceptual level' (Mahon and Caramazza, 2008, p. 61). In other words it remains unknown whether the motor system 'becomes activated prior to, or rather only subsequent to, access to an "abstract" conceptual representation' (p. 62).

based on knowledge rather than automatically responding in kind to body language. In other words, empathy is not mime, neither are its bonds to be tied too tightly to the emotion side of the cognitive-emotional range (see arguments for a more cognitive and analytical understanding of how empathy works in Goldie, 2003 and Currie, 2006).

It is obvious in one sense that sensorimotor processing is not essential for the functioning of emotional understanding, empathy and abstract conceptual thought. Mahon and Caramazza discuss a patient with lesions (the apraxia I have already mentioned) that do not allow him to use sensorimotor knowledge in order to use a hammer or any other tool: 'The patient might be able to recount the history of the hammer as an invention, the materials of which the first hammer was made...The patient may even look at a hammer and name it...But when presented with a hammer, the patient is profoundly impaired at demonstrating how the object is physically manipulated to accomplish its function' (2008, pp. 67–68). This suggests that a lot of important interpretative knowledge to do with history, materials, quantitative analysis and symbolic associations, active in the normal processing of art (and perhaps even the emotional attachments or aversions one might have regarding hammers), is not reducible to or dependent on sensorimotor processes – so why base a neurocognitive art theory that purports to give us a deeper understanding of art upon such processes?[3]

Showing how important body language is in art is not the same as saying that this is *the* most important aspect of the art experience and, to be fair, Freedberg does not espouse this approach. Putting the body and emotions back into art interpretation provides a balance with other more 'cognitive' art historical approaches that emphasise contextual knowledge as important ways to understand art, using aspects of social history or art historical comparative method. Freedberg stresses, quite rightly, that these approaches, the cognitive and the emotional, are not opposed to each other and that we should strive to integrate them for a fuller understanding of art. It is in the spirit of this attempt to integrate cognition and emotion that it would be entirely appropriate to offer examples of a range of subtle

---

[3] Mahon and Caramazza conclude: 'the neuropsychological evidence in no way resolves the issue of how concepts of concrete objects and actions are represented in the brain, beyond establishing that sensory and motor information plays, at best, a supportive but not necessary role in representing concepts. From the foregoing, one thing is clear: the goal of developing a theory of concepts will not be served by collecting more of the same data. One more fMRI experiment demonstrating that the motor cortex is activated during action observation or sentence processing does not make the embodied cognition hypothesis more likely to be correct' (2008, pp. 66–67). The same might be said of embodied approaches aimed to show how sensorimotor processes are activated during emotional or aesthetic experience.

emotions that seem to interact with abstract concepts to do with art. However, neuroscience is not yet up to the task of integrating these different yet complementary responses to art, and Freedberg struggles to get right the balance between the cognitive and sensorimotor.

Freedberg's approach to Rogier van der Weyden's *Descent from the Cross* (*c.* 1435), for example, tends to place too much emphasis on aspects of the facial and gross features of embodiment (facial expressions, gestures of the hands and arms) and foregrounds strong emotions such as fear, sorrow and disgust – which have been studied by neuroscience – to the detriment of composite and more subtle but no less important emotions – which neuroscience has yet to begin to understand. Emotion psychologist, Paula Niedenthal, explains that it is a well-known principle in emotion psychology not to confuse emotions with how they are reported or perceived: 'emotions are not one single thing (like a facial expression, or the report of a feeling state), not a rigid program' (2006). This is especially so because emotions have component parts that combine differently, depending on the context or stimulus; we use general emotion concepts to describe subtly different combinations of experience. I would like to suggest that Freedberg's identification of empathy as a mirror neuron response to Rogier van der Weyden's *Descent from the Cross* ignores many emotional subtleties that cannot be explained by a strong sensorimotor theory of aesthetics.

Rogier van der Weyden's *Descent from the Cross* gives us the opportunity to be somewhat disinterested from the emotions depicted than we might be if we were actually experiencing a crucifixion, and far too easily do art historians gloss over the differences between direct experience of the artwork and the event it portrays, and the different readings that are possible arising from photographic reproductions of the work. Aspects of execution, stylisation, traditional iconography and abstract composition help to stimulate a whole range of less obvious modulations of emotion – ones linked more closely to cognitive processes – but these are decidedly more difficult to trace to neural correlates than the more dramatic emotions flagged up for discussion with the sensorimotor approach to art. In van der Weyden's deposition scene, the way the Virgin Mary's hand suggests a failed attempt to curl around the skull indicates a peculiar cognitive and emotional ambiguity. The way in which the skull and Mary's nonconscious body seem to create a physical hierarchy of states amounts to a priming procedure that causes there to be a type of pattern completion leading us to think about what is next: the lifting of the body over death and oblivion, or a move in the opposite direction?

Figure 13. Rogier van der Weyden, *Descent from the Cross*, *c*.1435 (oil on panel). Prado, Madrid, Spain, The Bridgeman Art Library.

The way in which the painter has cleverly concealed or underplayed hands and garments also creates a feeling of graceful and effortless levitation that belies ordinary sensorimotor commitment. In terms of composition, the way the body of Christ seems to float unnaturally above the Virgin Mary's body, a posture that seems to imitate hers underneath in a dancelike movement, tends to lift the emotional gravity of the depiction to a message of hope in resurrection, especially because we expect the Virgin Mary to regain consciousness, and it is reasonable to make an analogy between her state and Christ's. Is hope an emotion? This line of reasoning reads sensorimotor action symbolically. In addition, there is resignation and introspection and, of course, on the outer wings there are tears and grief. Within the gross identification of sorrow are ranges of intensity and difference that go unremarked. We often believe that we can identify the core emotional content of a scene or situation, thereby capturing its essence. In fact, the latest neurological research into emotion suggests this tendency to essentialise emotion is part of a well-known 'emotion paradox': 'How is it that people can automatically and effortlessly see anger, sadness and fear in others, and experience these emotions...even though scientists have not located them clearly and consistently in the brain and body?' (Feldman Barrett, 2006, p. 49). Furthermore, 'there is accumulating evidence that words ground category acquisition and function like conceptual glue for the members of a category', thus emotion words 'serve to reduce the uncertainty that is inherent in most natural facial behaviors and constrain their meaning to allow for quick and easy perceptions of emotion' (Feldman Barrett et al., 2007, p. 328).

One of the problems underlying the sensorimotor approach to art is the ambiguity involved in reading what we assume to be an unequivocal emotion but which may, in fact, have various qualities, compounded by reading body language and gesture, which are also notoriously polysemous. Scientific research fails to provide consistent support for the idea that there is a discrete motor programme (which would move facial features among other things) activated by emotions that is universally understood (Carroll and Russell, 1997, p. 714). Folk psychology assumes distinct boundaries for emotions, while most of the recent neuropsychological literature indicates that emotional states such as sadness and anger can overlap and can be seen as composite forms or categories bringing together a range of properties that are carved up differently, depending on the situation.[4] As William James observed, 'not all instances that people call "anger" (or "sadness" or "fear") look alike, feel alike, or have the same neurophysiological signature' (Feldman Barrett et al., 2007, p. 328). When we call a face or gesture 'sad' or 'angry', we are often being approximate, interpreting or parsing a complex social experience or visual scene rather than considering the fine-grained variability that can lie underneath the apparent signals. There are questions over the value of art historical approaches that attempt to reduce the range of expressive possibilities depicted in artworks to the identification of well-known emotional percepts. On the other hand, there is little doubt in the value of trying to convey the range and dynamism of cognitive and emotional components depicted in art, if the art allows it.

Freedberg insists that viewers of van der Weyden's painting 'have no difficulty in recognising the emotions quite precisely' (2011, p. 345), a

---

[4] Take, for example, the fact that in Turkey, 'sadness and anger are properties of a single emotion category called "kizginlik"' (Mesquita, 1993). In addition to this: 'In the English language there are between 500 and 2000 words that refer more or less to emotions (*shame*), affective of valenced states (*tranquillity*), and cognitive-affective states (*vengeance*)... However, in Malay...there are about 230 emotion words, and in Ifaluk...there are only about 50' (Niedenthal et al., 2006). Clearly, therefore, there are enormous cultural differences in how people understand emotional states and how they are signalled and communicated.

rhetorical flourish describing a coherence that does not sit well with the psychology: 'for some theorists to conclude that lack of response coherence within each category of emotion is empirically the rule rather than the exception...a plausible explanation is that scientists have failed to observe stable and reliable response clusters because they are not really there' (Feldman Barrett, 2006, p. 34). This suggests that emotions, signalled by facial expression and body comportment that Freedberg wants us to believe viewers find automatically legible through mirror neurons, are, in fact, phenomenally and subjectively interpreted, not the result of some biologically determined empathy hinging on the action of mirror neurons.

Empathy is knowledge dependent. We can only allow it to flourish if we know its target deserves it and, fortunately or unfortunately, this is often mediated by moral beliefs, cultural prejudice, age and a host of other factors. The action of mirror neurons and observing the actions of others are not the same as consciously attending to an emotional percept and experiencing empathy. Of course, we may experience blunt empathy automatically, but there are a number of cognitive inhibitions or facilitators that are pivotal for empathy to become interpretable, and this last move is not dependent on mirror neurons but on our abilities to infer the likely content of other people's minds, higher cognitive processes of interpretation associated with the prefrontal areas (Stuss et al., 2001). Empathy is also tremendously variable and dynamic, and is likely not to be an on-off switch; it can appear as a spike of emotion or it can have a slowly spreading activation that involves many other cognitive processes (especially if we are considering the artistic depiction of emotions, not just attending to the emotions themselves).

As with many other emotions, it would be wrong to think of empathy as a simple or unitary event with a typical (or stereotypical) profile. Research suggests that there are component processes in every emotion, and very often these constituent parts (conceptual, perceptual and affective) do not cohere. Niedenthal (2006) summarises this view: 'various components can be elicited by different objects or events and proceed independently, or else combine in innumerable ways to produce highly nuanced emotional experiences'.

The authors mention that there is also the problem of how emotions change quickly, so even if emotion components seem to cohere, later processes come into play to decouple them. Thus, espousing the view that art is just an expression of an unproblematic unitary emotion would be to claim that art is caricature, a kind of 'fixing' of an emotional state as a stereotype. This brings into view how traditions in art employ conventions to read emotions that may be different from how we experience them in real life situations. For example, Carroll and Russell (1997, p. 174) remark that even though people almost never rub their abdomens when hungry, mime and, by extension, visual art are required to adopt conventions that are culturally acquired in order to be easily identifiable when, in fact, in many situations individuals choose to hide their emotions. The authors make a strong distinction between prototypical patterns, known as facial expressions of emotion that exist in the world of theatre and in the mind of the observer as *cognitive prototypes*, as opposed to the mundane reality of actual facial behaviour that occurs during everyday emotional episodes. Despite this, we persist in thinking that these prototypes can help us to interpret any facial expression in any situation. It is clear, however, that artistic conventions in painting (a static medium) and in life (which is not) are also an important distinction to keep in mind when speaking of natural sensorimotor dispositions to read body language and facial expressions. Importantly, there are significant differences in how certain kinds of art depend for their effect on 'freeze-framing' or clearly signalling a coherent emotion, while others depend on the variables of a group of emotions, a type of polyphonic series of different emotional types. This is also complicated by images in contemporary art that, in their attempt to explore the complications of aesthetic emotion, often bring together emotional components that seem to clash or hang together awkwardly. This is often a deliberate strategy to encourage us to reflect on possible knee-jerk reactions, preconceived ideas and emotional sureties.

In other words, the decoupling of 'molar' emotion components seems to be deliberate in various contemporary artworks. Marcus Harvey's *Myra Hindley*, 1995, is a good example of all the issues involved here, and offers an opportunity to discuss psychological research into emotion response with regard to a well-known, perhaps even notorious contemporary artwork. The painting depicts Myra Hindley, the British serial child killer, and is a huge portrait based on her criminal mug shot. It has been described as 'sick' and 'disgusting' with various protests staged against its display at the Royal Academy in London, and the painting itself was vandalised. Many thought the painting was headline-grabbing and exploitative, and some even thought that the painting glorified or glamorised the subject. From a distance, one is struck by its huge starkness, which seems confrontational. Hindley's enormous black eyes loom over the gallery space in a hard, cold, fixed stare, creating somewhat of a chill. Closer up, however, the picture becomes pixilated with a mottled effect and, even closer, one begins to recognise that the component parts of the painting are children's hands – or hand prints – the kind one would see in

Figure 14. Marcus Harvey, *Myra*, 1995 (acrylic on canvas, 396.2 × 320 cm). Photograph by Stephen White, Courtesy of White Cube.

children's paintings in nurseries. In fact, they were made with a plaster cast of a child's hand, in two instances stamping the pupil of each eye. The eye/hand contrast create quite an impact, a kind of binocular rivalry between the concepts of seeing and revealing and covering the eyes;

gesticulating, yet having the image of the hand reflected on the retina, changing the interpretation of who is looking at what. It is also the 'artistic' hand.

Apprehension, unease, anger are emotions premised on the first encounter with the image that vary over the course of the experience of the artwork. Yet even these already quite complex emotions begin to decouple when more information is gleaned from the image. Just as a distanced view of the image brings together its component parts, inviting strong emotional coherence, the close-up view begins to dis-integrate the easy identification of both the subject matter and any unitary emotions attached to it. The view of the children's hands, which seem to both reveal and blot out the image, are accompanied by feelings of revulsion or disgust that either overturn indignation and anger, or deepen them.

Here, the cognitive processes involved greatly determine both the cohesion and character of subsequent emotions. Some viewers walked away with bitterness and contempt (if press reports on the subject are to be believed), either partly to do with closeness and familiarity with the details of Hindley's role in the murders (some viewers were even among victims' families), or to do with a general contempt in the British media for contemporary art. Compounding these responses, no doubt, was the venue, the Royal Academy, a site renowned for celebrating aesthetic beauty and acknowledging artistic value. For others, the incongruity of the institutional setting would have been easier to resolve with the know-ledge that the appalling etchings of Goya's war series, Turner's *Slave Ship* and Picasso's *Guernica* demonstrate clearly that art never declines the opportunity to explore the negative emotions of disgust and revulsion. However, it is difficult to think of one's art history in charged moments and in the toxic atmosphere created by tabloid sensationalism surround-ing the exhibition.[5] Yet, the sight of the little handprints in Marcus Harvey's painting wield a significant power, at least for some. They help to flatten attention spikes of alarm and disgust into waves of sadness. For the children's handprints signal the presence of the dead children, and the effect is strangely quietening. The close-up view of children's hands, stubbornly accusing, are in conflict with the looming presence of Myra Hindley. Each handprint is a small yet powerful presence (each one a *punctum*, as Barthes would have it), and together, as a group, they form the anatomy of a tragedy. There is a kind of binocular rivalry

---

[5] It is ironic that the show was titled 'Sensation', which alluded to its deliberate attempt to shock those who thrive on scandal: sensationalist tabloids and their readers.

(more accurately, a cognitive-emotional rivalry) that exists between the fragmented details of the handprints and the optical mixture of the Moors Murderer. At the same time, there is an uneasy alliance where the individual identity of each handprint seems in danger of being lost in the overcrowding of details. At a higher cognitive level, the conviction emerges that each handprint appears as a kind of document, an indelible presence that points to the simple fact that Harvey's painting is not a monument to Myra Hindley but to her victims.

The contrast of the close-up versus long-distance view is more than a cheap trick borrowed from Seurat. It allows the viewers to switch attention from Hindley to the children, and for both murder and victims to be co-present in an uneasy tension or struggle. This struggle is emotional as well as visual, depending on how the image is identified. Whose image should we memorialise here, Hindley's or that of her victims? This epitomises the dreadful quandary that memorialising the victims cannot be separated easily from the knowledge of how they died. There is no easy way to mourn, the picture tells us; it is not some unitary, easily settled state; it has a course that is filled with many concepts, feelings and memories, refusing to provide the kind of emotional 'resolution' we traditionally expect of art.

The complexity of Harvey's work is typical of many contemporary artworks that are received with scepticism. At first glance, they seem simply to be provocative and shallow, yet are in fact 'difficult', providing obstacles to the easy identification of aesthetic, moral and emotional types and sureties. In many ways, this work can be seen as a psychologically complex painting that dissects automatic reactions even after provoking them. It shifts the focus on the viewer's autonomic or perceptual responses to art, and surprises us because it seems to make us critical of our own habitual responses. It is, perhaps, also an attempt to guard against the overexposure of the violent images we witness from day-to-day, which Warhol believed simply make us indifferent. We may tend not to be indifferent to Harvey's painting precisely because of its irresolvable tensions and the way it questions art's relationship to cultural memory and trauma, an uneasy alliance we see in Christian Boltanski's works, many of which use black-and-white photographs of faces of victims of the Holocaust to create altarpieces or shrines with lamps or candles. These works bring to mind Adorno's often (mis)quoted remark that 'Poetry after Auschwitz is barbaric', which is taken to mean a crisis in art's ability to respond to the scale of human tragedy.

Harvey's work questions the obvious, inviting us to reflect on our initial emotional identification, and with the fragmentation of the image on closer inspection, the initial, strong emotional response fragments. In a sense, the dual visual effect (strong image/fragmented image) matches the emotional response (strong emotion/fragmented emotion). It is significant that although Freedberg sees a blindingly obvious emotional signature in the characters' bodies in van der Weyden's painting, which he suggests is a response that we are biologically hardwired to have, on closer inspection the facial expressions of nearly all the figures in the Rogier van der Weyden painting are difficult to read. The Virgin has fainted, she is now without emotion, oblivious, presumably overwhelmed by emotion that only knowledge of the story would tell us is grief. Various glazed or downcast eyes in other figures conceal emotions; there is a slight knitting of the brow depicted in the expression of one face, Joseph of Arimathea holding Christ's feet. It is a mark of the artist's wisdom that he has not succumbed too much to the temptation of trying to convey emotion through the histrionics of gesticulation. Instead, the calm faces invite the viewer to interpret, evaluate and reflect on difference. It seems, in fact, more natural that in such circumstances most of the faces are not even up to the task of revealing the scale of the shock. Only the two women whose facial expressions are difficult to see, standing on either side of the painting, Mary Salome with a handkerchief on the left and Mary Magdalene on the right, seem to strike poses traditionally associated with grief or pain. These figures help to identify the chord; they frame the stage and the emotional subtleties contained between them.

As contemporary viewers, we may be less convinced or able to empathise fully with Mary Magdalene on the right, for her pose now seems to be a theatrical gesture of supplication or despair, something that viewers in the fifteenth century would perhaps have been more able to identify with, yet the power and nuance of this has been lost through time. It may be a naturalistic attempt at a conventional pose, aspects of which indicate how the sensorimotor theory of understanding is contingent and open to interpretation. The two figures who try to support the fainting Virgin Mary may be construed as having feelings of sympathy but from a sensorimotor and purely functional point of view they are only preventing her from hitting the ground. There is nothing in their body gestures or faces that is an unequivocal expression of particular emotions or their intensity. Of course, we are free to read these movements using a whole range of our own emotional subtleties but the sensorimotor action is primarily concerned with shifting weight or stooping down. A great deal of categorisation and interpretation is going on beyond the capabilities of mirror neurons that may automatically respond to body movements; in fact, one would have to ignore them in this case to impute mourning or sympathy to their actions, instead of sympathising with the weight they have to carry.

It is not at all clear that sensorimotor processes differentiate semantically in this way (Jacob and Jeannerod, 2005).[6] What we are apt to see is guided by what we *cognitively* understand is going on in the scene as a whole; we interpret more than the literal sensorimotor actions depicted for each figure. Yet Freedberg seems to suggest that the reason why we experience compassion for the figures in van der Weyden's painting is due mainly or exclusively to the natural, biological way in which we respond to the body postures of others, regardless of our conceptual knowledge. Referring to the painting, he writes:

Its hold on its viewers, even in the fifteenth century, would most likely not have depended on knowledge of its subject matter, or even on personal experiences related to the emotional connotations of the scene or of the story represented. Rather, it would have depended, just as it does today, on a set of cortical responses that have little to do with context, whether historical or connotative, but everything to do with the connection between sight of the bodies and movements of others and the viewers' sense of their own bodies and movements (Freedberg, 2011, p. 345).

A crucial part of Rogier's skill lay in his ability to make his viewers instantly recognize the sadness of those whom he portrays by the evocation of corresponding feelings through the excitation of those parts of the brain responsible for the activation of corresponding movements of the body (p. 344).

Nevertheless, what if we were told that the dead Christ was a murderer, or that the Virgin Mary was, in fact, the dead man's accomplice and that the figures holding up the Virgin Mary are going to take her away to stand trial? How would we read the sensorimotor and emotional valence of the painting then? Why would people assume that the corpse is being taken down rather than being hoisted upon the cross? Without knowing the proper details of the story, would we even know that the dead person has any relationship to the ladder, or that he had not died, in fact, of some dreadful disease that causes wounds to weep? We need to know the framing of the 'story' to make any sense of what our mirror neurons

---

[6] It is difficult to use an exact model for how sensorimotor processing affects perceptions and concepts because this suggests a causal chain where there is plenty of neuropsychological evidence that the direction of cause and effect is reversible: conceptualisation can affect perceptual processes and sensorimotor response. The case of identifying sympathy in the body language of those figures holding up the Virgin Mary is an inference that is purely conceptual in nature, based on our knowledge of the story. Besides this interpretation of sensorimotor action that interprets the meaning or intention of those actions, it is true that explicit categorisation goals influence how sensory information is sampled and processed in the visual field (Sowden and Schyns, 2006); yet emotions (especially affect) aid categorisation and other cognitive domains. See Feldman Barrett, 2009, pp. 11–12, for a summary of the relevant neuroscientific studies.

might be doing, and our mirror neurons could be misleading us. It might be argued that the figures in the painting show too much reverence for the dead Christ to be read as carrying an executed criminal, but the reading of such reverence requires more time and cognitive resources and cultural interpretations beyond immediate response valorised by the strong sensorimotor approach or, indeed, by formalist art historical approaches.[7] If we were to shift the whole argument to a consideration of what the viewers would have felt most in response to this painting in the fifteenth century, we would have to consider how appropriate or 'natural' emotional and perceptual responses are conditioned and mediated by cultural knowledge. This weakens the appeal to the non-contingent transparency of body language that Freedberg and Gallese emphasise.

Only with contextual knowledge of a scene or an event are we able to piece together causes for emotions that are essential for us to understand them. When processing bodies and expressions in the visual field, we make approximate estimates of the specific emotions that may be involved, which might allow us to commit fully to empathy. Even then, however, we tend to elaborate and explore further the variable range of emotions that are possible in us and in the objects of our attention.[8]

Wilson-Mendenhall et al. (2011) suggest that emotions are not states with hard boundaries. Emotions are not as fixed as figures depicted in paintings. This is key, because the real artistry in Rogier van der Weyden's *Descent from the Cross* is not that it *fixes* grief throughout the painting by freezing postures of the same emotion, but rather that it suggests what might happen after it is triggered; for example, a series of transformations: dawning awareness, smouldering resignation, the blinding darkness of loss, confusion, indecision, oblivion. A consideration of the figures reveals not only different emotional qualities and depths but also the suggestion

---

[7] Let us not forget that Rudolph Arnheim (1969), Clive Bell (1914) and Roger Fry (1924), in various ways, also tended to emphasise the importance of formal composition arrived at through a model of direct perception unaffected by contextual, situational and conceptual processes, which we now know exert important influences on our attentional focus. What we search for in the visual field and, importantly, what we report on, and how we interpret what we think we have seen, top-down processes, affect perception. For philosophical arguments as to how immediate sensations of pleasure and judgements of beauty are strongly affected by knowledge conditions, see Muelder Eaton (2006).

[8] We often learn this complex differentiation through lexical concepts. Note: 'conceptual knowledge about emotion that is necessary to support emotion perception is not available to young children, so that children's early emotion concepts do not support the perception of distinct categories of emotion like anger and sadness. Children do not possess the full adult taxonomy of emotion concepts until the age of 5. Two-year-olds favor a few emotion labels (e.g., "happy" and "sad") to describe the entire domain of emotion' (Feldman Barrett, 2006 p. 39).

of the temporal unfolding of emotions. This is not perceivable with sensorimotor decoding, yet is achievable through a conceptual evaluation of the story and probabilistic models of the range, intensity and duration of emotional responses of groups in events such as these, resulting in a more encompassing empathetic interpretation.

The stylistic aspects and compositional principles in Rogier van der Weyden's image lead to the exploration of emotional diversity. There is a rise and fall, a modulation of emotion, nuanced and enriched by the kind of cognitive processes that intervene, to do with how things are depicted and not only with what they depict. The variation of rhythms and forms suggest a sense of dignity and resignation but these concepts are not sensorimotor. Apart from Mary Magdalene's striking pose, there is no convincing muscularity, as Freedberg believes. In fact, the figures seem weightless, the hands and arms are patterned into a looping series of reciprocal gestures; it is an aesthetic game that smoothes the edges of raw emotion. Rather than picking out only the salient features expressed by body and gesture, one can and does take one's time to play on a scale of emotions, perceptions and concepts. We examine various aspects, panning over the surface of the painting, taking in what the picture has to offer as a whole. Even if one were inclined to fall for the gut reactions suggested by the first glance, the tears behind handkerchiefs, the lowered eyes, this evens out to many other kinds of emotion beyond the narrow range described by Freedberg. This allows one to avoid the notion that the correct way to read the painting is by focusing on grief in a circular way – and with the same intensity – as a discrete emotional state, when it is clear that the artist is able to create aggregates, complementaries and subtle variables.

This is not to say that grief or pain is not particular, sometimes visceral and convulsive, or persistent and debilitating. In this vein, the artist has managed to convey a knowledge of idiographic differences: that some people seem to explode visibly with emotion shown externally and with a variety of postures and gestures, while others implode and internalise their deepest emotional responses, betraying little or no body language. Are we to assume that the latter are heartless because they are not signalling clearly? Perhaps, instead, it might be appropriate to consider what Roland Barthes has to say on grief: 'Each of us has his own rhythm of suffering.' This brings into view the problem that, in art history, associating a blank face with an emotion not only assumes a great deal about the figure portrayed and the artist's intention, it also essentialises the work of art *and* narrows the range of responses that might be open to the viewer.

The painting's theatrical space seems rather cramped and flat, and most of it is taken up by the drapery. Much of the painting's allure arises from the treatment of the textures and patterns, the subtle contrasts of colour and luminosity, the ripples in the drapery causing spikes in attention, generating erratic saccades and suggesting fibrillation, yet there are gently undulating areas. This description of the drapery's expressive values is both an intellectual and emotional decoding, dependent on sensorimotor input and conceptual blending, but shows that the gaze is not shackled to the limbs and gestures for empathy. As Freedberg rightly acknowledges, Aby Warburg's *Pathosformel* suggests that flowing drapery can reveal inner emotions (Freedberg, 2006, p. 28).

There is, of course, a detailed history in German aesthetics dealing with empathy, from Vischer's coining of the term *Einfühlung* ('feeling into') in the nineteenth century. Controversy over how to define the properties of 'empathy', the term used by Titchener in 1909 to approximate the concept (and which loses some of the power of the original in translation), has dogged its use and continues today. The term *Einfühlung* was far from being agreed in the exacting circumstances of nineteenth-century German aesthetics; some art historians, such as Wölfflin, intended it as a cerebral association of ideas whereas Vischer as a sensorimotor (and possibly mystical) involvement with form. These different emphases, theorising empathy as a sensory or conceptual involvement with the formal properties of art, have given way to the prevalent modern psychological usage, linking empathy to various kinds of feelings for others. Even here, and as I have been stressing, there is disagreement between psychologists regarding the functional aspects of empathy, whether to define it, for example, more as a cognitive phenomenon instead of being just an affective state. Lamm et al. (2007) emphasise that affective states are mediated by cognitive and motivational processes, suggesting that empathy is often a cognitive-emotional hybrid.

This complements my argument here, that empathy is a set of variable cognitive processes and affective states that art is able to bring into play beyond the narrow view that empathy arises *primarily* as recognition of sensorimotor actions. This is so in a dual sense: there are cognitive (that is, non-sensorimotor) aspects of emotion that require us to conceptualise the situation of others using rational inference. For example, rather than just isolating facial expressions, we run scripts as to the reasons why such a 'situation' has occurred. Secondly, closer to Warburg's *Pathosformel*, we are able to experience empathy as a conceptual involvement in the *configural* properties of the image as an overall composition. While this may depend on sensorimotor processing of the contours of shapes and forms, this does not mean we conceptualise the whole composition in terms of simulating the use of our bodies. As I have shown in earlier pages, empirical evidence reveals that chess experts remember chess positions better than novices mainly because they perceive the chessboard as an organised whole rather than a series of single pieces, and this is what I suggest happens in the viewing of artworks with many individual 'pieces' such as van der Weyden's painting. While it is true the artist has depicted many fine details such as facial hairs and tears streaming down cheeks, experts would tend to switch from fine-grained to coarse-grained viewing and back again in order to gain an overall appreciation of the work beyond simple recognition. Experts are able to switch from a kind of viewing that involves precise focal points to a configural viewing that involves considering the relationships between these fixed points. Based on empirical research, Augustin et al. suggest that 'experts process artworks more in relation to style, whereas non-experts refer to criteria such as personal feelings' (2007, p. 135).

In terms of expert configural viewing and encoding of the scene, the eye is free to wander; it picks out rhythms, stops and starts and makes relationships that suggest moods and emotional ranges. This is sensori-motor involvement but it is not the gross kind suggested by mirror neurons that identify the limbs and actions of other bodies. Gracefulness of form, of course, comes into it, and so does the horizontal, frieze-like extension of the painting and its shallow space, the seduction of rich fabrics and their colours, their triangular folds, integrated with various concepts to do with art such as facture, style and conventions. The glossy surface and treatment of the paint erasing the trace of the artist's gesture, and the translucency of the pigments seem precious and as hard and inanimate as a jewel. Thus, to state that '[t]he painting shows how emotion can only be fully expressed through the body itself' (Freedberg, 2011, p. 344) is an exaggeration, for there are many kinds of emotion that can be expressed without an appeal to the semiotics of gesture.

In many empirical studies, it has been shown that emotion words can prejudice the perception of a face or an action (Feldman Barrett, 2009). This is despite the fact that in most situations there is ambiguity and variability in emotion *and* in the physiognomical signatures that are supposed to convey them.[9] Thus, to valorise a form of art history that presumes that there is a direct way to perceive embodied actions because, biologically, we are inclined to do so, is a great oversimplification. The use of language is crucial to understanding emotion. Feldman Barrett suggests, for example, that 'individuals with emotional expertise who have

---

[9] According to William James, 'variability within each emotion category is the norm' (Feldman Barrett, 2006, p. 42).

differentiated categories corresponding to the words "irritation", "frustration", and "annoyance" would experience and perceive a greater variety of emotional states than those who treat all three words as interchangeable with "anger"' (Feldman Barrett, 2009, p. 1296).

However, there are different kinds of languages; we need not just rely on the gross aspects of body language. Even collecting together groups of inanimate objects can convey emotion categories, so why insist on the primacy of mime? It is not that Freedberg is blind to the notion of an emotional range, expressible beyond the body's musculature, for he senses this in his own description of the detail involved in the work, suggesting the artist's loving care bestowed upon a whole range of features, answered in kind by the art historian: 'There can be no doubt about the artist's skill exhibited in the painting. The folds of every piece of cloth – but especially the whites – are painted with crisp precision; the variety of colors, some saturated, others delicate and subtle (like the lilacs and greens of the Magdalene's garments), testify to the technical prowess of a painter who paints almost every head of hair, every beard in a different way' (Freedberg, 2011, p. 344).

The empathy, the real emotional response of quality displayed here, which is not acknowledged by Freedberg perhaps because of a sense of modesty, is his own obvious pleasure in these details, which stems from the guidance of his knowledge. His appraisal of the artist's skill in rendering a wealth of detail and variations in texture, colour, rhythm and mood is very much part of a refined emotional response, and one that the artist himself possessed; other artists of the time would have detected these devices, across several centuries. Yet this subtle emotional investment, both the artist's and the art historian's, is set aside as secondary to the fireworks: the embodied effects of extreme emotional states used as evidence to read coarse emotions, ignoring another set of fine-grained emotions springing from a more considered cognitive-emotional understanding of the details, which training and expertise reveal. What are the neural correlates of such sensitivity? How does the overall beauty of a painting and the pleasure it affords affect the sensorimotor reading of empathy or distress Freedberg privileges? How does aesthetic emotion and expertise affect attention and the pattern of visual inspection beyond the obvious? According to various empirical studies: 'Experts spend significantly more time looking at background features, the composition, and the color contrasts, whereas untrained viewers spend more time looking at individual figurative elements and exploring figures in the centre and foreground' and, interestingly, 'there seem to be two specialized routes for processing human bodies, one of which processes bodies in a configural manner...and another, which appears to be specialized in the processing of specific details of body posture' (Cela-Conde et al., 2011, p. 45).[10]

How do we translate these empirical results into analyses of art? In van der Weyden's painting the 'non-expert' response would be to focus on the bodies and to identify emotions; while expert viewing would be concerned with background details, interrelationships, overall chromatic and figural composition, using working memory to sustain an overall conception of variability rather than easy identification. Expert viewing would enjoy 'the problem' of expression, using previous knowledge of compositional types and conventions in comparison – this is perhaps closer to how the artist conceived of the overall scene. The non-expert view might have been what the artist was aiming for at first glance, yet increasing familiarity yields further 'complications' for viewers in all historic periods. Art historians are adept at both expert and non-expert perspectives. This model also works with Harvey's *Myra Hindley*. Non-expert viewing reveals easy identification and little concern for facture, technique or complications in composition.

We can either privilege immediate emotional responses to art, reading what we believe to be clear emotional signifiers as a sign of art's value, or we may privilege the many subsequent processes involved in adding meaning to these effects, both in the same sitting, or during a lifetime of considerations, which, perhaps naturally, take us further away from romanticising 'the moment', the immediacy and primacy of embodied responses over different kinds of experience. Obviously, art can be valued for a whole range of responses depending on strong, weak or perhaps even non-existent sensorimotor stimulation or empathy. This goes against the notion that emotional response based on body language is necessary and sufficient for a definition of art, as Freedberg seems to imply:

Automatic empathetic responses constitute a basic level of response to images and to works of art. Underlying such responses is the process of embodied simulation that enables the direct experiential understanding of the intentional and emotional contents of images. This basic level of reaction to images becomes essential to any understanding of their effectiveness as art (Freedberg and Gallese, 2007, p. 202).

On this view, how would one evaluate the 'effectiveness as art' of Duchamp's readymades, Kosuth's works, the conceptual works of the Art and Language Group, and a host of other conceptual artworks that require little or no empathetic or sensorimotor response? It could be said

[10] Experts also attribute greater reward value and engage self-monitoring strategies to a greater extent than non-experts (Feldman Barrett, 2006, p. 46). For other empirical studies of expertise in art appreciation, see Locher et al. (2001) and Hekkert and van Wieringen (1996).

that not only does Freedberg overemphasise the importance of empathy in art, but that he also promotes a particularly simplistic form of empathy. As Currie remarks, '[s]uppose someone is making a difficult decision, but does so coldly, without emotion. I can be said to empathise with that person's decision when I recreate his or her unemotional decision' (2006, p. 215). It is doubtful that this kind of empathy has much if anything to do with sensorimotor processes. Thus, while I empathise with Freedberg's approach, even though I am not convinced that one needs to imply a hierarchy of values placed on emotions that can be traced to motor representations more easily in order to make the point, it is likely that my kind of empathy, which has to do with the broader picture, has nothing at all to do with the neural correlates of action recognition.

As with most emotions, empathy has a number of registers, some closer to sensorimotor response than others. As Currie notes, 'empathy is just part of our overall experience of the work...It does not signal unthinking absorption or submission to authorial will' (2006, p. 220); but also, 'I do not think that it is definitive of empathy that it exclusively concerns feelings' (p. 215). Not only is empathy integrated into a number of critical, rational and imaginative processes beyond the naïve and formalist notion of the direct perception of body language, but it also has a number of emotional allies with a great variety of differences. None of these needs to be signalled with arms and legs or facial expressions that emphasise fixed mental states. It might be thought that my analysis of two very different artworks, van der Weyden's *Descent from the Cross* and Marcus Harvey's *Myra Hindley*, in the same breath is frivolous and possibly irresponsible. Yet what the contemporary artwork teaches us is in stark terms, without the seduction of the window onto reality of van der Weyden's illusionism, and is that things are rarely what they appear to be at first blush, as if we were biologically meant to have an instant understanding of the work. As with Harvey's example, contemporary artwork presents seeing as a special problem or challenge, a display of technique that is not transparent, through which a commonplace figure of empathy is identified. Facture, materials and composition complicate emotional identification, disassembling immediate sensory response. If van der Weyden's painting were so easy to identify and essentialise, there would be nothing to learn about emotion or art.

Rather than wrongly assuming that emotions are based on particular brain areas, or are detectable primarily from fixed classes of bodily actions, facial reactions or nervous processes, recent studies show that conceptual processing, rather than being an optional supplement to emotion, helps to *constitute* them. Conceptual categories (genre, type of place, type of scene, tradition, culture and script, for example) provide emotion with numerous situational examples (or 'situated conceptualizations', as neuro-cognitive psychologists call them), without which our emotions could not be experienced meaningfully (see Feldman Barrett, 2006, 2009; and Wilson-Mendenhall et al., 2011). Rather than a discrete module implementing an emotion, emotions appear to result from distributed circuitry throughout the brain: 'Within this distributed circuitry, diverse brain states for a given emotion arise, each corresponding to a different situated conceptualization' (Wilson-Mendenhall et al., 2011, p. 1109). Counter-intuitively, rather than having a core set of fixed properties, our emotions are continually nuanced by contextual and situational conceptual processing that involves a massive interconnectivity of memory, semantic, sensorimotor and nervous systems, each of which, in itself, does not constitute 'an emotion'. To isolate and emphasise sensorimotor involvement in this wider connectivity would be misleading. Many of the brain regions associated with emotional states are not functionally specific to emotions and are used to represent non-emotional concepts as well (Wilson-Mendenhall et al., 2011, p. 1124). In other words, emotions are holistic phenomena. Rather than having core, fixed features, much like categorical concepts, emotions can be composed of different physical and mental resources depending on the situation, context, task, linguistic nuance, personal slant or acculturation through which and because of which the emotion is experienced in the way that it is: 'because there is not one bodily signature for each emotion, the same body state across different situations can be conceptualized as different emotions, depending on the situated conceptualization active to interpret it...when a situated conceptualization stored with an emotion concept becomes active, it has multiple concrete effects on perception, action, and internal states. It produces the [physical aspects of] emotion' (Wilson-Mendenhall et al., 2011, p. 1108).

Of course, my next move here may be predictable: when experiencing art, we habitually speak of how artworks may stimulate certain emotions and sensations. Yet, compatible with these recent studies, the particularities of each artwork will help to provide and configure a number of 'situational conceptualizations', which will give these emotions (and their succession, layering or overlapping) a particular *character*. An artwork may not only function as a situational conceptualisation helping to trigger an emotional state, but may also provide opportunities for its dynamic development during the experience of the artwork, in the inspection of other artworks and in the day-to-day experience of emotions beyond art. Thus, 'an instance of emotion (i.e., a situated conceptualization) is a compositional representation constructed from basic psychological components not specific to emotion' (Wilson-Mendenhall et al.,

2011, p. 1124). That is to say, components such as visual data, sensations, stored concepts and linguistic operations are not emotional in themselves, but may be reconfigured and assembled in different contexts to create the heterogeneous set of bodily sensations or word triggers by which we usually recognise – or name – a particular emotion.

The suggestion is that emotions do not exist outside of the situational examples in the world that contain them and stimulate and structure them. Even when we simulate emotions imaginatively in our experience of literature, film or art, we use situational examples. Situations are always more than the identified emotions we associate with them; they require a whole number of resources that are not emotional to sustain them:

Emotions such as anger, sadness, and fear, and even broad categories such as positive and negative affect, are likely to be generated via the interplay of more basic processes in perceptual, attentional, and mnemonic systems that are not unique to emotion (Kober et al., 2008, p. 1022).

In addition, these resources are not fixed for each emotional state in every circumstance where we believe that emotional state is to be experienced. On this view, emotions are emergent from but not reducible to these situational examples.

We think emotions are types that can be defined by a list of features, yet they are always experienced in different ways depending on circumstance. For convenience, we call *fear* a certain number of characteristics, which we assume the listener understands (but who will inevitably use different situational examples to illustrate). Thus, there is:

> fear of a cockroach
> fear of death
> fear of failing an examination
> fear of God

What is common to all of these examples? If we posit a core set of physical attributes (quickening pulse, sweating, feeling uncomfortable), these do not define fear (they can also define arousal). The situational examples are indispensable to the definition of the emotion, yet they are very different from each other – note, this is all to do with the rather 'basic' notion of fear – how much more complicated it would be if we were to discuss the modalities of bemusement.

Although such studies indicate that emotions are indeed very complex phenomena, they are complex by virtue of the fact that each emotion is relational, composite, extremely variable, contingent and irreducible, and if it is to be reduced and dissected into its composite parts, is no longer an emotion. This does not stop writers and artists from frequently analysing emotions using emotional concepts that are integrated, revised, combined and retrieved from massive stores of cultural and personal memory and through the contemplation of art. The point, however, is that the way in which we are able to explore and experience such emotions is by means of situated conceptualisations – networks of heterogeneous, multimodal and amodal resources – which may be activated in reading literature or in viewing contemporary art.

If an emotion has relatively little or no perceivable visceral effect, where mental resources are primarily engaged with higher-order cognitive processes, for example, then in the study of the abstract concept, LOVE, it might be argued that we are engaged with an emotion concept rather than feeling it. Might we not call this an 'offline emotion'? How does this tally with the cognitive dimensions of emotion that have been studied by Damasio's (1995) research into somatic markers, which I have mentioned are thought to influence reasoning and decision making, or studies that indicate emotions can influence such higher-order processes as categorisation (Versace et al., 2009) and attention (Hayhoe and Ballard, 2005; Kästner, 2004),[11] and long-term planning (with the help of the prefrontal cortex)? Much of this amounts to a model of emotion that stresses cognitive-emotional interactions and integrations, rather than characterising them as separate (Feldman Barrett 2009; Pessoa, 2010a).[12]

The amygdala has been associated with emotional response traditionally, when it is clear that it is also important for cognitive-emotional interactions because it applies values to affective information. It is also connected to the prefrontal cortex for higher cognitive processes of analysis. Parts of the amygdala (the area has different components with different roles) have a feedback connection to the visual cortex so that not only does it monitor affect arising from visual processes but it can also redirect such processing resulting in attentional spikes. This is obviously a key mechanism in the visual inspection involved with certain kinds of performance artworks that involve the demonstration of stress, pain or discomfort, as we might experience observing a performance piece by Paul McCarthy, Ron Athey or Marina Abramović, where feelings of caution and being alert to the consequences of such acts are also aroused. It is likely that these performance artworks would arouse a sense of urgency and immediacy, responses that Freedberg describes for Rogier van der

---

[11] These studies suggest that our visual attention is nuanced by inner motivations and goals, top-down bias in the frontal and parietal areas, along with environmental factors.

[12] 'many of the effects of emotion on cognition are best viewed as interactions between the two such that the resulting processes and signals are neither purely cognitive nor emotional. Instead, the "cognitive" or "emotional" nature of the processes is blurred in a way that highlights the integration of the two domains in the brain' (Pessoa, 2010a, p. 439).

Weyden's *Descent from the Cross*, even though for most viewers these strong emotional responses are muted by the stylisation. Pessoa goes on to explain that the amygdala establishes affective significance, differentiating the salience from less affective stimuli; thus, rather than characterising this brain area as an emotion producer, it helps to prioritise and evaluate affects for processing in other areas (Pessoa, 2010b, p. 3422). It is because of this that it is unlikely that the amygdala would be employed less with the obvious sensorimotor signalling of emotions in Rogier van der Weyden's image than with the emotionally blank faces. Moreover, it is relativity that is key here, for heightened emotional effects can be achieved as much by contrast between images or faces as by the inherent features of individual artworks, which provide combinations of 'situated conceptualization'.

Empirical evidence suggests it is 'unlikely that the amygdala will map specifically to emotion.' Instead, they think it corresponds to 'broader and more abstract dimensions of information processing including processing of salience, significance, ambiguity and unpredictability' (Pessoa and Adolphs, 2010, p. 780). Thus, the amygdala is more likely to be employed in the cognitive-emotional analysis of art rather than simply being the neural substrate for fear or other strong emotions. While there are numerous studies associating a dysfunctional amygdala with mood disorders, this has less to do with the internal structure of the amygdala and more to do with its broader connectivity with other structures that help to create emotion. While the amygdala plays an important role in encoding value, it does this not in isolation but as part of multiple systems of reward associated with prefrontal areas.

2.3   Dynamic interconnectivity

Currently, neuroscientific and embodied explanations of art and culture represent a number of widely different techniques, themes and approaches: single-cell studies in the visual cortex (Zeki, 2009), arousal mechanisms in Ramachandran and Hirstein's approach (1999), mirror neurons and the sensorimotor groundedness of emotional response in art in Freedberg and Gallese's work (2007), and the embodied approaches to art and literature in Lakoff and Johnson's work (1980, 1999). A significant problem with these different approaches is that they have not been joined up with other studies of different brain areas beyond the visual cortex or sensorimotor areas that suggest what routinely happens when we experience different forms of art. This consists of an interconnectivity of different kinds of thoughts and sensations that challenges the notion of matching discrete parts of our complex mental and cultural life to localised brain areas. To isolate one or two areas of activity, as these different approaches do, is not simply a neutral way to limit the field of inquiry into particular focused areas of research. Isolating areas of experience and thought often provides a distorted view of the overall aims, purposes and effects of larger conceptual tasks in cultural experience. This localisation approach, which relies on fMRI scanning of particular brain areas, has been strongly criticised. William Uttal (2001) believes that cognitive processes, particularly the more complex ones, are largely indivisible and 'cannot be analysed into components, modules, or faculties, because of the very strong interactions between what may only be apparently different aspects of cognition' (p. 215). Furthermore, he states that the localisation of activity associated with a certain cognitive process in one part of the brain 'does not exclude the participation of other regions in the process' (p. 217).

   The brain is naturally an integrative and relational system that functions with massive interconnectivity between its regions and with the nervous system, action and social cognition. Approaches supporting dynamic interconnectivity instead seek to see how these brain regions interact and cooperate, thereby providing the basis for an examination of the complexity of experience that art most often helps to stimulate, rather than dividing experience into functions or fragments that do not seem to join up. This is particularly important because it is the dense interconnectivity of cognitive and sensorimotor processes involved in experiencing contemporary art that helps to make such art absorbing and meaningful. Relational knowledge accounts suggest instead that it might also be wise to adopt taxonomies of different kinds of connections and relations involved with higher-order cognitive processes involved in art.[1]

Raymond Tallis questions whether 'love' can be traced to 'bits of brains' as Zeki proposes, when even 'sophisticated neural imaging...cannot distinguish between physical pain and the pain of social rejection: they seem to "light up" the same areas'.[2] The fallacy of fMRI scans is that 'the areas that light up are regarded as "the centre" for that experience, emotion, or propensity' (Tallis, 1996). Additionally, Eric Harth writes, 'almost any macroscopic physical event that involves the intervention by a human brain cannot be fully understood by just following the chain of cause and effect beginning with elementary neural events' (2004, p. 114). This last point is significant because it implies that what happens at the elementary level of neurons is not necessarily an indication of what happens at the higher levels of complex cognitive thought.

It is important to realise that even when identifying a function for a brain area, it does not follow that a given brain area is specialised to perform one simple function: 'activity in the component areas may shift in response to different conditions of processing' (Figdor, 2010, p. 425). More forcefully, Sporns points out that early neurology divided the brain into distinct cortical areas but recent studies show that these distinct areas could easily be subdivided hundreds of times: 'How these areas are interconnected is a largely unknown...Currently the most promising avenue is provided by diffusion imaging techniques which are beginning to provide human connectivity maps...the cerebral cortex comprises

---

[1] Uttal (2001) argues that there are serious problems with trying to localise cognitive processes in the brain precisely because a proper taxonomy of mental processes has yet to be agreed or developed. Tempering some of Uttal's rhetoric, however, Hubbard (2003), reviewing Uttal's work, suggests that 'To localize macrolevel cognitive processes like memory or mathematics to specific neural substrates is clearly an untenable goal (as Hughlings-Jackson noted over 100 years ago) and very few researchers in cognitive neuroscience are still pursuing this simplistic goal' (p. 30). Clearly, there needs to be a middle path where localised brain studies can be put into larger contexts as we often see with meta-analyses of cognitive research, as I do here.

[2] This is echoed with more technical detail by Carrie Figdor: 'in fMRI, the blood-oxygen-level-dependent signal does not distinguish excitation from inhibition...or neural codes that involve timing and synchronization. Thus, images can indicate areas that are active not because of what they are doing but because they are being prevented from doing something or are trying to do something but not succeeding' (2010, p. 429).

clusters of densely and reciprocally coupled cortical areas that are globally interconnected' (Sporns, 2010, pp. 45–46).

In philosophy, Figdor supports the view held by Friston (2002), Sporns (2010) and Uttal (2001) that complex conceptualisation such as that involved in experiencing art requires and stimulates broad neural interconnectivity, or 'multiple realisation', as she puts it. Multiple realisation opposes 'localisation' – a common research paradigm in neuroscience in which a particular brain region is solely responsible for a single cognitive task (2010, p. 422). Localisation is the kind of research neuroaesthetics is based on. Reviewing the neuroscience literature, Figdor makes the distinction between holists (who believe the whole brain or large areas of it are involved in cognition) and integrationist researchers such as Friston who 'investigate the ways in which co-activated anatomical regions influence each other's activity' (p. 422). Thus, it is clear that a wellspring of support for the broader and interactive context of cognitive processing rather than its atomisation has led to not only the cooperation of various specialisms across neuroscience, psychology and philosophy but also to an approach that is able to give equal weight to many of the different yet integrated aspects of conceptual production involved in viewing art. This kind of conceptual work relies less on matching aspects of conceptual content with particular brain areas and more on 'multiple realisation' (Figdor, 2010).

A 'dynamic systems approach' to neuroscience (Egan and Matthews, 2006) would put single or group cell experiments into context. This is needed because: 'cortical areas are typically involved in more than one function...functional responses in the cortex are highly context-sensitive...no cortical area operates in isolation but is connected to many other areas by anatomical long-range connections ("association fibers")'. The authors go on to state that 'The upshot is that the behavior of a particular [brain] area cannot be predicted and explained from local microstructure alone' (Egan and Matthews, 2006, p. 385).

A statement on this matter that strikes at the heart of the problem for neuroaesthetics is the following by philosopher Jakob Hohwy, who insists that trying to map brain areas to particular functions is mistaken, yet always seems to make the newspaper headlines that 'often make it appear as if one coloured blob superimposed on a standard brain can show what love or crime (or whatever) is. Rather, it is fundamental to brain function that each area of activity is connected to other areas, that the same area is recruited for parts of a number of different functions' (Hohwy, 2007, p. 318).

Hohwy goes on to suggest the superiority of explanatory models that adopt neural interconnectivity rather than local activation.

Neuroaesthetics is vulnerable from criticisms within neuroscience for assuming a crude relationship of parity between higher levels of conscious experience and neural correlates, which has been called a 'matching content doctrine'.[3] Kosslyn quips, 'we simply do not know enough to exclude the possibility of multiple roles for any piece of cortical real estate' (1999, p. 1290). To be fair, Zeki himself concedes that high-level concepts engaged in art are 'difficult to study at the level of brain cells [and that] where the concept itself resides is problematic' (2009, pp. 53–54).

It seems that neuroaesthetics and embodied approaches in recent art history and philosophy stemming from this narrow base of localised, neuroanatomical activations traced by fMRI studies or sensorimotor chauvinism should take note: multiplying such studies will not lead to a deeper understanding of the cognitive psychology involved in contemplating art. Tranel et al. (1997) add their weight to the wide neural connectivity approach for conceptual production, reporting on empirical evidence that suggests that conceptual thought involves the integration of separate items of knowledge in particular brain sites, for example, producing categories such as tools, animals or persons. However, Tranel et al. warn us that: 'the sites should not be seen as "centers" containing conceptual knowledge. Rather, each site should be seen as part of a multi-component system...The critical finding is that separate sites contribute differently to concept retrieval' (1997, p. 1324). The emphasis on brain interconnectivity is a welcome development in neuroscience because it allows for the dynamic and continually changing diversity of conceptual thought that we experience while looking at art that connects different functions, desires, emotions, sensations and rational thought and deduction. It thus seems important that neuroscientific studies on single cells are cross-referenced with studies of other brain areas and in conjunction with cognitive psychology concerned with conceptual production, which art clearly demands. Conceptual processing emerges from the cooperation of multiple cortical centres, which can cooperate flexibly for certain tasks at hand using local and global processes of specialisation and integration, respectively. An integrated approach to

---

[3] Some even doubt the validity of matching perceptions to neural correlates: 'contrary to certain claims, there are no known examples of neural-perceptual content matches. Second, there are reasons to doubt that any subpersonal level, neural representational system could match a personal-level, perceptual experience in content, and hence reasons to doubt the truth of the matching content doctrine – not simply as a philosophical thesis, but as a methodological one guiding neuroscientific research' (Noë and Thompson, 2004). On this view, neural processes cannot explain the particular, personal and subtle character of phenomenal experience just as it cannot explain where concepts, or indeed, consciousness are located in the brain.

understanding art needs to provide the perceptual experiments of Zeki and Livingstone with conceptual context and orientation.

Even in doing this, it would be wise to heed Merlin Donald's warning about the very objective of explaining artistic experience in terms of neuroscience intent on focusing on perceptions: 'Such an endeavour would not be unlike a particle physicist's trying to track every electron in, say, a roomful of people in a cocktail party. Why would one want to do this? It would explain nothing about cocktail parties or people. Nor would such an analysis explain a work of art' (2006, p. 13).[4] Donald's point seems valid if we were to follow any discrete or isolated line of inquiry that fails to take on board the complexity of how we experience art beyond perceptual and embodied experience. Breaking down art or the art experience into single neurons in the visual cortex will not do: art is a massive coordination of social and cultural contexts that influence nonconscious as well as highly complex self-conscious processes. Pylyshyn writes: 'the meaning of a complex thought must be derived from the meaning of its constituent parts, which means that thoughts must be *compositional...* together with the rules of composition (or syntax)' (2006, p. 437). Even more important, thoughts must have *systematicity*: 'This means that if an organism is capable of thought at all it must be capable of having sets of related thoughts' (p. 437). Thus, whatever happens in the visual cortex during optical experiences of art, a great deal more is going on in other parts of the brain concerning the organisation of conceptual systems, memories and semantic production, as well as the modulation of sensations and emotions.

It is important to note that there are objects in the environment that may play active roles in supporting, affecting and constraining the functioning of localised brain areas. Thus, to look solely to these brain areas as causal without rigorous reference to what they are processing puts us at a disadvantage in trying to understand neural events. Perceptual cues in the environment can work as 'affordances', which Gibson (1977, p. 1979) regarded as properties of the environment or objects that afford or anticipate being used in particular ways (grasped, pulled or pushed – automatically we know that a string cannot be pushed). Philosophically, Heidegger's assumption that tools have inherent properties that suggest or invite acculturated behaviours (which allow us to communicate with traditional knowledge structures) is a similar idea. Yet, as I have been at

---

[4] This sobering thought is also echoed by cognitive psychologist Robert Solso: 'higher-order cognition is the result of contributions and interactions that engage billions of neurons located throughout the brain, whose collective electro-chemical psychological actions are not known at this time' (2003, p. 132).

pains to show with contemporary art objects, art often uses this accultur-ated and tacit knowledge for what, in the short term, seems to be irra-tional ends in order to make visible such automatic processes of recognition. Art objects often do this by suggesting affordances (grasping, twisting, turning, balancing) that are at odds with object identification, so we become aware of our spreading sensorimotor activations as objects of intentional (often conceptual) thought. Our engagements with art rou-tinely reveal how affordances function, and they encourage us to work around them in order to conceptualise objects or hybrid objects as parts of a complex message or as a prelude to a dreamlike engagement.

For Greeno et al. (1993), affordances could be extended beyond Gibson's original usage for ecological psychology to include many cul-tural and conceptual nuances suggested by objects or environmental situations. Because artworks can depict concrete objects or situations beyond their own facticity, along with the basic affordances suggested by the objects referred to, they can also suggest highly acculturated afford-ances, sometimes in unison with these concrete objects or with other depicted aspects, gestures or configural information. To the expert agent, at least, there are also affordances in abstract and conceptual art that indicate how they are to be understood. In other words, contempor-ary art objects substitute affordances for 'aesthetic affordances' outside of ordinary usage, a system of invariances based on background knowledge of affordances. As Kirsh suggests (2009, p. 295), the research explaining how such affordances are picked up is in great need of development but it seems that practice and expert systems, which can range from activities such as cooking to interpreting the visual aspects of a Picasso painting, play crucial roles. As important is the way that we 'alter the cue structure of the environment to stimulate new ideas' (Kirsh, 2009, p. 300), as we might do while baking a cake, drawing or painting, or using computer software. This suggests that we actively change cues and affordances in the environment, while also being led by them.

People will, of course, just want to react to art in the way they see fit without considering the nature of response. Nevertheless, there are many who analyse these kinds of reaction *as part of* their involvement with art, something that I argue conceptual and contemporary art increasingly invites us to do. Consistent with general semantic properties of concepts, when one concept is being processed by a subject, related concepts are also activated for possible use. We might not be conscious of the possible choices there are for conceptual development or combination, and instead may choose to remain intuitive and habitual with our conceptual response to works of art. It would be true to suggest that, as a result of this, if we were to continue to rely on tried and tested methods of conceptual combination involved in viewing art, there would be fewer opportunities for learning new interpretational strategies, not to mention our ability to take on board innovation in art. Some ability to reflect upon our psychological processes concerning how the body is involved with conceptual integration and development is thus not only necessary for personal growth and for the appreciation of new trends in art, but is also essential for supplying us with a sense of agency and choice, while lending depth and meaning to our social interactions with others as well. The need to combine various approaches to understanding art, which draw upon different regions of the brain, the body and social factors, therefore, is essential in understanding the integrative processes that situations in art provide routinely.

2.4   Convergence zones

Going beyond brain localisation, Damasio (1995) suggests that brain areas can be characterised as the combined action of convergence zones (CZs). This strongly suggests that many brain areas beyond the sensori-motor system are involved in our experiences of objects, especially in art where the objects depicted may also have symbolic and cultural associations attached to them. One need only think of a simple concrete concept such as MIRROR or MASK, LION or SWORD, to consider how many different mental operations are needed to sustain even a simple interpretation of their import in a painting.

How are we to understand the neuropsychological underpinnings of various experiences of art that seem to indicate a systematicity that cannot be confined to one area of the brain alone? One way is to posit massive neural interconnectivity and another is to provide a more structured approach that somehow tries to steer a middle course between localised brain functions on the one hand and a radical interconnectivity of all brain functions on the other. As we have seen, some aspects of Barsalou's work (2009) seem to cede ground to weak embodiment theories and CZs. According to Damasio (1989), CZs are non-sensorimotor areas in the brain such as the anterior temporal lobes associated with the semantic processing of auditory and visual stimuli, parietal areas (spatial processing) and the prefrontal cortex (rules, categorical production, planning, multitasking, self-monitoring of mental states). According to Simmons and Barsalou (2003), these CZs help to organise the sensorimotor-based situations and simulations that go to make up conceptual thought. Damasio assumes a hierarchy of CZs with higher- and lower-order CZs, the former less dependent on sensorimotor information. In a linguistic context, Barsalou uses this CZ theory to suggest that a fully fledged sensorimotor simulation need not be activated every time a word is heard in a sentence. Parts of a sensory experience that might be relevant to a word such as 'painting' would be selected for 'shallow processing': 'As comprehension proceeds, representations of individuals develop, as in the perception of a physical scene' (Barsalou, 1999, p. 605).

The combination of abstract and concrete concepts in a sentence does not mean, necessarily, that the same kind of information is being coded with different amounts of complexity but that there are different codes, one more pictorial and the other symbolic. The former could be processed in a deep manner by sensorimotor areas, depending on the meaning of the whole sentence, or in a shallow manner in terms of grammatical logic, relational concepts, categories, analogies and some metaphors in the latter case. This chimes in well with Paivio's dual coding theory (Paivio, 1986; Vigliocco et al., 2009), which suggests that the difference between concrete and abstract words lies in the stronger presence of sensory and motor information for concrete words, whereas linguistic logic and emotional and affective content distinguish words that are more abstract. A thorough review of recent neuropsychological studies suggests that semantic production is the result of a neural network that involves the left prefrontal cortex, the temporoparietal junction and the temporal poles bilaterally (Pobric et al., 2007, p. 20138). Together these areas act as a CZ, which is able to process diverse kinds of information.

Importantly, neuropsychological approaches based on the connectivity of differently realised and combined bundles of information will be more successful in explaining how the brain and body interact with art when combining perceptible, concrete aspects with non-perceptible or non-perceptible abstract connotations. A broader, pluralistic kind of approach in psychology is required to study such a diversity of multisensory, concrete and conceptual aspects of the contemporary art experience. Such an approach in cognition and psychology has been proposed by Meteyard and others: 'Whereas concrete knowledge would be grounded in our experience with the outside world, abstract knowledge could be grounded in our internal experience. Abstract words tend, on the whole, to have more affective associations than concrete words, and the greater the affective associations, the earlier those abstract words are acquired' (Meteyard et al., 2012, pp. 13–14).

The authors also believe that abstract concepts can be learnt from linguistic communication that is schematic and coded, casting doubt on strong embodiment theories. Different semantic tasks presented to us by artworks may involve short or long periods of attentional exertion, therefore allowing for a deeper exploration of cognitive, affective and sensorimotor resources, depending on how much time a viewer of art is willing to spend in order to achieve that immersive experience. It seems that more research into neural CZs would account better for these immersive experiences. Meteyard et al. (2012) maintain that there is an increasing body of work that demonstrates a gradient of 'abstraction': 'as one moves away from primary sensory and motor cortices, more complex conjunctions are captured...We find ourselves supporting a position where primary sensory and motor regions are not activated during routine semantic processing (in opposition to strong embodiment) but may be so for deeper processing related to imagery' (2010, p. 14).

It seems, therefore, that CZs are the way to go in neurocognitive psychology if we are to understand many kinds of complex experiences of art, whether this art is conceptual, contemporary, Baroque or Wagnerian. Each requires a flexible and pluralistic neuropsychological approach that acknowledges the combinatorial complexity of such art and the differently coded types of information and representation that this requires. At the moment, however, there is disagreement as to how CZs work. Stronger embodied views such as Barsalou's maintain that CZs are to be found close to sensorimotor areas and are dependent on them. Weaker embodiment theories, supported by a number of empirical studies, place more of an emphasis on the categorising power of the prefrontal cortex[1] and the anterior temporal lobes responsible for processing the semantics of words and pictures.

To get some idea of the complexity of brain resources involved in a CZ, one need only understand that the temporal lobes are involved in auditory perception and are also associated with the processing of semantics in hearing speech and vision. The temporal lobe is also connected to the hippocampus, important in long-term memory. The ventral part of the temporal cortices appear to be involved in the visual processing of complex stimuli such as faces (fusiform gyrus) and scenes (parahippocampal gyrus). Anterior parts are for visual processing and are involved in object perception and recognition, and receive projections from multiple sensory areas but not from motor areas (Damasio, 1989, p. 124). Characterising the role of the anterior temporal lobes is 'complicated by the fact that it is not a homogeneous structure, but rather contains numerous anatomically discrete regions, each of which may play a distinct role in the acquisition, storage, and manipulation of conceptual information' (Martin, 2007, p. 30).

---

[1] Some very grand claims have been made for this area. Michael O'Shea suggests that much of what makes us human, creative, civilised resides in this part of the brain (2005, p. 62), and that this area is larger in humans than in any other organism and has evolved dramatically faster and more substantially than any other area, so that 'a positive feedback loop in which natural selection favouring creative intelligence became linked to an ever more extravagant expression of that intelligence' (p. 63).

2.5   Word and image in contemporary art

These psychological studies of word and image processing in the anterior temporal lobes (ATLs) do not usually deal with visual artworks that juxtapose images and words. What neuroaesthetic and cognitive psychological approaches ignore consistently is a major aspect of many kinds of art: the interplay of word and image. This is not only something that has a long history in many cultural traditions (see Camille (1992) for illustrated medieval European manuscripts, Clunas (1997) for Chinese scrolls, and the journal *Word and Image* for many other examples), but it continues to be a major aspect of contemporary art practice.

Joseph Kosuth's *Art as Idea as Idea (Art)*, 1967, is a photograph (48 × 48 in) mounted on board. The artwork is visible and yet, if understood as a gallery label or dictionary entry, it is referring to art as an absent, invisible or abstract concept. It piques interest by inviting a perceptual examination of the shapes of the letters as 'art', yet also invites us to override this response, encouraging us to reflect on the nature of vision and art. There are many works of art that use puns and word games to present the viewer with visual paradoxes. One of the earliest examples is Magritte's *The Treachery of Images* (*Ceci n'est pas une pipe*), 1928–1929, which, according to Zeki, 'goes against everything the brain has seen, learnt and stored in its memory' (1999, pp. 46–58). Yet this 'going against' is pleasurable and conceptually interesting. It also acts as an important and influential schema for many subsequent artworks. In Kosuth's image, we alternate *reading* a text with *seeing* an image. We also read the words 'human skill' and 'execution' in the text presented, concepts which have been extended by Kosuth to include 'quoting' and recontextualising words, an act of quoting that he wants us to consider is also indicative of art. The artwork adopts a mutually reinforcing strategy: it suggests a reading between the lines and its visual equivalent, an understanding beyond optical sensation.

One could say that in Magritte's famous painting of *The Treachery of Images* a relationship is suggested between the two perceptual cues, pipe and text. However, if I were to understand these perceptual cues as

Art (ārt), sb. M.E. [a OF. ı – L. artem, prob.
f. ar-- to fit. The OF. ars. nom. (sing. and pl.).
was also used.] I. Skill. Sing. art; no pl.   ı.
gen. Skill as the result of knowledge and practice.   2. Human skill (opp. to nature) M .E.
3. The learning of the schools ; see II.   ı.
†n. spec. The trivium, or any of its subjects
- 1573. b. gen. Learning, science (arch.) - 1588
†4. spec. Technical or professional skill - 1677
5. The application of skill to subjects of taste,
as poetry, music. etc. ; esp. in mod. Use : Perfection of workmanship or execution as an object in itself 1620.   6. Skill applied to the arts
of imitation or design. Painting. Architecture.
etc. ; the cultivation of these in its principles,
practice, and results. (The most usual mod.
sense of art when used simply.) 1688.

Figure 15. Reconstruction of Joseph Kosuth's *Art as Idea as Idea (Art)*, 1967 (original, photographic enlargement on compressed styrofoam board, 45 1/2" × 45 1/2"; 115 × 115 cm), present location unknown.

IMAGE and WORD, I could also assume that the painting depicts the abstract concept of REPRESENTATION. Here, the conceptual blend suggests that Magritte's painting is a representation of REPRESENTATION. The subject of the painting is a highly abstract concept. Usually, representation is used to denote something that is absent, but the painting's text denies that it is representational in this way by stating the truth: the painting of the pipe is not a pipe. In being a representation of REPRESENTATION, it is 'being itself', so to speak, and is not absent. Meanwhile, the words themselves that lead us to become aware of the problem are also representational; they represent a truth that the pipe is not real, and yet the words are part of the painting. One part of the painting (the 'text') seems to be denying the veracity of another part (the 'pipe'), while revealing a truth (that the pipe is a fiction). The painting thus manages to be both factual and fictional, allowing the first of these terms to state the nature of the second, but the second element also serves to give the first something to refer to. One cannot help but think that to describe or experience the painting solely in sensory terms would be to miss out on many of these twists and turns, which are premised on a number of propositional and analogical relationships, as well as transitive inferences. Understood primarily as a complex logical problem concerning representation, Kosuth's work would require amodal kinds of processing along with the sensorimotor action of reading (an action that, itself, could become thematic and treated conceptually).

Recent studies have also shown that artificially suppressing activity in the ATLs (using a technique known as repetitive transcranial stimulation (rTMS)) selectively disrupts semantic judgements for both words *and* pictures (Lambon-Ralph et al., 2007; Pobric et al., 2007). This is interpreted to mean that the anterior temporal lobe is responsible for the underlying psychological process of meaning creation common to looking at pictures and reading words. If meaning creation were restricted to the visual cortex while looking at pictures, then performance would not be affected by damage to other brain areas outside of the visual cortex. In Kosuth's work, which relies heavily on words and images, *reading becomes the subject of visual art*. We read about concepts that point to our perception of the letters and words in the artwork when normally these are invisible to us. The only other times we are conscious of the shapes of the letters as a theme is with extraordinarily calligraphic feats, when the font is unusual and, even then, we might suppress this perceptual quality in order to read the script. In Kosuth's works, the very meaning of the words points to their appearance; conception and perception (or 'ception', as Talmy puts it) seems difficult to separate. Martin (2007, p. 34) remarks that one of the vital areas at which research in cognitive psychology should be directed is how object conceptual and lexical representations are linked. It could do worse than beginning with the interplay of lexical and object categories brought into play by Kosuth and the scores of other contemporary artists who exploit word and image responses.

The processing of spoken words (hearing) and images (seeing) can cross modalities in reading, and this synthesis of higher-level meaning is itself not modal (but amodal), according to Visser et al.: 'Although modality specific cortical areas play an important role in semantic processing, information needs to be combined across modalities to allow the correct conceptual relationships to be discerned independent of surface similarities. This is because semantically related objects, such as a banana and a kiwi, may be dissimilar in several key modalities (e.g., shape, color, texture)' (2010, p. 1092). This appears to bring together and explain the kind of modal and amodal processes that would cooperate in some of the meaning creation involved in viewing Kosuth's conceptual works, but not in all of them.

Kosuth named his works 'analytical propositions' where, following the early Wittgenstein, the artwork or language is supposed to enclose itself in propositional self-dependency, isolated from any external contingency making a claim to being a self-sufficient statement, visually and conceptually self-evident. Kosuth's *Clear Square Glass Leaning* (1965–1967) consists of four square pieces of glass upon which are placed the words of the title of the artwork. As with many of Kosuth's works, this employs word labels to reference the material substrate upon which the words rest, in a kind of self-reflexive loop, trying to bracket out external references. However, the work also asks us to consider the phenomenal qualities of reading and how the perceptual features of the letters, their typeface and size, and the squareness and shiny aspect of the glass, its perceptual and material features, seem to become transparent when we focus on the conceptual meaning or look through the glass to the wall underneath. *Four Colors Four Words* is a neon artwork in four colours and although the letters do not bear any resemblance to the things to which they refer, the syntactical arrangement of four words and four colours appears to be iconic. In addition, the neon light tends to beam out a message of 'illumination'. The difficulty that the artwork creates for us is epitomised by our hesitation in answering the question: 'what does *Four Colors Four Words* refer to?'

This is similar to Jasper Johns' various paintings of coloured words on patches of different colour, creating an interesting dissonant effect. This is interesting because there are various psychological tests that are designed to achieve a similar incongruent effect, which reveal that activation in the anterior cingulate cortex (ACC) area of the brain is associated with error detection and conflict resolution. Interestingly, the ACC is also associated with the reward system, so feelings of pleasure result from solving a problem and so help motivate subjects to seek solutions. A typical conflict-inducing experiment is the Stroop task (Pardo et al., 1990), which involves congruence: the word BLUE (written in blue) or incongruence (BLUE written in yellow). This is exactly what is involved in paintings by Jasper Johns (see his *False Start*, 1959). Activity in the ACC is also indicative of suppressing mind wandering; hence, Magritte, Kosuth, Nauman and Johns, among others, intuitively grasped that certain word–image juxtapositions would hold the attention of viewers and help to structure their attention in order to create conceptual complexity as well as visual interest. This, undoubtedly, helps to explain some of the fascination that word–image art holds for us, the mutually reinforcing action of perceptual stimulation and conceptual elaboration generating complications. In many of these works, however, it is clear that perceptual experience is deliberately reduced in favour of the theme of the relevance of perception.

At higher levels of abstraction and relational knowledge, the congruence or incongruence of word and image running through many of Kosuth's works is premised on Wittgenstein's early logical positivism, on the one hand, which valorised the self-sufficiency of propositions, where Kosuth attempts to suggest that art is its own reference with no hidden messages, transparently public. On the other hand, the work seems to undermine this pure conceptual logic, with the conundrum of word games, a polysemy that has more in common with the later Wittgenstein of the *Philosophical Investigations* (1953) where the philosopher suggested how language use and contextual situations make concepts relative. Interestingly, it also plays off a naïve understanding of direct perception (the irrefutable facticity and self-evidence of the words) and conceptual sophistication. This word–image interplay shows that Kosuth's work involves several levels of cognitive and perceptual processing. It builds upon a system of relational knowledge that groups together what we know of his works over several years, as well as wider connections to other systems of thought involving Wittgenstein, Magritte and other artists' works, and public signage and neon.

In Kosuth's work and more recently in the neon works of Tracey Emin, Cerith Wyn Evans and Jason Rhoades, semantic processing occurs both at the level of the text and the image and, interestingly, at the higher level of cognition, which considers how the interplay between these different modalities functions. The left lateral temporal cortex is supposed to house a verbal language-based semantic system, while the right lateral temporal cortex represents non-verbal spatial or otherwise imageable concrete concepts. This is consistent with the dual coding system of Paivio (1986), who suggested that concrete abstracts rely more on imagery, whereas both abstract and concrete concepts can be processed in a language-like code. More recently, an extensive meta-analysis of nineteen neuroimaging studies concluded: 'Results clearly suggest a greater engagement of the verbal system for processing of abstract concepts, and a greater engagement of the perceptual system for processing of concrete concepts' (Wang et al., 2010, p. 1463).

I have mentioned the key role that the ATLs play in generating and organising meaning for both words and pictures. Yet, it is likely that this is supported by the prefrontal cortex and other brain areas to encode semantic networks containing abstract concepts such as REPRESENTATION. The system of relational knowledge that enhances and varies the production of meaning is made more complex by the fact that it can extend over different art forms, and the modality associated with each art form, but this seems to have been anticipated by Kosuth's word image strategies. With his *Art as Idea as Idea (Art)*, and in Bruce Nauman's neons, the image–text relation can be manipulated at the level of perceptual, phenomenological and sensorimotor exploration, especially when the image part, the mounted photograph, is attended to. It is

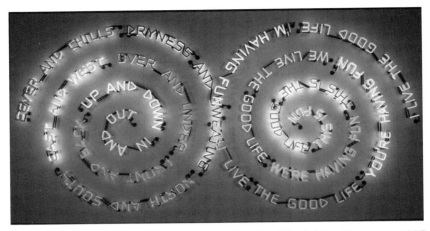

Figure 16. Bruce Nauman, *Having Fun/Good Life, Symptoms*, 1985 (fabricated neon, H: 175 × W: 334 × D: 34 cm). Carnegie Museum of Art, Pittsburgh. Purchase: gift of the Partners of Reed Smith Shaw and McClay and Carnegie International Acquisition Fund. © ARS, NY and DACS, London 2012.

also processed linguistically when the meanings of the words are focused on. Our categorising is skewed because we are encouraged to read about art as well as to look at it as an image. The work also seems to suggest an explanation, a speech utterance. This complex cross-modal experience situates a system of relational knowledge consisting of similar artworks, not only among different artists but within the series of works Kosuth titled *First Investigations* (after Wittgenstein's *Philosophical Investigations*), in which *Art as Idea (Art)* is situated.

Conceptual production is an objective of many of Bruce Nauman's works, although such works may also happen to be visually attractive at a superficial level. Bruce Nauman's *Having Fun/Good Life, Symptoms*, 1985, consists of two sentences of coloured neon words in spirals that simulate a joint movement, the doubling of the spirals suggesting eyes that create a feeling of vertigo. Thus, the work is not body neutral; it has an effect on the body reminding us of our embodiment engaged in standing vertical while trying to read words that are upside down and while referencing words to do with affect, location and action. It also makes us conscious of how long it takes to read the work, for its phrases seem to unfurl slowly, considerably complicating the psychological process of mental rotation, word recognition and schemata involved in anticipating meaning. This phenomenal experience of reading is further complicated by a feeling of ever-tightening sentences that seem to escape capture and the anticipation of meaning.[1] The way words unexpectedly light up in groups in rapid succession induces a sense of urgency to the reading.

The artist's choice of words represents abstract concepts grouped together to produce a good mood by using positive-sounding words on the right and negative ones on the left. Thus, abstract concepts are combined with the stimulation of affective and embodied responses, along with important spatial effects. I have discussed how the latest research in psychology shows that concepts can be distributed in both modal and amodal areas. They are sustained by coordinated operations of organising functions in frontal areas, linguistic processing areas (ATL), along with parietal areas that move around or notate modal demonstrations. Barsalou considers such a possibility when he states: 'certain physical artefacts exhibit a kind of "perceptual productivity", using combinatorial and recursive procedures on schematic diagrams to construct limitless complex diagrams. In architecture, notations exist for combining primitive schematic diagrams combinatorially and recursively' (1999, pp. 592–593).

Similarly, a deceptively simple artwork such as Nauman's appeals to at least four major systems of processing: rational and semantic, sensorimotor, spatial and emotional. The work seems to draw them out and relate them to each other in unexpected ways. However, we should not assume that visual experience here is coded along purely rational lines. On the one hand, artworks, traditionally and with modernism, have been examined for their syntactic, schematic and spatial organisation of perceptual data, which often encourages formalist art theorists such as Greenberg to value spatial and perceptual processing as a way of organising conceptual thought above all other kinds of art. On the other hand, Dada, conceptual art and contemporary art challenged the dominance of an aesthetic system based on visual formal structures as ideological rather than natural, and have attempted several strategies to resist these kinds of aesthetic judgements based on traditions of visual order. Thus, Nauman's work carefully balances syntax with semantics as a way to encapsulate this conflict. He creates a word and image interplay that is not simply an orchestration of sensory effects. By suggesting the *subpersonal* mechanical processes of grammar and syntax in sentence construction, he parodies the 'genius' of formal design principles valorised by modernism, in purely visual

---

[1] The work resembles Jasper John's painting, *Device*, 1962, with two rulers or paint mixing sticks pinned to the canvas that he used to smudge a range of colours into two blurred circles, suggesting eyes or windscreen wipers, and the notion that the painting is measuring or painting itself.

terms: the two spirals that intersect reinstate the primacy of visual and spatial order over semantics. This means that the visual and spatial, by their very configuration, impose a meaning onto the words, which also exert their own presence and meaning by the collocation in sentences and contrasting pairs.

The colours of the neon, flashing on and off at different times, present another ordering system superimposed on the work. As in a puzzle, the work offers a structured means by which to dissect a complex experience that commands an impressively diverse range of our psychological resources spread over brain, body and situation. Given that the work can be returned to and re-examined, it helps us to think about several semiotic systems (chronological, chromatic, semantic, syntactical, spatial) and how they intersect, complications that cannot be kept in the mind easily at any one time.

The result is an iterated process of metacognition where we read the codes, examine how this affects our mental states and discover more about how the codes interact with each other. With relatively simple means, Nauman has managed to reinstate the visual into contemporary art, yet not in ways that would necessarily reinstate the traditional aesthetic values of visual pleasure and formalism involved in the contemplation of the work's physical properties (the work seems to stimulate vertigo, if anything). Instead, we might consider that it is rewarding to elaborate aspects of various conceptual systems sparked by the artwork, based on processes of metacognition and the systematicity of language, the complexities of which are anchored in the dynamism of the artwork.

As well as the more obvious reading of the text in a linear sense going into the spiral and in the reverse direction coming out, the words can be read as they are stacked vertically above each other, cutting across the spiral. The multidirectionality of the work in its visual configuration is increased by the fact that there is an impulse to read backwards, as well as randomly, flitting from one spiral to another, picking out words and creating one's own associations. The work demonstrates the longstanding belief in conceptual art that the viewer helps to construct the artwork. It promises to be continually manipulable and variable, not least because there are also suggestions of feelings, beliefs, parodies of advertising jargon, Pop Art references and aphorisms. This is where the structures of relational knowledge begin to emerge within the psychological response.

Nauman designed the work to light up and switch off particular phrases on each side, introducing motion and dynamism to the work, and to create a series of temporal stutters and associations that interfere with the ideal of ceding control of the word order to the viewer. Instead, as in a conversation, we need to adapt expectations constantly, and this again shows how Nauman is intent on stressing contingencies, suggesting inter-subjectivity, instead of the logical positivism of a definite message. On the right, the words suggest the cardinal directions, prepositions: up, down, in, out, which interplay with the potential mental rotations required in reading the texts. The text on the left is worrying, not only suggesting illness (fever and chills, dizziness, dryness and sweating) but also seeming to add to the difficulty of the puzzle, whereas on the right, the text is a series of self-congratulating, banal statements associated with the feel-good factor that many advertising campaigns aim to achieve (such as 'the good life', 'I'm having fun'), which makes the artwork seem more light-hearted and 'fun'; a playful puzzle. The artist thus is able to manipulate embodied, emotional, intellectual, art historical (referencing Pop Art, Op Art, Kosuth), ironic (advertising messages, hypochondria) and aesthetic responses, along with philosophical references (the parody of logical positivism, Wittgenstein and semiotics). In short, Nauman has communicated a theory of mind effectively with visual and lexical means.

In terms of organising knowledge, the work shows global, 'between-systems' connections (Goldstone and Rogosky, 2002) to other artists such as Joseph Kosuth, Dan Flavin and many others who have produced neon works, as well as within-system relations where Nauman references his own previous neon works (in particular, another famous neon spiral piece with the looping sentence, *The Artist Helps the World by Revealing Mystic Truths*, constructed in 1967). There is also a within-work system of relational knowledge, in terms of words and concepts that can reference each other. In literary terms, the work is intertextual, an interdigitation of features of other works within new contexts and assemblages, working against the isolation of the artwork. These across-system communications also stress the social and linguistic aspects of conceptual art.

Each artwork will draw out sensorimotor processes, but the ways in which between-system considerations are staged are more likely to be amodal, coding groups and relations and types of relations rather than committing to action in any isolated, sensorimotor manner. Instead, these ways of connecting situations in art are formed by mental processes such as propositional logic, analogical modification, abstract concept combination and inference. These amodal connections allow us to shortcut or bypass the processing of sensory actions and situations in order to engage with a number of possible ways of organising relational knowledge. However, we are always at liberty to turn our attention to the perceptible qualities of the work. As with many contemporary artists, the sensual and intellectual combine but, importantly, not in order to create an indiscriminate phenomenal state. Instead, there is a structured passage between strong and weak sensuous and emotional engagements, which we often step outside of during rational problem solving and metacognition.

Many psychologists valorise the faster processing of concepts with the aid of concrete or modal situations as the normative way that we use concepts. Yet, the difficulties involved in problem solving and organising concepts that do not employ obvious sensory input or concrete situations to grasp them are just as 'natural'. Abstract concepts *are* more difficult to process than concrete concepts or concepts without situational or back-ground representations. Nevertheless, such difficulty is pleasurable in games and puzzles, emotionally rewarding and profound in art, and is a crucial process routinely activated in study, employment, and scientific and philosophical invention and discovery. It is the rapid connectivity between tokens and exemplars in a formal and amodal sense that allows for efficient conceptual abstraction and elaboration, and the ability to experiment with possible options and to be flexible with such procedures; these are the kinds of operation Nauman's work requires. Encounters with art and science frequently present us with opportunities to apply these rapidly connected networks of concepts against the ordinary, auto-matic or 'stock' associations between concepts that require little creativity in everyday experience.

Some of this is conceded by Barsalou and Wiemer-Hastings (2005). Quoting from lesion and neuroimaging studies that locate the processing of abstract concepts in left frontal areas, they write: 'In these studies, participants usually receive isolated words for abstract concepts not linked to particular situations. Thus, retrieving situations should be difficult, and word associations could fill the conceptual void. Consistent with this account, left-frontal areas tend to be implicated with word generation processes' (2005, p. 134). These areas of the brain are presumably active in the following processes, described by Wiemer-Hastings and Xu: 'Abstract concepts are *relational* concepts, which are likely linked to an extensive number of other concepts...The rich connections between abstract concepts are reflected by the fact that many of their "features" are often abstract concepts themselves' (2005, p. 733).

In a sense, the semantic theory that 'the meaning of a concept is given by its role within its containing system' (Goldstone et al., 2005, p. 286) suggests that the *system* provides meaning, and not the individual lexical units, concepts or metaphors on which Barsalou, Lakoff, Johnson and others focus in order to show perceptual grounding for each unit. As I have mentioned, Nauman's work requires the cooperation of several containing systems that are manipulable. We can view it from within-system and between-systems perspectives, yet we can also understand it in terms of syntactical (spatial) and semantic (linguistic) codes. The perceptual grounding for a sentence or conversation is much harder to justify using arguments that ignore conceptual webs and amodal organising principles. By extension, this is true for art, as we have seen in Nauman's neon, which provides a 'containing system' for individual units of meaning, either for different objects depicted in a work of art or between groups of artworks, enhancing the meaning of these individual units. This would mean that both context and lexical units, as well as categories and the relational aspects of concepts, are processed rapidly and efficiently, especially if we can refer back to the artwork so as to lighten the load on working memory. In Nauman's work, each visual code will activate different but complementary brain areas and provide a system of complex relations where words will represent abstract concepts that will be given extra meaning by their positioning within the artwork. This will stimulate spatial (parietal) and ATL activation, as well as memory areas and the prefrontal cortex that will have to integrate different stimuli.

Visser et al. (2010) suggest that the overarching meaning of a sentence, its rapid expression in speech and comprehension, or rapidly presented visual stimuli, and even their fine-grained meaning, are processed not directly by the sensorimotor system but by the ATLs. Vigliocco et al. (2009) suggest that abstract concepts are learnt implicitly or explicitly through language learning, dictionaries, definitions in speech and conversation. Sensorimotor processes need not be employed for these tasks all of the time. This suggests some sort of internal representation of word meaning of an amodal sort. Firth (1957) suggested that '[y]ou shall know a word by the company it keeps', and that we learn at least part of the meaning of a word from 'its habitual collocation' with other words. This is an important way of learning abstract concepts based on systematic relations in domains such as sport, tools, technology and art. Art, however, can present a combination of such domains in one artwork, as we have seen in Nauman's work, where our absorption is premised on several interconnected systems of cognition. Making explicit how these kinds of artworks produce such immersive effects on the viewer requires that we integrate studies in spatial, visual and linguistic cognition, as I have tried to do with my analysis of Kosuth's and Nauman's works.

2.6 Models of aesthetic cognition

In the following pages, I evaluate various models of aesthetic cognition in cognitive psychology that are possible candidates for use in conjunction with the broader picture of neural connectivity sketched earlier. Turner (2006) provides a map that is supposed to indicate a conceptual blending, which occurs when we focus on a distorted figure of a woman in Picasso's *Les Demoiselles d'Avignon*, 1907. The author argues that we have a conceptual constant schema of a woman's form in our minds that we continue to identify through Picasso's distortions of such a form, and that this causes there to be a conceptual blend of constant and variable aspects (2006, pp. 93–114). However, such a study would need to be augmented with more complex conceptual mapping many times over before it begins to do justice to the subtleties of Picasso's painting. By focusing on the concrete concept of a woman's *body*, any consideration of other important concepts, which undergraduate students are taught routinely to consider in the study of this painting, is omitted. These concepts are the use of exotic material such as African masks, the evocation of erotic desire in the depiction of a brothel scene and the classical European tradition of the nude in art. These treatments of the female figure are, in fact, multiple conceptual and cultural perspectives (or stereotypes) of women in art history. Picasso paints multiple *perceptual* perspectives (viewpoints) that indicate these various conceptual filters. Picasso attempts a 'double vision' of women: he allows the plurality of perceptual viewpoints of the physical bodies to stand for the multiplicity of ways in which women are conceived culturally and with abstract concepts. Thus, Turner's conceptual constant is, in fact, a series of constants that Picasso intends us to treat thematically and critically, that is conceptually, as types. As I have shown with the analysis of Jenny Saville's work, art history frequently brings together these perceptual and conceptual levels in mutually strengthening relationships. Turner and others do not take up these opportunities for studying the intricacies of Picasso's painting, or examples of abstract concepts in contemporary art.

Brandt (2006) suggests that the sensory and perceptual processing of the brushstrokes of a Monet painting allow the viewer to see a pond and its reflective surface. Brandt's analysis does not go beyond a play of optics concerned with surface effects assumed to form aesthetic response. With Impressionism, matters to do with brushstrokes, sense impressions and emotional registers, with occasional reference to the concept of self-aware visual inspection stimulated by the 'reflective' surfaces of water (itself an age-old trope), are viewed as the contents of art. Crucially, however, context-rich information (knowledge about the artist; cultural, political and philosophical concepts), which is typical of the art experience, is left out of the schema in favour of a notion of the artwork's self-evident 'logic of appearance'. This is odd, because these contexts in themselves are conceptual networks that have a hugely important bearing on the meaning of these paintings and on the notion of a painting's contents.

Brandt's model is a phenomenological blending of art's material and haptic factuality, referred to as a 'base space', with its 'presentation space' and its 'reference space'. Thus, in the case of Monet, we might have a painting depicting a pond with clouds and light reflected in it (a base space), which also brings to mind the reflective or dreamy qualities of paint (a presentation space), as well as referencing a summer's day and other thoughts – a blend which the author describes as 'a photohaptic synaesthesia'. The underlying yet unacknowledged diagrammatic schema the author suggests for such works is closely related to Husserl's tripartite *Bild* (the material foundation, canvas, wall, paint), *Bildobjekt* (the type of thing, picture, photograph) and *Bildsujet* (the thing depicted – rabbit or hare, house or mansion). Brandt suggests a similar three-part blend but, unfortunately, pays little attention to the fact that the blend at the level of the reference space is mediated by the categorical and stylistic knowledge of other artworks. It is this level that forms a far greater part of the art experience than research in this area suggests.

Some of these omissions have been addressed by Leder et al. (2004) and provide a useful psychological model of aesthetic processes for showing how a great number of mental operations co-occur during the art experience. This model, however, does not venture to indicate how different kinds of concepts are integrated into conceptual systems, which we routinely access during our experience of artworks. Leder et al.'s model is as follows: perceptual analysis → implicit memory integration → explicit classification → cognitive mastering → evaluation → then back to perceptual analysis (loop). This provides an overall holistic view of different stages but without any detail of what happens in cognitive mastering or how evaluation takes place in terms of the structuring of concepts. This model suggests a reciprocity between bottom-up processes (perceptual processes that recognise complexity, contrast, symmetry recognition in the visual field) and top-down processes (conceptual, categorical and attentional organisation from memory areas or areas responsible for reasoning and planning in the brain), which modify or interpret these bottom-up processes so that active perceptual exploration occurs at the behest of 'executive' signals, instead of responding passively. The top-down processes have been divided further into more specific processes the authors have called 'implicit memory integration' (where recognition of forms or situations depicted in art are integrated or compared with examples from previous experience). There is also 'explicit classification' (the processing of style and content of the artwork); cognitive mastering (the processing of art-specific information where personal taste might intervene); and evaluation, where aesthetic judgements are made in conjunction with feelings of reward or satisfaction. Part of this model also suggests a feedback loop where: 'modern art empowers loops of processing in which hypotheses concerning the meaning of an artwork are continuously altered and tested until a satisfactory result is achieved. The processing of these loops can be pleasing itself and essential for aesthetic experiences' (Leder et al., 2004, p. 500).[1]

It is interesting that the authors speak of 'modern art' with its aesthetic bias towards formalism and perceptual experience. This model is particularly useful for the kind of art that requires perceptual exploration and is rich in perceptual details. It is less applicable to performance art or conceptual or contemporary artworks that downplay perceptual experience. Even when perceptual details do form the basis of psychological processes involved in aesthetic experience studied by Leder et al., and some room is afforded for the role of top-down conceptual processes, this role is still restricted and lacking in detail with respect to the great range of different kinds of concepts (not just art concepts or judgements about beauty) involved in conceptual and contemporary art. The kind of processing that questions the observation of perceptual details (and, therefore, style), which is common in contemporary art, is not addressed by these psychological models. Indeed, Christoff et al. (2009b) states that the anterior part of the prefrontal cortex responsible for abstract thought is engaged in aesthetic appreciation of an artwork, a process that involves 'an attentional *shift away* from perceptual features and towards highly abstract

---

[1] This is similar to Martindale (1984) who proposed that the hedonic value of stimuli is associated with processing their meaning. However, as I argue later, this does not take into account the pleasures of ambiguity and polysemism afforded by postmodern and contemporary art that work against 'essentialising' meanings.

aspects of the perceived artwork and associated *internal* experiences' (p. 99; my emphasis).[2]

However, Cupchik et al. (2009) do look at various kinds of conceptual integration and categorisation, placed into three processes – stylistic categories, art-specific information and aesthetic categories – which they suggest are themselves objects of aesthetic contemplation. Aesthetic experience can thus result in the self-monitoring of conceptual production or categorisation as well as idiographic categorisation that one supposes can be pleasurable in itself, as we have seen with chess (Chase and Simon, 1973; de Groot, 1978) and extensive specialised knowledge (Glaser, 1994). Chatard-Pannetier et al. (2002) showed that antique dealers had much more categorical complexity for furniture than groups of librarians, using different reasons to put them into categories beyond perceptual similarities. This suggests that the sense of agency arising in the creation of conceptual complexity, categorisation and relational knowledge may often be more enjoyable than exploring perceptible qualities or notions of 'retinal' beauty although, of course, these pleasures may be combined.

Leder et al. (2006) and Augustin et al. (2007) questioned subjects with little or no expertise of art and studied their responses to paintings, both with the aid of stylistic descriptions provided in the experiment and with these descriptions withheld. Subjects responded positively to the explanations of stylistic descriptions. It is difficult to know, however, what part of the descriptions were important in helping the subjects respond positively towards the paintings. Clearly, only relatively low levels of 'aesthetic' experience to do with simplistic notions of style are being studied here, which are often confused with facture.

Both Leder et al. (2006) and Cupchik et al. (2009) emphasise stylistic considerations as an indication of aesthetic value when, clearly, in many contemporary artworks ignored by the authors, style is no longer a 'natural' aesthetic category at all, as we can see with readymades or performance artworks. One might even go so far as to state that the *aesthetic* project of contemporary art is continually to challenge the kind of aesthetic processes assumed to be natural in these empirical studies, particularly those based on the configuration of visual perceptible qualities as a system of rational authority, 'message' or meaning creation. As the artist, Joseph Kosuth famously stated: 'Being an artist now means to question the nature of art. If one is questioning the nature of painting, one cannot be

---

[2] Referring to Christoff et al., Ramnani and Owen state that 'By "internal" they mean representations that are stimulus independent, and in this sense their account resonates with our view that the aPFC [anterior prefrontal cortex] processes abstract information without reference to lower-order information (such as sensory input)' (2004, p. 191).

questioning the nature of art…That's because the word "art" is general and the word "painting" is specific. Painting is a kind of art. If you make paintings you are already accepting (not questioning) the nature of art…The "value" of particular artists after Duchamp can be weighed according to how much they questioned the nature of art'.[3]

Neuroscientists hold that neuroimaging techniques can be used to examine aesthetic experience. Yet this can only be done if it is assumed that aesthetic experience is itself an uncontested category. Many psychological experiments assume that aesthetic categories can be found in art or in the brain, but they do not direct their attention to the neural correlates and cognitive processes involved in challenging aesthetics and redefining them. It is an empirical problem because psychologists may be looking for the wrong thing, isolating part of a more complex process and overemphasising its importance in the overall process of experiencing artworks. It is interesting that psychology and neuroscience do not yet seem ready to take on this 'new' definition of art that is a fundamental characteristic of contemporary art in terms of the psychology of both its production and its reception: this is the deconstruction of art, beauty, ethics and identity as categories. I am using the term deconstruction here as a critical strategy that analyses hidden assumptions behind propositions, and which attempts to create new categories and relations between concepts while making explicit the stereotypes and power structures inherent in traditional aesthetics. Contemporary art consistently seems to value creating problems for aesthetic categories such as skill, pleasure, authenticity, precious materials and significant form, and it often does this by bringing together objects and materials beyond oil paint, watercolours and acrylic, which are not usually considered art. This process of creating problems and questions is often premised on rational induction and relational knowledge (an art historical knowledge based on both comparisons and contrasts with other works). Deconstruction should be seen as a psychological complex of creative thought and problem solving based on analogical modification (where previous artworks are altered and reconceptualised in new contexts), relying also on aspects of metacognition and art historical relational knowledge.

Leder et al.'s experiment (2006), in which the different responses are recorded for titles of works provided or withheld, is based on the aesthetic dogma that titles are extraneous to the 'true' visual aesthetic form of an artwork. Yet a majority of these paintings were designed for those with knowledge of the references that such paintings are able to stimulate

---

[3] www.ubu.com/papers/kosuth_philosophy.html Accessed 1/03/2012.

through titles (and, as I have demonstrated, with various word–image artworks). Titles have become intrinsic to many contemporary artworks (see Barbara Kruger's work, for example) and provide opportunities to build references to other paintings in art history or to cultural contexts. Dividing off the visual from the lexical in art seems in many cases mistaken because both are seamlessly blended into the art experience, as are many other more extrinsic aspects. Isolating 'the visual' from the cognitive is thus riddled with problems, especially in participative and performance artworks that involve the improvisation of social situations and interactions as part of the artwork. Titles, speech and communication, the gallery space, the viewing body and the frame are not merely factors that mediate aesthetic experience or value; in many artworks they *are* the experience and value, as integral to the artwork as its material substrate if, indeed, it has one.

Martin Creed's *The Light's Going On and Off*, 2000, is a room in the Tate Modern, London, where a light went on and off every five seconds, an exertion for which the artist won the Turner Prize in 2001. We do not normally think of a blinking light as art, and this invitation to do so may be infuriating, uninspiring or witty, making the gallery or 'art' disappear and reappear. The work 'blinks' between appearance and disappearance, art and reality. However, the blinking also references the viewer's gaze and the fact that she, too, can make reality or art 'disappear'. This is a play on the binary between visibility and invisibility, the former showing us emptiness in a gallery, the latter repeating emptiness in a different light and 'reproducing it'. The art is 'dematerialised' but the concept remains and can be staged in any gallery anywhere in the world or in any number of galleries at the same time. This questions some of the premises of psychological studies, by de Araujo et al. (2005), Leder et al. (2004) and Plassmann et al. (2008), of how titles and labels affect aesthetic appreciation. After all, in Creed's work, all that seems to be evident in the artwork is the title. This work is part of a tradition in contemporary art that attempts to make the gallery visible and central as an important producer of art rather than disguising this power. Hans Haacke's *Recording the Climate in Art Exhibition*, 1970, emptied out the gallery of exhibits to leave only the props and equipment. In *SILENCE*, 1988, curator Michael Fehr emptied out a gallery completely in order to make visitors aware of the gallery as an institution and physical presence that stages art, rather than persisting in seeing the institution as a 'neutral' background force.

As I have been arguing, although it remains an important research project to explain people's feelings involved with aesthetic experience, these feelings do not need to be matched to the artwork's appearance itself but to the series of concepts that it references, or the series of 'acts' the artist or her agent executes that may not be, in themselves, aesthetic or pleasurable. Hence, these studies may be too earnest, leaving out much of contemporary art's irony, parody, strategies of disengagement, entropy, repetition and accumulation, indifference, repugnance, pessimism, deliberate obscurity, irrationalism and esotericism, all of which are contemporary art's major themes and effects, brought about by particular perceptual cues which, in themselves, are not always to be taken at face value as aesthetic content. Such themes and configurations of the visual field, along with the eight major trends given in the introduction, seriously undermine current empirical models of aesthetic engagement and judgement. It may indeed be surprising to psychologists that in interviews with contemporary artists, and in recent art historical works, the words 'beauty' and 'pleasure' are avoided because they have negative connotations, suggesting frivolity, the absence of conceptual complexity, ahistorical and generalising tendencies, and scopic pleasure above ethical concerns.

Ultimately, in these psychological models, the absence of metacognition, the evaluation of self-generated information encouraged by contemporary art, is also telling. I have mentioned the narrativisation of the gaze. This is a key point to consider here, for such art is not simply about stimulating a sense of reward or interest in order to go back into the work to search for more perceptual details in a feedback loop. Many artworks aim to make us aware of our habitual perceptions as problems and they help us to bracket out these 'natural' impulses or to frame them as the target of attention, where cognitive operations of reasoning and categorisation and relational knowledge come into play. The idea is to gain a sense of agency or choice in the processing of visual information in a world already saturated with a visual order of codes and formulae that trigger rewards. The work of Andy Warhol and, later, the collages of Barbara Kruger amply demonstrate an awareness of these issues. Kruger parodies advertising images using caustic one-liners pasted across them to interfere with the power of the visual message, making a problem out of the notion of reward so highly valued in psychological studies. I have shown how this sense of reward is thought to be conditioned by structures of advertising and entertainment biased towards (male) scopic pleasure, highlighted in the work of Cindy Sherman. Marina Abramović's performances and a whole host of other artists' works are similarly committed to questioning the rewards of optical pleasure and the identification of style upon which psychological and institutional models of aesthetic value and connoisseurship are based. This is perhaps why this kind of metacognitive mechanism, this interrogation of automatic and habitual visual literacy, although recognised by Leder et al. (2004, p. 504), has been left out of

Figure 17. Norma Jeane, *#Jan25* *(#Sidibouzis, #Feb12, #Feb14, #Feb17...)*, Venice Biennale, 2011. Courtesy of the artist and the Di Gropello collection. Photograph by Tommaso Zamarchi.

their model. In fact, it should have been given far greater prominence as its role in contemporary art is crucially important.

I have mentioned the social dimension of 'participative' art. This also complicates psychological models of aesthetics. In some cases, the artwork may be seen to be a co-creation of the viewer and the artist. The artist provides an external structure or framework, a gallery space, venue, materials and props for the viewer to step into to manipulate to her liking to create meaning out of the situation with a sense of agency and creativity. The work of Kaprow's *A Furniture Comedy for Hans Hoffman*, 1958, created a series of rooms with furniture in them and invited viewers to rearrange the furniture. Many Fluxus event scores and instruction cards invite the viewer to make their own art. In a similar vein, *Cut Piece*, 1967, invited members of the audience to cut portions from Yoko Ono's garment until she was left almost naked. The work is thus a kind of 'subtractive sculpture', which puts the audience in the act of creating the work while other viewers watch – or consume – the spectacle. It was also meant to evoke a sense of social responsibility or culpability involved in viewing and acquiescence, creating problems out of the notions of witnessing and consent, inaction and agency, in the context of the Vietnam War.

Norma Jeane's *#Jan25 (#Sidibouzid, #Feb12, #Feb14, #Feb17...)* exhibited at the Venice Biennale, 2011, was a large slab of bright red plastic modelling clay that allowed viewers to come into the room, break bits off and stick them on the wall in any way they liked. After several weeks, the room was covered in a mass of wriggling red lines on the white gallery wall with names, broken phrases, political statements, figures and faces, animals and cryptic clues, all resembling a seething mass of graffiti struggling for space. Called 'participative' art (Bishop, 2006), and theorised by Nicholas Bourriaud's 'relational aesthetics' (1998), this consists of art practices exploring cooperative acts between individuals in art making, placing an emphasis on human interaction as the subject of art. This kind of art hopes to transform the viewer from a passive consumer, the subject of empirical science, into an actively and socially engaged participant. Here, the viewer is assumed to be an entirely different entity from the one presumed in psychological experiments concerned with aesthetic experience.

2.7 Relational knowledge

In contemporary art, relational knowledge involves categorisation and conceptual integration. I have mentioned a within-system kind of relational knowledge, and an across-system or between-system relational knowledge (Goldstone and Rogosky, 2002). To complicate matters further, artworks may often have both within-system and across-system connections. The following sections deal with the basics of relational knowledge, which I build up into more sophisticated analyses of art in Part III. Doumas clearly puts relational thinking at the heart of human cognition: 'Relational thinking – thinking that is constrained by the relational roles things play, rather than just the literal features of those things – is a cornerstone of human perception and cognition. It underlies the ability to comprehend visual scenes...learn and use rules...appreciate analogies...between different situations or knowledge systems...understand and produce language, science, art, and mathematics' (Doumas et al., 2008, p. 1).

While this is true, it does not give us enough detail of how this relational knowledge is structured or what the properties of these *relations* are and how they arise. For example, very young children have an intuitive understanding of basic relational concepts such as 'occludes, contains, collides with, and supports' (Doumas et al., 2008, p. 2). This involves moving from feature-based representation (similar to what Duchamp, in art, called the 'retinal') to relational concepts ('non-retinal' logic), which focus on *how* features are related, not on the features themselves. Similarly, those who interpret artworks from sensorimotor perspectives would emphasise these as feature-based representations. However, seeing artworks from a contextual and relational knowledge point of view requires that artworks are evaluated more for the potential they possess in alluding to other artworks in many different ways – in other words, from the point of view of the *different kinds* of relations they afford.

Conceptual blending comes some of the way to answering these questions and it has an important role to play in the construction of relational knowledge. Psychological models not only detail how concepts are mapped onto one another but also attempt to theorise about the kinds of relations that are employed when grouping or blending concepts. Blending, inference and analogy depend on matching some but not all of the features (contents) of one entity to another, discarding some and including new features for new conceptual material to emerge. This is called 'mapping', where the points and coordinates of one entity are mapped onto another, leaving out some or allowing others to emerge. When an artwork modifies or otherwise engages with aspects of another artwork to create visual correspondences, there is also much that is left out of such a mental mapping process of comparison, and new aspects are added. Similarly, inference involves making a series of logical conclusions from premises assumed to be true. These conclusions are structures 'mapped' onto premises. Artists may work by responding to an artwork and modifying it, eventually to create something quite different. Picasso's numerous studies of Velázquez's *Las Meninas* are a good example, where the artist preserved the configural relationships of the original while changing colours, style and proportion, leaving out the naturalist style of the original for hard graphics. The result was a modernist Picasso mapped onto *Las Meninas*, where the older painting was recognisable through this analogical modification. This aspect of artistic production is also appreciated by the viewer, whose ability to analyse the general gist of a scene with coarse-grained, configural attention will still allow her to interpret the 'situation' of one artwork through the situation of another. This is built up into quite complex systems of references to other artworks, which I have called relational knowledge. While at first glance this kind of visual correspondence between artworks might seem to reinstate the traditional aesthetics of optical inspection, in many contemporary artworks correspondences are achieved through conceptual, non-perceptible relations.

Psychological studies of the thought processes underlying inference, comparison, analogy and metaphor help to provide details of how this occurs. These are some of the fine-grained ways in which complex entities are grouped together to form systems of relational knowledge. For the purposes of clarity, these studies, to which I will turn my attention shortly, deal with isolated examples of mapping rather than the kind of complex relational knowledge that is active routinely during our experience of art. In reality, relational knowledge would involve many more examples of artworks than just the mapping of one artwork onto another. In addition, there are *different kinds* of relations, or different ways of mapping. There could be a relation that occurs at the level of visual appearance: formal correspondences (art historians are fond of identifying a figure's pose as indebted to earlier artists, for example). There could also be a relation at the level of a situation (this could be a mythological scene, for example, which references certain conventional ways in which the scene has been treated in art historical traditions). Furthermore, it could be that one painting causes others to occur, as I have shown with Picasso's series of paintings inspired by Velázquez's *Las Meninas*. When elaborated by several different kinds of works, such a group of works can be called a system of relational knowledge. Yet such a system is not merely the grouping of artworks together, based on shared affinities of perceptual features, but is also the way in which an artwork depicts abstract concepts. Although different in perceptual details, one can put artworks together in a category if they aim to express the same or similar abstract concepts. For example, one would put some of Kosuth's works dealing with Wittgenstein's philosophical investigations in the same category as a work by Martin Creed that also references the philosopher's concepts. In such cases, as Wiemer-Hastings and Graesser (2000) show, abstract concepts may be grasped by the 'abstract structure' of the situations used to understand them. The different situations I have given examples of here are structured by *types of relation* such as causal, temporal, spatial and semantic.

It must be noted that these types of relation are not necessarily mutually exclusive. Some artworks can be put into a system of relational knowledge using all of these types of relations, and even this short list is not exhaustive. According to Halford et al. (2010), the kinds of relations that help to structure relational knowledge should have the following core properties:

1 'structure-consistent mappings': cognitively principled and consistent ways that enable analytic cognition over and above the simple matching of content (lower-level similarity), 'they promote a selection of relations that are common to several relational instances, which is a major step towards abstraction and representation of variables' (p. 497);
2 'compositionality': the ways in which component parts of complex entities are related and retain this relatedness, and where we are able to extrapolate logically from these relations and add to them to make the entity more complex, using the same compositionality;
3 'systematicity': for example, 'John loves Mary' implies the capacity to understand 'Mary loves John' (p. 499).

Apart from these core properties (1–3), relations between concepts can be premised on reasoning processes such as proposition, transitive inference,[1] recursion,[2] relational categories (such as parenthood/children),

---

[1] 'Transitive inference: Given that the relation r holds between A and B, and between B and C, then if r is a transitive relation, we can infer that r holds between A and C, that is ArB and BrC implies ArC' (Halford et al., 2010, p. 497).
[2] 'Higher-order relational representations, with lower levels embedded within higher levels and the same operation being performed at each level, form a basis for recursion' (Halford et al., 2010, p. 499).

planning³ and analogy. Note that the following definition of analogy uses
a pictorial example well suited to art's ability to preserve structure consistency over several examples using different elements: 'consider a picture analogies task that comprises picture A, in which a boy restrains a dog
that chases a cat, and picture B, in which a tree restrains the dog that
chases the boy. In a relational match, "boy" in A is mapped to "tree" in B
because both restrain the dog. In an element (featural) match, "boy" in A
is mapped to "boy" in B' (Halford et al., 2010, p. 500). Note that in this
example, visual resemblance of a crude kind need not be operative. A few
elements brought together by the artwork may suggest causal relations or
intentions and abstract concepts. The pictorial example is, however, quite
simple compared with situations presented by artworks. Here, a picture
would be visually inspected while another picture in long-term memory is
being accessed in order to execute the comparison or mapping. Thus, it is
simply misleading to suggest that what is going on here is primarily an
embodied experience based on sensorimotor processes. Although many
artworks do appeal thematically to such experience, relational knowledge
need not be restricted to this theme.

   Kemp et al. (2010) use the word 'theory' to refer to 'a system that
specifies a set of concepts and relationships between these concepts...
many kinds of concepts derive their meaning from the roles they play in
theories' (p. 166). An important part of a curator or art historian's work is
to find a 'theory' emerging from an overview of several artworks in the
artist's oeuvre, a period or in group shows and, indeed, to cross reference
these with other artists' works that seem to create larger and more complex 'theories' of art.

   It is important to keep in mind that an artwork brings together a number
of visual features that can be grouped together differently. For example,
we can group together objects depicted in a certain colour or in terms of
their category (landscape scenes). Or we may group together objects that
belong together in terms of function, or objects that belong together as
part of a semantic group (objects that symbolise the life of Christ, for
example). We may also group together various readymades associated
with different artists that do not resemble each other in the least. The
point is, any aspect of an artwork, or any artwork in a group, can play
the role of causing a particular grouping or category to be activated, and

³ There are different kinds of planning, ad hoc and methodical, following a pre-prescribed
plan that does not deviate from the model. In both cases, there is the ability to mentally
extrapolate from the given, however, that is present in terms of external evidence, diagrams, art or notebooks. 'Planning depends on creating sequences of actions or operations
that transform the current state into a goal state as well as on representing relations'
(Halford et al., 2010, p. 501).

the same aspect can play different roles in different groupings. In other words, an object or an aspect of an object can be categorised in more than one way. In artworks that intend us to think counter-intuitively, there may be no obvious way by which a more 'natural' category inclusion will be preferred over another. In fact, we might be very interested in the psychological effects of an aspect's or object's potential to have multiple category membership (as Oppenheim's 'fur cup' amply demonstrates).

Each artwork within a group of artworks, or each feature in one artwork, can be read sequentially in a number of different ways, having a different value in each reading. This manipulability of an artwork's perceptible features will work in cooperation with how it constrains this manipulability: it is probable that a still-life picture featuring a glass of water might cause a spreading semantic activation that could contain concepts to do with transparency or thirst, but it is unlikely to set off connections with teddy bears. However, even with certain constraints, considerable manipulability will be possible (we can look at other objects in the picture or continue to ponder the meaning of the glass). This is no different from using the same sentence and placing stress on different words each time the sentence is read, producing different meanings, as we can see in Kosuth's neon art work, which glows in four different colours with the words 'Four Colors Four Words'. We may stress the sentence in the following different ways:

Four Colors Four Words
Four *Colors* Four Words
Four Colors *Four* Words
Four Colors Four *Words*

This is not to mention putting stress on groups of words (such as *Four Colors*, as opposed to *Four Words*). Placing the stress on different elements of the artwork allows the artwork to be 'read' differently and its component parts to be *seen* differently. Moreover, the syntax could be mentally rotated to change the order of reading the artwork. There is also a phonemic closeness between *for/four*. Kirsh (2009) calls these different ways of changing the cues of the material object in the environment (putting stress on different parts) self-cueing. The idea is that, by changing the stress or sequential order of viewing the artwork, one can change its meaning, causing semantic activation in various directions. As the neon lights for each word are different colours, this also adds complexity to the work. In addition, one begins to wonder why there is no acknowledgement of LIGHT or NEON in this work, if the artist is being thorough and consistent with his aim of having a self-enclosed mapping of words and visual elements without surpluses. The artwork points to itself and this is a consistent theme in the artist's works, as we have seen. Kosuth wanted to limit, as much as possible, the notion that the artwork points to a prior or absent reality outside of the work, thereby attempting to produce the presence of the work and nothing else. Yet we still bring certain expectations and scripts to the artwork; it reminds us of advertising, stimulates memories of lonely, late-night cityscapes and we feel the warmth of the neon on our skin.

2.8 Analogical processes in relational knowledge

The social community, institutions and organisations, technology and the material anchors of art can act as external stores to support an individual's relational knowledge, allowing new experiences, encounters, contrasts, comparisons and concepts to emerge. However, serious questions remain as to how exactly working memory allows for the dynamic binding of these different entities and domains. As Halford et al. ask: 'What specific working-memory process determines whether two representations are in structural correspondence?' (2010, p. 503). The question focuses on the fine-grained ways in which the internal features of an artwork might be understood to share analogies with the internal relations of other artworks in order to create relational knowledge. The psychology underlying analogical thought processes seems to be helpful here, as well as the work done on the psycholinguistic processes involved with metaphor, which also involves the cross-referencing of elements for new conceptual material to emerge.

Significant research on how analogies are mapped psychologically has been conducted by Gentner and Kurtz (2006). Although the authors show that objects and object attributes, as well as relations between objects, enter into the structure mapping process, it is the ability to match object relations rather than object attributes that is more important for successful analogies. Gentner and Kurtz suggest that this matching has a high level of systematicity and that these processes are also important for creating new representations: 'Consider the simple arithmetic analogy 3:6:2:4. We do not care how many features 3 has in common with 2, nor 6 with 4...but only the relationship "twice as great as"' (Gentner, 1983, p. 156).

We do not have to process the detail of the attributes of the things being compared but rather the similarity of the respective relations mapped from domain relations to target relations. This can be taken as an example of how we can skip sensorimotor processing; not only are the abstract concepts immediately understood without an appeal to embodied or concrete concepts, but we are wont to process the syntactic relations between each part of the analogy, rather than object attributes that might require sensorimotor involvement.

According to Gentner (1983), most metaphors are relational comparisons: Shakespeare's metaphor of 'Juliet is the sun' does not mean that she is 'yellow, hot or gaseous' but rather that 'she appears above him, bringing hope and gladness, etc.' (1983, p. 162). It remains to be seen whether the visual equivalents of metaphor or analogy in art are to do with attribute comparisons or relational comparisons. Those who consider art to be yet another example of how embodied experience grounds abstract conceptual knowledge would stress attribute comparisons, while those who would prefer to see art as part of a system of abstract relations, would tend to lean more towards relational comparisons. Yet, it seems important to consider that we can experience an artwork in both ways. We can understand the artwork in a deliberate, intentional sense or in terms of gist and relational and contextual references where the examination of attributes may be based on non-thematic appreciation of embodied experience. The preponderance of relational comparisons militates against the notion that sensorimotor processes and neuronal feature detectors are necessary and sufficient primary engines of the art experience.

Empirical studies of analogical mapping processes (Gentner 1983; Holyoak and Thagard 1995) do not usually look to art for evidence.[1] A study of two Japanese contemporary artists explains how their work developed over several years (Okada et al., 2009). The researchers used the model of analogical modification to explain creativity. External material anchors are assumed to be central in this analogical process, and can be used as evidence that analogical mapping can occur with visual aids in the environment, which are acted upon and manipulated far more commonly in the art experience when we make relational and knowledgeable connections between artworks *as viewers*. Thus, although Okada et al. make the point that analogical modification is an important part of the creative process, where artists alter previous artworks and features by creating a mental model, and where the old and the new are put into an analogical relationship, I would insist that this cognitive process is freely available to the art viewer and gallery visitor.

When viewing a work of art 'through' the perspective of the artist's oeuvre, and by comparing similar works painted by the artist in a series or in an exhibition of works, the viewer attempts to see the artwork through the eyes of the 'period eye'. This is a phrase used by Michael Baxandall,

---

[1]   However, see Bonnardel (2000) and Dahl and Moreau (2002) for the generation of design concepts, and Kennedy (2008) for preliminary comments on the commonalities of visual art and metaphor, which I evaluate and supplement in later pages.

who explains it as 'the interpreting skills one happens to possess, the categories, the model patterns and habits of inference and analogy' (1988, p. 29). Importantly, implied in this is the ability to look through somebody else's 'period eye'. Whether the viewer manages this successfully is not at issue here; another art historian, Jonathan Crary (1990), insists that this can never truly be possible. However, one can be constrained by the knowledge of what was available to the artist in his or her own historical setting. This would, for example, involve seeing Mondrian's *Broadway Boogie Woogie*, 1942–1943, in the context of the verticals and horizontals of New York city life, an urban energy and momentum that is somehow epitomised by the work rather than, say, using pixel technology to contextualise the work, which would be an anachronism. Yet, it might also be wrong to do this because, although the title of the work suggests this interpretation, we know that Mondrian methodically avoided representation in favour of a highly intellectual formalist abstraction involving relational principles. He also aimed to emphasise the concrete presence of the painting. Knowing this gives us the opportunity to see the painting differently but my example amply shows how the 'period eye' works and how it can be withdrawn for a flexible and exploratory experience of art rather than one that only follows the theoretical framework of embodiment, privileging it as *the* natural process of interpretation.[2]

There will be general and expert applications of this contextual knowledge. Again, one can refer to the relevant cognitive experiments on the visual behaviour of chess masters, which show how they are able to recall complex chess situations not because of their ability to memorise every detail but because of their ability to conceptualise the chess problem summarily. It is probable that this amodal coding of the chess situation in its intricacy is a computation that becomes habitual, based on lightning analogical reasoning using many other 'situations' stored as schemas in the long-term memory. Such tacit knowledge applied *in situ* is based on years of analogical processing. This is not dissimilar from how an artist or art historian becomes accustomed to seeing the 'larger picture' in their encounter with an artwork: they know what to look for, what the implications are, and they use a broad and deep system of analogies and theoretical frameworks in order to do so.

---

[2] One could associate the period eye to the 'framing' actions of the prefrontal cortex, which holds hypotheses in the mind: 'the frontal cortex intervenes both in the genesis of hypotheses and in the elaboration of critical judgement, both faculties being essential for viewing a painting' (Changeux, 1994, p. 192). For the period eye, however, this ignores other processes such as empathy that can cause us to see things from allocentric perspectives, or 'perspective-taking'.

The basic definition of analogical thought in the art context hinges on the notion of 'analogical mapping', which entails abstracting 'a similar structure or dimension between a source and a target, ignoring features that are different between them. However, in the context of creation, paying attention only to the similarities between them is not enough, a person also has to pay attention to the differences in order to generate a new target, i.e., to create a new thing or event' (Okada et al., 2009, p. 190).

Such mapping may be achieved randomly and in an experimental manner or by applying methodical rules and procedures. Obviously, the latter kind of constrained and intelligible analogical modification in art making and viewing is easier to provide an account for than the random process. However, it is important that we take into account how analogical reasoning can take place with the aid of material anchors, namely, artworks, rather than thinking of this process purely as an internal, amodal process of computation cut off from the world. Okada et al. identified three phases of acquiring expertise: 'constrained by external criteria', 'forming one's own internal criteria' and 'harmonious creation' (2009, p. 191). Analogical mapping is a key to the creative process, where perceptible features of earlier works are selected or filtered out and rearranged with new ones when creating works. A technique, concept or superordinate category such as STYLE, may be mapped onto the 'new' situation of an artwork and its perceptible qualities. Various mappings, adding different examples into the category of STYLE, will eventually change STYLE. In addition, it is important to remember that STYLE as a set of features can be mapped onto PAINTING, SCULPTURE, FASHION or BEHAVIOUR.

In theory, analogy may sometimes be a way of apprising oneself of 'relational commonalities independently of the objects in which those relations are embedded' (Gentner, 1989, p. 121). This is a crucial clarification to keep in mind for the analyses of artworks that follow in later pages. An abstract concept, FREEDOM, may be connected analogically to LIBERTY or to BIRD. A concrete concept can thus be mapped onto an abstract concept (or vice versa). This happens when providing concrete exemplars for abstract concepts. Yet we could also have a superordinate concept: FURNITURE mapped onto DOMESTIC, BEDROOM or TABLE or even TOADSTOOL, a poetic mapping using metaphor where a mushroom is the furniture of the forest. However, FURNITURE can also be mapped onto CHESS to yield some interesting new conceptual material concerning the rational organisation of a dining room or some unusual chess pieces. Thus, analogical mapping or modification will take the 'features' (perceptual or abstract) from one domain and map them onto another in order for

new qualities to emerge: this is what we call creativity. It seems important to stress the variable nature of analogical relations because they occur
across modalities and across different mental entities. For example,
'watching the news was a bitter experience' involves sensations as well
as abstract concepts that are not simply matched using visual similarities,
which would lock us into the old game of privileging the perceptible
qualities of art. I try to explain how some of these different kinds of
entities and sensations may be mapped onto each other with regard to
one important artwork discussed in the following pages.

2.9 Carl Andre's *Lever*, 1966

Perhaps one of the most uncompromising works of Minimalism is Carl Andre's *Lever*, 1966, which, among other things, is a coming together of both low-level and high-level analogical relations. The work is a single line of 139 unjoined firebricks laid down upon the gallery floor. *Lever* is a material structure with sculptural and architectural aspects that are also part of a complex conceptual game. The title signifies a principle of mechanics, with or without reference to the body. As a rigid bar that pivots about one point and is used to move an object at a second point, it resembles the line of bricks that can also be seen as a bar. The title, *Lever*, thus adds metaphorical import to the work, suggesting that the line of bricks is a tool 'to lever' meaning from its heavy, material base. The metaphor neatly characterises two typical kinds of art historical analyses of Minimalism: an approach that (A) emphasises the facticity of its material base as a way to get us to consider our embodied facticity involved with this materiality and the space it suggests, and (B) emphasises conceptual combination and the creation of superordinate concepts. It is, however, possible to do a structure mapping exercise based on the art historical discourse analysis, whereby (A) is used as a source domain for (B) in order to provide a complex relationship between embodied considerations and abstract concepts but avoiding the reduction of (B) to (A). Instead, this relationship is best characterised as a series of analogical modifications or mappings with new representational content (C).

(A)   Embodied and phenomenological concepts (source domain)

Standard art historical interpretations of *Lever* (Archer, 2002; Krauss, 1981) emphasise how the work brings to mind the following embodied or phenomenal concepts:

(i) rough bricks, hard, industrial objects, texture
(ii) walking or stepping over (the line)
(iii) territory (the bricks divide the room into two halves)

  (iv) direction (verticality/horizontality)
  (v) bigger than human scale but thin, like a spine
 (vi) gravity
(vii) absence of plinth (flatness of ground)
(viii) visual similarity, self-same repeat
 (ix) temporal extension (counting the bricks)

These affordances provided by the art object can be understood as concepts which reference the body in such a way that we *feel* the immediate oneness of such concepts with our embodied orientation, position and self-reference.[1] Our body-reference is through an awareness built up of numerous concepts (i–ix), which may be experienced as embodiment and, when not attended to as 'themes', could be described as perceptions. Yet it could be argued that the artwork encourages us to process such perceptions in thematic ways, changing them into apperceptions and concepts about phenomenological experience brought to mind by the artwork. In other words, although the artwork may be designed to strip down conceptual thought in order to make way for sensory experience and perceptions, it soon becomes a complex production of concepts about how a reduced and constrained cognitive environment with relatively limited perceptual cues can lead to higher cognitive operations.

(B)   Conceptual approaches (target domain)

Concepts here could be built up by a series of negations or counterfactual examples in order to create a superordinate category of the 'artistic practice of Minimalism'. *Lever* suggests a 'razing down to the ground' of traditional categories of art by attempting:

1 A negation of the notion of the artwork as an expression of the artist's personality
2 A negation of artistic dexterity, traditional notions of craftsmanship, facture or skill
3 A negation of conventional notions of representation
4 A negation of traditional artistic materials

---

[1] '. . .a shift from the spectator/object relation where meaning is determined by the optical exchange across the visual field to a haptic or tactile phenomenology of the body as it encounters the physical world, a felt and lived experience of corporeality' (Bird, 1999, p. 96).

(C)   Mapping

Examples from (A) (embodied and phenomenal concepts) can be mapped onto (B) (abstract concepts). For example:

(iii) → 1 = yields: the artist has withdrawn traces of gesture and style as clues to revealing his intentions, yet the straight line emphatically divides the floor and confronts the viewer. Does the line of bricks suggest a rule in a game, a territorial demarcation? How does one play the artist's game, and not break the rules and 'cross the line'?

(vii) → 3 = yields: lack of traditionally understood markers of representation, the absence of the sculptural plinth separating ordinary from elevated art. An assemblage of randomly placed bricks would have a different psychological effect. Bricks here are 'built' into a line, reminding us of their function; bricks work in groups and are commonly used for buildings and architecture. This brings to mind the room, the floor, the building, the gallery in which the bricks are placed. Where, in fact, does the artwork begin or end, even though it seems to divide the floor, as a wall, into two parts. If this is a monument, what is it a monument to?

(vi) → 4 = yields: the absence of 'artistic' materials brings to mind the materiality of the bricks, colour, texture, dead weight, solidity, stubbornness, indifference to human touch and meaning. Is there a play on gravity as an impersonal force that keeps the bricks in place (there is no cement). The reduction of artistic facture or 'interference' is coupled with the concept of the readymade: an object not made by the artist and not considered in itself to be art, yet the institutional context or placement encourage it to be read as art.

(iv) + (ix) → 2 = yields: 'one thing after another', Donald Judd's phrase meant to capture the impersonal serial repetition of the new art in the 1960s. It also manages, however, to *represent*, by act and demonstration, the concept of a logical method or procedure followed strictly. Any embodied involvement here, from the point of view of this blend, would amount to perfunctory repeats, indicating a lack of volition, using the body as a tool for a logical method, expunging spontaneity and improvisation and the model of expressionism. The artwork has coherence, an internal logic not dependent on the contingencies of external, contextual factors. This blend is the purist, propositional interpretation of conceptual artworks as propositions (similar to Kosuth's work based on the early Wittgenstein).

These kinds of thoughts may occur in any order and will be accompanied by stray thoughts and feelings, negative or positive or irrelevant. There are personal permutations, contingencies and proclivities that might produce a different syntax with variable emphases in meaning, cooperative with the constraints of the artwork. The art experience, even with such an apparently 'simple' work of a few bricks, can be an agglomeration of embodied sensations interspersed with abstract concepts that are 'highly abstract, premised on a series of higher-order relations' (1–4) 'that connect the lower order relations' (i–viii) 'into a mutually constraining structure' (Gentner, 1983, p. 164). This is not just a question of comparing object attributes (the shape, texture, line of the bricks) or the phenomenal qualities arising from a consideration of these, but of ordering both the system of perceptions and phenomenal concepts into a series of analogical relations organised by (1–4), relations that are, in themselves, abstract concepts. The concept of artistic involvement or withdrawal from facture, for example, orders relations between the bricks as mechanically produced objects, and the placing of them into a line as the barest minimum of artistic intervention. In turn, the absence of the artist, signalled by the reduction of artistic style and signs of intentionality, questions a straightforward and unproblematic phenomenal experience of embodiment. However, if we were to use an aspect of relational knowledge (the classical pilaster column, the built environment, Minimalism), we may also achieve a 'transfiguration of the commonplace' (Danto, 1981).

The whole cognitive psychological structure involved in the interpretation of *Lever* is not rigid or fixed. It is fluid, yet somewhat constrained or anchored by references to the artwork in the environment, which provide a limited number of reference points, although we do not have to dwell on the optical appearance of the work for these cogitations to occur. The artwork does constrain conceptual combination by forcing a particular order, temporal sequence or syntax: the attributes of bricks and perceptual thoughts about them may be read in any order, unlike a sentence that is more effective in presenting the order by which it is to be understood. *Lever* does present a context or mental space that constrains and causes there to be particular conceptual combinations. The artwork helps to group together related concepts (note how I have grouped together (i–ix) and (1–4), for example) and causes there to be a systematicity that arises out of structural relationships between the different cognitive processes implied in each grouping. This is in harmony with many aims of Minimalism. As Sol LeWitt declared: 'The system is the work of art; the visual work of art is the proof of the system. The visual aspect can't be understood without understanding the system. It isn't what it looks like but what it is that is of basic importance' (LeWitt, 1969).

The way in which materials such as bricks are organised by a systematic logic and structure engages with our sensorimotor processing of their appearance. We are also able to analyse the significance of the way in which an artwork is arranged because we are familiar with the intentions of other Minimalist artworks, especially Sol LeWitt's procedural art that emphasises *a priori* knowledge. Yet the 'system' LeWitt speaks of is also relational knowledge: we learn that looking at a Minimalist sculpture is not a precious kind of reification of the object into visual perfection or the intricacies of scopic pleasure; instead we learn to question this impulse and to puzzle over the systems of knowledge and processes of economic, social and material flux, which seem to be 'snagged' by the artwork.

From the perspective of psychology, the system-as-art-experience may be organised into different cognitive processes (perceptions, sensorimotor action, phenomenal feeling, categorical abstraction), which may be combined, using structural mapping concepts, into analogical relationships to each other. Each viewer will compare and contrast examples from or create analogies between these different cognitive processes in different ways; some viewers will have fewer and others greater examples for each group, and there will be differently composed superordinate categories. Others will find the lack of visual stimulation afforded by a line of bricks to be an example of the failure of modern art (or will not be able to accept that it is art in the case of Michael Fried). Others will see it as an elegant structure that, with an economy of means, eloquently and systematically within the mythos of the classical column, extends the aims of so many modernist artists concerned with questioning traditional aesthetics. For *Lever*, one *does* need to understand one's art history and one's relational knowledge does need to be brought to bear if one is to get more out of this work. However, that is not so say that the visual opulence of a Dutch still-life, bristling with illusionist detail that stimulates the senses, is any less a work of art than Andre's *Lever*. In any case, sometimes understanding a work of art is more important than the dilemma of whether one likes it.

The relational knowledge that allows us to glimpse the elegant systematicity of Minimalism is extended further by intersubjective communication, by reading a book on the subject of Minimalism, by having several different experiences of other Minimalist works that are variations on a theme, and these experiences will mediate and abstract this systematicity across different instances. What I am proposing here is a different emphasis in the psychology of art, which suggests that our fascination with art, why we might find it beautiful or meaningful for a whole number of reasons that differ from person to person, will involve the kind of structure mapping outlined earlier and importantly, *systematicity*. This mapping does not simply occur in a conceptual domain where these concepts are of the same kind. The mapping of a phenomenal concept TALL onto another phenomenal concept STRAIGHT, which are relatively low-level mappings, may also be elaborated by superordinate concepts, so that we have, for example,

BALANCE or UPRIGHT mapped onto CLASSICISM, and higher-order mappings: CLASSICISM onto MINIMALISM.

Both (i–ix) and (1–4) are seamlessly meshed into our experience of such work: it seems churlish to emphasise that higher cognitive relations are more important than lower ones, or vice versa, in order to characterise art, or to state that one is causal for the other, especially given the complexity of the mappings presented in (C), which are more than the sum of their parts.

Importantly, the artwork's perceptual cues will help to determine the relationship between these cognitive formations and the contents of each grouping of different kinds of concepts. For example, the way in which the bricks in *Lever* are lined up (rather than made into a circle) constrains or helps to organise a number of phenomenal concepts that can be grouped together and mapped onto superordinate categories about artistic practice and culture in a way that organising them into circle, throwing them into a pile or titling the work 'hospital' might not. The work is informed by art history and knowledge of the grid as a repeated form, a seriality that references assembly lines and conveyor belts, those quintessential processes of industrialised production that are the antipathy of creativity, yet 'here' become conceptually creative. *Lever* also engages with concepts of the built environment, temporal progression, brick by brick, the many in the one. Each artwork will constrain the character of our conceptual combination for that art encounter and, yet, a particular kind of conceptual integration lies behind the creation of each artwork.

Our experience and understanding of *Lever* today also frames our conceptualisation of other artworks. It might invite us to consider the uproar caused by the purchase by the Tate Gallery, London in 1972 of Carl Andre's *Equivalent VIII*, 120 firebricks placed on the floor in a rectangular format, and again in 1998, when Danish artist Per Kirkeby installed his bricks in the Tate Modern. Alternatively, these works remind us of *Lever*. In terms of discourse analysis concerning Kirkeby's work, we can do no better than quote art critic Lillian Pizzichini of *The Independent* who wrote: '*Brick Work* 1998 is laden with references, both autobiographical – to the great Grundtvig neo-gothic edifice – and geological...Its double-helical shape is based on Kirkeby's own sketches of DNA molecules. It is undecorated (Denmark is a Lutheran country), so the clarity of the structure sings out' (Pizzichini, 1998).

The structure mapping I have employed to understand the psychological processes involved in experiencing *Lever* can easily be used to show the structures of concepts and perceptions underlying Pizzichini's writing, which we learn to elaborate effortlessly in a seamless manner while reading about it, and in a tacit and rapid manner while engaged directly with the artwork. Kirkeby's work, however, is itself a structure mapping of Carl Andre's Minimalist work onto his own contemporary analogy in order to create interesting surpluses of meaning which include, among other things, using bricks as metaphors for DNA molecules (an interesting twist on how Minimalism is supposed to reference the body). The reference to Grundtvig Church, designed in 1916, made from six million bricks is 'peculiar to the ancient Danish tradition of brick-laying. [Kirkeby's] childhood impressions of this church have informed the whole of his artistic career', writes Pizzichini. The work is clearly architectural as a well as biological. It also references geology (Kirkeby was once a geologist) and, at least in the writer's mind, the Lutheran antipathy for ornate embellishment and visual and sensory overload. The restraint of classical Minimalism here is culturally specific, ideological, ethical and personal. Thus, although the work manages to reference nearly all of the phenomenal and sensorimotor concepts listed in my description of *Lever* (i–ix), in addition, it manages to suggest various scientific, religious and aesthetic systems as overarching superordinate categories that can draw upon (i–ix) in different ways. Thus, there is nothing absolute or essential about (i–ix) – the framing of these by superordinate concepts will change how they appear to us. Importantly, *Lever* helps us to see, interpret and become more involved with Kirkeby's bricks and to look again at *Lever*.

A recent work by New Zealand artist Kate Newby, *You Make Loving Fun*, 2009, continues the work of *Lever* with interesting analogical modifications. Like *Lever*, it is a line of bricks, this time, cemented and vertical, wedged between floor and beam, running up a wall like a pilaster. The work's perceptual cues invite conceptualisation of Carl Andre's *Lever* as something now assembled and made to stand up from its slumber, as if brought to life. Furthermore, as if to add a spark of life to the column, the artist has planted grasses in between some of the bricks. Whereas Andre's *Lever* was aimed at the viewer's body and the phenomenal experience of movement, territory and ground, Newby's column of vertebrae points to life itself: the land of the living, the grasses breaking through inanimate industrial materials, a natural force that viewers, when they notice this unexpected detail, respond to as if discovering a quiet secret. This is especially so as the bricks might easily be mistaken for a part of the gallery architectural structure, breached by what seems to be an opportunistic growth not part of the plan of man-made territories and structures. Yet also brought to mind is the memory of the artist, Ana Mendieta, famous for her mapping of the body onto grasses and on the earth, who fell to her death from a bedroom window after an argument with her husband, Carl Andre, creator of the row of bricks known as *Lever*.

Figure 18. Kate Newby, *You Make Loving Fun*, 2009. Courtesy of the artist, Chartwell/AAG and Sue Crockford Gallery.

Much in common with the sentiment of bringing new life to inanimate Minimalism is Mona Hatoum's *Hanging Garden*, 2008, in which bags of soil are put into sandbags in order to create a wall usually employed for trench warfare – through the bags, grasses grow. There is an eerie sense that the place it 'depicts' has been abandoned and lost in time or that nature is reclaiming the soil in the present and future. There is a sense of arrested time, things 'hanging' in the balance.

A garden, a place of peace, may result, but it is a strange garden. *Hanging Garden* immediately brings to mind army checkpoints designed to halt the flow of peoples, cultures, goods and time by producing a blockage, a territory, and the artist has indicated that her intent was to reference the war in Iraq.[2] As with Newby's work, here there is an

---

[2] 'This work can be seen as an oblique reference to the continued state of war in Iraq. Sand bags are a very familiar site in the Middle-East. They are supposed to be temporary structures used in times of war. The implication here is that they have been around for so long that plants started taking root in them. It is a poetic piece. There is something hopeful about life sprouting in the most inhospitable environment.' Correspondence with the artist, 18/04/2012.

Figure 19. Mona Hatoum, *Hanging Garden*, 2008 (jute bags, earth, grass, 140 × 90 × 603 cm). Photograph by Jens Ziehe. Courtesy of Daadgalerie, Berlin and the artist.

unchanging state of inanimate Minimalism, talking to a (brick) wall. However, in these works the wall is made organic and biological and, therefore, the art object seems to grow. The grass seems to mark different states of change: 'grass grows' and will continue to do so with brazen indifference to all and sundry.[3] In *Hanging Garden* there is a sense of both a place divided and contested, and a place as a marker of duration. Victor Burgin writes: 'Locations...are fixed by definition, but the actual spaces to which they refer are in continual flux and so impossible to separate from time' (Burgin, 2009, p. 12).

---

[3] Hans Haacke's title for an earlier conceptual work where he brought into the gallery, in 1969, spaced layers of turf formed into a sculpture.

The rhizome-grass shows us time but it is indifferent to showing, except that it 'pokes through' a man-made territory. Hatoum arranges a three-dimensional space and material facticity. With earth and grass she makes the artwork a continuous variation. It is a space we can walk in or around, a freedom denied to others. While it is a territorial marker, there is a growth that passes through it to deny its authority. The grass seems to defy the territories we artificially carve up to create an 'us' and 'them', a human and a non-human.

The way in which these different artworks come together with interesting analogical mappings of perceptible details and associated concepts creates a system of relational knowledge active in the viewer and communicable to others. There may be those who object to art being characterised as a rational system of analogies that underlies the logic of art interpretation, as I have demonstrated here. An alternative, however, to analogical-based combination is the 'case-based approach', which is less about feature indexing, searching, matching and transference (which may be based on systematic rules), and is more improvised as a situation with irregular or awkward features and relations: 'Goals in the situation at hand activate stored cases that specify requisite actions along with attributes of the case that might influence the success of various action alternatives' (Scott et al., 2005, p. 81).

Art interpretation requires that we learn to take notice of these hints; but it does not require definitive conclusions, sometimes merely the acknowledgements of possibilities. As with Murphy and Medin (1985), the idea here is that, rather than matching features in origin and target domains of mental spaces as I have shown with *Lever*, which suggests only the basic underlying processes of analogical thought, it is possible that entire strings of event structures and recalled phrases might be adapted to a new situation *intuitively*, based on the task at hand, improvisation, creative problem solving or a risk strategy. What is also involved is experimentalism, a trying on for size, a throw of the dice, a theoretical or hypothetical approach, which would require a making-do with materials – a *bricolage* – rather than an inflexible systematicity.

2.10 Metaphor and art

One of the more effortless ways in which we combine concepts, related to analogical processes, is the use of metaphor that brings together two seemingly incongruous entities and blends them to create emergent meaning. There has been much research in cognitive linguistics as to the psychological underpinnings of the use of metaphor and also much debate as to whether the underlying cognition is fundamentally embodied or more abstracted and recombinable in its linguistic complexity with only partial dependence on sensorimotor processing. Lakoff and Johnson (1980) believe that underlying the use of metaphor are image schemas that also determine our language more generally, as well as concepts and cultural forms.[1] On this view, an image schema is a kind of fundamental shape or form that is premised on how our bodies engage with our environment in terms of embodied actions (up, down, forward, backward, through, upon and inside). There are neural configurations, activated online or offline in our sensorimotor areas, that help us 'to grasp' concepts. For example, Johnson speaks of the abstract concept THEORY that he claims is often grasped by using concrete concepts such as BUILDING. A THEORY might have a foundation, supports, buttresses, a framework, it may be dismantled; the basic image schema is a block or rectangle that can be built *upon* or taken apart. A CATEGORY, meanwhile, is a CONTAINER with smaller objects *inside* it. As we can see, language is an elaboration of a neural circuit concerned with how we can use our bodies (grasp, touch, go up, down, through, inside). On this view, even complex moral concepts (to be MORALLY UPRIGHT/A FALL FROM GRACE) depend on metaphorical elaboration derived from body position and experience or projection of movement of limbs and positions in space. Lakoff (2006) has even attempted to show that certain visual artworks can be reduced to an image schema. For example, he analyses a picture of a mother and child by the artist Corot to show that its

---

[1] The problem of defining images schemas is, as Zlatev points out (2010), compounded by the problem that there is no agreement about these theoretical entities.

underlying image schema is 'containment', a sensorimotor enactment of an encircling of the arms. It might be assumed that contemporary and Minimalist artworks would similarly rely on Lakoff's 'embodied concepts', but this is too quick.

There are various critiques of Lakoff and Johnson's embodied approaches to cognitive linguistics and philosophy, such as by Haser (2005), Mandler (2010), Pinker (1997) and Zlatev (2010). The common thread running through these criticisms is that both authors over-inflate the importance of sensorimotor processes in the brain as the most important aspect of metaphor, while presenting over-simplified characterisations of traditional representationalism or linguistic complexity that do not depend on the exercise of sensorimotor areas. In Zlatev's critique (2010), cognitive linguistics of this kind is seen as lacking sensitivity to the complications of lived, phenomenal experience, reducing language and culture to a largely unconscious neural system, stressing the barest literal core of utterances traced to sensorimotor areas. The core component may have little to do with intended overall meaning, which might even be at odds with such a literal component taken out of context, or the core component may be intended ironically. Explaining sentences using sensorimotor image schema here would be misleading. Largely ignored are semantic interactions in social situations and many of the nuances of feelings, intentions and timing that contextualise utterances. In short, both Lakoff's and Johnson's understanding of embodiment reduces the richness of intersubjective and phenomenal experiences to mechanistic formal patterns based on an over-simplification of neural connectivity. Itkonen writes: 'For years now, leading representatives of theoretical linguistics have been arguing that humans, being guided by a blind "language instinct", can be described in physicobiological terms...this conception has been shown to be fundamentally false. Humans are also, and crucially, social, normative, and conscious beings' (2003, p. 151).

It is axiomatic that the use to which metaphor is put and the structure of metaphor itself are separate entities. In the former case, we may derive judgements as to whether the metaphor is appropriate. Importantly, the structure of the metaphor may also be judged to be successful or weak (or 'mixed'). In both cases, these evaluative processes can be associated with aesthetic judgement, distinct from the sensorimotor processes that might be stimulated by the metaphor. This is also a general point about aesthetic judgement, although it may be applied to perceptible qualities. The structure and reasoning of the judgement is not, in itself, perceptual process. Such judgements of style or taste involve interventions of cultural memory, rational inference, analogy, categorisation and, in many cases, specialist knowledge in many walks of life. Such standards may themselves be complex rules or superordinate concepts that need not rely on embodied processes of metaphor. Mixed metaphors, purple prose, the bringing together of various versions of metaphor or extended metaphor complicate the picture. Contemporary art – as well as poetry – is replete with examples of counter-intuitive and highly abstract uses of metaphor and extended metaphor. As I show in later pages, some artworks may be seen as using extended metaphors initiated by earlier artworks in order to 'extend' relational knowledge well beyond embodied metaphor.

Johnson writes that 'philosophies are built out of conceptual metaphors' (2008b, p. 51), which are all 'body-based' and 'truth is a matter of how our body-based understanding of a sentence fits or fails to fit our body-based understanding of a situation' (p. 45). Yet the concept of the body is problematic and open to different meanings. As a superordinate category, it can be given a whole host of concrete concepts to explain it, if one is to read the psychological, phenomenological and feminist literatures, yet Johnson continually appeals to one definition of the body in its biological sense, as if one body fits all.

Against Johnson, mention could be made of how concepts such as RELATIONSHIP or ORGANISATION are superordinate and may be grasped without experiencing concrete situations or metaphors. We do not have to characterise RELATIONSHIP using a metaphor at all to understand what it is. The concept DEMOCRACY will be understood very quickly in a sentence such as 'the adoption of such legislation assures democratic practice', where no metaphor is needed. In addition, understanding 'dead' metaphors that are familiar to us and do not need literal computation may be 'very much like understanding individual lexical items, via direct access' (Glucksberg, 2008, p. 9). Metaphorical action language, for example 'grasping a concept', need not activate sensorimotor areas any more than non-motoric language (Rüschmeyer et al., 2007). This amounts to a form of coding or compression that allows us to skip the 'embodied' sensorimotor acting out of metaphors in order to engage with the overall meaning of a complex sentence rather than dwelling on a literal metaphor enclosed within it.

In an fMRI study, Chatterjee et al. (2010b) contrasted spatial metaphors in sentences such as 'the man fell under her spell' with more concrete sentences, for example: 'the child fell under the slide'. They found greater activation in temporal areas and in the prefrontal cortex for spatial metaphors as compared to literal sentences. They conclude that temporal areas process motion in increasingly abstract ways, removed from perceptual networks (p. 100). Importantly, Mandler (2010), using arguments from empirical studies in developmental psychology, notes that spatial schemas do not have to involve sensorimotor input and suggests that spatial image schemas should remain distinct from motor image schemas and should not be treated as the same mental operation. Although we often do use sensorimotor information to grasp frequently used abstract, spatial concepts beyond sensorimotor-based situations, this information is not necessary and sufficient for such concepts.

Even our seemingly most embodied concepts – love, sex, the body, life, food – are extremely complex, some of them involving extended metaphors: a network of different kinds of metaphors, some of them 'weakly intended' (Sperber and Wilson, 2008). A metaphor stimulates a number of strong or unequivocal meanings, while those that are 'weakly intended' can do this with the addition of other implications creating polysemy or ambiguity, often used to explain 'poetic effects' by relevance theorists interested in metaphors in literature and everyday speech. Low (2008) laments that such theorists tend to focus on individual expressions in isolation, ignoring complex extended metaphor that can exist over whole texts. Another term for extended metaphor sustained by a whole text or body of works is 'mega metaphor' (Werth, 1999). An example is Umberto Eco's *Name of the Rose* that uses codes, manuscripts, libraries and reading as metaphors for aspects of knowledge and power, as well as referring neatly back to its own status as a book organised in chapters.

An 'overall account' of a corresponding visual artwork would not ponder an individual detail of a sensorimotor action (as Lakoff attempts with his analysis of Corot's mother and child, 2006), as much as the overall configural composition and its relation to other compositions, or postures in other artworks. This would enable viewers to judge influences, cultural traditions, the artist's knowledge of art and the study of older masters in order to gauge innovation and meaning that arise over and above the perceptual details. To appreciate such complexity and to be absorbed by it, we must learn not to fixate on single metaphors alone, or on the perceptible features of lexical or visual structures, but 'to see' the web of relations they indicate.

2.11 The structures of metaphor in art

Gentner and Bowdle's structure mapping of analogy (2008) has also been used to analyse metaphor. The authors show that the comprehension of metaphor works rapidly from early stages of 'blind' directionless comparisons to increasing direction and consistency in later stages with an interesting systematicity. Take, for example, the metaphorical phrase used as an example by the authors, which I analyse as follows:

> Patience is bitter, but its fruit is sweet
> M1   /   M2

If we divide the complex metaphor into two parts – patience is bitter = M1, but its fruit is sweet = M2 – we can see that a source domain is posited, PATIENCE, which is an abstract concept linked via a propositional relationship to a target domain, to a sensory or phenomenal concept of taste = bitter. This is already a very interesting juxtaposition of two different operations, a stored memory of what we know of an abstract concept, PATIENCE, mapped onto the phenomenal concept of bitter-tasting to yield: 'patience tastes bitter'; taste is being used for 'experience' and bitter for unpleasant. This first metaphor (M1) becomes a base or source for another metaphor, M2: the reward for waiting is a sweet fruit. REWARD is an abstract concept mapped onto the phenomenal concept of sweet-tasting.

The overall metaphor employs two nested metaphors (M1+M2), each with a source and target. The first metaphor is to be made into a source for the second, which becomes its target. In this way, the metaphor depends on a structural mapping not of concrete objects but of two corresponding or coupled relations: A is to B, and C is to D – but with a transformational and causal directionality whereby D 'grows' out of A, B and C. The complication is that fruit is, strictly speaking, a superordinate category. Thus, in one deceptively simple metaphor a number of different kinds of thoughts and relations are calculated rapidly. We may dwell on imagining the taste of bitterness or sweetness implied by the metaphor but SWEET is itself a metaphor for REWARD or PLEASANT.

Yet the automatic comparison of coupled relations would be primary in enabling us to understand a further twist, which I believe is fundamental to our accompanying judgement about the metaphor as an aesthetic experience. The unspoken of *Patience is bitter, but its fruit is sweet* is that PATIENCE IS A PLANT, it takes time to grow and to bear fruit. It is this aptness and implied meaning that makes the metaphor elegant, because waiting and growing are implied to be cooperative here, an implicit blending of two abstract concepts so that the first is transformed from a waiting state into waiting productively; that is, growing. However, added to this is a self-reflexive element: the relative complexity of the metaphor is worth the time of working it out to gain the subtleties of its meaning. In other words, the metaphor's complex structure, its form, not only implies its meaning but anticipates its effects; its full meaning takes time to unfold and then its outcome transforms everything before it into a felicitous phrase that began ominously.

Already, one can see that psychologists of metaphors often think in 'longhand', analysing a large number of diverse processes triggered by such metaphors that may be thought, read or spoken rapidly without any consciousness of how these diverse processes are related to each other. But only one part of this complex operation can be called 'embodied' as this has been understood, using arms, legs and eyes. The complex workings of the brain are also embodied. This complexity is, of course, also evident in even larger composites with intricate subroutines, such as those involved with extended metaphor and metalepsis. Before we advance to such complications, however, let me ask one important question at this juncture: Is there a visual equivalent of *Patience is bitter, but its fruit is sweet*, requiring similar mental operations and complexities?

Some psychologists show that there are serious problems with analysing pictorial or iconic images in terms of metaphor. Kennedy (2008) believes in the superiority of imageless thought for logical operations: 'Images stimulate thought but are not capable of being the actual engines of thought' (p. 459).[1] Yet Kennedy does accept that some pictures might work metaphorically, if we accept that many pictures try to communicate implicit understandings:

Picasso's powerful *Guernica* supplies objects of wartime, defenseless people, an eye in the sky and more. Many things make it metaphoric, including the eye in the sky.

---

[1] Kennedy cautions against too easy a slide from the textual to the pictorial and shows problems in comparing lexical metaphors to visual ones. The visual illustration of 'a really big hand'; 'falling in love'; 'burning desire' might not efficiently convey the ordinary sense of the metaphor. Irony as a purely pictorial example is also hard to show unless we have a title, text or some prior knowledge that creates the contrast between what we know and what appears to contradict it, so vital to irony. This ignores the importance of titles in contemporary art, however. Kennedy also states that when people claim that pictures are metaphoric, they mean this metaphorically (2008, p. 460).

The possible expansion would use all of these objects and possibly more. The form of the sentence [written metaphor] could well be "the wartime tragedy is a...". Agreed, the sentence is not in the picture. But the picture is a part of a communication, though the structure "the...is a..." is implicit (Kennedy, 2008, p. 460).

However, this ignores an important complication, that the visual arrangement of a painting can be 'read' in syntactically variable ways (from right to left, for example) to produce different implications. Moreover, what could also be invisible in art are not just the propositional contents designated by 'the...is a' but concepts that are implied 'outside of the frame': the bombing by the planes, the destruction on a mass scale of which the picture is a metonym. Visually, this is as automatic as the montage technique in film; we assume that a woman is looking at a painting of *Guernica* even if one frame shows a person with a sad expression launching her gaze at something outside of the frame and the next frame shows a full-screen shot of the painting. We do not need to see her head turned round, with body, head and nose directed at the painting, to see that she is looking at it, and we understand that this is what she is thinking about.[2]

It is this automatic recognition at the psychological root of metaphor that leads us to wonder if there is an equivalent automaticity in painting or sculpture. A great many contemporary art objects require that we interpret them quickly, often automatically, although sometimes after extended periods of voluntary and focused thought: a range of early to late processes that employ analogy, inference, comparison and categorisation, often although not exclusively, without any recourse to words (even when artworks contain them). Art's 'metaphors' are rarely too wordy, yet they may be laboured. Their meanings are understood intuitively in many cases, without the need to translate them into their verbal equivalents. When we see, for example, Mimi Parent's *Maîtresse (Mistress)*, 1996, we see a whip, its lash fashioned into two plaits of hair. We do not process 'the whip is like plaits of hair' (a simile), nor do we need to think of the whip's plaits, because to do so would be perfunctory. We are likely to rehearse grasping actions and swishing sounds, yet these hardly exhaust the uses to which the artwork can be put.

We have, by now, understood the metaphor (which could also be read as a metonym or a personification), so the exact description is immaterial, for we do not translate the lightning action of visual experience into words. The instantaneous visual appeal makes linguistic processing superfluous,

---

[2] Compare this with the fact that understanding 'occurs automatically without conscious control' (Johnson-Laird and Miller, 1976, p. 66); and 'linguistic input automatically triggers semantic analyses' (Glucksberg paraphrasing Fodor, 2008, p. 69).

Figure 20. Mimi Parent, *Maîtresse (Mistress)*, 1996. Collection Mony Vibescu: courtesy of Alain Kahn-Sriber. Image: courtesy of Manchester City Galleries.

and there are all sorts of other, more weakly intended meanings that are suggested, equally wordless and instant, in our silent encounter with the art object. Yet one must put this lightning visual processing into words if one is to try and communicate something of the nature of thought. The girl's plaits imply a particular abject kind of embodiment, suggested by scalping, yet this is contradicted by the fact that, as a whip, the object is also capable of being used as a weapon against this kind of softening empathy. This fits neatly with the sadomasochistic implications of the piece. As always, the assisted readymade splits meaning or fuses two or three instantly identified objects or parts of objects together as one object. It is this visual process that I am suggesting depends on the underlying psychology of metaphor studied in the psychology of language. Furthermore, assisted or altered readymades reference the larger art movements that made them famous, Dada and Surrealism, which adopted them to achieve instabilities in meanings and new ways of creating them. They bring to mind dream objects, using what was thought to be a way of reproducing Freudian condensation (a compression of significations attached to tokens or objects in dreams that could be 'unpacked' when translated into words in the waking state, demonstrating their density of meanings). Yet, even in our waking state, lexical metaphors are condensed. If we were to dwell on sensorimotor understandings of some words, our computation of complex sentences would be slowed down considerably. If our inspection of art images depends on a lightning recognition, a kind of compression must also be present here.

I have already examined the 'visual mechanics' of Oppenheim's *Lunch in Fur*. In another example of Oppenheim's work, *Ma Gouvernante/My Nurse*, 1936, the artist ties together two white shoes with used soles turned upwards for display, placed on a silver food tray. Oppenheim put chicken leg frills on the stiletto heels, almost as if to dress the rudeness of their bare protrusions. Metaphors abound: shoes are chicken breasts, feasting is sexual, the shoes' freedom of movement, the bondage suggested by the strings – all these interpretations are instant and wordless in the visual encounter. However, it is possible to add to the visual communication numerous texts and words that frame our experience of the work. Oppenheim wrote that the idea this readymade evoked is 'thighs squeezed together in pleasure'. The fact that the shoes are turned up so we can see the soles reminds us of what it must be like to see them from underneath, perhaps catching the nurse with her lover, *indelicto flagrante*, or inspecting her corpse on an operating table; a typical Surrealist device of juxtaposing sex and death, or sex and food. The titles of both Mimi Parent's work, *Maîtresse*, and Oppenheim's *Ma Gouvernante* have already primed trains of thought about absent female figures of authority, an absence for which

Figure 21. Meret Oppenheim, *Ma gouvernante – My Nurse – Mein Kindermädchen*, 1936–1937 Photograph by Moderna Museet, Stockholm. © DACS 2012.

the objects substitute in ways that bring to mind the mechanics of the fetish. There is also some word play: *Maîtresse* brings to mind both the humiliating status of being a mistress and also the sexual role play of dominant woman with a whip. The associations arise also with '*ma tresse*'/tress/mattress, and invest the object with the dreamlike ability to metamorphose. Thus, although bereft of words and much like dreams, visual imagery can trigger a spreading semantics of puns and wordplay as we experience in dreams.

There is also important contextual information: it is reported that, in a rage after discovering her husband's infidelity, Mimi Parent cut off her own 'tresses' in order to create the work. This kind of contextual knowledge always adds layers of meaning to our experience of contemporary art. Such objects depend on dragging knowledge of some event into the gallery space, into the art object itself, which the object is seen to document. The cutting of hair is a feminist trope. Frida Kahlo's well-known self-portrait showing her seated among shorn locks of her hair snaking the floor was painted in 1940 shortly after divorcing Diego Rivera. We have also seen the use of hair in many of Mona Hatoum's works, with *Keffiyeh* and in *Pull*, 1995, where one is invited to pull a plait to see how it affects the image of the artist opening her mouth in surprise on the screen. In many cultural traditions, the shaving of heads can mark mourning; it denotes humiliation, it compromises identity or strength, at least in the story of Samson and Delilah. This artwork seems to be a counterfactual imagination of the biblical story, with the man in the role of betraying the woman in Mimi Parent's case. The presence of the artist's hair, fashioning part of the artist's body into an art object, is another trope that has travelled from the traditional cultural signifier of a lock of hair (a lover's sample of hair to remember them by) to Adrian Piper's hair and nails saved in glass containers: *What will become of me?*, 1976, and *Loving Care*, 1992–1996, a video of a performance by Janine Antoni, who mops the floor with black dye in her hair to parody action painting and housework, creativity and chores.

Furthermore, Mimi Parent's careful plaiting of the hair is a 'parting' of ways. At first blush, it seems comical and after reflection, rent with sensations of anger, mourning, pain, while ironically referring to the pleasures of sadomasochism. The artwork is also framed in such a way (with a brass tag nailed to it) that it suggests something of a hunting trophy pinned to a wall mount, referencing the husband's 'conquests'. In addition, we have the skinning of an animal, the harsh detachment of a body part (two plaits associated with a young girl), as a metaphor for detaching a husband or wife from one's affections.

So, all together, Mimi Parent's *Maîtresse* deftly balances multimodal sensations (the softness of hair, the stinging lash of a whip), strong emotions or rejection, cruelty, anger and self-hurt with the callousness of hunting, humour and irony, shared with analogies referring to Oppenheim's and Kahlo's work, with which it forms an alternative feminist art history, as well as nudging towards the fairytale of Rapunzel and the biblical story of Samson and Delilah, which it reverses. It also engages with word puns, flirts with sadomasochism and the fetish, and serves as a document of an act and a monument to a betrayal, yet as a trophy, it suggests a male possession or something that could be used by a man or a woman.

Put into diagrammatic form, one can begin to appreciate the psychological complexity of the art encounter, much of it wordless, some of it systematic without referencing the body, some of it referencing the body and sensations of pain and betrayal, or role-play involved with wielding a whip and projecting power and subjugation, and some of it engaged in word play. Note that the aspects of embodied concepts referring to the body or sensations and the word play are only part of a densely patterned and textured art experience. There is also a series of associations that we bring to the art experience that nuances meaning and provides us with a fascination built upon a kind of inter-repulsion of concepts. In other words, the marshalling together of concepts and sensations during our experience of artworks is not always to be seen as harmonious. It is often contradictory, as are the artist's feelings of loss and betrayal mixed in with anger and creativity: both her execution of the artwork and her thinking it through are a kind of therapy that is also available to us.

Many kinds of mental operations are involved in a typical art experience. Mimi Parent's *Maîtresse* shows us that to isolate metaphors, as many theorists do, in order to make grand claims about how they structure complex meaning can only really deliver a partial view of a much more detailed and complex process of meaning creation. These cooperate and blend in some cases to become composite entities in order to generate new meaning on the fly. An important point here is that art and literature tend to avoid conventional uses of metaphor or analogy, almost as an implicit *raison d'être*: the innovation or elaboration of conventions seems to be consistent in many examples. Gentner and Bowdle maintain that 'a metaphor undergoes a process of gradual abstraction and conventionalization as it evolves from its first novel use to becoming a conventional "stock" metaphor' (2008, p. 116). They maintain that there are two strategies of comprehension: comparison of source and target terms through structure mapping, which usually happens in novel situations, and in more conventional cases (dead metaphors, for example), source and target are processed using categorisation. This might involve using the source as a category in which the target term fits, or using the whole metaphor in a more complex construction, in metalepsis, for example. In such cases of categorisation, these stock expressions 'have stable non-literal meanings that can be accessed directly without needing to be derived anew' (p. 117).

Conventionalisation will mean that active interpretation of a metaphor's meaning will be suspended for retrieval of stored meanings (Gentner and Bowdle, 2008, p. 117), presumably in order to create more complex meanings that are the result of new categories and blends. Against the stock sensorimotor and embodied responses, these cases show that one does not always process such metaphors extempore in terms of acting them out using gross body movements or mirror neurons, which would amount to a literal interpretation of the metaphor.[3] It is interesting that in none of the examples given here, where I have examined

---

[3] There is some disagreement between theorists as to how categorisation and comparison occur and in which circumstances; see Glucksberg (2008) and Gentner and Bowdle (2008) for overviews with different emphases. Gentner and Bowdle's career as metaphor

Oppenheim's and Mimi Parent's works and the system of analogies they imply, are conventional metaphors employed. Yet it is also equally true for both artists' works that literal and sensorimotor responses are disseminated among a plethora of other strongly or weakly intended meanings. In both cases, it is almost as if our 'natural' categorical processes *and* comparative processes come under scrutiny as part of the theme or demonstration the art object is intended to convey. Thus, in terms of comparison, we are forced to conclude that the artwork is a kind of visual and material metaphor for 'plaits are whips' although, conceivably, it could be used as an actual whip upon which, presumably, its metaphorical status might magically disappear. The problem here, though, is that if we insist on calling it art, and framing it, as Mimi Parent has done, then its metaphorical status reappears.

The categorical process arising from Mimi Parent's *Maîtresse* might be *my cut plaits are an artistic medium*, which would invite us to form a novel class inclusion assertion: the conventions governing what art uses for its materials and processes, or what actually counts as art, can now include cutting one's hair or plaiting them and affixing them to a handle to create art. As in many cases, novel class inclusions can allow us to experiment with important abstract concepts, such as 'art' or 'medium', which could involve new cultural understandings. It is interesting that Mimi Parent's use of human hair in the art object is an actual, demonstrated fact, rather than simply a metaphor, although its metaphorical sense can be retained while rephrasing the artwork as *an artist's paintbrushes are her plaits*, which invites us to think metaphorically about how an artist's tools are an extension of her body. The advantages of doing so seem to allow us the pleasure of imagining a more personal and poetic connection that the artist might have to her art and to her tools, a connection that does not seem to be a ploddingly literal description of a fact. Although this could also be true if we recall the artist Janine Antoni painting with her hair, as a parody of masculine abstract expressionism. Hence, in both cases, we can see the artwork or its performance as factual and innovative in changing the categories of 'art' and 'medium'. In Parent's work, the inclusion of plaits and whips suggests radically different tools for art's facture as well as forming the material substrate of the artwork, yet there is also an artistic process involved with the metaphorical association of hair with paintbrushes. This may be intimated visually without words but is strengthened

theory assumes that novel metaphors are understood through the process of comparison and structure mapping and conventional metaphors through the process of category inclusion. Glucksberg, meanwhile, doubts that novelty is the deciding factor and, instead, supports the view that considerations of aptness decide which process is adopted: 'Different metaphors will have different careers' (p. 79).

by later lexical elaboration and acknowledgement, which the artwork might imply but certainly does not state. What it does state lexically is '*maîtresse*' as a title on a metal label, affixed to the artwork. This may suggest that, like the plaited whip, a mistress is another kind of tool or trophy displayed in a museum. This mechanism is premised on the interplay of words and images that combine to create interesting metaphorical possibilities dependent on conflict, contrast, comparison, integration and blending processes. A kind of equivocation allows the metaphor of '*my plaits are whips*' (for pleasure or punishment suggested by *maîtresse*) to be sustained while also retaining a notion that the artist is literally in earnest, a facticity to which art is loath to commit wholly, lest it be accused of being blunt, or worse, didactic.

What is clear is that, involved in the interpretation of such a complex work, both processes of categorisation and comparison are evident with significant amounts of unresolved play between literal and figurative meanings. My analysis of Mimi Parent's work brings into view another consideration that taking the time to think about the consequences of a metaphor or its visual art equivalent can lead to important innovations in categories (*plaited hair is an artistic medium*) while, at the same time, *plaits are whips* or *plaits are paintbrushes* manage to preserve the poetic benefits of figuration. It seems important that we recognise, however, that the artwork is a materialisation of metaphor. When we look at Mimi Parent's artwork, which activates a creative equivocation, we can see it in different ways: 'seeing as' as a category innovation for art, or 'seeing as' as a poetic image. However, this 'seeing as' most probably does not entail the suggestion that our categorical or comparative processes should be put into words, which would distinguish each process clearly.

What is also evident is the achievement of the artist: with quite simple means, she has managed to stimulate a number of associations and an awareness – a pleasurable awareness – of how this is brought about. We might enjoy something similar while watching a puppet show; even though we can see the strings, the puppeteer manages to allow us a glimpse of the puppet's life, while revealing her own dexterity and expressive power.

Visual art and poetry thus may function in ways that make us aware of our relatively automatic or conventional processing of metaphors, sometimes by parodying it or, in the case of the readymade, by objectifying it as a simple tool for novel and more highly abstract processes of thought involving the creation of new categories. Thus, art encourages us to participate in novel meaning creation, often by allowing us to step outside the subpersonal use of conventional metaphors, which suggests a lack of agency. In this respect, feelings of involvement or absorption in the artwork may be the result of experiencing novel relationships between concepts (categorisation and integrations) or novel comparisons of the attributes of concepts.[4] The artwork 'comes alive' for us when we feel that we play a part in meaning creation while attending to it, and this feeling can be activated when we attempt novel conceptual integration of which metaphors are a type.

---

[4] This reflects some of what Gentner and Bowdle presumably mean when they state that structure mapping may involve 'matching nodes at any level of structure, from higher-order relations to concrete perceptual attributes' (2008, p. 124).

Part III

Body

3.1 Embodied approaches to art

Conceptual elaboration, like language, is not a private matter, a point that could be supported further by Wittgenstein's well-known arguments against private language. Many examples of contemporary artworks allow us to see how relational knowledge can also be shared and it is thus not a purely mentalistic, internalist system. It is the body that allows us to be physically situated in the world, and to combine internal and external resources effortlessly and fluidly. 'Embodied' approaches in psychology, philosophy and art emphasise the role of the body in constituting thought, even highly abstract thought. In this section, I review the literature and evaluate its importance for our understanding of contemporary art.

I have already presented many arguments from empirical studies that question extreme sensorimotor chauvinism (Chatterjee 2010b; Machery 2007; Mahon and Caramazza, 2008). Most of these studies show an important appreciation of sensorimotor processes in cognition but they also reveal the most objectionable aspect of Johnson's approach (2008a), which is to divide the world into pragmatists and representationalists, ignoring a middle path that allows for representational pluralism (de Bruin and Kästner, 2011; Dove, 2009). Yet even those who are keen on arguing for the primacy of perceptual and sensorimotor processes in conceptual thought (Barsalou, 2009; Damasio, 1995; Simmons and Barsalou, 2003) accept that 'convergence zones' involve many other brain areas outside of sensorimotor processes and are responsible for very important cognitive functions. In previous chapters I have discussed how contemporary artworks draw upon semantic and linguistic processing of the anterior temporal lobes as well as parahippocampal areas for personal memory. Drawing upon the work of Chatterjee (2010b), Fuster (2003) and others, I have shown how the prefrontal cortex is emerging as a very important area of research into the complexity of organising long-term goals, self-monitoring (Christoff et al., 2009a) and decision making, when the prefrontal cortex resolves attentional conflicts and helps to bring about rule-oriented behaviour.

I have returned continually to examples of relational knowledge that organises large groups of concepts into systems. These cannot be fixed to precise sensorimotor contingencies, especially if we take an overall view of their complexity. Like many contemporary artworks, such relational knowledge systematically attempts to parody and re-categorise such processes for rich ambiguities of exploratory experience, reflection and social exchange. To suggest that the whole conceptual system of both abstract and concrete concepts involved in experiencing an artwork such as Tracey Emin's *My Bed* or Matthew Barney's baroque and densely topographical *Cremaster Cycle* is to be explained by analysing sensorimotor processes would also clearly be wrong. We might explicitly draw upon embodied metaphors or image schemas to explain, for example, the desire to travel to the moon, the sense of what is right, the feeling of who I am or what features of contemporary art make it contemporary. It does not follow that the *meanings* of these examples are the same as how we explain them using figures of speech that, when taken literally, imply sensorimotor processes. As Chatterjee states, 'the claim that motor simulation *determines* or is a *core attribute* of the understanding of actions is quite different than the claim that our *experience* of actions influences how we understand those actions' (2010b, p. 90).

Johnson argues that the meaning of art is intrinsically connected to the body: 'Human thinking is a continuous feeling-thinking process that is forever tied to our body's monitoring of its own states' (2008a, p. 98) and abstract concepts are grasped by our sense of being embodied. Our language and art making is dominated by conceptual metaphors and image schemas that are expressions of bodily sensations and projections. He writes: 'Many philosophers are reluctant to extend embodiment to all meaning. They are captivated by the dream of a pristine language – a language carefully defined by its literal concepts free from the alleged taint of bodily processes' (p. 221).

What are the consequences of this approach for understanding something more complex than metaphors, but which skilfully employs many of them, such as poetry? Johnson analyses Neruda's poem, *Gentlemen*

Without Company. I will take only a small section of the poem to discuss Johnson's treatment of it.

> The homosexual men and the love-mad girls,
> and the long widows who suffer from a delirious inability to
>   sleep,
> and the young wives who have been pregnant for thirty hours,
> and the hoarse cats that cross my garden in the dark,
> these, like a necklace of throbbing oysters,
> surround my solitary house, like enemies set up against my
>   soul,
> like members of a conspiracy dressed in sleeping costumes,
> who give each other as passwords long and profound kisses.

Johnson states: 'Neruda does not merely develop its theme conceptually, in the thin air of intellectual connections. Rather, it digs down into. . .the implicit meaning of a situation and lets itself be carried forward by the palpable images, rhythms, and contours of felt experience' (2008a, p. 220); and the 'necklace of throbbing sexual oysters' is something Johnson hesitates to explain, 'for fear of diminishing its incarnate realisation of sexual longing'. The poem is a 'tsunami of felt images. . .a squirming mass of sexual eroticism'. The problem with these phrases is that they purport to bring out simple embodied realities but are, in fact, words which betray a complex conceptual elaboration. This involves theories of a 'thin air of intellectual connections' (which refers to the common definition that abstract concepts are intangible and imperceptible), which is contrasted to 'digging down' (using imagery of the solid earth and embodied, concrete concepts). Furthermore, this metaphor is extended to suggest the concept of incarnation. It is unfortunate that Johnson actually acknowledges the conceptual development of the poem but chooses to ignore this for what he sees is its grounding in sensorimotor contingencies. The point is, however, that even Johnson's own embodied interpretation of the poem is based on quite complex abstract concepts that cannot be understood simply by appealing to sensorimotor processes.

To leave the complex meaning of Neruda's poem languishing at the level of throbbing embodiment here would be a travesty of the secreted pearls (the poet's 'pearls of wisdom'), which are absent from the poem but suggested by the oysters surrounding a solitary house, the place of self and identity where the poet himself resides. With this, we encounter concepts to do with marine fecundity and sexuality, the mother-of-pearl, oyster, an aphrodisiac; but does the necklace of oysters, the image–embodiment of the poem and its pulsating verse, bottle up or release sexual desire? If the world is the poet's oyster, does it contain or open up desire? It is not clear, and this is because desire, like the body, captures and enslaves, as well as offers us the hope of freedom and escape, sensuous experiment and liberation. Johnson's interpretation, fixated on the body, squanders this rich ambiguity. However, it also tells us much about embodied theories of art: that they are too polemical and fall too heavily on the side of body consciousness and *body imagery* as explanatory strategies for the deliberate polysemy of art.[1] In this verse, and in much of poetry, there is a tension between the body experienced as arms and legs, head and torso, skull and skin, and sexual eroticism *and* our escape from its circuitous pleasures and functions, by dreaming of other embodiments in the world besides ours (cats and oysters, for example), which may yield other meanings. These non-human embodiments, surreal and uneasy, may promise us the use of our bodily sensations, suggesting a libidinous encirclement, but they also free us from the *sensus litteralis* of this impoverished interpretation. If all poetry or art were intended as Johnson supposes, we would soon tire of it because it would continue to keep referencing the same thing: the body.

Self-reflexive consciousness will address, and a prereflective kind of consciousness will simply presume a functioning body witnessing art, yet the art itself is often primed with its representations to remind us of such a body and its functions. The embodied approach is a valuable strategy against the notion of the 'inner chamber' of the mind, disconnected from the body, with its abstract propositional symbols codifying thought. However, foisting a human body schema upon animals and anthropomorphising inanimate objects is only one simple way to respond to a poem. It is taken for granted that sensorimotor processes not only produce patterns in poems and paintings but that these art forms also produce sensorimotor patterns in us. It seems that this circularity is all there is to this approach to art. Yet, the poem could as easily be read as a skilful engineering of over-abundance that suggests entropy. Neruda's poem is not simply first and foremost an attempt to entrench sensorimotor processes, a repeated listing of the same obvious eroticism, but is a strategy to destabilise the automaticity of such visceral responses as the foundation of knowledge, an ideological literary interpretation veiled as natural and evolutionary.

One can look at the early and middle parts of the poem that deal with arousal and delirious peaks of energy, and then the poem's images begin to suggest unattractive and unhealthy undertones: 'and he strokes her legs sheathed in their sweet down with his warm hands that smell of cigarettes. . .the bees have an odor of blood, and the flies buzz in

---

[1] Lakoff and Johnson might insist that the imagery of the necklace confirms their 'containment' image schema, but this hardly helps us to appreciate the complex set of mythopoetic concepts that spring from the image of the necklace of oysters.

anger'. Johnson only seems to take away with him the sex, yet the abiding value is bittersweet, as we become conscious of our gut reactions and sensations as inadequate. To be fair, Johnson mentions 'troubling images' and themes to do with frustration and being smothered by sexuality, complex concepts that are equally if not more central to the meaning of the poem, yet are not satisfactorily characterised in terms of sensorimotor experience, which is perhaps why they are treated as if they are of no consequence. For Johnson, the real meaning of the poem is the immediate arousal of visceral responses. For others, these are effects employed for a longer-term conceptual strategy: to get to the meaning of the poem.[2]

Besides the many references to how eroticism also turns ugly or suffocating, at the end of the poem Neruda reaches beyond his elegant descriptions of unthinking impulses and encounters, to the end of all sensorimotor activation and towards abstract concepts of death (a concept that is not disembodied, just differently embodied beyond the reach of sensorimotor experience). The poet's obsessive-compulsive images begin to fall from their high beds to a grave encircled by flowers 'like mouths and rows of teeth' threatening to swallow up the poet and his words forever:

> and still more, the adulterers, who love each other with
>   a true love
> of beds high and huge as ocean liners,
> this immense forest, entangled and breathing,
> hedges me around firmly on all sides forever
> with huge flowers like mouths and rows of teeth
> and black roots that look like fingernails and shoes.

What Neruda communicates to us is that, although we are trapped by our urges and carnal desires, and by the limits of our embodiment, these things also provide the inspiration for a poetic imagination that is not only a sublimation of sorts but is also a vitally important improvisation over the sensuous scaffold of poetry. Neruda's gallery of images serves to illustrate a life cycle from unthinking simple pleasures to a dawning self-awareness, and thence to a moral decay, which leads to the contemplation of death.

Sensorimotor and embodied explanations of meaning have their place. They remind us that we are embodied in a strong sense and that this is

---

[2] Thus Johnson writes that 'In poetry and prose, there is much meaning beneath and beyond concepts and propositions. In the visual arts, it is images, patterns, qualities, colors, and perceptual rhythms that are the bearers of meaning' (2008a, p.234). Yet one could equally and justifiably reverse the formula and claim that beneath the bearers of meaning there is conceptual content. However, it is, in fact, wiser to claim that both conceptual and perceptual aspects cooperate to produce meaning.

crucially important in understanding the urges and drives of our mental life connected to poetry and art. However, just as it would be wrong to suggest that poetry is all disembodied intellectualism, we should not claim that a heightened awareness of the sensorimotor engagement is the *raison d'être* of art and art criticism. It is one thing to point to our embodied functions involved in our experience of art, but descriptions of sensorimotor responses should not be confused with literary criticism. They may be an important part of it; but poetry and art also have the power to jolt us out of our sensorimotor expectations in a process of active and creative conceptual complexity, providing self-reflection on life, ethics, emotion and human nature, which should not be confused with the sensory tools used to help us explore these difficult concepts.

Perhaps the biggest problem with embodied interpretations of art is that they often do away with a huge amount of diversity when it comes to experiencing, imagining and interpreting it. Art invites us to imagine greater feats than the discovery of a poem's hidden sexual organs and ejaculate – an approach that is similar to the worst excesses of reductionist kinds of psychoanalytical interpretations of art that see penis envy and Oedipus complexes around every corner. Art can be expansive, enabling us to go beyond the circularity of finding 'our' embodiment through art, which, it is supposed, we are neurologically primed to find. With effort in the pursuit of meaning, we can go beyond the self-evident to imagine differently abled, gendered and aged bodies and even ones transfigured into the stars. The imagination is not limited to body references or themes, or bound tightly with a fidelity to sensorimotor processes and an anthropocentric view of nature or even to normative assumptions of what the human body is capable of, or should be. As Chrisley and Ziemke (2003) state, there is a lack of coherence in what various people mean by 'embodiment'; all they seem to have in common is their rejection of a (simplistic characterisation of) classical representational cognitive science.

It is true, as Johnson proposes, that the old formalism of traditional art may be characterised as an attempt to divest sensuous and embodied experience from idealised disembodied judgements of beauty and form (Kant's disinterestedness). Both Lakoff and Johnson's formalist understanding of cultural objects and their emphasis on the importance of image schemas in metaphor, however, create an 'embodied formalism' that goes against the grain of many conceptual artworks. There is also the problem that this embodiment is assumed to be primarily neutral and universal, veiling ideological presuppositions of normative embodiment. It must be noted that most of Johnson's arguments for embodiment, his characterisation of Neruda and the universality of this experience

illustrate a particularly masculine embodiment. The answer to universalising formalism in contemporary art has been to reject the opticality of
formalism as a claim to truths self-evident to all, by developing artworks
that are anti-formalist or conceptual and based on different kinds of
bodies. More particularly, against embodied formalism we should look
to the many contemporary artworks that show embodiment – and, by
extension, formalism – to be highly contingent and mediated by the
specificities of gender, sexual orientation and ethnicity, which question
universalising (yet strangely masculine) claims for a 'standard' or normative embodied language and visual art.

3.2   Phenomenological approaches in art history

> Ours is a culture based on excess, on overproduction; the result is a
> steady loss of sharpness in our sensory experience...What is important
> now is to recover our senses. We must learn to see more, to hear more,
> to feel more...Our task is to cut back content so that we can see the thing
> at all.   (Sontag, 1995, p. 222)

Sontag's influential essay makes a plea that can be read in a number of
ways: as a somewhat naïve attempt to achieve a *tabula rasa*, an erasure of
acculturations for an ideal state of embodied sensory 'truth', or as an
attempt to escape the corrupting power structures of language (even
though the plea she makes is itself polemical and highly conceptual).
Theorists of embodiment (Merleau-Ponty's phenomenology, in particular) were popular among artists such as Donald Judd and Robert Morris
in the 1960s who aimed to escape purely optical experiences in the
Greenbergian tradition. Art history in later years continued this trend
(Jones, 1998; Krauss, 1981; Michelson, 1969; Potts, 2000). It is important, however, to note that in this period the controversy surrounding the
debate over the relevance of phenomenology to art was based on a number
of assumptions about the psychology of art that continue to influence art
historical approaches today. An interesting remark by Vickery (2003), for
example, claims that Minimalist art redefined modernism 'as a quasi-
science of practical phenomenology' (p. 127).

While Robert Morris defended the new Minimalist sculpture (works
such as Carl Andre's *Lever*) as a way to reflect on the structures of
perception espousing gestalt principles, Michael Fried (1967) attacked
such artworks as being virtually indistinguishable from brute objecthood
which, given its scale and dominance in the gallery space, forced the
viewing subject into a self-awareness of her own body with regard to the
art object. In fact, many defences of Minimalism make this last point one
of its virtues. For Fried, such art created a 'theatricality of objecthood',
preventing cognitive activity that it was art's duty to provide in contra-
distinction to the cognition available in ordinary life. Minimalist sculptures, he argued, were an empty shell of perception without such content.

Fried condemned the mundane 'presence' of this 'literal art' and with his mentor, Stanley Cavell, valorised the 'presentness' of modernist art as a cognitive engagement beyond the self-evidence and solipsism of perception. Modernist art, instead, was supposed to move us, to provide special cases of objects that we invest with value, find absorbing and treat with respect, as we would other people, providing an exchange between two entities.[1] On this view, the profundity of an encounter with otherness is not possible with Minimalism and phenomenology, which merely provides perceptual experiences of oneself. In addition, modernism was defined by Fried (1967) and by Cavell (1994) as continually creating a new vocabulary by which to make viewers think, and as a critique of traditional art and its conventions.

Both the defence of the phenomenology of art and Fried's attack on it are essentialist and tend to oversimplify. Perhaps one of the weak points of Fried's argument, and also something that is overlooked by those supporting Minimalism, is that in many ways the formal, historical and cognitive strengths of modernist art were continued, not abandoned, by Minimalist art (a point made by Hal Foster, 1996). It could be said that Minimalist art achieved a new vocabulary by which to construct meaning, as did Pop Art. Minimalist art, as well as many contemporary immersive artworks that engage with Minimalism's principles in different ways, should benefit from blending some of Fried's axiological arguments about the efficacy of modernism with a weaker sensorimotor phenomenological explanation of Minimalism. As we have seen in my earlier analysis of Carl Andre's *Lever* with regard to analogical thought, the work invites phenomenal qualities, experiences of embodiment *and* phenomenological analysis of these, along with relational knowledge of modernist art.

As I have been arguing throughout this book, sensory perceptions of artworks rarely, if ever, occur in isolation and are accompanied by conceptual analysis, emotions and memories that help create a range of different qualities of experience. It would not be correct simply to refer to this range of engagements as 'embodied'. It goes without saying that the body, in cooperation with the environment, is the medium for these different aspects of experience, yet it need not be characterised first and foremost as a sensory body; it is also a conceptual body that moves in and around the environment in a conceptual as well as a sensory exploration. The following is an analysis of a 'classic' Minimalist artwork that has been considered most often in phenomenological terms, but I aim to show that corporeal motor movements and sensory engagements with artworks are

---

[1] For an excellent summary of this topic, see Vickery (2003).

Figure 22. Anthony Caro, *Early One Morning*, 1962. Barford Sculptures Ltd. © Tate, London 2012.

also intertwined with conceptual knowledge in a mutually reinforcing relationship.

In the same year as Sontag's plea for the primacy of sensory experience, the sculptor Antony Caro completed his *Early One Morning*, 1962. Depending on how one approaches it, one is halted by a large metal cross painted red at one end, and a large square sheet of flat metal, held upright (much like a road sign or blackboard, although also painted red) at the other. Connecting the two ends is a long metal bar about twenty feet long, held over the floor about the normal height of where a lorry chassis might be, and there are two curious little metal stools towards the 'blackboard' end, propping up another flat metal sheet, reminding one of a bed or two pupils sitting in a classroom. This is just below the 'blackboard'. There is also another horizontal, flat plate propped up by the bar. In a gallery space, it seems to invite us to walk alongside it, or at least we imagine how long it would take to do so; and all of this taken in with one glance.

From a child's perspective given its dwarfing scale, it seems like a climbing frame to play on, with smaller and thinner metal bars sticking out diagonally to break the strict verticality and horizontality. The sculpture is also tall. One walks around it, puzzled, trying to understand its use, as one would try to understand a machine or a tool, how it works, how it is to be used. We understand it in terms of the mechanics of action, weight and counterweight, enclosed spaces and open spaces, hard edges and corners, nuts and bolts, bars and metal plates, corners and joints, and in terms of direction. Its function cannot be discerned readily because it is not built to manufacture anything obvious and it does not seem capable of moving; in that sense it seems to be a disused tool, a museum remnant from a golden age of agriculture no longer needed. Its mechanical appearance, however, also suggests an architectural built environment. Hence, the conceptual blend between machine and room produces the impression of the skeleton form of some kind of vehicle. However, this blend is based both on highly cultural traditions of reading structures and how to project one's body inside these different traditions accordingly. At the same time, our movement in and around and imaginatively through and above the structure drives further cultural and imaginary concepts. One wonders whether this is an old or new way of contemplating what a sculpture is or can be.

The sculpture's crossbars mark its length and breadth, suggesting intervals, a rhythm and a sense of time, which we mark or it seems to mark with our physical inspection of it. This is complicated by the experience of reading about Caro's work in the art historian Rosalind Krauss' text, which includes an image of Caro's work. The text may also be punctuated by stops and starts, certain temporal intervals that may be integrated with the visual inspection of the sculpture (the reading becoming a somewhat 'diaphanous' experience that 'frames' the visual inspection). In such a case, the time-based metaphors of the text ('intervals') affect the visual flow of the optical experience: metaphor making here is both spatial (inspecting the image) and semantic (linguistic processing), with different amounts of multisensory processing also in play.

As we walk around it, or imagine doing so with various mental rotations, it seems to change shape and the vertical and horizontal lines slowly converge into different patterns and configurations. Our movements around the sculpture seem to compose it, bringing different aspects of the sculpture into view, which is also a form of active interpretation, helping to assemble and disassemble our overall sense of the sculpture's three-dimensionality, a case of juggling attentional foci. Such an embodied involvement with the sculpture makes us conscious of our bodies locked in a cooperative dance-like encounter, where the sculpture seems to move with us or wrap itself around us. The artist himself referred to it as a kind of dance and the title of the work is a song. We are conscious of our depth perception (we can see through it and the parts furthest away from us seem smaller than they did when we were at that end). Our body position creates a different sculptural form, our walking helps to create different sculptural relations and a sense of past moments that contain different compositional relationships.

What are some of these compositions? Viewed from the side, the sculpture invites us to become intimate with it, walking alongside it. Although it towers over us, the way in which it is divided up seems familiar, like an architectural plan. It seems to remind us of the frame of a house or a room, the large vertical plate at one end could be a wall, the flat sections before it, a bed, the cross at the other end, a window, and the bits in between, furniture. The sculpture, seen from the conceptual view of architectural space seems like an abstracted form of a bedroom on the ground floor. Referring to this sculpture and applying a phenomenological understanding of art, Rosalind Krauss wrote that one is reminded of its bars and parts as 'a post-and-beam system that is common to most of our built environment' (1981, p. 188). I seem to be able to fit into its spaces coherently if I imagine these spaces to indicate rooms as we might expect reading a blueprint. Moreover, this proposition seems to fit quite nicely with the sculpture's title, *Early One Morning*. Notice that this interpretation is based on imagining the body in the extended opened out spaces that the sculpture and its measurements, vertical plane, and horizontal divisions and intervals seems to suggest, and we respond in intuitive ways to its orientation. The sculpture's lines and spaces force us to read it in particular ways to do with tool use, habitation and time, enclosed (halted) and open (fluid) space. It references the body's scale and its ability to walk, to lie down, to stand upright. We become a measure for its scale and it becomes a measure for our experience of the work that is intimately bound up with the capabilities and projections of our bodies, but understood as a normative body.

This perceptual awareness is accompanied by intuitions of passing time; time seems to unfold in experience and space. Within what we perceive in the immediate present is a retention of perceptions just past, and this retention in the present overlaps into the perception that is coming to be (Husserl calls this 'protention'). Imagine a stone has been thrown; we retain a knowledge of where it was thrown from and its flight in the air, and we can predict roughly through its velocity and trajectory where it will land. Thus, perceptions are not isolated from others or fixed alone in time but flow into each other, continually becoming different.

The sculpture's perceptible cues suggest games with horizontality and verticality, as well as degrees of depth. We can lie 'flat on our backs' with it or ponder its uprightness. In this way, the getting up and lying down actions that we project within the sculpture's spaces give us very different apprehensions of the sculpture's nature. As Krauss writes, the 'thin tubular elements become the major visual factors within this view of the work, partly because their fanlike configuration seems to enact that transposition of horizontals into vertical' (1981, p. 191). In other words, the sculpture's bars seem to suggest not only vertical and horizontal directions but stages of transformation, of gradually becoming vertical from a horizontal position, of getting up in the morning, for example, and this is where I think we approach some of the reasoning behind the title of the work, *Early One Morning*, although it is entirely plausible that its placidity and silence are also being alluded to, as well as the song.

The sculpture invites conceptual interpretations: cultural, pictorial, architectural, mechanical, phenomenological, all of which are supported by the 'use' of our bodies as an indispensable reference point for actual, physical interpretation-as-experience. However, folded into this is the metaphor of getting up in the morning. Krauss writes that the 'change from horizontal to vertical is expressed as a change in condition of being' (1981, p. 192). *Early One Morning* seems to encapsulate the concept of the domus, the built, lived, environment, and Heidegger's being-in-the-world, even while taking in the real environment of the gallery space that seems to join on to its open spaces. The sculpture itself is open 'physically and spiritually', as the artist said, and its 'furniture' and intervals of crossed beams mark the temporal extension of our experience as well as a sense of distance and perspective. As a room or series of rooms enclosing and conceptualising our embodiment, it tends to bring to mind the quotidian and routine spaces of our lives to which we become accustomed. Additionally, 'walking the sculpture' from one end to the other (a kind of uncanny division of space that seems familiar although abstract and detached) seems to make us conscious of our habituated kinaesthetic response to space, time and demarcations in the visual field. Our 'living' – our being-in-the-world – seems to be reflected back to us as a theme (viewed pictorially) and as a lived experience outside of the ordinary (moved in and around horizontally). Yet the mechanical view of the structure suggests an obsolete relic and abandoned civilisation. The title, *Early One Morning*, suggests a revelatory quality and the cross/window at one end also suggests a religious reference, a chapel with altarpiece at the front, with some sort of marriage ceremony occurring (with the ritualised, steady walking at intervals also implied); yet I have also mentioned that we can think of the sculpture as a classroom (with blackboard in front). Whether chapel or classroom, bedroom or abandoned wreck – weakly intended scripts and schemata that the sculpture activates – the actions of our bodies are regulated accordingly or 'tried on for size'. The sculpture constrains our projections into it, creating an interesting interplay between the capture of the body in its manipulable structure and the liberation from thoughts of the body that conceptual transformations often require. Much of this interpretation of the work brings together modernist formalism with phenomenology, as well as reflections on cultural and social categories. The sculpture seems to call for it with its series of affordances.[2]

Various anthropomorphisms are exercised upon it and the artist himself referred to it as something 'stretched out', which implies a reclining figure, although it is resolutely abstract. Yet it also produces self-monitoring: the sculpture's perceptual cues, its structure and length, the play of its vertical and horizontal planes and its scale, help to create the conditions whereby the viewer becomes aware of her own body interlocking with the sculpture, a presence that fits within its preconceived spaces and completes it. Yet there is a circularity in this, as the viewer is invited to project her body schema within the sculpture in order to become aware of the human body schema as the model of the sculpture's address.[3] Perhaps the only way to break the circularity is to retrieve aspects of art historical relational knowledge and cultural critique in order to turn away from the exclusive emphasis of embodiment as the primary vehicle for interpretation.

Returning to Caro's sculpture, we walk alongside it weaving our perceptions and concepts with its intervals. At one point, however, looking at the sculpture head-on from one of its ends, this fluid temporal and physical extension seems to collapse into one flat compacted view. When we stand still directly in front of it, it suddenly appears as if we are looking at a painting in a gallery (yet we can also believe this to be a window onto reality in the traditional illusionary sense). As Krauss suggests, the sculpture tends to become *pictorial*.[4] This concertina effect consists of the planar sculpture collapsing into a flat graphic aesthetic with its square sheet of metal suggesting a pictorial frame. Because the pictorial or diagrammatic mode of presentation gives us an illusory feeling of being outside of it, we feel no longer anchored by the sculpture; the

---

[2] This chimes in with another art historian who speaks of Caro's sculpture as both anti-traditional yet it 'draws upon historical resources [and] speaks in a grammar we already possess: the grammar of bodily movement and gesture. For the historical practice of sculpture always revolved around our understanding of the human body, or more accurately our experience of the body' (Vickery, 2003, pp. 124–125).

[3] A similar point is made by Amanda Boetzkes (2009, p. 699) concerning phenomenology and Tony Smith's sculpture, but more importantly, she claims that the notion of installation art is 'haunted by the possibility that it will merely satisfy perceptual expectations and stabilize the spectator's pre-existing sense of her or himself' (p. 703).

[4] 'There are, then, two ways of relating to *Early One Morning*. The first is to experience it as a physical construction...The second alternative arises from standing directly in front of the work and thereby experiencing it pictorially' (Krauss, 1981, p. 191).

pictorial view 'disembodies the eye', yet now places us in a gallery space. This is key, because it shows that Caro's work was able to appeal both to Fried's modernism, which prized formalism untrammelled by social or embodied references, while it could also be seen to engage with phenomenological appeals to the perceiving viewer's body, suggesting perhaps that the longstanding conflict between disembodied formalism and embodiment in art history and criticism is over-egged. They can cohere in our experience of the same sculptural form; we do not have to choose. In fact, to slip from one to the other frame of mind and back again is surely one psychological explanation of how the sculptural work is able to absorb us.

The 'flattened' sculpture seems to unfold when we walk alongside it but there are still transformations of form and mental rotations that lead to different aspects of design history, from architectural space, to lorry, to machine, to gallery space, to relational knowledge of other artworks. Our ongoing perceptions continue to transform the sculptural object but added to these are comparisons with the abstract paintings by van Doesburg, a de Stijl-designed chair or Malevich's Suprematism, for example. These form a base of relational knowledge that further enhances the encounter, along with phenomenological and formalist theory.

Another strategy enabling us to build richer conceptual appeal into what otherwise might be a cul-de-sac, where embodied phenomenal experience becomes both the subject of and the interpretational mode for the artwork, is Richard Serra's works, sculptures that literally can take hours to walk around in remote landscapes, works that tend to dispense with the house as the model to organise embodied experience. Instead, especially in those large works that sit upon and clearly indicate the gradients and contours of the land on a grand scale, the earth is disclosed by the work of art, 'the earth' being disclosed in 'the world', as Heidegger would have it. Our encounter with the sculpture is not restricted by our habitual sense of space associated with the house and living rooms and the body; we confront the earth enframed by the sculpture both as material facticity and as conceptual construct. The sculpture does not appeal to the sense of lived cultural space or enframed space, but to the open-ended, unfettered and unbounded space around the sculpture, which seems to have a presence within its undulations. The land's contours dictate the curves of the sculpture. The sculpture becomes an encounter between the earth and its concrete qualities and abstracted cultural forms, an encounter that fashions the sculpture as a particular thing. The constructions Serra attempts are highly technical in terms of engineering and the architecture, making the Caro sculpture seem like a handcrafted maquette in comparison. Serra deals with issues concerning territory, site, sight, memory and culture, and walking within the land. The sculpture's structures seem to follow the lie of the land: we step outside of the house and outside of the gallery to walk on the earth, which is a kind of primordial encounter, yet we are also displaced by the sculptural object. The 'natural' morphs into the built environment but the latter is not a depiction of the former, but in fact is shaped by it. In Serra's work, we need to act, to engage with the sculpture as a site for 'perception in action' (Noë, 2005), matching a sense of what is unknown about the sculpture and what it conceals with a sense of discovery achieved by engaging with it as a journey. Boetzkes (2009) attempts to show that this sense of discovery avoids the reflexivity of a body-centred approach to the art encounter. I take this to imply that the art experience could work, psychologically, in terms of a creative process, not so much as a purely self-generated creativity but one that arises out of an interplay between what one knows in relational knowledge and what one can learn from the artwork's difference.

The starring role in Serra's tacitly psychological theory of art is that action itself, although embodied, is never settled enough to 'find a home', as it does nestled in the embrace of Caro's work. Instead, action 'out there' in the big landscape, which also consists of being able to see for miles around, levers us out of the self-image of our body and into an unpredictable world. One could argue that this elevation of action as an unresolved process – much like desire – re-inscribes the body as the locus of action. Serra's works attempt to disrupt total visibility of the sculptural object; his works are usually too large to take in from a single-point perspective. He cedes authorship to the land, allowing the sculpture to follow its contours, and all of this is cultural, conceptual and theoretical. Yet there is the stubborn residue of the body, it is still the *urdoxa* behind the work, reconstructed through actions and opticality brought together in order to restore the body as the site of disclosure and the object of the sculpture's address. The sculpture's spaces are designed to prime ergonomic or gestalt sensations, even if staggered over a duration, a journey, in which we forget ourselves.

The sculpture is made coherent by piecing together memories and perceptions of its profiles. The unification of walking time and the space of the landscape is achieved by the body or its displacement. The alterity (Irigaray, 1993) or 'presence' (Fried's term) of Serra's constructions is contained in their towering and dominant presence, where one struggles to encompass them or one becomes ensconced by them. A fundamental tension occurs where, on the one hand, the sheer material monumentality and the metal twisted with forces beyond human scale evoke a vision of Burke's sublime where one's body schema unravels. On the other hand, one struggles to find a reference point from which one can reclaim a sense of one's centredness. What Serra's work achieves is to disarm pre-emptive interpretation. In many ways, only 'doing' a Serra sculpture can explain the experience. It is its own best model.

Krauss suggests that an attitude of 'humility' (1981, p. 283, and emphasised by Boetzkes, 2009) should allow a passage to open between the viewer and the artwork. The aim is to suspend our prejudging of the artwork with an attitude of humility where we do not force our interpretations upon it in an egotistical manner. A related idea is the philosopher Gadamer's metaphor of the 'fusion of horizons' (*Horizontverschmelzung*), where one finds agreement between individuals. Coming to such an agreement means establishing a common framework or 'horizon' that, in phenomenology, explains an intersubjective situation that is reciprocally constraining: 'The horizon is the range of vision that includes everything that can be seen from a particular vantage point...A person who has no horizon is a man who does not see far enough and hence overvalues what is nearest to him. On the other hand, "to have an horizon" means not being limited to what is nearby, but to being able to see beyond it' (1997, p. 302).

This is particularly interesting when we consider Richard Serra's *Shift*, 1970–1972, a sculpture consisting of a series of walls built on the contours of the land, which plays games with the visibility of the horizon and where we might expect the horizon to be. There is no one-point perspective that would dominate it. Krauss (1981) offers a complex analysis of this sculpture as an intersubjective experience that Serra himself claimed arose out of an experiment of two people walking towards each other on a plot of land from opposite ends. The land rises at the centre, making it difficult for the two people to remain in each other's sightlines. However, despite the unevenness of the land that threatened to obscure their shared gaze, they trace a path and it is this path that becomes the plan for the sculpture. The orthogonals of the shared gaze influenced the final positioning and direction of the sculptural walls. The sculpture, therefore, seems to be a material trace of an intersubjective exchange between two people and their interactions with the land rather than a structure planned from one point of view. The sculpture thus brings together the facticity of the land, the shared human gaze, walking, desire, mapping, memorialising, nature, art. Embodiment is part of this, but it cannot explain the whole of it.

An intersubjective exchange between people is a fusion of horizons where each person exerts an active influence on the shared conversation, either by actively structuring it or by actively listening and remaining silent in structured ways. The situation is not the same for an artwork that does not listen in structured ways. Krauss' attitude of humility that we are supposed to adopt in understanding art implies inattentive psychological processes or mind wandering (Christoff et al., 2009b, p. 99) where one is opportunistic or open to various analogical possibilities (Bar, 2004), taking the lead from the artwork rather than prejudging it. The mechanism of this mind wandering is a topic I return to shortly. It is difficult to avoid the thought that this attitude of humility resembles a somewhat naïve faith in the *tabula rasa* idea: that one can prevent thoughts about what one knows from entering the mind in order for the space to be filled by the other. It also seems perverse to think that one can force mind wandering to occur, especially if such wandering is meant to be free and unplanned. There is a fine line between exercising rational, familiar processes when examining an artwork and relinquishing rational control to allow intuitive and imaginative engagements to occur, and many artists alone before the canvas have attempted to walk this line. For the viewer, success in being able to balance empirical knowledge with creative thought, and new meaning also depends on the artwork. This is perhaps a measure of its success. In terms of psychology, this process of exchange with the artwork may be similar to analogical modification, where the features or relations between features that are known to one are re-situated or mapped onto the differently configured perceptual features of the artwork, creating new emergent material from the blend of pre-existent structure and unfolding context. This is what is suggested in *Shift*: a knowledge of an aesthetic plan kept in touch with shifting geographical experience. Ad hoc modifications require a balance between maintaining known structures of knowledge and 'tinkering' with them, replacing some of their features with new features from the ongoing experience suggested by the artwork.

These aforementioned analyses in art history are a tacit theory of creativity and conceptual production, and are implicitly about the preferred psychology one should try to adopt towards an artwork in order to question preconceived ideas forced onto artworks and in order to avoid the solipsism this implies. In short, what is valorised in many of these artworks and theories of art is the process of adjusting schemata in cooperation with new experiences of the artwork. Another way to understand the process of changing schemata is to view it as a form of creativity. In the following pages, I attempt to evaluate four ways in which creativity arises from an encounter with the art object:

1 Action as perception: ongoing unpredictable engagement with the artwork. This approach has recently found common ground with 'enactivism', particularly in the work of Alva Noë (2005). Creativity here is thought to be an ongoing experience of the artwork based on sensorimotor actions and engagements with the art object, contingent actions

that cannot be preconceived. However, it is doubtful whether this approach can avoid reductionism concerning contemporary art, as I discuss later.

2 Krauss' 'humility' (1981, p. 283) suggests that a fully egotistical approach to art based on simply confirming old knowledge structures is an obstacle to creative interaction with artworks. I examine some allocentric psychological processes as part of my discussion of action as perception.

3 Various feminist interpretations of phenomenology (Irigaray, 1993; Jones, 1998; Young, 1980) have shown that traditional phenomenology assumes that the subject is male, and suggest different nuances of female embodiment not taken into account in many phenomenological texts, Merleau-Ponty included. For Irigaray, making these distinctions is part of constructing a positive alterity and she is particularly keen to show how oppressive this assumption of normative sameness can be in gender relations. I examine how contemporary art destabilises sameness and phenomenology's assumption that there should be a normative body as the subject and address of art, disclosed in the art experience. This means looking at art that makes the body a conceptual problem, not a given. It also means creating problems for representation, for such art makes visible different bodies and lifestyles traditionally blanked out of art history. Creativity here is about creating new meanings from experiences of different perspectives.

4 Balancing what one knows with being open to what one does not know. This touches upon a number of important issues in psychology to do with how creativity arises, how attention is exercised, what constitutes the self. In later pages, I narrow down this focus to the topic of how self-consciousness is mediated by experiences of art showing how art encourages us to imagine different selves. I then go on to look at inattentive mind wandering, which is akin to losing oneself with a creative openness to various possible understandings of the 'situation' provided by art. The rearrangement of one's system of relational knowledge, which may also be the fundamental way in which we organise the self, occurs *in cooperation with* aspects of new knowledge found in the artwork. Thus, there is an interesting reciprocity between innovation and finding oneself in the situation provided by the artwork.

3.3   Action as perception

A recent case for privileging action in the world and in art comes in the form of Noë's theory of 'perception is action', which has sparked much controversy in psychology and philosophy, and has the potential to make inroads into art history, as phenomenology once did. One of Noë's best-known sound bites is 'Consciousness is not something in our heads it is something we do' (Noë, 2005). This is an 'enactive' account of engagement with the world, which challenges the notion that the world is neurologically coded in elaborate detail by showing that the use of our sensorimotor skills *in action* is, in itself, perception and understanding perception, so that the 'world is its own best model' (a much-quoted phrase from Brooks, 1991, p. 139). One does not just see the world checked against some internal representation. Instead, we naturally explore the world with our bodies and therefore experience perception as an ongoing engagement with the world. Seeing becomes a way of acting, perceiving action (intersubjectively in others and 'offline' sensorimotor processes) and acting in the world, moving inside, around and among objects, buildings, sculptures. Important for art is the assumption that bodily action is also interpretation.[1]

As with Johnson's embodied approach, it is interesting to see how Noë applies this enactive theory to art, for this too reveals certain weaknesses in the general approach. Noë interprets the sculpture of Richard Serra. Noë chooses Serra's work, *Running Arcs (For John Cage)*, 1992, three large plates of steel, each about ten feet high and forty feet wide, embedded into the hillside. Each plate is curved and stands either leaning forwards or backwards to produce alignments and disjunctures that can be best explored using the body in and around the sculptures in the site-specific environment. Moreover, because one needs to use one's sensorimotor actions to explore the environment in this way, this sculpture perfectly illustrates Noë's argument that sensorimotor action is perception.

---

[1] Noë acknowledges his debt to the art historian Rosalind Krauss, whose phenomenological interpretations of Serra (1981) largely prefigure his own (Noë, 2000, p. 129).

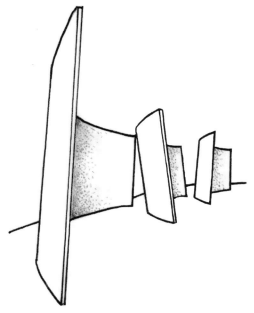

Figure 23. Drawing of Richard Serra, *Running Arcs (For John Cage)*, 1992.

On the enactive view, we can only really perceive sculpture if we involve our sensorimotor system on- or offline in the process. To perceive a sculptural curve is to imagine what it would be like to feel it, follow it, be surrounded by it; we project our sensorimotor actions onto the object and understand it as a series of potential, physical interactions. Grasping the practical contingencies of action and perception allow us to know the intrinsic qualities of the sculpture. For Noë, how things look is *constrained* by our sensorimotor knowledge. Of course, this may be right, for we do come to know many objects by acting, moving and using our limbs as well as engaging our senses, moving in, around and through these objects or imagining our bodily actions involved in this manner. Nevertheless, it does not follow that how things look to us must always, in all cases, be constrained by the actionable part of our sensorimotor knowledge.

The work is a memorial to John Cage, the composer, who died the same year as the sculpture was completed and to whom it is dedicated. Noë suggests that the work stops at our discovery of our perceiving bodies; that Serra's aim is purely to provide us with an opportunity to illustrate how we perceive with our bodies when, in fact, this is only the basis for a lot more thought that is possible. To cut the development of thought off at the point where it merely illustrates Noë's action in perception argument is unfortunate. The discovery of perceptions Noë describes as the outcome of Serra's work is only Serra's starting point. We can see an indication of the other avenues of thought that the work opens if we go back historically to the reception of *Running Arcs* by art critics of the time: 'It is an exceptionally sensuous sculpture, and to walk along and between the conical curves eliding into one another was an exhilarating experience, partly because of the implied danger of those overhanging, twenty-ton walls, but mainly from the sheer grace of their placement. This was the first time Serra had used three rather than two or four curves and the result was unusually lyrical' (Godfrey, 1993, p. 161).

The quote begins with perceptions of Serra's work that are entirely in consonance with Noë's schema of bodily self-reference during exploring the artwork actively (a comment on the sculpture as sensuous, a body awareness caused by its great size, weight and overhanging tilt). Then there is a rapid escalation of thoughts that converge upon the concept of 'graceful placement' referencing dexterity, surely ironic given that the sculpture is so monumental and immovable that any sensorimotor process needed to 'place' the sculpture would be futile. Yet the reviewer reveals the complex thought that the sculpture is not only about scale, site and placement referencing the body, but is 'unusually lyrical'. This refers to Cage and his music, and is truer to the intention of the artist to provide an opportunity to explore the material embodiment of music, not merely a confirmation that one explores the world with legs, arms and craning necks.

Serra's work most probably references Cage's *4'33"*, a three-movement composition for any instrument (note that Serra's *Running Arcs* is also three 'movements' of curved metal, cupping the air). The score instructs the performer not to play the instrument during the entire duration of the piece, throughout the three movements. While it is being 'performed', *4'33"* thus turns the attention of the audience to the sounds of the environment. One precedent for this conceptual music was Robert Rauschenberg's series of white 'empty' paintings done in 1951, which would reflect back light conditions and the movement of shadows in the surrounding location. Cage's *4'33"* is 'silent' and yet is as sensitive to its surroundings as Rauschenberg's silent 'blank' canvas. Serra's *Running Arcs* may be seen as a transmedia reference to both of these works of art. In all of these works, the common thread is the undermining of action, author and egocentric performance and, in contrast, the coordination of conceptual *action* available to anyone as an observer/auditor is invited.

The spaces that the work creates are public and subpersonal. The silence that unites them is sculptural, aural and invisible. Serra's work is not merely to be understood by moving around it, or within it. One must use long-term memory referencing other works and similar experiences and emotions and, importantly, one must allow concepts to interrogate others in long- and short-term memory, all in order to process meaning well beyond the circular notion that the work of art should remind us of our sensorimotor experience while we are having it.

Of course, bodily exploration may reveal new spatial and orientational complexities, but this does not mean we have to keep our interpretation of the sculpture at that level of exploration, for there are many non-sensorimotor conceptions we actively explore by shifting our attention from egocentric body-sculpture interaction to questions about the inanimate. Not only does the graceful placement and alignment of Serra's sculpture figure forth a massive, precisely attuned musical instrument (left unplayed in Cage's formulation), its heavy metal *capable* of a sonorous tintinnabulation that we may wish to recall from personal experience, but also the precision by which the tips of the sculptural forms are appointed remind one of Stonehenge or the pyramids and the ancient ways in which we measure the rotation of the earth and the paths of stars, and align our buildings and monuments to them. We are reminded of the fashioning of metal and fire, gravity and the torsion of materials to create vast cities and machines, and the glorious 'purposeful purposelessness of art', as Kant put it – a vast face of undulating metal that need not be 'used' or pressed into service for goal-directed action. It is a monument to a silence, as is Cage's *4'33"*, which it references, a parody of a monument, a monument that parodies movement and refutes the notion that sensorimotor contingencies must dictate aesthetics. The sculpture does not simply reference the body; Serra's work gives us a sense of the history of human technological, artistic and conceptual achievement and, uncannily, a vision of how that history will be memorialised in the future. It anticipates and dispels the 'classic' phenomenological interpretation of sculpture that severely circumscribed the sculptural project for decades. We need sensorimotor involvement only at the very lowest levels of this realisation, before the sculpture subtly begins to undermine the solipsism that it is the reassurance of embodiment that we extract from this encounter with art.

It might be that Noë's attempt to bond the sensorimotor system with seeing is too strong. Prinz remarks: 'When I see an ice cream, I imagine tasting it: that does not show that my vision is intrinsically olfactory. Likewise, when I see a tomato, I imagine grasping it from all sides, but that does not mean that vision is intrinsically motoric' (2006, p. 8). Prinz

also points to the fact that people with motor deficits can see and understand the world 'and people with perceptual deficits can act in it' (p. 10).
An important part of Noë's enactive approach, as well as some simplistic
attempts to show that aesthetics are extended into the world by sensorimotor knowledge (Myin and Veldman, 2011), attempts to explain that
sensorimotor knowledge qualifies as conceptual knowledge. This greatly
simplifies the complexity of concepts and conceptual systems. We might
examine the perceptual cues in artworks using our actions but there is also
much going on in rationalising attention for longer-term goals (prefrontal
cortex) and processing semantic subtleties and memories (temporal poles
and the hippocampus) – more than enough neural interconnectivity to
conclude that conceptual knowledge is more than perceptual action of the
sensorimotor system exploring the world as its own best model.

3.4 Contra-normative embodiment

Although I have provided various criticisms of simplistic sensorimotor accounts from phenomenological perspectives, Anjan Chatterjee offers strong neurological arguments against localised claims made for cognition that favour a strong role for sensorimotor areas, the wrong emphasis for an understanding of contemporary art. 'I take as axiomatic,' he writes, 'that exquisitely developed sensory and motor systems are not sufficient to embody complex human cognitive capacities. Otherwise animals with demonstrably more acute sensory systems and more agile motor systems than humans would be expected to have minds more subtle and sophisticated than those of humans' (Chatterjee, 2010b, p. 83).

Although it is commonplace in the literature and research on mirror neurons to cite evidence from fMRI scans that sensorimotor areas of the brain light up when subjects process action verbs (Kemmerer et al., 2008), lesion studies clearly show that even if motor areas of the brain are damaged, individuals do not demonstrate conceptual deficits (Chatterjee, 2010b, p. 86). Importantly, the interpretation of actions need not be based on processing the action itself but may involve many other conceptual processes: 'Despite not knowing how to swim, I can watch Michael Phelps at the 2008 Olympics and have some understanding and even appreciation of the event. My understanding might be different than that of my 16-year-old competitive swimmer nephew. He might simulate some of the movements as he watches Phelps compete. Instead, I might watch the event and also ponder the social pressures on such a young man' (p. 90).

Much of this suggests that the processing of action concepts favoured by some enactive accounts may not necessarily be explained by the involvement of the sensorimotor areas. Indeed, Chatterjee conducted a series of neurological experiments, concluding that 'Relational thinking in the form of X pushes Y, or X is above Y, gathers flexibility by being referentially promiscuous. There are many possible referents for X and Y. Inserting possible referents for X and Y must mean that relational thinking bleaches out the sensory and motor details of specific actors and objects. Our data suggests that the neural underpinnings of this bleached action representation lies within the posterolateral temporal cortex' (2010b, p. 95).

These results are important for art history as they point to the weakness of embodied and phenomenological interpretations of art and conceptual thought, many of which focus on literal examples of embodiment without seeing the system of relations these examples imply. It is important with examples of contemporary art, such as installations and sculptures that require our moving in and around the art object, that we do not reduce the meaning of the art object to our experience of moving. Chatterjee goes on to review several other neuroanatomical experiments that suggest abstract, grammatical and relational responses to action concepts, in addition to or not dependent on sensorimotor processes. This casts doubt on some of the strongest claims made for action as perception as primary for the art experience.

Rather than assuming that the body is a fundamental, universal given, one of contemporary art's strongest themes, built upon older traditions of science fiction fantasy or nightmares, is to stimulate thought about how human bodies can change as a result of scientific experiments and social developments. The body is shown to be under duress, in a process of transformation and impermanence, for example, as we see with the French artist Orlan who films herself having plastic surgery that deliberately disfigures her face. Orlan shows how the body, rather than being a natural given that determines identity, can be a medium for constructing concepts whether they are ideas of beauty or stereotypes. She makes a spectacle out of her performance of changing her body image, a deconstruction of the normative beauty of film icons. This is a 'staging' of narcissism but it is also real, the mutilation many women are willing to go through to achieve the ideal self-image, standardised by overexposure to stereotypes in mass entertainment.

These challenges to the assumed coherence of the human body are sustained by various 'post-human' artworks that encourage us to visualise a future world where biogenetic engineering produces unrecognisable human hybrids, as we see with Patricia Piccinini's fleshy sculptures, which are strange animals that seem half-lactating human, half-pig. Similarly, in Jake and Dinos Chapman's *Zygotic acceleration, biogenetic, de-sublimated libidinal model*, 1995, a typically nightmarish science fiction sculpture made of fibreglass, several female figures are fused into one torso with many legs, and appear to be driven, as the title suggests, libidinally, to activate their motoric capabilities simultaneously in all directions, threatening to split them apart. Although some of the concepts involved in this abysmal vision of human survival will be realised by motoric knowledge, this is not what clinches it for us. Our conceptualisation of why motoric sense is thwarted here hinges on our knowledge of science fiction horror stories, Surrealist dolls and biogenetic mutants, rather than privileging phenomenological engagements. In these cases, as with Stelarc's technological extensions of his body and implants of wire circuits, the body itself with its motor capabilities becomes a contested field not only theoretically but also physically.

Johnson and Noë's embodied and enactive interpretations of art encourage a sense that embodiment is a universal, biological series of facts that inform phenomenal experience, even though the phenomenal experience they often describe is insensitive to different kinds of bodies. Both art historians and scientists have begun to see the body as a series of contested concepts rather than just a normative entity from which automatic and 'natural' cultural expressions in literature and art sprout. Many art practices, particularly performance artworks, make issues of gender, race, ethnicity, differently abled bodies and marginalised lifestyles and choices visible and explicit. The making visible of these different bodies in art is: 'a sign of protest against an abstracted and normative body image that is most often white and male. The particular body image [as opposed to a normative one] acquires a political dimension and the explicitness of a particular body image serves as a metaphor for the pain of social, economical and political discrimination, and as a reaction against the normativity of "accepted" body images' (de Preester and Tsakiris, 2009, p. 367).

The body is not just a given pre-existing and uncontested reality that the (traditional) artwork addresses and which can be found unproblematically in the spaces of minimal art. Neither is it a biological common denominator we return to in art, culture and language as a universal mute language of understanding. There are always variable individual, cultural and psychological contingencies that complicate the ideal encounter of the body with the art object, however 'uncomplicated' the artwork or the theory are. 'The body' as it is experienced is always filtered through the imaginative and transformational power of art and, indeed, the way in which contemporary art has managed to make different bodies the centrepiece in many artworks helps to make the body a relational knowledge system. Moreover, art situates the relational knowledge system that is the body, extending it into the world of art as a series of diverse images and practices that destabilise the underlying values, aesthetics, racism or sexism associated with the normative body. Far from being a biological system that determines artistic and cultural behaviours, the superstructures of culture, history and art continually act upon the body's facticity in order to change it, whether this is cosmetic surgery, tattooing, circumcision, increased medical knowledge or a whole host of other disciplines and desires exercised upon and through the body.

The body is a system of relational knowledge: it can be seen as a species, child, differently abled person, man, woman, Caucasian, a self and an identity (or the producer of one), metaphysical, noble, savage, genetically enhanced, biological, autoimmune, sensorimotor, chemical, muscular, skeletal, circulatory, cellular, subcellular, evolutionary, socially interactive, the measure of an aesthetic system, psychological, kinetic, a nervous system, something awake, something that sleeps, a chiasm of touching and being touched, a site and conduit of energy, a sex object, geometrical, linear, planar, dismembered, reassembled, gestural, facial, emotional, a tool of consciousness (or consciousness one of its tools), a unit, a whole, composite, individual, a poetic field of signs or a work of art.

Many of these descriptions are correlates of distinct disciplines forming a vocabulary and a method of practice and inquiry, elements of which can be deleted or supplemented, rearranged and recombined in any order to provide a new direction and new discoveries about brain, body and world. In art history, the spatial, visual and aural arts continually recombine various concepts about the body as an expressive tool and as a method of inquiry. Art rearranges the images through which we are supposed to 'know' the body and makes us aware of our will to order and classify. This also helps redefine what we mean, exactly, by 'embodiment' and, in this vein, asks a great number of important questions relevant to many other fields of inquiry.

In other words, art can often be used as a tool in questioning embodiment, not merely confirming preconceived ideas, schemata or stereotypes. This means that art, ultimately, has an important part to play not only in altering our conception of the body but also in making us aware of the various ways of struggling against methods of control and power that subjugate the body by promoting advertising and entertainment images of preferred, normative bodies. This kind of saturation leads women, for example, to look at their own different bodies as inadequate (Fredrickson and Roberts, 1997). This is implied as much in Jenny Saville's *Plan* discussed in Part I. Feminist contributions have led the way in redefining phenomenology as a way to understand many different kinds of experience, avoiding the fundamental subject (Idea of a body) assumed to be *the* body, engaging with the particularities of difference. Writers have questioned *who* it is, exactly, we mean by the term 'the body' when we use such a term in philosophy and psychology. Luce Irigaray and Judith Butler were instrumental in pointing out that when we talk about 'the body' we should not just assume that the body means white male bodies or sexually attractive female ones, and neither should we forget that bodies are extremely diverse, and this diversity can lead to different ways of thinking phenomenology.

What art does is to provide a space where these varying kinds of phenomenological understandings of the body and identity can intersect, in order to create an intersubjective experience: a method of becoming more aware of other people's phenomenologies of the body. This involves simulating 'the body' imaginatively from the point of view of other people different from us, which allows us to value and respect difference. It puts into central focus people's lives or ways of living that are normally marginalised by the mainstream projection of images of the body that pander to traditional, conventional and hegemonic notions of what is right, proper, important or beautiful.

The difference between the body as a 'natural' subpersonal basis for human knowledge and the body as a contested conceptual system seems to be explored as a fundamental duality in many contemporary artworks. Psychological approaches characterise this difference as *body schema* and *body image* (Gallagher and Cole, 1995).[1] One's *body schema* is automatic: we exercise it unthinkingly most often and our brains are evolved to have a knowledge of coordination, limbs, posture and so on. This is distinct from the *body image*, which is social, learnt consciously or nonconsciously from relations with others, advertising, cultural practice, gender acquisition, what we think is expected of us and projected by our desires and ambitions ('I want to be a dancer', for example). The more complex *self-image* shares a strong relation to body image (especially in terms of gender identity and sexuality). Self-image includes rather more non-visual aspects (self-esteem, confidence, self-loathing, social status). We are often encouraged to conform to standards of body image and self-image by the family, school, cultural traditions, science and technology. Rather than lump together these important distinctions as 'the body', contemporary art explores the relationship between body schema, body image and self-image, and these relationships are explored, using both psychological and aesthetic considerations, in the following pages.

I argue that phenomenological approaches to art, along with embodied cognition and enactivism, are more at home emphasising types of body

---

[1] '[The] Body schema can be defined as a system of preconscious, subpersonal processes that play a dynamic role in governing posture and movement. [Body image is] most often defined as a conscious idea or mental representation that one has of one's own body ([p.] 370)...The body image consists of a complex set of intentional states – perceptions, mental representations, beliefs and attitudes – in which the intentional object of such states is one's own body. Thus, the body image involves a reflective intentionality' (Gallagher and Cole, 1995, p. 371). This reflectiveness comprises the situation where the object and the subject viewing it are the same.

schema instead of complexities of the body image, an image that is complicated by processes of social cognition. The complex superordinate categories of the self and other require the support of semantic and analogical reasoning as well as a complex relational knowledge; in short, many more resources than sensorimotor systems. Although individuals will undoubtedly engage with vast stores of information available to them in art and literature to elaborate body images in relation to others, this reliance on external supports is made all the more meaningful when built upon prior experiences of such artworks and earlier conceptualisations, which become objects of thought in themselves.

Perhaps the strongest questions that action as perception and the enactive approach have to answer are posed by contemporary artworks that show that there are many different ways of understanding action, rather than assuming it is something that we just do with our stereotyped bodies. The rationale behind valorising action in perception as an aesthetic theory was taken to its extreme by critic Harold Rosenberg in the 1950s. Action was seen as the key to understanding what was thought to be the universal historical destiny of America's action painters, such as Jackson Pollock and Willem de Kooning. Added to this was the assumption that men were better at taking action than women whose actions in painting were less explosive and apparent, as with Agnes Martin's delicate mechanised grids and Helen Frankenthaler's arbitrary washes where colour is allowed to take its own course through the 'action' of absorption by the canvas and the principle of gravity, which the artist worked with cooperatively. In these examples, the conceptualisation of action is considerably complicated.

Thus, action in aesthetic perception in this period was folded into the heroic trope of masculinity but with various practices that contested the notion that action was a purely sensorimotor event. Contesting the concept of action in these ways helps us, even today, to be careful not simply to conflate a particular characterisation of action in perception with aesthetic value that might assume inadvertently that varieties of passivity and inaction are somehow obstacles to aesthetic experience. However incoherent it must appear, inaction is also a form of acting in the world, whether it is refusing to budge in peaceful protest, or actively suppressing the outward signs of interest in order to provoke responses or avoid them, or to *imply* approval, or to signal subordination – all of which we can see in many performance works that require the artist to execute repetitive or perfunctory actions that express powerlessness and anomie. I have mentioned Yoko Ono's celebrated *Cut Piece*, 1964, which consisted of the artist sitting motionless while audience members approached her in order to cut pieces of clothing from her body with scissors. The performance was supposed to be a reference to the Vietnam War as well as a feminist statement of resistance and self-containment. It was also a staging of an alternative to the heroic masculinity of action painting espoused by the previous generation of artists.[2]

Dance valorises complete stasis as a way to punctuate the flow of movements and to provide intervals. In addition, importantly, contemporary artworks are often at pains to foreground the diverse kinds of action and its relation to evolutionary function. Action is often depicted as having a problematic relation to normative behaviour and, as always, contemporary art offers counterfactuals: the gestures and actions in dance or performance are not rational or intuitive, automatic or natural; they are symbolic, cultural and conceptual, relying on relational knowledge as well as counterintuitive and imaginary nuances in order to think beyond their literal embodiment. Thus, for example, the well-known performance work by Shigeko Kubota, *Vagina Painting*, 1965, is a performance/painting where the artist crouches over a canvas laid out on the floor with a paintbrush attached to the crotch of her underwear, applying red paint to the canvas. The suggestion is that she is symbolically painting with her genitals (female genitals usually thought of as inactive without being penetrated) as Jackson Pollock was symbolically painting with his, bringing into public view and into the realms of art the taboo subject of menstruation. Making the vagina visible and a topic for public discussion was a strategy adopted by feminists in the 1970s for many reasons, some of them psychological and to do with the male objectifying of women's bodies. Fredrickson and Roberts (1997) explain: 'Sexual objectification occurs whenever a woman's body or body parts, or sexual functions are separated out from her person, reduced to the status of mere instruments, or regarded as if they were capable of representing her...In other words, when objectified women are treated as bodies – and

---

[2] Sitting on a chair, men are more likely to sit with legs wide open than women, who will often sit with knees closer together. Embodiment and space in a men's shower room will be quite different from a woman's sense of embodiment and space in a woman's changing room. Generally, women commonly experience themselves as objects, or passive recipients of action located in space, with more contained limb movements in most social settings, whereas men project themselves outward into space and express limb movements more emphatically as a sign of normative masculinity and self-objectification (for empirical tests supporting this view, see Frederickson and Harrison, 2005; and for theoretical discussion, see Butler, 1989; de Beauvoir, 1949; Jones, 1998; Young, 1980). Visible traces of this kind of gendered embodiment may be seen in the gestural work of abstract art of the 1950s and 1960s, as described here. Of course, there are many personal and cultural differences but no more than standard phenomenological or embodied accounts of 'the body', which attempt to represent the body as gender neutral.

in particular, as bodies that exist for the use and pleasure of others' (1997, p. 175).

Contemporary artworks play a key role in challenging this process of objectification because they provide images that ask us to question our viewing habits and assumptions and serve as alternatives to cultures that are visually 'saturated with heterosexuality'. This is said to be partly responsible for encouraging particular, sexualised depictions of women and girls, which they tend to internalise (Fredrickson and Roberts, 1997). Seen in this light, art contests public space dominated by these images and offers alternatives. Shigeku Kubota's *Vagina Painting*, Carolee Schneeman's *Vagina Scroll*, 1975, and the making visible of the vagina in Judy Chicago, Hannah Wilke and many other artists' works may be seen as attempts at showing women's bodies to be capable of more than being objects for the gaze. Instead, they are recast as artistically and intellectually productive in ways that the phallus is assumed to be for men.[3] Objectification is parodied and shown to be an instrument of scopic pleasure instead of being veiled as 'reality', or the woman's body is withdrawn as an opportunity for objectification to take place.

That the masculine, heterosexual gaze is anticipated and catered for in traditional art is an issue further complicated by homosexual psychology. Keith Boadwee's *(Untitled) Purple Squirt*, 1995, is a performance piece where the artist used his anus for action painting. Amelia Jones refers to these examples against normative action as the 'Pollockian performative feminised and homosexualised' (Jones, 1998, p. 92). The point in Kubota's action painting was to emphasise that the vagina is not a passive, inactive entity, or lack, as it is traditionally regarded in Freudian psychoanalysis. In many artworks in the 1960s and 1970s, the vagina is no longer characterised as something that needs to be acted upon or shamefully repressed and is foregrounded in order to displace the trope of male, phallic power. In Boadwee's case, or in the case of Robert Mapplethorpe's whip and in many self-portraits showing him penetrating himself with the handle of a whip, and in many of Ron Athey's performances, these are actual and symbolic acts that refer to anal sex.

These acts of feminising and 'queering' of contemporary art provided 'representation' in art history (as opposed to under-representation or censorship), playing on the notion of representation. Additionally put

---

[3] For example, Schneeman said of her now iconic performance work where she took out a scroll from her vagina to read to the audience: 'I thought of the vagina in many ways – physically, conceptually: as a sculptural form, an architectural referent, the sources of sacred knowledge, ecstasy, birth passage, transformation'; in other words, basic aspects of embodiment were thought of conceptually and culturally, not simply at the level of embodiment.

into question were traditional concepts of normative action for evolutionary or procreative purpose, which are often underpinned by male heterosexual value judgements and beliefs about sex. These contemporary artworks, and many others, amply question the equation of overt gestures of heterosexual expression with normativity, and encourage defiance in the case of marginalised groups who recode gestures for their own purposes – and this is against the notion that action is primarily 'natural'. Action becomes contested, intersubjective, variable *in principle*, contingent and symbolic rather than typical (or stereotypical). This kind of contemporary art valorises action as an imaginary exploration free of direct evolutionary justifications. In none of these cases is an appeal to sensorimotor processes sufficiently explanatory. In the last case alone, action is freed from being a tool for some other purpose: it becomes one with the exercise of the imagination, as it is in dance.

All of these examples (with the exception of Agnes Martin and Helen Frankenthaler) are assembled by Amelia Jones, as well as some others (Benglis, Saint Phalle and Kubota) to show a whole category of artists whose works form a system of relational knowledge of artworks that questions assumptions regarding the legacy of patriarchal values and normative masculinity proposed by Greenberg and Rosenberg.

3.5 Disguised bodies

In many contemporary artworks, the body is masked or made artificial (Cindy Sherman, Claude Cahun and Nikki S. Lee) so that the problem of identifying what is a 'true' body image becomes the substance of the experience of these artworks that continually ask us to refrain from simply confirming our knowledge structures. The challenge for making different bodies visible in art, for example, gay, African–American or differently abled, is to avoid reinstating stereotypes and to encourage imaginative perspective-taking. Similarly, in literary studies, critical theorist Mikhail Bakhtin spoke of polyphonic voices and there have been psychological arguments for literature playing the role of exploring difference (for a review, see Mar et al., 2008), which I argue are transferable to visual art. For contemporary art, this has meant elaborating a number of visual strategies and techniques, such as priming early recognition processes, which would happen when viewing a well-known painting, Manet's *Olympia*, 1863, for example, and, on closer inspection, to subvert this by revealing that the woman is in fact a Japanese man, as we see with Yasumasa Morimora's photograph of him 'performing' *Olympia* as a tableau, 1999. Morimora's artistic technique intuitively contrasts early perceptual processes with later visual cognition and questions 'natural' or automatic embodied responses. Yet, such an appropriation of a cultural icon by Morimora, who seems to be 'camouflaged' by art history, puts his own visibility into question, and this is the point: even though this act of appropriating a well-known image by which to disguise his own functions on the principle of a conceptual blend, it is an uneasy one, for our facial recognition system has trouble making out the identity of the sub-ject. However, body image, subjectivity and identity are not fixed or essential but changeable and mediated by schemata and intersubjective exchange and by our categories and expectations concerning art. There is both recognition and misrecognition involved here, which Morimora wants to suggest occurs at the level of cultural encounter, when Americans meet Japanese, for example. On the one hand, Morimora destabilises our recognition of a stereotypical image of a woman by inserting his image into the scene. On the other hand, his own presence as a gay, Japanese other is made virtually invisible, as it is in the history of art, except perhaps until now.

As with modernism, we are supposed to read a new visual language of the body image from other subject positions in conjunction with these artworks. However, with postmodernist interpretation, the systems of concepts and cultural markers are put into doubt. There is irony and a parody of stereotypes, as we see in Lyle Ashton Harris' 'Constructs', which explore and destabilise African–American stereotypes, or in Catherine Opie's *Pervert*, 1994, where she poses under a black mask, the flesh on her chest bleeding from the word 'pervert', which has been cut into her skin. In these cases, stereotypes are paraded as stereotypes, or bodies are shown as objects of opprobrium, anticipating the judgements of the stereotyping gaze.

Cindy Sherman's work is central to any discussion of the conceptual construction of gender and how images, particularly photographic images, are powerful ways of conveying messages. Sherman is important in using the photographic apparatus to parody naturalised stereotypes of women but her images also suggest the psychological internalisation of such images when consumed. Fredrickson and Roberts (1997) explain that this internalisation is a psychological corollary of a process of object-ification where: 'girls and women are typically acculturated to internalize an observer's perspective as a primary view of their physical selves. This perspective on self can lead to habitual body monitoring, which, in turn, can increase women's opportunities for shame and anxiety, reduce oppor-tunities for peak motivational states, and diminish awareness of internal bodily states' (1997, p. 173).

Sherman's 'self-image' seems both staged and yet an accurate social commentary. Her photography is a kind of 'mockumentary' of private and public impulses. Intriguingly, Sherman's 'poses' have at least four levels of presentation: Cindy Sherman as Sherman; Sherman playing an unknown woman; Sherman playing an unknown woman playing an actress; Sherman playing an unknown woman playing an actress through the eyes of the male gaze. Thus, Sherman is able to present a series of simulacra (note the reference to Baudrillard, the French philosopher who theorised that the play of images of mass media continually defers the real for the reality of the hyper-real) with no clear 'truth': all the 'self-images' here are a series of masks with the self continually being elusive.

Sherman photographs or 'documents' stereotyped body images and simulated 'naturalised' body schema in order to reveal the artificiality of film roles. Her photographs are artificial duplicates of artificial film stills, which are artificial self-images of artificial women. Importantly, her poses are performances but they are also *mental* or eidetic performances: a mental image she has in mind (or she pretends a housewife might have in mind) if she were dreaming or imagining herself to be an actress. It is interesting that this dizzying series of duplications, which reminds one of Russian dolls, may be compared with Hitchcock's *Vertigo*, where the actor Kim Novak is required to act as an actor in order to enable her to escape the entrapment of the male gaze, which also co-opts a series of internal-isations (when a woman imagines she is being looked at by a man and, therefore, poses accordingly).

In effect, Sherman destabilises any phenomenological approach to images because we can never be sure what is being represented and what is being experienced. We are unable to understand the work using the body as a basis for interpretation, and so embodied approaches here are fraught with problems because her photographs are a series of pro-jected body schemas and images that obscure the body rather than reveal its facticity. In this sense, her work is worrying because it suggests that any such facticity is always presented, or self-presented, and through a tissue of lies, through layers of fantasy, veils of social power and desire, and through the interpolation of mass media semiotics. Sherman's staged photographs imply there is no 'essential' identity, woman, photograph or body; instead, these images are a series of impulses, desires, entrap-ments and escapes working on each other in an elaborate system.

Claude Cahun's photographs may also be seen in the same terms as Sherman's work but they are not restricted to the visual language of cinema. Instead, Cahun gives free rein to the imagination in a way that suggests irrational and subconscious desires. One senses the construction of a different kind of subjectivity in her work, often dispersed and even nomadic. Sherman destabilises phenomenological understandings of her work and suggests that subjectivity itself may only be a play of fiction controlled by the male gaze, internalised by women, and regulated or projected by the language of cinema and photography. Her work is particularly attuned to reflecting back the social rootedness of stereotypes, whereas Claude Cahun's images are purely fantastical and marvellously irrational, also centred on escaping phenomenological generalisations. The difference is that while Sherman's deconstruction of the feminine is rational and is based on a methodical observation of public icons, Cahun's self images are whimsical, passionate and deeply personal. They draw upon the creative resources of an unbounded imagination, as Irigaray (1993) believed should be the strategy adopted against a system of patri-archy; that is, a system of displaying images of women for the pleasure of men in many realms of life. Whereas Sherman deals with the bored housewife's pipe dreams, Cahun mines the deeper and more anxious levels of dreams, somnambulism and nightmares. Sherman shows us the structures of the trap, how it is logically organised, while Cahun tries to show us a line of flight by fashioning a new language. Sherman's photographs have a hierarchical structure, a regress of social masks seamlessly fixed into one iconic 'film still'. Cahun's photographs are split, fragmented and disguised, as if trying to escape categorisation and object identification; identity as a theme seems to flow in all directions with abrupt juxtapositions and nonsensical lacunae.

3.6   Queer objects and invisible bodies

In earlier chapters, I have shown that object identification and integration occur at the level of nonconscious processes, as perceptions, concrete concepts and abstract concepts, and as part of complex categorical knowledge. I have also shown how hybrid objects such as Meret Oppenheim's fur cup challenge the automatic ways by which we often execute this multi-level object integration. Seen in the context of artworks that destabilise normative images of the body and sexuality, the fur cup is a gendered or even 'queered' object. There are many objects and symbols that become associated with normative body images: one only needs to think of father's day cards (with fishing rods, footballs or golfing references) and mother's day cards (sewing and gardening equipment or fashion apparel). The body image in these examples of popular visual culture is often constructed without the literal depiction of bodies. In what follows, I look at the psychology behind the strategies of some contemporary artists who have found ways to question normative object identification in visual culture by absenting the body and using hybrid objects to destabilise normative object identification.

Amelia Jones makes the important point that the body in art is never completely legible and self-evident (1998, p. 34). This would risk believing, wrongly, that the body is a concept consisting of a core set of features that are transferable across different minds and instances, and this is the basis of the belief in a 'normal' body image that is promoted in advertising campaigns and entertainment channels, and assumed in many embodied approaches in philosophy and psychology. In fact, some artworks imply the body; for example, Kara Walker's black cut-out silhouettes or Ana Mendieta's *Silueta* works, 1973–1978, which use traces of body forms in the mud or sand or as a ring of fire. The body is, in fact, absent or invisible, a silhouette. In both examples, the works do not point to 'the body' as uncontested truth but rather to its elusiveness and contested nature. Amelia Jones speaks of the photographs of Mendieta's body traces in the landscape as a 'double lack' (1998, p. 35). Both Mendieta and Walker's works suggest the presence of bodies, yet also, equivocally, their absence.

To this we can add Gonzales-Torres' work, where he photographed pillows and sheets hollowed out by the weight of bodies no longer present, putting these on dozens of billboards in New York in 1992. All these cases in contemporary art act as examples of different ways of resisting essentialist tropes based on the easy recognition and consumption of the normative body.[1] In Gonzales-Torres' case, when many people were dying of AIDS-related illnesses, his photographs on billboards of absent bodies were eloquent memorials refusing to sensationalise and make a spectacle out of diseased bodies. Mendieta's traces in the land point to the impermanence of the body itself and its relationship to the earth. Walker's parodies of black silhouettes are as flat and artificial as the stereotypes that underpin them (Joselit, 2003). In performance art, where the body plays a central role as both medium and subject (a modernist paradigm), far from being a universal sign understood equally by all, reducible to a common biological definition, it becomes a question mark, something that is shown to be a construct within a system of signs that creates cultural, spatial, ethical and imaginary responses that are far from univocal. This polysemy, producing images that are not essentialising, is a key trope in postmodernism and it presents important challenges to psychology and phenomenology, and to Johnson's brand of embodied philosophy, which assumes that embodiment is naturally discoverable in art and literature rather than contested.

Jones also speaks of art interpretation as being about intersubjective exchange (1998, p. 34), which is consistent with the desire to go beyond the solipsism of having one's own beliefs and attitudes concerning the body confirmed rather than questioned by the artwork. This art interpretation at a higher cognitive level consists of processes of transvaluation that depend on conceptual combination of one's own concepts and those intersubjectively exchanged. Psychologically, the process would involve negotiating one's own relational knowledge with ongoing aspects of performances. In these works, the retrieval of concepts to do with the body, art, gender, ethics or death would not simply be reconfirmed but recontextualised and modified. I would suggest that the process of questioning stereotypes can be described psychologically as a case of combining schemata and that it is, therefore, creative. As with conversations where we exchange experiences with others, encounters with visual art or performance often present unexpected scenarios that question stereotypes and expectations. In these situations, we cannot simply rely on past

---

[1] In the language of psychoanalysis, these images reveal the problem of narcissistic tendencies in the scopic drive. By removing the fetish object from view, the images make us conscious of our withdrawal symptoms, our desire to construct an image of the body.

conceptual schemata to make sense out of them; we must create new ones
by combining concepts with the alterity of the artwork, and this allows us
to step outside of the narcissism that confirms our stereotypes and beliefs.
Intersubjectivity of this kind is not just social. It is an opportunity to create
new concepts by which we understand embodiment and subjectivity, by
modifying and extending existing structures of relational knowledge. This
is a chiasmic relation whereby one changes one's knowledge in order to
adapt to a new situation, which, in turn, helps to constrain the process of
change.

Gerry Cupchik reminds us: 'It is this process of de-autonomising
perception from the cognitive bias of everyday life that constitutes a
first step in the aesthetic education' (2002, p. 179). One attempt to
achieve this is the example of Tracey Emin's provocative artworks,
which prompt some commentators to ask difficult questions that disturb
the traditional schemata associated with women and art: 'Emin has seen
a lot of humiliation, public and private…"I paint because I am a dirty
woman", the artist Marlene Dumas once wrote…But what does it mean
to be a dirty woman? To be sexual? To wank, to menstruate? There is a
great deal about menstruation, including withered, bloodied tampons in
a vitrine, and Emin's writing on the subject' (Searle, 2011). It is clear
that what Emin manages to achieve is not just inflaming a bourgeois
sense of propriety and beliefs that art should achieve unity and coherence, categories and assumptions that the works here allow us to disen-
gage from and objectify. In addition, unpalatable themes of abortion and
rape, bodily processes of menstruation, visceral processes and responses
that are supposed to be left out of aesthetic experience, here take central
stage in her art. What has become increasingly clear is that responses
from people who resent this focus on these processes and realities,
responses that are often abusive and sexist in the extreme, have also
become part of her focus. Thus, Emin's work allows us room to reflect
on what it means to have a woman's body in a society that predominantly
purifies its public places and advertising and entertainment spaces where
women's visceral and unglamorous bodily processes are banished from
view. It also allows us to contemplate the fear and aggression generated
when the pure spaces of contemplation or scopic pleasure are 'defiled' by
such impurities. Emin redraws the boundary between pure and impure,
personal and public, comfort and exposure, aesthetic unity and fragmentation, moral continence and fluidity. Much of our conceptual
combination here is premised on the artworks' ability to coax us out
of habitual object identification: this is a public neon sign, this is a
blanket, this is a bed, this is a body, this is a woman. Beyond the pale
for many commentators are Tracey Emin's *The History of Painting*,

1998, and *Every Part of Me is Bleeding*, 1999, which feature tampons in glass boxes. Yet this is part of a whole category of realist and feminist artworks that deal with similar subjects.

Judy Chicago's *Red Flag*, 1971, is a mainly monochrome print of a woman removing a tampon that is coloured red. The affect here works on the response to blood and to the colour red but, also, it is a deeply ingrained social taboo, a kind of visual obscenity that makes a political point about what is permissible and, therefore, visible in art and in public generally. It still shocks less, however, than Goya's etchings of war. In Emin's work, we have ordinary and natural biological processes that seem to be associated with dirtiness and abjection all the more because they are out of place in art. One could say that the categorical concept of art is violated and that this violation is associated with uncleanliness. However, viewed from the perspective of feminist aesthetics, the menstrual blood of shame has been used to paint a revolutionary flag (as the title suggests), held over the sterilised body of aesthetics.

It is interesting that, psychologically, what is also happening here is a transvaluation of colour that goes beyond the mere processing of the visual cortex. Martin writes that although colour detection begins early in the visual processing stream, 'active color perception seems to require more extensive neural activity extending anteriorly into the fusiform gyrus [a complex area associated with facial recognition]. One function of this region may be to provide a neural substrate for acquiring new object–color associations and representing those associations in the service of conceptual processing' (2007, p. 32). This gives us some idea of how Chicago's complex play on the colour red would activate a number of brain and body responses such as visceral effect (insula and nervous system with emotional mechanisms) along with conceptual processing of its artistic, political and phenomenal associations. Yet, all of these need to be put into larger and more complex systems of relational knowledge to do with artworks and traditions of the body image questioned or constructed by them, even when the body is absent.

An installation work that courted affect, visceral responses and fears to do with hygiene or outrage concerning how the purity of art had been compromised is Judy Chicago's *Menstruation Bathroom*, a well-known installation work that has been influential for Tracey Emin's work. Knowledge of this installation piece tends to take the shock value out of Emin's work. It features a bathroom with menstruation products and clothes. The room itself seems to be a private place that one trespasses with one's gaze but one also enters the room and is present and embodied in a way that Minimalism does not allow. The display was a white bathroom, bottles and jars on a shelf, a bin with 'used' tampons, and a clothesline. The work tends to jolt men, especially, out of their unthinking assumptions, which many artistic traditions encourage, that art naturally is directed at men, that art is *for* men. This work plainly is not.

These works are not to be reduced to mere object identification or the identification of a physical process (one that is usually erased from the public arena), but it is important that one does not lose a sense that these objects seem to be in 'the wrong place'. In so doing, they provide us with the opportunities to challenge, that is, to rethink our categories of what the body is, what a woman should be, what is appropriate as an art topic or as an object in a gallery, what defines artistic style and what is to be allowed into the aesthetic domain. The treatment of the topic of menstruation by these artists becomes a system of interrelated concepts that bring into focus an aesthetic tradition of exclusion that is particularly male. Duchamp's toilet humour demonstrated with his urinal, *Fountain*, and Manzoni's *Merda d'artista* may have challenged the threshold of what is permissible in art many years before, but even these works may be seen to form a conspiracy of silence when it comes to excluding female equivalents of these works. In this sense, Judy Chicago's *Menstruation Bathroom*, 1972, functions in the same way as Duchamp's *Fountain*, feminising the toilet and Duchamp's iconoclastic gesture while appropriating its power. This is how relational knowledge works. Importantly, all of these works are very different from Minimalist sculptures, which were supposed to help make us aware of our embodied facticity in very 'clean' spaces, accentuating notions of purity and the temple. Any specificities that might reference such earthy themes such as menstruation allow us to see that the embodiment that Minimalism had in mind was idealised and classically sealed: it depended on excluding any thoughts that bodies could be leaky.

Continuing with similar themes but with a quite different approach is Joana Vasconcelos' *A Novia (The Bride)*, 2005, constructed for the Venice Biennale. It appears to be an elegant turn-of-the-century chandelier at a distance but when one approaches it one can see that it is made of thousands of tampons wrapped in cellophane that reflect the light like cut glass. Not only are traditional aesthetic judgements possible here, assumed to be 'distinterested' or objectively neither male nor female, but there is also a particular, embodied process specific to women that is being referenced. It also acts as a switch from assumptions to do with the purity of light imagery and hygienic disembodiment to the suggestion of a mass-produced commercial product that soaks up blood. The title also suggests the festivity of the bride (as well as references to Duchamp's *Large Glass*) and the coming of age for a woman who has had her first

Figure 24. Joana Vasconcelos, *A Novia (The Bride)*, 2001–2005, with detail. (OB tampons, stainless steel, cotton thread, steel cables 600 × 300 cm). António Cachola Collection, Elvas. Work produced and restored with the support of Johnson & Johnson.

period. Additionally, the work stimulates imaginary thoughts of what the chandelier would look like if 'used'. In this sense, it mimics advertising strategies to allude to tampons without actually showing them by disguising them or depicting them as abstract and clinically clean. The work is a parody of euphemisms.

In concert with these works but on a more sombre note is a recent series of works entitled *Isilumo siyaluma* by South African artist Zanele Muholi. '*Isilumo siyaluma*' is a Zulu expression referring to period pains. At first glance, the works appear to be intricate floral or geometrical symmetrical patterns that stem from a central point, much like kaleidoscope images in various shades of red and pink, but this quickly turns into a feeling of repulsion when one realises that the red ink is an image of the artist's own menstrual blood. In *Case 200/07/2007, MURDER*, one can see that the closely bunched up lines that originally appeared to be an intricate pattern

Figure 25. Zanele Muholi, *Case 200/07/2007, MURDER*, from the series *Isilumo siyaluma*, 2007 (digital print on cotton rag of a digital collage of menstrual blood stains). Image courtesy of the artist and Stevenson Gallery.

are fingerprint marks. As with many contemporary artworks, the artist leaves an 'indexical trace'.[2] The notion of human tissue sparks a strong visceral effect thrown into a cognitive dissonance by the overall aesthetic

---

[2] 'As distinct from symbols, indexes establish their meaning along the axis of a physical relationship to their referents. They are the marks or traces of a particular cause, and that cause is the thing to which they refer, the object they signify. Into the category of the index, we would place physical traces (like footprints), medical symptoms, or the actual referents of the shifters. Cast shadows could also serve as the indexical signs of objects' (Krauss, 1977, p. 70).

frame.[3] Attractive and beautiful in the traditional sense, the prints are digitised images of the artist's thumbprint in blood, printed on cotton rags and repeated in a radial pattern. While Muholi's pictures deal with these personal feelings to do with menstruation, they are also public demonstrations of mourning and loss for lesbians in South Africa who are victims of 'curative' rapes, some of whom have been brutally murdered. It makes for harrowing reading:

Between March – May 2011, three young black lesbians under the age of 25 were brutally murdered in various townships. Nokuthula Radebe (20), her body was discovered on Monday 28th March late afternoon around 5pm by kids playing in an abandoned building in Everest Thokoza, Ekurhuleni . . . her friend Simangele, who saw the body before it was taken by police, say that Nokuthula's pants were pulled down. . .Her faced was covered by a plastic bag and she had been strangled with one of her shoelaces.

Noxolo Nogwaza (24), Tsakane, Johannesburg. Her body was found lying in an alley in Kwa-Thema around 9am on Sunday, April 24 2011. Her head was completely deformed, her eyes out of the sockets, her brain spilt, teeth scattered all around and face crushed beyond recognition. Witnesses say that an empty beer bottle and a used condom were stuffed into her genitals. Parts of the rest of her body had been stabbed with glass. A large pavement brick that is believed to have been used to crush her head was found by her side.

Nqobile Khumalo (23), KwaMashu F-section, Durban, went missing on May 4 and her body was found in a shallow grave near her parents' home two days later.[4]

Muholi's images obviously signify on a number of emotional, conceptual and aesthetic levels, as well as performing acts of commemoration and restitution, engaging with the other feminist works that outwardly deal with menstruation as a way of destabilising the sterile dominance of aesthetic philosophy and high modernism. One could argue, following some ideas in traditional aesthetics, that if one needs to know about the context to understand the art (even though the patterns stand on their own in terms of aesthetic interest), this detracts from its value. However, this 'extra' material by which we make an overall judgement about the efficacy of the artwork *is* now admissible as a factor in that evaluation, given the wealth of conceptual artworks that play on titles and relational knowledge, aspects of which, admittedly, can be gleaned from newspapers and art history books, as well as gallery catalogues. Yet one could argue that contextual knowledge and symbolic meaning have always been important

---

[3] There is a kind of synergy here with Mark Quinn's celebrated sculptural busts made of casts in which he poured his own blood which he then froze to allow them to be freestanding. These frozen sculptures are like death masks carrying the imprint of the artist's contours and features, as well as being formed by the artist's blood.

[4] www.blankprojects.com/1111-zanele-muholi

in our understanding of a depicted scene if it is not to be reduced to the superficial qualities of its design. Moreover, Muholi's work suggests that sometimes we have an ethical responsibility to find out more, rather than breaking off with a knee-jerk reaction, pleasurable or otherwise. How else might the artist have commemorated her anger and despair? By painting the scenes of rape as she imagined them? In this sense, Muholi's work seems to betray the utmost restraint and decorum. The image restores order in its forms but the violence and affect bleed through the material substrate, threatening chaos.

The other complication is that it is at this point where I begin to have sympathies for embodied approaches to aesthetics, because to deny that the colour red and the fingerprint refer to human blood and embodiment would be the same as ignoring the murdered women being commemorated here, in favour of enjoying the design qualities of the work, taking our scopic pleasure without considering its consequences. Instead, the fingerprints remind us of criminals taken into custody, yet because the bloodied fingerprint is made into a kind of kaleidoscope of flowers, it also suggests the binary fission of mitosis, a series of mirror images, a symmetry referring to same-sex relationships, which are also instances of splitting. The work is thus commemorative yet also creative, suggesting the teeming life of the blood and elemental forces, and, as a fingerprint, it is a document of what has happened in the world that may otherwise go unremarked and unpunished. It is also an affirmation of identity, a truth that has a kind of beauty of its own.

With Joana Vasconcelos, Judy Chicago, Tracey Emin and Zanele Muholi's works, we alternate our attentional focus from attention to embodiedness to a state where embodiedness becomes a background hum, and from object identification to symbolic association, depending on whether we are aware of our perceptual processing of egocentric space and materiality, or whether we are more aware of our mind wandering away from such processes to concepts, categories and memories that might appear to be unrelated to present experience, but which are, in fact, part of it. Cupchik writes that aesthetic experience integrates 'qualitatively different *material sensory* and *symbolic qualities* into a *coherent* whole [and] provides a cross-modal challenge for both the artist and the audience' (Cupchik, 2002, p. 179). Although there is some truth in such a general statement about both traditional art and the works just described, there may be too much emphasis on coherence and resolution (of the senses) as ideals. In my analysis of Zanele Muholi's work, I have suggested processes of organising cross-modal experience along with a complex weaving of symbolism and affect with materials and expression, the ethics of viewing, that problematise multisensory experience, taking us nearer to self-reflection. This extra layer of experience involved with art need not form a coherent narrative with sensory unity (although it often does) but can be critical of such Romanticist aesthetics that unthinkingly valorise a coherence of senses with concepts. Instead, *A Novia* and the *Isilumo siyaluma* series are discordant, offering optical pleasure but also making a problem out of such promise. One could argue that Muholi's work is solely an intuitive exploration of emotions, yet the execution of the work is also about iterations and evaluations involved with a theory of mind furnished with different kinds of activity: conceptual, sensorimotor, embodied and emotional, condensed into simple visual means.

This is typical of contemporary art: providing the appearance of a traditional kind of beauty while being continually critical of it, threatening to replace it entirely with irrational, biographic, ethical or referential perceptual cues, yet we return with a renewed understanding of the possibilities of form. Art conducts a self-interrogation with its layers of representation that deliberately spoils aesthetic purity and modernist formalism. In this, the principle is not so different from Bataille's elevation of *bassesse*, base materiality, or Jean Genet's aesthetics to the realm of art.

Something of this may be found in the notoriety of Tracey Emin's *My Bed*, 1998, associated with dirt and stench in the national press, which used phrases such as 'urine-stained sheets', 'heavily-soiled knickers' and 'used condoms'.

Deborah Cherry (2002) compiled a summary of the reception of this work and shows that an entirely different response is possible:

[*My Bed*] is a thoughtfully composed assemblage of items...The linen is both rumpled and smoothed, bright white and stained; beside the soiled items are pristine objects such as the glistening clear glass of the vodka bottles. If encountered in daily life, all these items would exude distinctive and powerful smells: sweaty feet, stinky ashtrays, stale body fluids of semen, blood or urine. But *My Bed* emits no strong odour. Nevertheless a stink metaphor, already in circulation for Emin's art, drifted around *My Bed*...The bed becomes a stage for occasions and events: sexual abuse and harassment, terror and physical danger, strife and conflict, fear and oppression; it was surrounded by stories of love, abuse, sex, abortion, desertion and promiscuity. The voices in the texts do not necessarily all add up to a narrative of a singular self (Cherry, 2002).

Seen in this way, *My Bed* is uncomfortable viewing, not because of its suggestion of the body's fluids and smells that destabilise categories of art dependent on multisensory harmony and the classical sealed body, hygiene and higher moral purpose, but because it acts as an embarrassing, perhaps even appalling, portrait of a woman in depression after having had an abortion. The psychology behind all this is more complex, social, cultural and personal than we have assumed is possible for contemporary

Figure 26. Tracey Emin, *My Bed*, 1998 (mixed media). Courtesy of The Saatchi Gallery, London. Photograph by Prudence Cuming Associates Ltd. © Tracey Emin. All rights reserved, DACS 2012.

art. As with many contemporary artworks, *My Bed* primes a number of 'private' or personal automatic scripts or schemata to do with the body, the bedroom, the private world of sleep and introspection, yet its place in the gallery exposes our schemata and upturns our sense of appropriateness. The bed becomes a spectacle, dissected in public, a place where social interaction and mores are played out on a stage on the basis of a few perceptual cues. In psychological terms, *My Bed* works against multisensory pleasure or reward and normative body schemas and, instead, courts a broad cognitive-emotional range from contempt to empathy. The bed is a refuge from the world, yet here there is no shelter from the glare of public outrage. It seems as if part of Emin's self is on display here, that it has been offered up to the public. Importantly, it lays bare processes of objectification of women (as it objectifies Emin's identity), draws out stereotypical responses to women and shows how this is related to aesthetic categories of art's moral purpose, narrowly defined. In this sense, the work is intuitively an exploration of social psychology as well as self-objectification, and it is also a kind of excavation of conscience, a kind of therapy. It allows various anthropomorphisms: we can perceive a portrait through inanimate objects and detritus. This is greatly in excess of the various lower levels of cognition involved in scene and object recognition I have discussed in previous pages, and which are here destabilised. Here, and in many contemporary artworks, 'objects serve as props on the theatrical stage of our lives...as markers to denote our characters for others...we derive our self-concept from objects' (Wallendorf and Arnould, 1988, p. 531).

The bed is made into a crisis of identity, exposed to the public. The identification of *My Bed* as an object draws upon art theory, psychology and sociology, as well as art historical relational knowledge: the bed may be framed by several thought processes that seem to transform it into different kinds of objects with variable purposes. What is striking in the installation, and what some misguided commentators have seen as slovenly housekeeping, is the impoverishment of the objects by the bedside and the lack of care with which they are treated. They suggest an attitude of withdrawal, a low self-esteem, and an estrangement from object attachments and interest in the world and what it has to offer. However, this interpretation is based on momentarily accepting 'the literal', that the bed and the objects around it are clues to some sort of crime scene. Yet, seen as a depiction of depression, the objects and their arrangement become expressive tools and materials for the artist's inventiveness. *My Bed* plays a dual role, as a kind of parody of a traditional still-life and as the bearer of a new visual language of therapy in creativity. Even though each object viewed separately speaks of despair, the whole arrangement and its premise are an orchestration of concepts and ideas.

Many artworks are thus *discursive*, using conceptual integration of various references (and the concomitant conceptual associations for each reference) as a key aspect of the experience, questioning the proposition of an 'aesthetic perception', and raising philosophical, social and cultural concepts well beyond even art knowledge. They may also question philosophical traditions. Tracey Emin's *My Bed* comes at the end of a long tradition of questioning the universalising tendencies of the more sterile and impersonal aspects of Minimalism and phenomenology: that the body is a given rather than something that is contested in social space, that we might have visceral responses to the bed because it challenges our view of what is permissible as a self-portrait of a woman.

The woman's body, so often put to use as the nude – that object meant to absorb the gaze and offer back delight in every sinew – is withdrawn here, leaving only *Persona*, the brand name printed on a contraception product that we see lying on the floor next to the bed. *My Bed* plays with levels of fiction as Cindy Sherman does. It seems to parody product placement and identification and to reference the gaze of the camera in reality TV and documentaries. *Persona* is accompanied with the following information:

> Hormone Free Reversible Contraception
> Assists in Identifying Ovulation to Aid Conception
> 94% Accurate When Used for Contraception

As it can be used for both contraception and conception, its inclusion in *My Bed* is equivocal. It may also refer to conceptual art, a process of creative conception that overcomes the depressing entropy that *My Bed* seems to signal. Like many 'sculptures' or memorials, *My Bed* largely depends on what the viewer brings to the space. It is a blank slate waiting for the viewer to inscribe it with meaning and it reflects back this inscription, whether, in the case of the tabloids, it is a circular kind of disgust and loathing, or whether, for those more wary of judging others, it represents a state of besiegement. Not remarkable at all for how it appears to the eye, in fact deceptively ordinary, as are many artworks to the untrained eye, it allows us to ponder the dynamics of the sensationalist press and the nature of scandal, misogynism and opprobrium. A whole range of emotional investments and social habits rise up to encircle the bed, becoming in a sense its very themes. Phenomenology, psychology, enactive and embodied approaches to art should not regard the body (and the intimate objects associated with it) as given. These artworks show that the body is politically, socially, sexually and aesthetically controversial.

3.7 Contemporary art and the self

I have suggested that neuroaesthetics, and enactive and embodied theories, have vastly underestimated the complexity of art because of a simplistic model of the neural correlates of the art experience and by overplaying the role of sensorimotor action as part of the viewing experience. Without relational knowledge, which can include artistic, theoretical and cultural references, *My Bed* would be a purely optical or visceral experience without semantic production and the experience of immersion this entails: it would remain just a bed. In fact, however, *My Bed* is powerful because it is personal and intersubjective. As Cavell (1994) insisted, artworks are special kinds of objects that can be understood better when acknowledged or taken seriously, as we would in our face-to-face encounters with other people. This requires that we question preconceptions, strive to offer the benefit of the doubt and acquire an attitude of openness. In this way, art can be seen as some kind of exchange between different selves, helping to structure self-knowledge.

In what follows, I review cognitive and neurological explanations of how we achieve self-referential processing as a basis for structuring self-knowledge. I want to suggest that many kinds of contemporary art encourage a process of exploring 'the self', either by challenging prevalent notions of what this should be (from a moral or scientific perspective), or by emphasising the open-ended nature of the exploration itself. The experience of the work of art is akin to enjoying the exploration of the self as something unresolved, which may or may not dissipate when one has left the gallery space.

Philosopher Jakob Hohwy (2007) posits three cognitive tasks that seem related intimately with the self:

1 Self in agency and bodily movement – sense of 'mineness' and index to a minimal sense of 'mine', or I am here.
2 Self in perception – reality testing, the ability to distinguish between cause and effect, reality and deceptive appearances.
3 Self in planning and action – being able to focus attention and select from a large number of signals in the environment in order for higher

purposes or goals to be achieved, matching to an internal state of desire, preference or plan.

Hohwy believes that these three aspects are present in a thin sense of self and in thicker 'narrative senses' of self, suggesting that whatever the complexity of incoming signals, these three things have to be present for self-awareness during complex art encounters or self-monitoring one's states (during one of these encounters). This is an attractive schema because it suggests that the self need not be constituted in its richness during every moment of experience, neither does a rich sense of self need to be held in the mind constantly while experiences of the world in all their myriad diversity are matched to it. In other words, we do not match all of these features of experience to each and every part of a rich sense of self. Instead, we experience the world and feel that a self is experiencing it with these three simple indexical points present, which allow us to feel 'present'. Presumably, this would be held in place by working memory and the prefrontal cortex while attending to objects and events differing from the rich sense of self, which is available on-tap if required.[1]

By extension, it could be that active consciousness may amount to a few salient concepts (or indexical points) kept uppermost in the mind and immediately blended by the prefrontal cortex: 'me', 'now' and 'real', for example, by which we 'own' or 'act upon' an event or object in the environment attended to, or to our occurent internal states. It is important, of course, that the contingencies of our environment – our situatedness in the world – will help to provide, in their own ways, particular phenomenal qualities that will determine the character of first-person experience, helping to trigger other concepts or emotions retrieved from memory, blended with this retention of indexical points. While our ongoing processing of the world in which we are situated may be richly detailed and quickly changing, the indexical points will be maintained as constants alongside such processing, either as strongly thematic or as a background hum.

Following Hohwy's three points, I might experience Damian Hirst's cows in formaldehyde as a novel experience that references my own 'being there'. I might even be thematically conscious of this for a moment when I see a reflection of my self in the glass tank holding the specimen, and I might walk around it to gain a sense of my own agency in

---

[1] The question is, however: are the minimum aspects of a sense of self sketched by Hohwy present during the experience of a thick sense of self or are they somehow subsumed by the experience of a thick sense of self?

discovering what it is.[2] Secondly, I might monitor sensory experiences and attenuate them according to the visual details to see how 'real' the cow is, and I might decide it is not a representation, that it really is a carcass, which I can then pronounce 'dead'. This might provide the basis for a sense of my reality and enhance my sense of being alive in order to make such pronouncements. Thirdly, I might relate this experience to abstract concepts, my long-term knowledge, my desire to learn more about the concepts of contemporary art, or curatorship and display and its uneasy alliance with the storage of laboratory specimens, death and the corpse, flesh and food, the contemporary transformation of the tradition of the *momento mori*.

Hohwy's schema is attractive not only because it is parsimonious, in the sense that we do not need massive amounts of working memory to maintain a rich and elaborate sense of self while we process all of the details of the art object, along with its conceptual ramifications. It is also attractive because it allows the perceptual details and processes (*perceptual reality testing*, as Hohwy puts it) to be part of a larger process of conceptual thought – that the perceptual reality testing does not *become* the *raison d'être* of the art experience or the objective of the artist, but a subroutine in the processing of the 'big' concepts: contemporary art, meaning, life, death.[3] Hohwy's point, however, is that both perceptual and conceptual processes, however much one decides to give them a primary or subsidiary role in evaluating the art object, will contain, roughly speaking, the three elements described here as a basis for describing *my* experience, or the artist's; *her* experience of producing the artwork, accompanied by episodes of mind reading. I am not going to defend Hohwy's exact definitions but I do find the basic idea attractive: that the self can be formed by schemata attached to (or framing) variable ongoing perceptual experiences or conceptual complexities such as 'the self', 'culture', 'identity' or 'art', which momentarily, especially when perceptions and concepts are combined, bring together a feeling of being-in-the-world.

---

[2] As Hohwy suggests, and in line with traditional phenomenological accounts, this account of mineness as an unfolding sensory experience is related to temporal extension, similar to listening to music 'where one does not just hear one note at a time but somehow at any moment incorporates both past notes and anticipates future ones' (2007, pp. 5–6). This compares well with Merleau-Ponty's account of the music of the body and self.

[3] It is undeniable, also, that these indexical points that are held in place by the working memory can be brought to bear on an occurent analysis of abstract concepts such as SELF or CONSCIOUSNESS. Alternatively, we might accompany these cogitations with indexical points that are allocentric, which would attribute ongoing phenomenal experiences to different experiencers.

It is interesting that this schema of the self seems to espouse a reductionist argument of a 'thin' self, composed of feelings for the three aspects of mineness, agency and reward, which seem possible to explore psychologically. At the same time, it also posits a 'thick' narrative sense of self, which subsumes these core aspects and allows more complex notions of selfhood to be possessed, acted upon and explored while engaging with ongoing experience in the world. These are dynamic processes that cannot be fixed or localised without misrepresentation. It is worth asking if a similar twin theory might be pursued for art, in the sense that one does not need to have all of one's detailed abstract conceptual concepts entertained while looking at a work of art, but simply a few core details that allow the art object to be tagged, parsed, integrated into different conceptual structures in later moments, or that work as framing devices held in the mind while various cogitations are elaborated. Certainly, this comes close to Barsalou's argument concerning simulation: concrete situations do not represent the whole series of instances that are possibly associated with an abstract concept such as VALUE, but only a few key aspects, enough to be getting on with for the task at hand.

Hohwy suggests that when perceived causes in the environment are deeply unexpected, the feeling of 'mineness' would be 'replaced by a feeling of bewilderment and alienation towards the offerings of the sensory system – the minimal self would begin to fragment. . .one would lose track of, so to speak, where the mind ends and the world begins' (2007, pp. 7–8).

These unravelling sureties are a frequent and often necessary experience when we confront absorbing experiences of art that purposefully *undermine* reality checking, part of which is affirming the self against such reality checking. Interpreting objects, motives and events in the world goes hand in hand with a sense of self and agency, supported by such acts of discernment. These acts are self-acts. Art is a place where, for a short period, experimentalism, browsing, exploration, revision, change and surprise are possible. If the prefrontal areas of the brain are involved in the monitoring of mental states, as Christoff et al. (2009a) have suggested, there are also times when such monitoring goes into a state of mind wandering, an expansive state where Hohwy's three-point agenda for selfhood is suspended: one loses the self, either in an immersive environment configured by someone else or in a state of continuous differentiation where mineness and agency, as well as longer-term plans and goals, do not work as efficiently and effectively as they are supposed to, according to psychological models.

Complicating Hohwy's model are postmodernist theories of the self and literary theories such as Bakhtin's 'polyphonic novel' (a coherent psychological theory of experiencing the intersubjective aspects of the self-concept through art). Such approaches suggest rather more complex dialogical approaches to 'mineness', agency and long-term planning: that these are nuanced by a whole system of relations to others and to culture. Bakhtin's concept of the polyphonic novel captures an important psychological process of reading that is familiar to us all: various characters, some of whom we identify with while others seem to be anathema to us, provide us with the opportunity to 'channel' voices within us. Psychologically, this is the problem of reading other minds and imaginative, allocentric projections. Both of these, however, will require a temporary diversion from egocentric processes of self-monitoring and prefrontal processes to do with long-term planning and assigning priorities and rewards, as well as memories associated with the self in the parahippocampal cortex. Inhibiting these processes could lead to the imaginary suspension of disbelief when reading novels. We adopt the subject positions of the characters, we 'speak' their words, and this creates an experience of multiple perspectives and role playing. An overall interwovenness, a plurality of simulations of self and otherness, is performed and mentally rotated so that we have a heightened awareness of the fictive and imaginative power of creating selfhood. The ability to do this extends the skills by which the self may be experienced. In contemporary art, being able to adopt or simulate different subject positions is similar to the polyphonic novel. We are always ourselves but if artworks are intersubjective, as *My Bed* suggests they might be, there are ways of imagining different selves. Theories of empathy are key here and empathy works by extending one's system of relational knowledge that constitutes a self, an extension that means adding new concepts while leaving others behind.

Hermans et al. write: 'In Bakhtin's view, individual speakers are not simply talking as individuals, but in their utterances the voices of groups and institutions are heard' (1993, p. 149). This touches upon what I have addressed earlier regarding the issue of the 'readymade' subpersonal cognitive processes that we adopt as part of our larger, personal cognitive tasks. It is thus also possible for simulations of selfhood to occur through others, or through the voices of institutions. These simulations are mediated by tradition, mores, an authority embedded in the text, along with stereotypes and role models – heterosexual, rational, hardworking, respectful of authority – which we might give our consent to or automatically accept, or we might reject such constructions as authoritarian and instead reach for a sense of self from acts of defiance and rejection, and achieve a sense of power in doing so. It is important that we keep in mind the fact that contemporary art inherits this discourse on power and identity, self and other(s), continually creating new problems for

Enlightenment notions of what makes a self. In fact, the artwork provides a space where polyphonic simulations of self blend or unravel.[4]

Hohwy's three points – agency, mineness and desire – similar to William James' 'nucleus of the me' (James, 1890, p. 400) may become the very target of a novel complex analysis, creating problems for such models. In other words, external objects, books and films have the power to affect self-conceptualisation. This happens not only with modernist novels and experimental films but also in contemporary performance artworks, where the works of Nikki S. Lee, Sophie Calle, Marina Abramović or Vito Acconci consistently focus on the troubling and problematic constructions of the self, somehow decoupled from desire and agency. These artists reveal that the self is not only intersubjectively mediated in social situations and internalised by the novel's polyphonic voices, but it is also a series of performances and experiencing others' performances. If one remains silent and motionless while watching a performing artist put herself into a dangerous position, one also learns a little about oneself, about what one is willing to give one's consent to, or not, as the case may be.

In terms of the underlying psychology of postmodernist and contemporary art, literature and film encourage us to ponder the difference between body schema and body image, and automatic response and volition, respectively. At a higher level of reflexivity, contemporary artworks encourage a perceptual and proprioperceptive sense of self (a prereflexive 'thin' sense of self) while experimenting with possible worlds and selves, engaging with a rich narrative self-concept. The self-concept represented or performed in contemporary artworks is a desire for an irreducibly 'pluralist' experience, avoiding essentialising polemics and embracing a notion of 'selves'. This may, at the same time, be accompanied by anxieties for a thin sense of self, which seems besieged by the polyphonic voices and challenges to agency. The 'postmodernist self' is viewed as entirely open to change and intersubjectivity, a conception that puts it in direct opposition to many psychological models of the self that posit – at the conceptual as well as perceptual level – a unified sense of self stemming from Enlightenment ideas and, later, liberal humanism where the self is associated with an autonomy and rationalism. The postmodernist self, which is a major theme in many contemporary artworks, represents (and in some cases succeeds in activating) a sense of selves in tension with self-doubt. As Christopher Butler puts it: 'What

---

[4] Hermans et al. (1993) conceive of the self as 'in the middle of a highly dynamic field of criss-cross dialogical relationships among possible positions, subjected to influences from all sides' (p. 98).

Figure 27. Yasumasa Morimura, *To My Little Sister/For Cindy Sherman*, 1998 (Ilfochrome mounted on aluminum 139.7 × 78.7 cm). Courtesy of the artist and Luhring Augustine, New York.

postmodernist theory helps us to see is that we are all constituted in a broad range of subject positions, through which we move with more or less ease, so that all of us are combinations of class, race, ethnic, regional, generational, sexual and gender positions' (Butler, 2002, p. 56).

Certainly, there are many examples in contemporary art that aim not only to decentre 'automatic' phenomenal processes that point to an experiencing self, but also to decouple such processes from a conceptual dissimulation of the self. The self is presented not only as a series of elusive simulacra, as in Morimora's *To My Little Sister/For Cindy Sherman*, 1998, but phenomenal experience of these masks of different selves, a series of levels of representation, also cause the viewer to go through several reality checking procedures, which point not to a unified viewing self but to a series of self questionings and combinations of possible identities; in short, a visual experience of the self in flux.

Morimura 'appropriated' Sherman's *Untitled #96* (Figure 12), which I discussed in Part I, in such a way as to suggest continual transpositions of a self: Morimora performs the role of a woman playing a film role, playing Cindy Sherman, playing a woman, playing a film role. These various 'masks' fit perfectly into the postmodernist theory of the self and simu-lacra: not only is the self elusive, it is also plural and yet 'appropriative' of previous selves and fictional roles. Role playing and public personas become part of a process of self-referencing, using multiple indexes (woman, transvestite man, film star, artist, performer) any or all of which can be combined. In processing these personae imaginatively, the viewer also acquires a sense of flux because her reality testing, by which a moment can be fixed as real in order to reflect on what one is looking at, is as elusive as the identity depicted.[5]

---

[5] Morimora even restages a well-known painting of a self-portrait of Frida Kahlo with himself as Frida and poses as Duchamp as Rrose Sélavy (Duchamp in drag), which was, in the first place, an attempt to destabilise unequivocal masculine identity. Morimora succeeds in layering appropriation with the politics of representation and the simulacra of the self.

3.8   The self and neuropsychology

The following is an examination of the neuropsychology underlying processes of self-reference that can be seen to support some of the previous observations regarding how the self is negotiated during experiences of art. Northoff et al. (2006) identify a group of brain areas known as the CMS (cortical midline structures), which consist of language processing areas, memory areas, areas responsible for spatial processing, sensorimotor areas, emotional networks (which themselves are distributed across several brain areas) and areas associated with reasoning processes. Importantly, the authors want us to note that there are no clear anatomically defined borders between these different regions. They come into play as areas depending on the task they are required to do, which is what I have suggested happens with the substructures of the self. All of these areas or, at times, only some of them are activated, depending on the type of experience of the self the subject undergoes. Broadly speaking, these types are: self-referential processing in the verbal domain; self-referential processing in the spatial domain (egocentric space and allocentric space); self-referential processing in the memory domain; self-referential processing in the emotional domain; self-referential processing in the facial domain; self-referential processing in agency and ownership of movements; self-referential processing in the social domain; self-referential processing in the sensory domain; and, importantly, self-referential processing in the area of the brain responsible for organising categories and rules (the prefrontal cortex). It is obvious that many of these domains overlap and create interesting complications. It is significant that the authors state that many processes of the CMS would be over and above the kind of simple sensory and perceptual involvement stressed by embodied and neuroaesthetic approaches to art.[1]

---

[1] 'Our review of neuroimaging studies reveals a set of commonly activated regions, within the extended CMS, during self-related tasks using a diverse set of sensory modalities. Activation in CMS must therefore be considered independent of the sensory mode within which the self-related stimuli were presented. Such sensory independence of neural activity in CMS

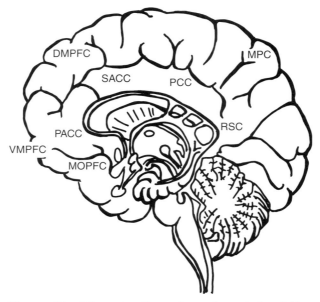

Figure 28. Schematic illustration of cortical midline structures. MOPFC: medial orbital prefrontal cortex; VMPFC: ventromedial prefrontal cortex; PACC: precortex and subgenual anterior cingulate cortex; DMPFC: dorsomedial prefrontal cortex; SACC: supragenual anterior cingulate cortex; PCC: posterior cingulate cortex; MPC: medial parietal cortex; RSC: retrosplenial cortex.

Thus, the self may be experienced in a number of distinct ways that may be combined. This is the kind of approach that I have adopted for explaining the art experience that would also involve a broad range of brain areas brought into cooperation to consider the particularities of an artwork, a dynamic interaction with the world. One could expect that viewing a Rothko painting might stimulate spatial, memory, sensory and categorical processes, as well as emotional responses, whereas

can be observed in all domains. This is paradigmatically reflected in the emotional domain. Regardless of whether emotions were induced visually, auditorily, gustatory, or olfactorily, they all led to activation in CMS...The same could be observed in the verbal and memory domains. Therefore, neural processing in CMS might be characterized by "supramodality".' (Northoff et al., 2006, p. 449). This is important in transforming simple sensory processing into more complex self-referential processing. The distinction is related to an unthematic or prereflexive sense of self or background hum that is present in simple sensory experience and the strong sense of self, or the object oriented self-reflexive self that subsumes and transforms such simple sensory experience into a broader neurological organisation.

Warhol's *Brillo Boxes* would likely stimulate a very different pattern of cooperation between brain areas and nervous, kinaesthetic and tactile responses. However, if an artwork manages to stimulate self-referencing processes, as it often does (the key work usually taken as the best example of this is Velázquez's *Las Meninas*, which features a mirror and characters depicted peering out from pictorial space at the viewer), then it is logical to predict that the CMS would be engaged in processing not only the 'experiential self' (Northoff et al., 2006, p. 441) but also the complexities of the painting. It is fair to say that the artwork will help spark such self-processing within the longer-term goal of interpreting the painting, a balancing of long- and short-term goals that the prefrontal cortex is known to facilitate. The commonly recorded response to this famous painting is a feeling of self-awareness caused by the mirror and the address of the figures in the depicted space. Such a response entails that we go beyond any fixation on the visual cortex or sensory areas as primary in the art experience. These areas would only play a part, for some perhaps a small part, in a larger composite functional unit such as the CMS, temporally extended in a way that fMRI scans normally do not record, calibrated as they are to give snapshots of fixed and compartmentalised mental functions executed under extremely circumscribed conditions.[2] An interesting experiment would be to repeat some of the tests in the literature involving self-referencing processes (listed in Northoff et al., 2006, p. 443). This could involve asking subjects to study *Las Meninas*, some of whom are primed for themes to do with bodily and conceptual self-awareness and others who are not primed. The tests could be repeated for expert and non-expert subjects. The authors go on to suggest that: 'Neural activity in the CMS was observed during self-related tasks across all domains. Verbal, memory, emotional, or social tasks related to the self were found to induce activation in the CMS. This suggests that CMS involvement reflects the self-related component, i.e., self-referential processing being common to all these tasks rather than the respective task-specific component, i.e., the domains' (Northoff et al., 2006, p. 450).

However, even when the CMS is at rest, there still remains significant activity that the authors suggest is due to a continuous experience (or

---

[2] 'imaging techniques such as PET and fMRI rely on short and discrete modes of stimulation in time which are therefore designed to show discrete rather than continuous neural activity in CMS. Future studies should directly compare discrete and continuous modes of stimulation with self-referential stimuli' – as they should in art experiences (Northoff et al., 2006, p. 45). O'Shea also remarks that fMRI measures blood flow but that face recognition can occur within about 300 milliseconds, 'whereas it takes seconds for blood vessels to dilate. It is possible, therefore, brief bouts of neural activity do not attract a blood surge' (2005, p. 122).

'stream of consciousness'), which might be related to the prereflexive
state, where one is only marginally self-aware. Firm distinctions between
past, present and future will probably not be foremost in the mind during
this state. Here, one could be said to be 'in the moment', distracted or
absorbed in a film, play or work of art. Yet there is also a different kind of
psychological absorption: we are thinking about aspects of ourselves in a
deliberate and thematic way, and ascribing aspects and attributes of the
external world to the superordinate category of the self, a representation
which, for the task at hand, will be partially sustained in the working
memory and compared with externally cued attention presented by the
artwork. In other words, art can present the opportunity for the viewer to
experience the absorption in an artwork where one temporarily suspends a
sense of the self and time, or it can bring these concepts to mind for
evaluation, explicitly related to the perceptual cues in the artwork (facial
recognition, emotional modulation, a sense of agency in creating metaphors or analogies) or the social context where the artwork is viewed.
There are, thus, different kinds of absorption in art. The sense of agency is
a complex issue, where any cognitive, embodied operation is ascribed to a
self who causes or 'owns' the thought process or embodied action. The
authors deal only with proprioperceptive ownership of embodied actions
and body parts when, in fact, there are many conceptual kinds of creative
combinations (metaphors and analogies, for example) where a sense of
agency is not only strong but also pleasurable, therefore involving emotional networks and areas of reward associated with the dopamine system.
However, there does not have to be a strong sense of self involved in the
actual reasoning processes employed in solving puzzles and creating
complex new categorical entities that can be possible in the interpretation
of artworks. In fact, a strong sense of self might present an obstacle to
dealing efficiently with some kinds of conceptual integration (Northoff
et al., 2006, p. 452).

Another way of putting this is to say that absorption in art is neutral as to
whether a strong sense of self is implicated in this absorption. There is also
the added complication that even a strong sense of self will be a type: a
sensory or proprioperceptive and body-specific sense of self (which I
argue is never given but negotiated with all our encounters with art), a
social self, a conceptual self (which may entertain thoughts about the
different selves mentioned in this sentence or be exercised using various
concepts in the verbal domain), an emotional or linguistically processed
self, and a remembered self (and past self-referential stimuli), parts of
which are encoded and retrieved by the autobiographical memory. There
will also be personal and habitual ways in which subjects tend to valorise
(or identify with) some distinct kinds of self-reference (emotional,

affective or bodily, for example). Many different combinations of these different mental selves, and varying intensities of each, are possible. What seems to support the underlying psychology of the postmodernist self of many voices is the following: 'the higher cognitive self, in each individual, may take diverse perspectives, yielding a multitude of voices that can rapidly take different viewpoints (i.e., yielding the concept of "dialogical self" – intrasubjective selves that speak to each other). This could lead to a variety of independent voices, taking different perspectives on the same situation' (Northoff et al., 2006, p. 453).

The authors indicate how difficult such issues would be to disentangle in most brain imaging studies: 'We are not yet in a position to argue that the CMS provide the central integrative mechanism – a clearinghouse – for all of the multiple self-referential perspectives' (Northoff et al., 2006, p. 453). It seems likely that each artwork will encourage different emphases in types of self-reference. Alternatively, the artwork will coax us into thinking allocentrically or abstractly when a strong sense of self is not being processed due to relative deactivation of the CMS. Those works that seem to fascinate and absorb us will allow us to experience both kinds of absorption, one after the other and back again with added interest. Importantly, we may leave the artwork with changed concepts about the body or the self, so that new external stimuli can be ascribed to this altered sense of self, whereas this ascription (or identification) might not have occurred without such an encounter with the artwork.

What triggers activation in the CMS (and self-referential processes) during the art experience and in certain kinds of combinations will depend on the stimuli art has to offer, and whether the subject can identify with them or, analogically, be able to see how this might be possible allocentrically. This can happen, for example, when art shows us different bodies and ways of living. There was much controversy in recent years when sculptor Marc Quinn won the competition to put a work, *Alison Lapper Pregnant*, 2005, on the fourth plinth at Trafalgar Square, featuring a pregnant, differently abled woman, Alison Lapper. Lapper was born with no arms and shortened legs. Many people responded positively to Quinn's statement that:

At first glance, it would seem that there are few if any public sculptures of people with disabilities. However, a closer look reveals that Trafalgar Square is one of the few public spaces where one exists: Nelson on top of his column has lost an arm. I think that Alison's portrait reactivates this dormant aspect of Trafalgar Square. Most public sculpture, especially in the Trafalgar Square and Whitehall areas, is triumphant male statuary. Nelson's Column is the epitome of a phallic male monument and I felt that the square needed some femininity, linking with

Boudicca near the Houses of Parliament. Alison's statue could represent a new model of female heroism. (Quinn, 2005)[3]

Others, however, refused to accept that aesthetic categories could be altered to accommodate such a sculpture. Yet *Alison Lapper Pregnant* can become part of our own personal experience and self-reference when recalled in future encounters with art that remind us of this experience. Whenever I use the image of this sculpture in my lectures to students, I know that there are various self-referential processes occurring in my brain. Self-reference here works for me not on the level of bodily self-reference but is related to verbal and conceptual categories I would like to ascribe to myself, to do with accepting difference, an acceptance others might see as patronising. My own ethical and empathetic responses to it are self-validating but they are also committed to a new kind of public sculpture and art that I can identify with as strikingly new rather than nostalgic (although of course many works, such as Antony Gormley's *Angel of the North*, manage to combine these qualities). Self-referencing processes for me viewing the sculpture seem to function on the conceptual level. Yet emotional responses are also possible; in a recent photograph of Alison Lapper with her baby son on her stomach, it strikes me as particularly poignant because she cannot physically embrace him whereas I could, and I cannot imagine how I can express intimate physical emotion without my arms. The picture sustains the impulse in me to embrace the child *for her*. Yet this immediate response is tempered and readjusted by what I see as a remarkable intimacy between them that cannot be bettered even by mothers with arms, and there is the shame of feeling that I should intervene for her, as if there was a lack. It is as if my self-referential processes, which originally reaffirmed my own embodied abilities to use my arms, die away in favour of an allocentric view and a recategorisation of the range of possible ways to express intimacy that are equal, if not superior, to my own. This is so because with the photograph, Alison Lapper was not only making public an intimate moment, the facticity of her body in relation to caring for her son, but the photograph also seems to thematise the very condition of photography: while it is capable of inviting the touch and empathy, and stimulating the urge to embrace, the photograph cannot deliver the tactile qualities it suggests. There is something in excess of representation between the mother and child that makes me feel my lack, the emptiness and solipsism of scopic power.

[3] Interview with the BBC: news.bbc.co.uk/2/hi/uk_news/england/london/4247000.stm Accessed 02/03/2012.

The photograph disables us and makes us aware of our inability to get any closer. We look but we cannot touch, and to desire to touch is already an imposition. It is not only the photographic condition that seems to be referenced here but also the condition of contemporary art that, in many ways, promises to broaden experience beyond the narrow confines of self-reference attached to the usual images of movie stars and models, images of the normative or superlative body that could even be said to represent the atrophy of aesthetics. My description of this photographic work demonstrates a series of transformations from body self-reference and visceral responses to social and emotional responses and finally to abstract concepts regarding representation, photography and art, a range of responses not carefully balanced in many embodied approaches. The photograph acts as a kind of 'hinge' (Jones, 2010) that swings between self and other in a phenomenal sense. The underlying psychology of this hinge is complex. The only way that seems to suggest how it might work is to imagine two flocks of starlings, one representing the self and one representing the other. They twist and turn as if they have one mind, rapidly changing directions of thought, and occasionally they pass through each other, momentarily becoming one flock. Each bird of each flock is a perception, concept, sensation or voice, and the flock is held together by the self as a superordinate category, one that can be intersected by others, losing or gaining some category members.

3.9   Losing oneself: mind wandering

It might be possible to understand how certain artworks help us to think about different subject positions and selves, and they might even help us to think differently about the concept of a self, but how far is it possible to 'lose oneself' in contemporary art? Recent studies in the process of mind wandering suggest how this might work. Traditional approaches to mind wandering assume that it is a deficiency or an obstacle to learning in classrooms (Smallwood et al., 2007), where working memory resources are diverted to processing internal representations rather than attending to external details. However, this may only be true for certain kinds of learning tasks. Reading a detective novel, solving a puzzle or reading a map are demanding tasks that require the application of rational learnt procedures, often applied in progressive or linear fashion. An art exhibition, painting or poem requires different learning processes and outcomes. Whereas reading a novel and solving a puzzle can be purposeful and pleasurable, these situations often require that we minimise distractions and keep an eye on possible solutions, evaluating each as they occur to us. This means that mind wandering needs to be minimised in order to reduce the load on working memory, engaged with evaluating possible fits for the problem at hand. In an art exhibition, in the process of examining a particular artwork, or when watching a film, there is no pressure to process incoming stimuli in a particular order, and quite often mind wandering is encouraged. For most of us, these examples are not demanding tasks.

In fact, various psychological studies suggest that creative insights occur in the 'resting' state when the mind is decoupled from demanding tasks that require our full attention (Christoff et al., 2009a, p. 8722). Furthermore, de Bruin and Kästner suggest that: 'the agent may engage in "offline" processing, while *controlling for* or *suppressing* "online" processing, to achieve the best result. Focussing on direct coupling (online processing) alone neglects the agent's ability to generate *new* and more *advantageous* conditions for relating to her environment' (de Bruin and Kästner, 2011, p. 7).

This is particularly interesting and important for understanding how we experience art because I have been at pains to stress that one of art's consistent qualities is to encourage an active interest in the artwork and a feeling of being immersed. How can mind wandering *away from* the artwork also be a form of absorption in it? The answer to this question presents an opportunity to fine-tune theories about the kind of immersion that contemporary artworks are able to stimulate.

A solution might be that, rather than thinking of absorption as a coupling with (attentiveness to) the *perceptual* details of the artwork and decoupling as an attentiveness to one's internal representations and mental states ('away from' the artwork), it is possible that we can be processing the artwork while not visually inspecting its details. After all, what is there, really, to see in Duchamp's *Fountain* anyway? Instead, along with de Bruin and Kästner (2011), we might think of the process as being a dynamic looping process of decoupling/recoupling, where two different kinds of absorption are experienced, one kind with perceptions and sensations in the foreground of experience and the other where full attention is paid to conceptual combination that the artwork helps to encourage. Of course, there may even be the feeling that the two kinds are in perfect harmony, that we are having a concept of a sensation or a sensation of a concept (Deleuze and Guattari, 1994, p. 199). These different kinds of engagement with the artwork may all qualify as part of the superordinate category of absorption, and our feeling of their duration will be affected by the pattern of their shifts in emphasis; we may also attribute this particular pattern to the nature of the artwork before us.

Absorption does not have to be premised on logical, linear procedures, egocentric experience or direct observation of the artwork, even though the artwork will provide the occasion for the mind to wander. Individuals generally fluctuate in their levels of explicit awareness of their own thoughts. We process thoughts even during conditions of 'rest', when we are not engaged in demanding tasks with the brain's default mode network, a collection of regions that are active when subjects are not involved in goal-directed behaviour (Bar, 2009). Mind wandering is most pronounced when there is a lack of metacognition or self-awareness; mind wandering, therefore, can occur with varying levels of self-awareness and executive control. The default mode network and the executive brain system have often been thought to be mutually exclusive or inhibiting, but it is clear that their work can overlap (Christoff et al., 2009a). Different works of art may encourage stronger activation of parts of the executive system than the default system: our minds might be encouraged to wander more when viewing a Rothko painting than it might a Francis Bacon painting, and there might be some interesting attentional shifts in viewing a photograph by Morimora. Yet, the research is clear, mind wandering (that is, non-goal directed behaviour and decoupling from processes of vigilance) still draws upon central executive functions (Baddeley, 1993, 1996; Teasdale et al., 1995). Many of these studies suggest that there are different kinds of mind wandering with or without metacognition, which are likely to play a key role in mediating spontaneous thought, and that there are personal memories supported by the parahippocampal cortex, which might be involved with other kinds of mind wandering. Certainly, personal memory has been shown to be active during artistic production (Kowatari et al., 2009). Alternatively, there are times where one is simply not conscious of mind wandering and is hard put to recall its intricacies.

It must also be noted that an added complication is that interpreting artworks can be creative. One can evaluate various interpretations known to one concerning the artwork, or one can evaluate one's own creative interpretation. It is likely that executive control mechanisms aiding analytical processes as well default mechanisms allowing for creative and emotional exploration will be highly correlated during the experience of art.[1] Metacognitive involvement will be more active in the evaluative process[2] rather than in creative generation, suggesting that one slips in and out of self-awareness during creative interpretations of artworks. In all likelihood, this switching from executive and evaluative processing to default associative and affective processing will be fluid and will probably work in the same way as the coupling/decoupling/recoupling theorised by de Bruin and Kästner (2011). This is in agreement with suggestions (Hasenkamp et al., 2012) that there is a dynamic cognitive cycle of four intervals: mind wandering, awareness of mind wandering, shifting of attention and sustained attention that iterates continually during a meditation session (and, I would suggest, during our contemplation of some artworks). The co-activation of the default mode network and executive control oscillates in favour of one or the other system, depending on each interval (see the dotted line in the following diagram).[3]

If one assumes that art can cause the mind to wander and also to be attentive, this would create different kinds of absorption: being absorbed

---

[1] It is suggested that communication between the two systems is supported by a frontoparietal control system (as well as the cerebellum), 'which may integrate information from and regulate the activity of two opposing systems that each process external environmental information and store internal representations' (Ellamil et al., 2012, p. 1789).

[2] Indicated by the activation of the rostrolateral prefrontal cortex (Ellamil et al., 2012, p. 1789).

[3] The model is complicated by the possibility of various transition states between the four mentioned here and switches between networks.

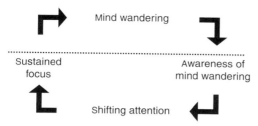

Figure 29. The mechanism of mind wandering.

and knowing one is being absorbed, where the latter is more likely to be identified as a distinteresed or distanced experience, and there are aesthetic arguments that can be mobilised in favour of one kind over the other. Inattentive conceptual complexity also begs questions as to how a voluntary or focused kind of conceptual combination (akin to puzzling and trying to find solutions) is different in the art experience from involuntary conceptual combination. As I have shown, artworks can jolt viewers out of their customary, habitual and involuntary thoughts, even though some of these might be deployed for other occasions. Inattentive thought, however, may be classified as such by being inattentive to perceptual details, or inattentive to how one is combining concepts in complex ways. It is clear that the ability to monitor internal states (attentive conceptual complexity) can function as a learning opportunity for future situations. Attentiveness to one thing will require a lack of attentiveness to another, yet mind wandering may be characterised as the deferral of commitment to one line of thought that excludes others.

Artists and those trained in looking at art will be able to spend periods of time switching off from clearly focused self-monitoring and thematic perceptual analysis. It is possible to focus on one point of a painting, for example, to experience shapes and forms in peripheral vision or by squinting, or turning the head to look askance, or closing one eye. These kinds of techniques help to offset automatic gestalts and habits associated with attentive viewing. While attending opening nights and private viewings of contemporary art, usually not the best of times to experience art with so many constant distractions, one can have a conversation while inattentively looking at details of artworks that one might not have noticed while paying full attention to them. This often happens inattentively, such as in listening to music while writing. Split-attention, randomness and distraction as well as free association are also processes that are required in automatist art, which is a kind of doodling where the mind, hand and eye seem to wander uncoordinated, creating what we often believe are chance happenings. These processes of free association indicate different levels of systematicity, more or less 'structured' mind wandering and memory retrieval akin to daydreaming or pipe dreams (Andreasen et al., 1995). Yet, with some meditative practices and in artistic production, more or less control or metacognitive awareness can be exerted on mind wandering. This might consist of a process of continually trying to distract or disperse firm ideas, mental images and shapes with diversionary tactics or formulae, contemplating the concept of change or emptiness or visualising one's breath. This harmonises with a psychological study by Hasenkamp et al. (2012), who examine meditative behaviour.

Christoff et al. (2009a, 2009b) understand mind wandering as a process of monitoring internal states, or one's own thoughts, but it is clear that one can do this with various degrees of rational control. There is much in the art experience that is concerned with the self-generation and analysis of concepts, and this 'internal dialogue' may be refreshed by reference to the perceptual details of the artwork. Christoff et al. capture some of the neurological underpinnings of such an internal dialogue, suggesting that the anterior part of the prefrontal cortex can process self-generated information such as a plan, past episode or working memory subgoal, 'information that cannot be readily *perceived* from the immediate external environment but needs to be generated internally' (2003, p. 1161).

This aspect of interpreting art has been neglected by neuroaesthetics and embodied and enactivist approaches. Many contemporary artworks, by Kosuth, Nauman and Martin Creed, for example, rely more on the analysis of internal states than external data in the environment. These internal states are analysed by the prefrontal cortex that lights up 'in at least two types of situations: first, when novel information such as inference, a hypothesis, a relation, or a plan, needs to be inferred, or self-generated; and second, when previous information from an earlier episode or experience needs to be retrieved from memory, or again, self-generated' (Christoff et al., 2003, p. 1166). Kosuth and Creed's work are examples of these types of situations and it is reasonable to assume that the same internal, self-generated processes occur in processing them, sometimes at the expense of sensorimotor processes, or in cooperation with some of them. As with these art situations: '[s]elf-generated information can be processed at different levels of elaboration. At one level, subjects can make implicit use of such information, without becoming aware of it. At another level, subjects may consider self-generated information explicitly, by deliberately focusing on it' (Christoff et al., 2003, p. 1166).

Nowhere has it been suggested that these processes are sensorimotor. This is because such information is highly abstract in nature: thoughts emptied of situational detail.[4] For example, mind wandering might revolve around the following topics or questions (mind wandering, of course, would likely not put these into words as I explain them here): 'How do we measure time within nothingness?', 'What is the difference between complete darkness and nothingness?', 'How does my mind represent nothingness?' We might consider these topics with Martin's Creed's *The Light's Going On and Off*, Malevich's *Black Square*, Ad Reinhardt's black paintings or Rauschenberg's white paintings. The withdrawal of perceptual details, that is, sensory deprivation, within a context such as a gallery, where we are primed to anticipate perceptual detail, can stimulate conceptual plenitude, where one is forced to imagine not mental images of landscapes, as we have seen with the reduced perceptual cues of Turner or Rothko, but abstract ontological concepts without words. The key thing here seems to be that the artwork is absorbing, but not in a way that has much to do with self-awareness or embodiment or an ongoing set of perceptions that construct a reality 'out there' – ways by which, tacitly, we come to understand that we exist. This kind of mind wandering with the aid of artworks is not uncommon. Importantly, also, awareness of embodiment and different kinds of embodiment continually fluctuate.

It might be thought that my description of mind wandering risks emphasising it too much as rational interrogation, whereas many traditions of art are at pains to dismantle such logical processes for a different kind of mind wandering as a stream of thought. We have seen how Oppenheim's fur cup is strongly situated in a Surrealist aesthetic, which, for many years, viewed mechanistic, rational and intellectual motivations for art as suspect and inferior compared with the power of affect and unexpected irrational juxtapositions and leaps. Yet even nonconscious thought in daydreaming and mind wandering depends on conceptual combination and structuring relations, and this happens even in our dreaming. Our dreams allow unusual 'irrational' object integration and structuring relations between concepts, perhaps because of the deactivation, largely, of areas of the prefrontal cortex (Muzur et al., 2002). These areas usually exert 'rational' control and apportion priorities for working memory, helping to resolve conflicting stimuli or to ignore irrelevant details that do not conform to a situation type or long-term goal. Importantly, these frontal areas are responsible for the *temporal order* or sequencing of retrieval of situation types, so that if this timing is skewed,

---

[4] We can rely on Christoff et al.'s neurological experiments (2009a, 2009b) to surmise that engagement from posterior to anterior prefrontal cortex indicates increasing abstraction away from the predominance of perceptual thought usually employed to justify conservative aesthetic categories, towards the evaluation of self-generated information.

objects will appear to be found in strange situation types or contexts. The syntax of conceptual combination is spontaneous and unreasoned and, as the Surrealists hoped for, is sometimes poetic and imaginative when accompanied by affect and reflected upon in later stages.

When the prefrontal areas do not function normally because of exhaustion through sleep deprivation, because of the influence of drugs or alcohol, or when there are lesions, 'surreal' affects and conceptual juxtapositions are common. This principle of 'irrational' categorisation is precisely what lies behind 'hybrid' objects such as Oppenheim's fur cup. The uncanny or uneasy feeling we might have in experiencing such an object must have something to do with how the object helps to remind us of our 'irrational' dreamlike categorisations, made uneasy to us because our frontal areas are active in our waking state. Oppenheim's fur cup, or the numerous 'situations' we find in installations in contemporary art, remind us of the principles of irrational conceptual combination we customarily adopt in dream thought, or which occur with sleep deprivation. Thus, the object's irrational syntax and grammar, how it brings things together that should not logically be together, is both familiar to us yet will not 'compute'. However, when familiar with this artistic strategy, as we often are with poetry's striking juxtapositions of words, the experience can be read as amusing or aesthetically pleasing. Either as a cup in a lap of fur, or fur in the 'lap' of a saucer, the work has a perverse logic, as many of our dreams do. What structures the underlying impressions of unease or fascination is a concept of the real, fractured by our familiarity with the syntax of the dream, at odds with the 'real object'. There is also our suspicion that, at some level, the 'real object' is itself a fiction, a break in the continuum, and that this difficult beauty can be accidental and unauthored.

Thus, even inattentive thought without self-monitoring might be quite complex and systematic. This is because the prefrontal cortex, responsible for problem solving and evaluation, as well as the temporal lobe remain active during some kinds of mind wandering. Christoff et al. (2004) suggest that mind wandering is directed at one's own internal cognitive states. Yet the authors also, intriguingly, suggest that 'thought continues to exist even when we are not observing it directly' (p. 629), which implies that, in periods of rest and mind wandering, we may be 'working things out' both emotionally and intuitively, rather than relying on tried and tested logical procedures (Kounios et al., 2006), which, certainly in the case of art, are not the only way to proceed. Relevant to a consideration of the thought processes brought to bear on the art experience is research that demonstrates that 'highly creative individuals exhibit diffuse attention allowing input of a greater range of environmental stimuli, in contrast to less creative individuals who tend to focus their attention more narrowly, thereby sampling a smaller range of environmental stimuli' (Kounios et al., 2006, p. 289). This coheres well with results presented by Cela-Conde et al. (2011, p. 45) that experts process configural and global shapes and forms rather than fixating primarily on particular details. The expert is able to fixate on particular, fine-grained structures when required, while working memory keeps the global representation in mind in connection with acculturated schemata and unusual aberrations.

The varying results of psychological studies suggest that there must be different kinds of mind wandering involving variable cooperative activations between different brain areas (Christoff et al., 2009a; Hasenkamp et al., 2012; Kounios et al., 2006). Binder et al. (1999) observed that rest-related patterns of activation included temporal areas responsible for semantic processing and, thus, some kinds of mind wandering involve conceptual processes of semantic knowledge retrieval, and the manipulation of represented knowledge and mental imagery, supported by the visual cortex. With a different emphasis, Christoff et al. reported fMRI results in the temporal lobe during non-task-related behaviour, indicating that long-term memory processes may form the core of spontaneous thought flow while prefrontal executive control may be secondary (2004, p. 629). Taken together, these results suggest that mind wandering may turn out to be important for theories of creativity, leaps of thought and creative interpretations of and interactions with artworks.

The literature on mind wandering suggests that it may well be a key artistic and interpretational process when it is employed for creative exploration. Patterns of activation for creative generation seem similar to such mind wandering. Whereas Ellamil et al. (2012) show that for creative *evaluation*, executive systems will play a major role; the default mode network as well as limbic (emotional) areas are involved in creative *generation* with low cognitive control, which, as has been studied with mind wandering, will also consist of spontaneous thoughts, memories and imagery. It must be noted that the creative process has many components and stages (creativity generation and evaluation being just two of them), and this will also be the case in the creativity involved in interpreting works of art and evaluating them. Brain regions and networks will contribute differentially to each step or component of the creative process but this has not yet been clearly mapped or understood (Ellamil et al., 2012, p. 1784). Mind wandering may only be one of these components but it is an important one. The obvious definition of 'creative' is that something novel arises, an idea, often in conjunction with manipulating or being manipulated by the body and the environment in a fluid process. This will mean not restricting oneself to rehearsing old ideas; it will certainly require that one is not limited to situational types or scripts. Ellamil et al. suggest an associative and constructive function for the medial temporal lobe memory regions, important in supporting semantic and episodic associations and simulations. This also implies that novel ideas and imaginary fictitious scenes and associations can be recombined with old ideas or memories in conjunction with the parahippocampus. This is in line with suggestions that creativity recombines pre-existing concepts (Weisberg, 1995).

The executive system provides cognitive control for deliberate analytical information processing and relevancy checking needed in the evaluation of creativity. Ellamil et al. (2012, p. 1784) cite many studies that show executive control in various creative endeavours including piano improvisation, creative story generation, word association, divergent thinking, fluid analogy formation, insight problem solving and visual art design. In all these activities, parts of the default system will also be active. In addition, Ellamil et al. cite an interesting anomaly from a study by Limb and Braun (2008), who found activation of the default network and deactivation of the executive network during improvisation by professional jazz pianists. I would like to suggest that the process of rapidly assembling relational knowledge in conjunction with experiencing or creating artworks also entails an improvisation of the default network with a deactivation of the executive network, although some artworks, and writing about them, would require much more deliberate kinds of analytical thought. The creative improvisation in viewing and embodied action might entail retrieving various related artworks in long-term memory in quick succession, creating new groups of objects, perhaps even creating hybrids of parts of artworks.

For mind wandering to occur, less driven or purposeful thought may be required while deferring long-term goals. Yet sometimes a sense of urgency will force the hand and create an impromptu choice when one is taking an executive decision under duress. Conversely, lacking a sense of urgency might allow emotional processing and gut reactions to play a part in creative solutions (Ellamil et al., 2012, p. 1790), or subjects may be detained by the pleasures of processing several possible scenarios and analogies, some stronger than others. Unexpected and unconventional analogical modification will be more likely to occur. This would happen, for example, in assisted readymades where one object would not normally be mapped onto another. The tolerance for unusual mapping of features between artworks in mind wandering may also be higher due to the fact that metacognition (a self-awareness whereby one is somewhat aware that one is mind wandering) may be offline, as I explained happens in dreaming. It is interesting, though, that many artworks such as the fur cup are already a material form of an irrational mapping (fur mapped onto cup). These kinds of objects, of which there are many, will sometimes be the result of the artist's own mind wandering, which we are at liberty to continue imagining as viewers, especially if our self-awareness is inhibited. While some of us are more susceptible to mind wandering, others learn how to achieve aspects of this as a technique of spectatorship.

Creativity is also able to capitalise on the chance encounters and connections associated with mind wandering and is, in fact, 'open' to nonsensical play and word association and we are able to reflect upon such creativity with purpose in later stages. Bar (2009) has suggested that we generate several possible analogies, associations and predictions for one input stimulus or problem (reminiscent of Dennett's multiple draft thesis), but perhaps the art situation allows this process to be savoured. Weighing up which of these to choose from and deferring others does not necessarily have to be a highly rational or automatic process, but could be an intuitive or emotional process, or even a game. Imagining how a solution might feel if we were to choose a particular interpretation or scenario might take several attempts. Certainly in metaphor theory, weakly intended meaning remains active during metaphor comprehension and, in problem solving, subjects maintain weak activation for the solution (Bowden and Jung-Beeman, 2003), alternatives that can be called upon to achieve insight. This kind of mind wandering may be more controlled (as it might be while engaging with a Kosuth work involving word and image) or may be closer to free association, and it may amount to a means of deferring immediate object identification and situation type. Our reward system might be more disposed to suspending preconceived ideas about an artwork in order to seek more complex meaning, which means abstracting away from the situation as a type.[5] This may also entail suspending strong commitments to a self-concept and metacognition, which might interfere with imaginative simulations of allocentric perspectives, or 'passive evidence accrual' (Kounios et al., 2006). This comes close to what Krauss calls 'humility' in art interpretation, which I have referred to in previous pages, where preconceived ideas and self-interest are temporarily shelved to allow for the differences of the artwork to come to the fore, leading to the possibility of 'mind reading' through the artwork

---

[5] Again, this emphasises Cavell's point (1994) about the art encounter as being a kind of encounter with another person. This is supported by empirical studies of preparatory brain states prior to problem solving (if we take, for argument's sake, an encounter with an artwork as a 'problem'). According to Kounios et al. (2006), subjects can adopt a frame of mind or strategy to solve a problem by being prepared to switch attention from the problem's central features to weaker, more remote or improbable associations in order to approach a solution.

occuring. In psychological terms, mind reading means the ability to infer the mental states of others, which requires a tacit theory of mind. For example, one can understand how someone might feel if we are well informed of the set of circumstances that have led to their predicament or caused them to produce a particular artwork. The ability to mind read is something that was demonstrably lacking in the responses of many tabloid commentators in their strong disapproval of Tracy Emin's *My Bed*.

There is much research to be done in the area of mind wandering, how this affects the experience of artworks, and how artworks present situations that can affect mind wandering. However, the fact that some artworks seem to constrain the systematicity of our creative thought, coupled or decoupled from the environment, brings into view important issues to do with situated cognition and art, to which I now turn my attention.

Part IV

World

4.1   Does contemporary art situate cognition?

In this section, I look at how contexts or situations, particularly those presented by artworks, constrain concepts and help to support certain processes of cognition. In doing so, I will look at new trends in psychology to do with 'situated cognition' – various approaches that place an emphasis on the social and environmental or 'external' influences on cognition.[1] In particular, I will evaluate whether such theories can give us any insights into the role of contemporary art in supporting cognitive processes. Cantwell-Smith (1999) explains that situated cognition regards 'intelligent human behaviour as engaged, socially and materially embodied activity, arising within the specific concrete details of particular (natural) settings, rather than as an abstract, detached, general purpose process of logical or formal ratiocinations' (1999, p. 769).

It remains to be seen whether, for an artwork, a gallery qualifies as a natural setting. I believe it does, and I will provide arguments for this in due course. Adams and Aizawa (2009) and Prinz (2009) point to various positions in situated cognition that can be characterised as strong or weak,

[1] This is not to be confused with general arguments about context sensitivity in art or the situatedness of different bodies. Situations give us specificities that work against egregious generalisations, contexts give us generalities that allow us to abstract and communicate differences and form principles. Although it is important for interactions between these tendencies to take place, whether a physical and concrete situation in the environment is a constituent part of cognitive process ontologically is what primarily concerns situated cognition here.

radical or conservative. It seems that a fundamental sticking point is whether 'situationists' hold that external props or scaffolds in the environment and situations (already a hugely complex and broad category) are *causal* for internal cognitive process or constitutive of them (that is, become constituent parts of these cognitive processes). Prinz holds that the first case is relatively uncontroversial; most cognitive theories of mind recognise that things happening outside of the organism in a social setting and in physical contexts can trigger cognitive processes that otherwise might not have occurred without them. What is controversial is whether, *pace* Clark (2008), Hutchins (2005) and Rowlands (1999), these external factors are actually part of (or essential for) these cognitive processes, and whether cognition is to be found outside the head. Can contemporary art be seen to constitute some of the cognitive processes that are directed at it?

Attempts to construct constitutive arguments for a situated cognition of art are a new research area. Myin and Veldman (2011) and Pepperell (2011) support the 'externalist' (or anti-dualist) view of situated cognition, that the art situation enhances (or is part of) cognition. However, they lean heavily on sensorimotor engagements to explain how this works, neglecting our ability to generate hypotheses, self-monitoring, analogical mapping, relational knowledge, induction and other cognitive non-sensorimotor processes involved in art. A good example of how situated cognition should proceed beyond narrow sensorimotor accounts is Currie's analysis (2006) of the modalities of empathy in reading literary fiction. In this view, empathy would be affected by the environmental controls of the story, yet sensorimotor involvement would not feature centrally in the exchange of cognitive processes involved. It is important to remember that while sensorimotor processes help us to access information in situations, much of the semantic content of the information is not understood using sensorimotor processes.

Artworks present extremely complex and coded (one might say, already cognitively compressed or constrained) material that will be accessed using vision or touch. The work may trigger higher-order semantics and relational knowledge not reducible to those access points, although an artwork's perceptual cues may provide pointers for the organisation of relational knowledge for the task at hand. The fact that the environment and cultural products almost always come in coded ways to aid completing tasks (Kirsh, 2009, p. 284) shows us that there are many kinds of situated cognition of variable complexity, artworks being perhaps some of the most highly coded. Some of this coding will rely less on sensorimotor engagement and more on relational knowledge. Similarly, complex maps can show political, geographical, climatic and economic sets of information. This multi-level coding that will be accessed with strong spatial and embodied processes will, of course, help us greatly to enhance our cognitive experience of a place, and such maps are the products of compressed cultural and expert cognitive processes (Tversky, 2010). Artworks could be seen in this light. In such cases, theorists of situated cognition tend to call all of the components (map, body, user, memory, cultural memory, expertise) a whole cognitive system. Yet it is hard to see how the polemical phrases suggesting how cognition 'leaks out of the skull' and 'is offloaded onto the environment' provide any precision or specificity in explaining what is involved in these situations. Simply repeating that the role of sensorimotor apparatus is primary will not do.[2]

Kirsh also agrees that theorists of situated cognition lack details as to how exactly an agent engages psychologically with an external resource. He writes that, as a negative theory outlining how abstract symbol manipulation and internal mental states do not generate and support cognition on their own, situated cognition has been a success. However, 'if approaches are judged by their positive theories, situated cognition has been a failure. All efforts at creating a substantive theory of problem solving [for example] have been underspecified or [are] fragmentary' (2009, p. 303). I believe that this is where studies of contemporary art can step in. What I intend to do here, with an examination of Duchamp's works, is to fill in some of the details that are lacking in situated accounts of cognition, especially situated aesthetics.

Insisting that sensorimotor processes are the bridge between the internal and external risks reduces aesthetics to the kind of 'retinal art' that Duchamp and conceptual art eschewed. Even in traditional art, which encourages us to study and enjoy the optical aspects of experience, in still life painting, for example, the 'perceptible details', jugs or glasses, are painted in particular ways that engage expert knowledge beyond the inspection of simple perceptible qualities. The artist has juxtaposed elements and painted them in a particular light, suppressing or highlighting

---

[2] A typical example is Smith and Conrey, who write that cognition is 'enabled by information processing loops that pass through the outside world as well as the mind, via perceptual and motor processes' (2009, p. 461). How does this work? How do sensorimotor and perceptual processes affect cognition; which parts of the brain are affected; which cognitive processes? How do sensorimotor processes affect conceptual combination? It is not enough to rely on Barsalou's account of how abstract concepts are grounded in situational examples to suggest that cognition is all sensorimotor; even Barsalou suggests amodal convergence zones. Many conceptual and categorical processes as well as speech utterances and semantic constructions in the temporal lobe areas abstract away from, parse or filter out sensorimotor processes; how, then, do we get from these non-sensorimotor cogitations to external situations and back again? One way is to look at the emergent properties of complex communication and the interactional mechanisms of individuals in groups, which cannot be reduced to sensorimotor processes.

particular details. It might seem as if we are merely presented with the facticity of perceptible objects, jugs and vases, but (a) we are conceptually interpreting notions of style, medium, expression, often imposing order and compositional principles upon a scene or discovering them with our relational knowledge of different ways of composing scenes; and (b) these help to produce meaning. Perceptual experience is thus assimilated into or organised by these complex conceptual categories. Although it might seem that it is sensorimotor engagement with the world that creates meaning, this is too quick: neither (a) nor (b) are sensorimotor processes. In empirical studies, Martindale reveals that processes such as those involved in (a) and (b) are attended to and remembered rather than the perceptible details, which are 'ignored and quickly forgotten' (1988, p. 27). Therefore, it might be more accurate to say that situated cognition brings together details of a situation that are accessed in a sensorimotor way and which provide perceptual details that are parsed or coded in such a way as to allow the mind to organise higher-level cognition, or the kind of expert knowledge commonly involved in viewing art. This is not the same as saying that situated cognition depends upon sensorimotor processes. This would mean seeing situated cognition in art as a distributed system similar to the following:

> *perceptible details of artwork* + *sensorimotor details* + *higher order cognition and semantics* + *relational knowledge*

To call all of this 'extended cognition' because these elements together result in a variable and ongoing cognitive process seems merely to be a generalisation that neglects how these different processes are involved with each other, which, in any case, may be open to idiosyncratic differences. Depending on the artworks, some of these individual processes will cooperate with each other without any significant sensorimotor involvement, so it is difficult to generalise about how art situates cognition using sensorimotor processes. In addition, artworks will be important for helping to stimulate a number of emotions, yet we would not claim that the artwork plus the viewer form an 'extended emotion'.[3] Another important complication is that some artworks require that we ignore the obviousness

---

[3] Although there is a case to be made that situations such as weddings or other social situations (Griffiths and Scarantino, 2009) strongly influence emotional behaviours, and films can be said to create moods. Still, it seems incorrect to state that we are sharing emotions with artworks or films. Nevertheless, it seems important that in all cases, even when individuals are convinced that they are 'sharing' emotions with loved ones, for example, we do assume that emotions are fixed states, that they have a dynamic variability that can be communicated. The intractable question, however, remains: in terms of situated cognition, is the communication causal for various internal cognitive or emotional operations, or constitutive?

of the perceptual details and use them counterfactually, as I have shown in previous chapters, which means conceptualising sensorimotor processes in non-normative ways, as we would the artefacts themselves. There are other artworks that do not even require that we study them perceptually.

Myin and Veldman (2011) insist that even conceptual artworks that seem to have little or no perceptual content are still dependent on sensorimotor processes: '[however] "dematerialized" contemporary artworks may be, they are still properly conceived as objects of visual attention. A full appreciation of them still requires going to the gallery and visually exploring them' (p. 58).

This suggests that these authors are not aware of works such as John Cage's *4'33"* (four minutes of silence), Fluxus event scores or conceptual works such as Robert Barry's *Inert Gas* series, one of which was a canister releasing spurts of helium gas into the desert (not a gallery) to illustrate that art can be, as he explicitly stated, imperceptible. There is even Tom Friedman's cursed plinth where the artist asked a witch to curse the atmosphere above a single white plinth on which nothing is placed (1992). There are a great many land art works that are not objects at all, such as Richard Long's walks or Vito Acconci's *Following Piece*. In Santiago Sierra's *Space Closed by Corrugated Metal*, Lisson Gallery, London, September 2002, the artist invited guests to his opening only for them to find the gallery closed by corrugated iron in order to illustrate what it must have felt like for crowds trying to get their savings back after the currency crisis in Argentina where the banks refused to open their doors to customers. This also references artist Robert Barry who declared in December 1969 that his Amsterdam exhibition would consist of staff locking out gallery visitors and appending a sign: 'For the exhibition the gallery will be closed.' Of course, one is at liberty to claim that this is not art, or even a parody of it but, by the same token, one would also have to discount many conceptual and performance artworks. I have mentioned Martin Creed's work. In addition, we do not normally consider the aesthetics of photographs that record performance pieces from the 1970s. If a mathematical or scientific equation can be elegant, it would be pointless to suggest that its elegance lies in the symbols that go to make up the equation when demonstrated. Similarly, many artworks severely limit perceptual involvement or exploration to a point where it becomes superfluous or unremarkable, as I have stated continually in this book. More recently, Tino Sehgal's Documenta 13 work at Kassel, 2012, consisted of withdrawing vision from performance works altogether by forcing visitors to grope around in the dark.

How can situated cognition, as an approach that tries to show in varying degrees how cognitive processes take place beyond the skin and are offloaded onto the environment, account for situations that have little or no perceptible qualities to allow the internal to latch on to 'the external' or vice versa? One way is to insist that our engagement with the world in situated cognition need not come down to sensorimotor action of a crude sort, that some thought is not contingent upon perceptual experience, or that there is thought, such as conceptual thought, that is *in excess* of or in cooperation with exploring the environment with offline or online sensori-motor processes. This is clearly the case with relational knowledge, conceptual integration, linguistic and semantic generation, rational induction as well as self-reflexivity. This does not mean rejecting the notion of an integration of external and internal processes but it does mean rejecting certain explanations of how this integration occurs. Myin and Velman's situational cognition thus represents a crudely reductionist account of situated aesthetics that betrays a very limited knowledge of contemporary art and the new aesthetic problems that it uncovers.

A short description of what is involved in viewing a piece of video art reveals some interesting aesthetic and perceptual issues which may be pertinent for situated cognition. Bill Viola's *I Do Not Know What It Is I Am Like* (1986) is a short film of an owl looking straight out at the camera. It moves only once and blinks occasionally but remains almost entirely still throughout the film, its gaze fixed on one point, while the animal's irises seem to dilate very slightly at certain moments. Slowly the camera zooms in to focus on a pupil where the reflection of the camera's looming presence may be descried. How does the artist encourage us to be absorbed in a film where *nothing happens*?

The owl is inspecting something it may not be entirely conscious of; it may be inattentive of the camera's presence. It does, however, seem perfectly fixed on a point in its visual field, one that happens to be the camera. One wonders, is it monitoring its own internal states, whatever they are? It has a presence that is entirely distinct, fixed; but what could it be thinking and is it possible to think nothing at all? It is so still for the five-minute duration of the piece that it encourages me to be still. It makes me think, what could I be thinking? The film seems to be a portrait of some kind of consciousness, and the owl is perfectly still, like a photograph. It only occasionally occurs to me that it is a running film, an image that captures the passing of time in a particular way, not through action normally understood. It helps me to reflect on difference and the possibility that animals can have a consciousness, or even that they sometimes can be deep in thought, or not thinking at all.

As a film, it is refreshing to note that a film director or an artist could film animals doing nothing, instead of performing tricks within structured plotlines. There is an attractive, mesmerising Minimalism and simplicity to this, something that we normally attribute to an iconic presence or charisma. Bill Viola did a whole series of similar films on animals that seem to do nothing (bison on the frozen tundra, for example), that remain still, seem to have inner lives.

There is some value in getting human beings to meditate on the inner lives of animals and many other artists have tried to do this in art history. Perhaps for those who have pets, this becomes a trivial observation; but for me, there is something attractive about being drawn into the utter darkness of a pupil, to get some idea of what the owl may be looking at. It tells me something about myself and the way I understand things through my own pupils. Yet the owl seems familiar to me, a feeling I am reluctant to think is merely a solipsism, and it is difficult not to imagine being there, to avoid imagining that the owl is inspecting me. It is a kind of 'internalisation' of the gaze, a mechanism that many artworks adopt where we simulate looking at ourselves as we imagine how we might be looked at.

It is important to note that these cogitations are not stimulated by mirror neurons. Movement here is the same as magnification – it may suggest approaching the bird, or the bird approaching us. Either way, this 'movement' does not determine the image alone, for the stillness of the bird and the time image, the image of duration and thought, seem to carry the burden of meaning. These thoughts are all mine, others will have different responses to the film, but it is not difficult to see how my thoughts are constructed logically from the visual material in front of me. Many of these thoughts are imaginary, based on imagining being looked at, and speculating on the consciousness of others. It is a 'theory of mind' experience, yet strangely held in check by thoughts of animal consciousness. Art encourages us to use our imaginations, sometimes surprisingly and creatively. The power of the image is sometimes that it can make us think about how we structure our thoughts with regard to the image. It helps us in a *situated* way to inspect our own thoughts and feelings and their relational structure, perhaps in a special, contemplative way, fixed on the visual, which might otherwise not occur, at least not in this peculiar way in connection with an owl.

Yet in performance art, this kind of interactivity or requirement that we treat the artwork as 'another consciousness' or as a theory of mind, which requires that the artwork itself responds to the cognitive processes of the viewer and can anticipate her needs, comes into focus more sharply. This idea reaches one of its finest expressions in art with Marina Abramović's *The Artist is Present*. As the MOMA website commemorating the event explains, 'every day the Museum was open between March 14 and May 31, 2010. Visitors were encouraged to sit silently across from the artist for a duration of their choosing, becoming participants in the artwork.'[4]

The artist's body becomes the body of the artwork, silent yet perhaps interrogative and interactive. It is something that can be seen as a social situation but one that is typical of a lifelong exploration of how to represent, actualise and abstract what it means to be embodied in art beyond ordinary facticity, which it would be ridiculous to reduce the encounter to here, but which is nevertheless a *conceptual* framing indispensable for the exchange between viewer, artist and artwork. Abramović is both passive and active, seeing and seen, as is the viewer. In this embodiment, one should say, extension, of Merleau-Ponty's 'chiasm' and Lacan's 'the object staring back', she enables art to become, literally at the same time, body schema and body image, perceptual and conceptual, public and intimate, still and silent, yet uneventful. It seems that whether Marina Abramović becomes a body, a person or an artwork depends on our conceptualisation but we are equally a medium for her transformation of us, and perhaps some of this realisation leaks into our own cogitations. The shared gaze, its simple facticity and directness, undoubtedly allows for a synchrony of cognitive functions in viewer and artist, and possibly even a matching of them. One might even say, figuratively, that they are sharing the same thought or way of thinking, that there is a perfect synchronicity; but are there any cognitive functions really being shared here? Is the notion of cognition not extending an artistic expression beyond the skull in *The Artist is Present*?

Watching the exchange between artist and visitors, it appears that there is both a vulnerability and consent, as well as a sense of responsibility to do with the power of viewing and appreciating how this gaze acts as an instrument in objectifying the other or, more remarkably, in looking forwards and reflexively at the same time. For Abramović, it must have been exhausting and disconcerting to look into the lives of so many others, either to feel or not to feel, to be able to speculate about emotions or recognise that a face is inscrutable or potentially charged with a huge range of emotional intensities, residues of which may remain to be detected by subsequent sitters. Both intersubjective difference and sameness are negotiated with the exercise of respect, suspicion or empathy.[5] Moreover, desire seems able to magnify or moderate any one of these states. Everything seems to

---

[4] www.moma.org/visit/calendar/exhibitions/965

[5] These more 'cognitive' kinds of emotion make the claims of situated cognition stark: 'An extended-emotion thesis potentially confuses the claim that the environment makes a causal contribution to a mental process with the more ontologically demanding claim that it is a constituent part of it' (Griffiths and Scarantino, 2009, p. 448).

be arranged around the shared gaze. Vicariously, I imagine what the viewer saw, what the artist saw, whether this was possible for them to think the same thought somehow reproducible in me – what can this possible thought be, except perhaps the thought of possibly sharing a thought? What are the cognitive underpinnings of such a common thought? The thought about the possibility of sharing a thought demonstrates a theory of mind, a kind of empty bracket in which any contents can be placed, but it does not require that it is actually reciprocated or shared. Whatever is going on in the artist's or viewer's mind is not cognitively shared, as we are fond of saying the gaze can be, and the artist's thought does not constitute the viewer's, or the other way around; the viewer is not extending the artist's cognition even in this intimate exchange.

To interpret the artwork as just another opportunity to realise our embodiment seems trivial. In this artwork, it seems key that viewer and artist (in fact, they are both viewers) are still and silent, and the exchange is pared down to its Minimalist essentials. Would it be true to suggest the artwork is constituted not so much by the viewer or the artist, as such, as by the shared gaze? This would certainly be a development of a major theme in contemporary art to do with the dematerialisation of the art object, the shared gaze, the optical exchange, visible in terms of its material substrate (person, eyes) but invisible in that we are not able to 'see a gaze'. This is a telling point for situated cognition, for it need not be bound too tightly to sensorimotor details. Viola's owl and Abramović's staring contest present situations that help conceptual thoughts to arise in abundance, even though perceptible details are pared down in each work, where stillness, uneventfulness, emptiness and the invisibility of the shared gaze become the contours of a situation that moulds a cognitive systematicity that may be reciprocated by the object staring back.

In terms of subsequent viewers' experiences of Abramović's performance work through various photographs and films that document it, there is a continuous coupling with aspects of the work's perceptual cues while, at the same time, there is a decoupling from other perceptual cues and background details that were available for the viewer and artist to see during the performance. As de Bruin and Kästner (2011) suggest, decoupling, that is, thinking about a perceptual aspect of the artwork and its conceptual import without having to actually observe it – as we might do while thinking about Duchamp's *Fountain* or *The Artist is Present* – is perhaps better understood as a dynamic, looping or repeating process of decoupling/recoupling. We can attend to a present or nonpresent artwork while engaging with conceptualisation. In other words, when situationists claim that we are attentive to the situation, this may be only a fleeting part of a much greater and complex task involving many other processes. The artwork is a situation, whether present or not, in the sense that it constrains my conceptualisation, which may attend to it directly (coupling with it conceptually) or work around it, or through thoughts associated with it (decoupling). The constraining is being carried out by my own cognitive processes: I am allowing the thought about an artwork and its qualities to be present within my working memory so that I can arrange a number of cognitive processes around it and with regard to it. The artwork itself may be so Minimalist and empty of details (as in *The Artist is Present* or *Fountain* and many contemporary artworks) that it is not necessary for my cogitations to be supported by a material anchor in the environment, in the literal sense.[6] When structuring my system of relational knowledge with artworks and references, which provides a context during the inspection of an artwork in front of me, these nonpresent artworks will also be lacking in detail. Thinking about the possibility of this – how we can think of the absent art object as an aid to our conceptual thought – would amount to a kind of decoupling and recoupling with the artwork before me. I believe that these are the kinds of issues and thoughts that both Duchamp and Abramović were keen to encourage in order to question naïve assumptions about 'the situation' as direct perception or the direct perception of embodiment. Sometimes individuals simply cannot rely on what is in front of them and will have to 'appeal to some kind of stand-in for what is currently absent…This enables the agent to inhibit reflex-like automatic responses to external triggers…by recruiting internal representations' (de Bruin and Kästner, 2011, p. 7).

It is important that decoupling does not mean disembodiment or decontextualisation (Clark, 2005). Clark also claims that even high-level reasoning is local and situated when decoupled from the immediate environment. This may be true for many occasions but it does not explain how these surrogates are arranged, categorised or given value, processes that may be encoded as rules with the help of amodal representations with the kind of convergence zones theorised by Simmons and Barsalou (2003), who I have mentioned cede some ground to some kinds of amodal representation. Theories of enactivism and extended mind, as well as neo-empiricist approaches that emphasise perceptual experience, generalise that situations, surrogates or artefacts make detailed internal representations unnecessary. However, they do not explain how we

---

[6] I do not think that Minimalism, performance art or readymades are any less complex conceptually than a Picasso; witness how much ink has been spilt on Warhol's perceptually unremarkable *Brillo Boxes*, and Duchamp's *Fountain*. While there will be many more perceptual details in a Picasso painting than we are able to keep in the mind at any one time, it is worth remembering also that not every perceptible detail is a cue for conceptual thought.

process such context-sensitivity, how we choose to couple or not with the environment or, indeed, how we pick out specific parts of the vast continuum of environmental contexts in order for them to be represented as 'sensitive': 'since anything can be relevant to a given circumstance, these mechanisms have to access all our long-term perceptual knowledge, without succumbing to some form of computational explosion...Since relevance is a semantic notion, syntactic views of the nature of our cognitive processes do not seem suited to explain context-sensitivity and relevance' (Machery, 2007, p. 30).

Yet attempts to integrate internalism and externalism in some enactive accounts by reducing concepts to perceptual experience with a bias towards the latter (Myin and Veldman, 2011; Noë, 2005), or by reducing embodied engagement with the environment to the brain's neural correlates (which remain the privileged partner) at the expense of how it is supported and guided by technology and artefacts (neuroscientific approaches), fail to produce a balance that preserves the complexity of conceptual formation (in the first example) and the dynamic connectedness with the environment (in the second example).

Many of our encounters with contemporary artworks in the environment depend on complex dynamic interactions between perceptions and concepts, which have been under-theorised. Perhaps only dynamic systems theories, applied to our understanding of the cognitive levels summarised by de Bruin and Kästner (2011) and also applicable to different neural levels (Egan and Matthews, 2006), along with pluralistic approaches to representation (Dove, 2009), can come close to providing a more equitable integration that does not involve isolating composite parts of the art experience in order to make them fit into the relevant theory.

Left out of the equation as well is the prereflexive reciprocity between agent and environment (what will be more familiar to art historians and philosophers as Heidegger's *dasein* or being-in-the-world), which is difficult to include in detailed cognitive models. Perhaps *dasein* may be thought of as a continuous or dynamic looping of coupling and decoupling/recoupling with the artwork, theorised by dynamic embodied cognition (de Bruin and Kästner, 2011), which is a continuous process of differentiation rather than static or 'pure' stable states maintained over particular time periods. I have mentioned how mind wandering most probably will have a key role to play in creative interpretations of artworks and in mediating metacognition. Pertinent to experiences of contemporary art that I have analysed in this book, coupling may be associated with direct processing of the perceptual cues of the artwork, while decoupling arises when processing various 'non-retinal' abstract aspects, such as with

Martin Creed's *The Light's Going On and Off*. At any rate, in order to do justice to the conceptual complexity of contemporary art, and as I have advocated with a pluralistic approach to representation, which includes aspects of both modal and amodal representation, art historians and psychologists will be more able to avoid the dangers of reductionism implied by enactive, situated and strongly embodied approaches if they adopt 'a mixture of enactive and representational processing'. While online processing is 'cheap' and efficient as 'it allows the agent to avoid building up "costly" internal representations', offline processing provides agents with more flexibility (autonomy) regarding their direct environment but it is also more cognitively demanding (de Bruin and Kästner, 2011, p. 9).

This more flexible notion of representation avoids the classical representationalism of complex symbol manipulation. Thus, dynamic models of interaction between enactive processes and decoupled (sub-)symbolic representations avoid distortion caused by polarising a strong embodied and situated approach and the classical information-processing approach, each of which trivialises what the other focuses on. Both have important roles to play, and cognitive psychology should address how they cooperate. Many of the schemata of relational knowledge involved in experiencing art should not be thought of as static or preconceived representations but as nonlinear, 'manipulable' (as Hutchins, 2005, states) dynamic decoupling/recoupling processes that are 'tweaked' with regard to the artwork attended, and which require the joint action of top-down and bottom-up processes. Therefore, there is an ad hoc element to schemata as well as a relatively constant core that can be relied on across different instances of looking at art objects, but even this core may change over time. The challenge for cognitive psychology and neuroscience is to provide empirical research into interactional and dynamic models that stress interconnections between top-down and bottom-up processes, perhaps viewing these interconnections qualitatively. Dealing purely with the interconnections between concepts or those between perceptions will not do. Contemporary art draws out, sustains and influences these interconnections between concepts and perceptions in ways that are not repeated in other domains of knowledge.

4.2   Evaluating situated cognition

Approaches to situated cognition (along with enactivist approaches) are designed to discourage the idea that there are complex pre-formed concepts stored in the brain as internal representations that are matched in the world or that help to form our view of it. According to theories of situated cognition, explicit conceptual reasoning plays a minor role in online cognition. As I have mentioned, the world is its own model; we need no duplication of it in our brains to recognise it (Brooks, 1991). Many contemporary artworks I have dealt with in this book encourage a broadly defined form of action using massive neural interconnectivity well beyond sensorimotor systems. Maybe this broader 'configural' view should count as a form of action, even if the sensorimotor part of this larger process plays only a minor part in it. This effectively goes beyond the narrow definition of action purely as a matter of arms and legs, head and eyes in movement (or such movement imagined offline), which many embodied or situated accounts depend on. As Prinz objects (2009, p. 422), being in a sensory-deprivation chamber where one is unable to engage with the world using one's senses or actions does not halt complex cognition. Situationists might counter this by insisting that, even there, projections and dispositions in the sensorimotor system are still being used (offline) to generate thought. Yet, the fact that cognition of a complex kind is possible, cut off from the sensory world, does show that we do not need to use, or imagine using, our arms and legs, head and eye movements to *generate* thought.

It is likely that top-down and offline processes, that is, higher cognitive and conceptual integration, work cooperatively with bottom-up perceptual processes and in motoric systems, which may be offline, imaginatively engaged with perceptual processes, or online, actively exploring artworks. These continuous and massively connected processes are perhaps better understood using dynamic models of embodied cognition (see de Bruin and Kästner, 2011). Dynamic models of interaction with the environment (Turvey and Carello, 1995) emphasise the agent's interaction with the specificities of the environment. For example, when having a conversation, cognition seems to be 'shared' between the speakers in a joint conceptual space, or cognitive processes rapidly interact with a dynamic environment as we see in the game of Tetris (Kirsh and Maglio, 1994).[1] Although this model 'speeds up' the notion of an iterated cognitive extension, it still inherits the weaknesses of various situated cognition theories in that the exact ways in which external resources contribute or replace internal cognitive mechanisms remains underspecified.

When Noë claims that consciousness 'is not something in our heads, it is something we do', one must also acknowledge that there is a lot of 'doing' in our heads in conjunction with artefacts and environmental aspects lying outside of it. Even our sensorimotor dispositions are in a sense 'in our heads', as the sensory deprivation chamber demonstrates. Although not denying that representations and conceptual thought exist, surely it is wrong to suggest that such thought 'is merely icing on the cognitive cake' (Griffiths and Scarantino, 2009, p. 440). Adding further details of what is required of situationist generalisations if they are to be plausible, Kirsh (2009) suggests that situated cognition currently does not address *how* and *when* people externalise inner states and 'interactively frame their problems, and cognize affordances and cues, and allocate control across internal and external resources' (p. 290). The implication is that a lot of 'internal' cognitive processes involved in temporal and prefrontal areas that control engagement with situated cognition and prioritise how we engage with aspects of the environment are ignored by theorists who focus only on the physical engagement with external tools and ways in which these seem to affect internal resources and priorities. A similar weakness may be discerned in many attempts to explain participative art, which assume participation to be primarily a question of bodies rather than the sharing of internal resources such as knowledge systems. Clearly, according to Kirsh, theorists for (and against) situated cognition have not yet satisfactorily joined up what is going on inside and outside the head, apart from going beyond figures of speech that indicate offloading cognition leaking into the environment (Clark, 2008).

Thought is physical action using regions of the brain, with or without other physical systems of the body and with or without manipulation of material objects in the environment or even imagined material objects. There are, in certain circumstances, situations in art and

---

[1] Clark writes about constructing a chapter for a book that contains 'all kinds of hints and fragments, stored up over a long period of time...as I move these things about...the intellectual shape of the chapter grows and solidifies. It is a shape that does not spring fully developed from inner cogitations. Instead, it is the product of a sustained and iterated sequence of interactions between my brain and a variety of external props' (1998, pp. 206–207).

further afield where knowledge arises without perceptual exploration. This is not to elevate the nonperceptual over the perceptual but to emphasise their mutually reinforcing action. In art, perceptual exploration, that is, exploration of what is perceptible, is processed in parallel with what may be imperceptible to the senses, such as abstract concepts and relational knowledge. Perceptions are only *part* of the interdigitation of different kinds of thought processes involving, for example, the self-monitoring of mental states, memory, rational induction, semantic complexity and many other processes that traditionally have been considered 'internal', in cooperation with external resources such as notebooks, computers, artworks and other minds. This is not, I think, in strong opposition to many kinds of theories of situated cognition, and is certainly in agreement with embedded cognitive approaches that emphasise the subject's interactions with the environment. This marshalling together of different kinds of thoughts, some of them involving manipulations of external resources, which I have been at pains to demonstrate in my analysis of contemporary art, is how situated cognition should properly be thought of, not by insisting on the primacy of sensorimotor action and perceptual experience but by examining how this cooperation works. Perhaps the biggest sin of omission in both embodied and situated accounts of cognition and art is any examination of how perceptual details provide us with cognitive conceptual complexity beyond the description of one or two simple concepts.

This integration of resources within *and* beyond the skin is made explicit in Hutchins' adaptation of Fauconnier and Turner's conceptual blending using material anchors, to which I turn my attention. I have hinted at how Carl Andre's *Lever*, the metaphorical associations suggested by Mimi Parent's plaits, and Kosuth and Nauman's semantic networks involved in words and images provide some examples of how thought is mapped onto external resources, detail for detail. What I attempt now is to look in more detail at how this works at a fundamental level, using some modern and contemporary artworks that link conceptual integration to language or artefacts without overemphasising gross bodily movements or perceptions as the most important link between internal and external resources, although there will be variable sensorimotor involvements.

Thus, the standard objections must be noted: that the notion of extending cognition 'outside the skull and skin' suggests that a lot of cognition goes on inside them as well, in order for it to be extended, which is not taken into account by theorists of situated cognition. It would be rash to conclude that such external props are active, have choices about acting, and are generative of their own cognitive processes that have a causal influence on the cognitive processes of the viewer, the 'coupling–constitution fallacy' (Adams and Aizawa, 2009). As Kirsh suggests, ideas and possible ways of interpreting the situation and the situated scaffold are evaluated: 'there is always a component of generating candidate actions and testing their adequacy' (2009, p. 292). Moreover, there are differences between using aspects of a situation unthematically for a task and attending to the same aspects of a situation thematically as part of the task, a double function offered by artworks. This evaluative and creative process, where we try out different ways of using objects, is itself worthy of study, as we have seen in the ways that psychology can shed light on how we interpret art. Perhaps the most that can be claimed here is that the viewer's expert knowledge allows an artwork's perceptible cues to be recognised, processed and contextualised by relational knowledge, and interpreted in order to allow the viewing subject's cognitive processes to be altered, if they are willing to have them altered, and they effect these alterations upon themselves. In such cases in contemporary art, this might well amount to consent where, as viewers, we allow the artwork to be understood momentarily as an other, where we imagine that the artwork seems to reach out to us. However, in such circumstances, the viewer/reader is in a process of interpreting, contextualising and actively supplying the artwork with significance, filling in its gaps and allowing aspects of the artwork that are not gaps, packages perhaps, to be parsed and coded within existent knowledge structures. The artwork does not, strictly, act upon us, unless, of course, the artwork is a performance where a performer may directly address us, but even this is complicated by whether the act is causal or constitutive of my cognitive states. If external information does appear to constitute my cognitive processes, it is only because, at some level, we consent to this appearance and cast the artwork in the role of something that 'supports' cognition; rather, it is *interpreted* as supporting cognition. As viewers and readers, we are still actively processing incoming signals to the best of *our* abilities, following the contours of our own peculiar characters and neural networks.

An interesting objection to this might be concerning memories, where Sutton (2009), for example, suggests that such inner representations and traces might not always be complete but be partial and context sensitive, so that perceptual cues in the environment can help to reconstruct them. This reverses Duchamp's well-known quip, 'it's not what you see that is art, art is the gap', because it suggests that we, as viewers, have 'the gap' supplied by the aspects of the artwork! Sutton also provides food for thought regarding how memories arise within the flow of a thinker's present desires and needs, as well as her 'forward-looking or anticipatory features and functions' (p. 229). This further suggests that the organism's cognitive processes provide meaning rather than the cognitive constancy of external resources so often suggested by theorists of situated cognition. Perhaps the strongest case for situated cognition comes in the form of Sutton's explanation of how memories are coded within social systems of values and influences, and are made to feel autobiographical although they are publicly shared. There is an important distinction between shared experiences or memories (on a train, or a bus), and collective or cultural memory, which accrues aspects of value, empathy and identity as well as abstract notions of history and time (2009, p. 227). Memories can also 'migrate': we might experience an account of another's memories that becomes our own. These examples may seem to support a notion of socially supported situated cognition, but because they are very much in the field of communication and social cognition, as well as memory, they also seem to go beyond the more particular claims of situated cognition that particular cognitive processes are supported by external sources even though most accounts of situated cognition fail to show, in any detail, how such 'support' is organised psychologically.

If one were to reject some strong theories of situated cognition, this does not mean that one has to deny that artworks that 'narrativise the gaze', that show us how we tend to look at things and conceptualise them, such as Velázquez's *Las Meninas*, are not cognitively informative. The work is composed in such a way as to address the viewer: many of the figures depicted are outward gazing figures. It teaches us about how gazes can be involved in an intricate network that can structure space and relations with suggested orthogonals (also involving the viewer). Such an artwork can have important cognitive effects on us and on how we process art in subsequent years. Surely, it is not right to say that the artwork is cognitive, that its gaze is directed at us, which suggests a subject–object confusion, although we are more willing to believe this in our engagements with other minds, dogs, or characters in novels whose inner cogitations seem to become ours.

There is no problem with suggesting that one's store of knowledge can be extended or reflected back to one by a close friend or a partner, whom you trust knows your thoughts through long experience and who can remind you of what you previously held to be true, which you have temporarily forgotten. It also seems fairly uncontroversial that books and diaries contain detailed access to thoughts which, when reading them, will aid reflection and generate further thoughts. Yet, in reminding you of what you said on previous occasions, a person will probably add her own interpretation or emphasis in retrieving your thoughts on a topic, and in subsequent situations will again add different nuances to that retrieved knowledge, depending on the situation.[2] Moreover, whatever one writes will be read in the context of a different present, and will no doubt be used cognitively differently. The so-called fixed aspect of the external 'cognitive' store can be carved up and used for different cognitive tasks, changing the nature of its previous cognitive support. The organism retains so much more of the greater share of the cognition processing, which also included deciding upon what qualifies as cognition. To claim that the external store is also cognitive merely seems to confuse matters. The external storage, artwork, novel, diary, will be intricately tied up with ongoing cogitations but it will not generate cognition in the sense that we, as readers or viewers, become extensions of the external storage and *its* thoughts and become units of its larger cognitive task. It is not thinking me, it has no cognition.

If cognition is to be defined as a larger cognitive task or purpose, it might parse information that will make my cognitive load easier, or more difficult. However, the overall task occurs inside my head and my prefrontal areas will help me decide whether I am still on course, and will help to direct me to cognitive support in the environment or lead me to ignore it as irrelevant. To share a thought with a book or a person does not mean that my cognitive processes, which are involved in generating that thought that is dynamic, are being generated by the book or the other person. We may share similar representations but not the same neural processes that support that representation. Situationists might mean that what is shared or supported by the physical environment are representational contents, not the neural circuits that enable them. Even so, these inner representational contents, the timing and quality of which an artwork will be able to influence and constrain, are only relatively stable.

In other words, there may be an overemphasis in situated cognition involved with external storage as permanent or fixed. In fact, it may only appear to be so and is dependent on how it is to be interpreted or used. There is a kind of time delay, in that a work of art configures with 'external marks' the intentional thoughts and aspects of the consciousness of the artist, and the viewer reconfigures these in a process of mentally and physically exploring the work. This in effect works as a *partial* cause of the ongoing cognitive state of the viewer, the other cause being the internal resources and knowledge base we have at our disposal, which we bring to

---

[2] As Griffiths and Scarantino point out (2009, p. 443) this is complicated in linguistics by diachronic (historical) grammatical organisation, which evolves more slowly than synchronic (contemporary, personal, improvisational) tendencies. Both synchronic and diachronic tendencies combine or interact in speech utterances. Depending on the situation, such tendencies and interactions will involve extremely variable cognitive processes.

bear upon this encounter between *different kinds* of resources. These 'external marks' may seem to change their character dramatically on subsequent viewings, or the cues themselves could change as they do with film or performance art. Our ability to recognise the change is due to us. Does the cognitive mechanism behind recognition change, depending on the thing recognised? What is the empirical evidence for this? Do the cognitive mechanisms behind how scripts, schemata or simulations are retrieved or coded in order to recognise a situation change their functioning (and, therefore, become something else), depending on the situation being attended? The prefrontal cortex is important for maintaining priorities over and above competing signals in order to complete tasks and projects. Do physical objects and environments drive cognition in this way? What is there in the situation that extends, adds or alters, in any way, the principles of how these cognitive mechanisms function, except by supplying them with different, more or less complex details to work with? Theorists of situated cognition need empirical support to answer these questions because only then can we speak of situations as cognitive 'in themselves'. Even in such unlikely scenarios, where we would find external stores that are cognitive 'in themselves', that is for their own purposes, one is still bound to ask, cognitive *for whom*?

4.3   Clark's extended mind

Andy Clark explains situated cognition as a break with the past, when the mind was seen as a series of internal states acting upon passive external resources: 'a good deal of actual thinking involves loops and circuits that run outside the head and through the local environment. Extended intellectual arguments and theses are almost always the products of brains acting in concert with multiple external resources' (1998, pp. 206–207).[1]

Is there anything in Clark's extended mind theory (Clark, 2008) that is helpful as a way to understand the psychology of contemporary art, potentially a strong candidate as an external resource for supporting cognition? I think there is, but there are also some problems. Compared with some versions (Kirchhoff, 2012; Wheeler, 2010), Andy Clark's (2008) version of extended cognition appears to be quite moderate. He has well-considered answers to many of the worries I have voiced in this book concerning agency and some of the key cognitive processes of representation and self-monitoring. Rather than taking Clark's more colourful phrases seriously, such as 'local mechanisms of human cognition quite literally bleeding out into body and world' (2008, p. 70), polemical comments that sometimes mar his often brilliant *Supersizing the Mind*, it is wiser to turn one's attention to his more balanced comments, which are often forgotten. Concerning the recruitment of external tools and resources, he writes: 'it is indeed the biological brain (or perhaps some of its subsystems) that remains in the driver's seat...it is the biological organism that spins, selects, or maintains the webs of cognitive scaffolding that participate in the extended machinery of its own thought and reasoning' (pp. 122–123) and acknowledges that 'The organism... remains the core and currently the most active element' (p. 139).

Clark is very clear that it is the brain's plasticity that is primarily responsible for the main process of cognition, 'without which the whole

---

[1] It is interesting that, in the humanities, the opposite it commonly held to be undesirable: that we are passive spectators, disempowered by the flow of information around us.

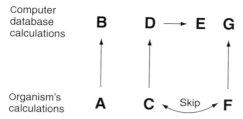

Figure 30. Extended cognition: the database metaphor.

process grinds to a standstill. There will be no new pens, or paper, and software packages when the human organisms all dry up and die' (p. 162).

Importantly, however, Clark insists that this cognition has a whole heterogeneous range of external material, as well as embodied and internal resources it recruits, that *altogether* effect the efficiency of cognition, so that without the aid of certain external resources (according to Clark, Linguaform, notebooks, gesture, for example) such cognition would still arise but it might have a lot more work to do. One of Clark's major purposes is to show how the integration of external and internal resources works. A key point here concerns an approach called distributed functional decomposition, which 'analyzes a cognitive task as a sequence of less intelligent subtasks...but it does so relative to a larger (not merely) neural organizational whole' (p. 202). This implies that some elements of cognition, such as the calculations of software programmes, arrive at the same results that we would when using our minds but we, of course, build those results into meaningful and more complex cognitive processes involving purpose and longer-term plans and goals. This seems like a fairly uncontroversial way in which some cognitive processes may be seen to be 'offloaded onto the environment'.

The flow chart attempts to sketch the cooperation between a human and an art history database for researching relationships between landscape painters in a particular period and country. A user inputs dates, type of work (painting), genre (landscapes) and country (A). The computer provides a selection of artists under these criteria (B), from which the organism chooses, narrowing down the choices to five artists whose careers overlap (C). The computer is able to provide the list of five artists picked and to display them in alphabetical order (D), but is also able to calculate from a probabilistic programme and suggest any similar titles of paintings or place names shared by these artists (E). The user chooses (E) and formulates a new question from the list of paintings displayed that have common titles. Thus, the organism can skip a part of cognitive subroutine (E) and work on narrowing down particular paintings that are by the same artists with the similar subject matter and titles to request more detail (F). Not only is the computer able to make inferences from a line of questioning, but it also selects works that are grouped together in terms of categories that would require more time and effort working only with a paper-based catalogue. One could imagine this taking place with databases of far higher complexity. The dynamic process of interdigitation allows for both mechanical and biological calculation processes and categorisation in order to share the cognitive burden of the task.

There is good reason, however, to make a distinction between a circumscribed, subpersonal task and a cognitive task, the assembly and trajectory of which – the framework of the task – is built and led by the organism, rather than being a discrete subroutine that can be used by anyone and for any purpose. While the organism integrates this into the overall task, the computer subtask takes part only in the organism's 'cognitive flow' because the organism has allowed it to enter that flow, otherwise it has no function in the greater scheme.[2] It is only cognitive because the organism uses it cognitively. The *overall* cognitive task can be said to be shared with the computer and one can imagine progressively more difficult tasks with more complex input from computerised subroutines helping the organism to achieve its long-term goal. Yet, even here, it makes good sense to resist the imagery of leaky minds. Clark would perhaps counter that this relies too much on an internal/external dualism between mind and technology. He writes: 'Much of what matters about human intelligence is hidden not in the brain nor in the technology, but in the complex and iterated interactions and collaborations between the two' (Clark, 2001, p. 154). This finds support in relational aesthetics theories that emphasise the flow of processes between individuals; the processes constitute the art, not fixed art objects, but social interaction. The diagram of the flow chart indicates how some of these iterated collaborations might occur. It relies on computer subroutines that are discrete units in an

---

[2] As Sutton remarks, paraphrasing Merlin Donald's criticisms of Clark's example of a notebook as a form of extended mind, 'information is stored there in discrete fashion, and representations in the notebook (linguistic or pictorial representations, for example) have no intrinsic dynamics or activity, are not intrinsically integrated with other stored information, and do no cognitive work in their standing or dispositional form' (2009, p. 197). In the biological system, the stored representations will continue to influence and be influenced by surrounding processes. The response to this from extended mind theorists is merely to say that not all external resources are static and that the differences between external and internal representations do not disprove extended mind theory, it just shows that cognition is able to rely on a number of variable and heterogeneous resources (2009, pp. 197, 200). However, the objection still stands and should teach theorists to be more particular about the external resources they choose as examples.

overall cognitive task decided and pursued by the user. The difference is that the separate units are like individual figures, while the use or purpose of the whole task is the configural framework.

As Hutchins writes: 'Stars and planets have an existence independent of people. Constellations do not. While an eye can register a pinpoint of light, seeing that pinpoint as a star is a cultural accomplishment' (2011, p. 446). Similarly, in the task to do with the art history database search, the computer provides the 'stars' while the user configures the 'constellations', a configural process that is a mixture of the user's own experience and cultural tradition. To be able to see configurally beyond the fragmented and successive details, to be able to join up all the dots, is a key cognitive and cultural process that occurs in the 'cognitive style' of the viewer of art or the user of a database. External cultural artefacts and programmes can help us to see the configuration of a larger cognitive task but it is realised and pursued as a longer-term goal by the organism, and in some cases by groups of organisms and their relations.

What remains to be seen is whether certain participative and performance artworks, where artists address viewers within strictly enforced parameters, or films or installation works that present a series of journeys through space, may be seen to take over the cognitive load of certain tasks in ways that are similar to the kind of looped iterations suggested by the diagram, or even in more advanced ways, by anticipating the viewer's needs, thoughts and desires and by manipulating shocks and surprises. In addition, it seems that another way of arguing from a situationist perspective for a subpersonal cognitive unit placed within or working alongside a larger cognitive task led by the organism is to look at how an artwork is placed into groups of works in exhibitions, collections, books and catalogues. Any particular artwork in such a grouping can function as a cognitive subtask placed into a larger cognitive whole as demanded by categorisation processes, the construction of themes and narratives based on relational knowledge structures. In this example, the form of relational knowledge for that particular visit to the gallery, or while reading a book on art divided into themes, will be situated by the 'syntax' or exposition of the works. In other words, how the exhibition is organised will help the viewer to think in certain ways. The reader's or viewer's relational knowledge contains within it a subpersonal unit (a metaphor or a readymade, for example), yet the semantic complexity of this unit is situated in the larger complexity of a book or exhibition (and in the viewer's mind). I attempt to provide some examples of how this might occur in later pages.

There are four interesting areas in art that both situated and extended cognition need to address if they are to be helpful in future empirical research on the psychology of art:

1 How are these subpersonal cognitive processes (overwhelmingly perceptual processes that are treated in situated and extended cognitive research) uploaded into larger cognitive wholes (such as conceptualisation processes) that are not subpersonal?
2 How do cultural and institutional constraints affect the use of subpersonal cognitive 'units' and the organisation of these into larger wholes?
3 The molar complexities of conceptualisation involved in the production and reception of art: how do they utilise subpersonal cognitive routines in ways that are different from other domains? (The complication here is that in the domain of art there is film, painting, sculpture, performance art and so on.)
4 What is the right balance between functionalism (cognitive processes or results that can be achieved across different resources or using different systems and contingencies or bodies) and creativity and innovation?

I hope to provide some suggestions as to how we might begin to answer some of these questions in my following analyses of some artworks.

Affecting many of these problem areas are concerns to do with idiographic differences affected by expert systems and the exercise of agency. Within extended cognition, recent debates seem to centre on the exact role to apportion to the individual organism's cognitive processes, as opposed to subpersonal routines that may be executed by tools and technological mechanisms. Clark seems to defend an interesting balance between the two that could be described as moderate and pragmatic, and appropriate for the purposes of explaining some experiences of art. Clark states that there is no 'inner homunculus' organising all of the cognitive activity; cognitive control is fragmented and distributed so that the interaction between different inner resources and external resources does not always have to be regulated by conscious supervision (2008, p. 137). The use of gesture can regulate and articulate speech, for example, and help us to think and communicate, but we 'do not consciously choose to gesture so as to lighten [the cognitive] load' (p. 137). In such circumstances, however, it is clear that cultural conventions, gender differences and idiographic specificities, that may have been learnt at some stage or acquired and have become second nature, play important roles. Cultural forms can speak through us, unbeknown to us, providing us with cognitive support that is unconscious to us. This seems true for the way that we acquire methods of responding to artworks. What is controversial, however, is whether these cognitive subroutines support preexisting cognitive processes or help us to acquire or alter such cognitive processes. Clark seems to suggest that fundamental cognitive processes are not altered by the recruitment of external resources. Such recruitment 'complements but does not profoundly alter the brain's own basic modes of representation' (1998, p. 198). However, some theorists of extended cognition disagree. Hutchins (2011) clearly comes out in favour of social and cultural practices as well as group interactivity organising cognition.[3] Gallagher and Crisafi (2009) speak of 'mental institutions' that strongly affect our cognitive processes, such as bureaucratic and legal practices, so that we seem to 'think through them'. For a recent summary of these issues, see Kirchhoff (2011), who also provides some discussion of how language learning alters basic cognitive processes. More recent theories of extended cognition place an emphasis on human interaction in groups (rather than individual minds), that carry the cognitive burden of a task such as navigating a ship (Hutchins, 2005) or orchestrating a play in a Shakespearean theatre (Tribble, 2005). The latter study is a good example of how participative practice in contemporary art theory and relational aesthetics (Bourriaud, 1998) can be explained in cognitive terms as a network of mutual support, complementarity and communication between individuals, able to anticipate needs and in some cases to think for them.

In terms of the cognition involved with art, it seems that a balance of such views is needed. In this regard, Clark asserts (2011, p. 459) that his analyses of internal and external integration is about the immediacy and pragmatism of such relations, where the brain plays a major role in assembling heterogeneous resources, while cultural practices are more influential in the longer term in the developmental and evolutionary sense. Hutchins, Gallagher and Crisafi and others insist that the brain and the individual are overemphasised as the major executive in terms of cognitive functions, and that extended cognition shows that such agency is largely distributed among multiple cultural and social practices, where our choices are made for us by the wealth of knowledge represented by medical, legal and bureaucratic structures handed down from generation to generation.

Traditional knowledge structures, the 'grammar' of visual language and various schemata, are often involved automatically in our processing of

[3] 'A practice is cultural if it exists in a cognitive ecology such that it is constrained by or coordinated with the practices of other persons. Above all else, cultural practices are the things people do in interaction with one another' (Hutchins, 2011, p. 440). This is, I take it, the cognitive equivalent of what the cultural theorist Homi Bhabha (1994) has been arguing for years: that culture is performative between people, not fixed substances but fluid, ongoing interactions and exchanges. The virtue of this idea is that it suggests that an artwork can also act as a situation structuring a cultural encounter between individuals. This concept has resurfaced in contemporary art theory in Bishop's discussion of Liam Gillick's work: 'This interest in the contingencies of a "relationship between" – rather than the object itself is the hallmark of Gillick's work, and of his interest in collaborative art practice as a whole' (Bishop, 2010, p. 263).

artworks. This subpersonal aspect to the psychology of art is not just a matter of cultural context and history; cognitive structures can become acculturated and dominated by expert systems. These processes are long term, taking time to affect neural plasticity. We do not change fundamental cognitive structures from painting to painting in an exhibition. The way that we learn to read and interpret artworks forms a continuity over instances, and we form scripts and schemata that may not be highly individualised: a kind of *lingua franca of* cognitive processes that we learn and share with communities and with the artworks themselves, which are configured to speak this language of expert systems and relational knowledge. My other concerns are to do with the more extreme kinds of extended cognition, which seek to show subpersonal units of cognition at work in our responses to art, in that they tend to trivialise creativity and innovative thought, which may eventually allow different assemblages of cognitive resources. At times, there will be a clash between internal cognitive resources and the environment: art is often cognitively challenging, seeking to make us think about stereotypes and tried and trusted ways of using our cognitive resources. For example, metacognition is involved in moderating aesthetic feeling and the rational processes of categorisation. If cognition is offloaded into institutions that act as subpersonal systems that think for us, how are we to reject legal systems and bureaucratic practices when they seem to be oppressive and need to be renovated or reformed? What allows us cognitively to step outside such impersonal machinery that seems to dominate our thought processes and fate? These fears were explored most famously in the surreal scenarios of Kafka's works.

There is no doubt that some of the subroutines of conceptual thought will be subpersonal, and various artworks will help us to offload the simpler cognitive tasks in terms of distributed functional decomposition, helping us to reduce the load on working memory while we construct a relational knowledge system in order understand a particular artwork. For those experienced in viewing art, subpersonal cognitive routines involved in the art encounter will be different from those of non-experts. An expert might not even look twice at Duchamp's *Fountain* while a non-expert might be puzzled by it. Some non-experts might study a Norman Rockwell painting and marvel at its realism, while an expert might dismiss it as meretricious and hackneyed and not worthy of any detailed visual inspection.

4.4 Conceptual blending

Although theorists of situated cognition list many possible kinds of external resources that can be used to free up working memory, conceptual blending, which is itself not a theory of situated cognition, can provide a more fine-grained account of how a concept is mapped onto a material anchor in the environment (Hutchins, 2005). Conceptual blending (or conceptual integration) is Fauconnier and Turner's (2002) theory of cognition, where component parts of a concept (these could be concrete aspects, such as dog in park) act as a source domain and are mapped onto components of another concept in a target domain (man watching dog through binoculars). This mapping creates a blended mental space (scene in science fiction film of man watching dog through binoculars) where new emergent conceptual material occurs (evil android dog tracked down by cyborg detective). The blend brings together these different compounds most often in largely non-conscious and subpersonal ways although, with complex thought, one can deliberate over such blending. Conceptual blending is a diagrammatic way of representing how the contents of one concept and its composite parts map onto another, so the relations between them are visualised. Another way of thinking about this is analogical thought, where two entities are compared in order for us to infer a third entity from the mapping of elements.

Lakoff and Johnson's theory of metaphor (1980) focuses on demonstrating how the source domain of sensorimotor schemas is mapped onto the target domain. However, conceptual integration explores higher-order mental concepts, which may not involve sensorimotor based processes. In other words, the source domain may consist of quite complex frames, scripts or situations (such as sport, restaurant, seminar) that are mapped onto either a more specific source domain (Italian restaurant in Soho), or yet another situation (sport + transport = buffet car in a train). I have already demonstrated how analogies and metaphors can work cross-modally, mapping concrete situations onto superordinate concepts and abstract concepts onto other abstract concepts.

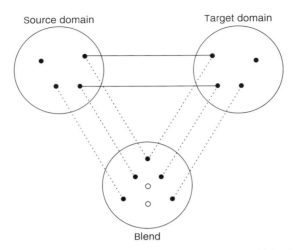

Figure 31. Fauconnier and Turner's conceptual blend.

An important link between abstract concepts as internal states and their relation to material anchors in the environment is made by the psychologist Edwin Hutchins (2005), who writes:

A mental space is blended with a material structure that is sufficiently immutable to hold the conceptual relationships fixed while other operations are performed...In some cases, the conceptual structures to be represented...are so complex they cannot possibly be given stable representation using mental resources alone...the elements must be somehow held (or anchored) in place. The 'holding in place' is accomplished by mapping the conceptual elements onto a relatively stable material structure. This is how a material medium becomes an anchor for a conceptual blend. (2005, p. 1562)

Although he does not reference art, many cultural products (loci, Japanese hand calendars, Micronesian navigation charts, and various sliderules and dials) provide stability and constraints, reference points and mnemonic support for concepts: 'Since conceptual models work by embodying constraints among conceptual elements, both memory and processing loads can be reduced if the constraints of the task can be built into the physical structure of a material device' (p. 1575).

There are many cultural artefacts and artworks that aid memory in many different cultural contexts (Mack, 2003) and some of these have been studied from the point of view of cognitive psychology (de Beni and Moè, 2003). Importantly, however, these mnemonic devices require acculturated and idiographic manipulation along with subpersonal cognitive operations. The perceptual features of an artwork can be used as loci for complex conceptual thoughts, memories, calculations and their relations. It is important to keep in mind that both art and Hutchins' examples do not provide a fixed map or coding of concepts or their relations. In the examples he gives, it is possible to manipulate the order of components of the tool or dial, and with art one can look at the details of a work of art in any order. Hutchins insists that material anchors provide the opportunity for manual manipulation, rather than there being a fixed symbolism at work. Similarly, art presents the opportunity for 'mental manipulation' within certain situational constraints: we can read a painting from right to left, or diagonally, and place a different emphasis on the objects, colours and relations depicted, yet the methods of depiction also suggest relations.

This interaction between individual with material anchors is related to an evolutionary theory of cognitive niche construction (Pinker, 1997) where 'humans create external semiotic anchors that are the result of a process in which concepts, ideas, and thoughts are projected onto external structures' (Magnani, 2007). The manipulation of external anchors in the form of artworks leads to new solutions, problems and opportunities for fresh thought.

4.5 Blending time

Even a deceptively simple process of telling the time involves conceptual mapping and blending but, interestingly for situated cognition, it involves a material anchor, the clock, upon which are exercised a number of conceptual operations.

The metaphoric mappings for telling the time shown in the diagram on the next page (Figure 32) project an inferential structure (the part–whole relations of quarter circles) onto the clock face, enabling quarter-hour relative time reading (based on a study by Williams, 2008, p. 19). Fauconnier and Turner (2008) study different ways in which the apparently simple metaphors of time involve intricate integrations of semantic networks for various uses: 'What we have come to call "conceptual metaphors," like TIME IS MONEY or TIME IS SPACE, turn out to be mental constructions involving many spaces and many mappings in elaborate integration networks constructed by means of overarching general principles. These integration networks are far richer than the bundles of pairwise bindings considered in recent theories of metaphor' (2008, p. 54). Reducing this emergent structure and these groups of mental spaces to image schemas, or to other primitives, does not allow us to understand the range of this complexity. Isolating embodied metaphors or concepts and reducing them to image schemas in an attempt to show the fundamental embodied underpinning of complex thought simply diverts our attention from the rapidly burgeoning intricacy of such thought, which integrates many different kinds of resources.

Such nuanced emotional responses arise in an engagement with an artwork that uses functional clocks: Felix Gonzalez-Torres' '*Untitled*' *(Perfect Lovers)*, 1991 (see Figure 33). This is a contemporary artwork that consists of one clock placed on the wall next to another, telling the same time, and identical with it in every way. Without knowing anything of the context of the artist's life or work surrounding the clocks, the immediate first encounter with the clocks is dominated by automatic and habitual responses we might have to a familiar face – the clock face – and its humdrum ordinariness. Yet here, doubled in this manner, the artwork is

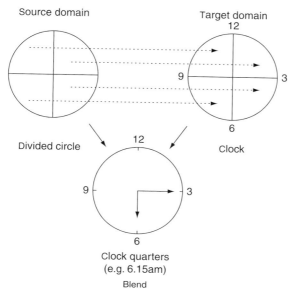

Figure 32. Conceptual blend involving geometry mapped onto clock time.

striking and unusual, and invites further thought. Perhaps for a split second I am uncertain, I am forced to check seeing double; reality must be coherent. The 'same-sex' doubling is also a splitting that suggests unity as well. There is a sense of expectation that any clock I single out for my gaze is momentarily mine, that it is there for me, to tell me, personally, what the time is; this is the notion of the clock's 'face'. The automatic, individual attention paid to a clock face or wristwatch is a personal exchange, it is a kind of recognition of something familiar, wherever the clock is found, the material anchor of the purpose foremost in my mind when I look at it. The twinning, then, is a splitting of my allegiance to a single entity, and there is now a kind of binocular rivalry. A rapid series of saccades multiplies from right to left and back again, attempting to balance, verify difference, achieve precedence – but to no avail. Is one time original, the other time counterfeit? Which is the doppelgänger, the foundling? Is this the fate of all art-as-representation, that it be considered a copy of a reality, staged and outside of time? Or is the undeniable functionality of the clocks – the fact that they are telling the time – able to disturb the cordon around art?

Yet surely they are unremarkably identical: viewers are assured that in paying attention to one, they may as well be looking at the other, in valuing

Figure 33. Felix Gonzales-Torres, '*Untitled*' *(Perfect Lovers)*, 1991 (wall clocks and paint on wall, overall dimensions vary with installation, clocks: 14 × 23 × 23.4 in. Overall two parts: 14 in. diameter each). Photograph by Peter Muscato. © The Felix Gonzalez-Torres Foundation. Courtesy of Andrea Rosen Gallery, New York.

one, they must value the other. All of these thoughts tumble out from each other rapidly and are shortlived, giving way to the overwhelming gestalt of symmetry. The harmony of the timepieces, once established, is restored to me. I am no longer in danger of bedazzlement and splitting; I now share their time.

The precision of each timepiece, the second hands in perfect synchrony, now seems like music: two precisely calibrated instruments in perfect time, where each clock is telling the time for the other, and there is something mesmerising about how one second, one minute, one hour are shared by the same clocks and, by extension perhaps, many others in the world. The subtle object identification tacitly acted upon the clock face described earlier is greatly enhanced by contextual knowledge, however, where the quotidian is transformed into art and an intellectual thought experiment into something else.

The artist's partner, Ross Laycock, died in 1991 of AIDS-related illness, the same year as Gonzalez-Torres brought together the two clocks as '*Untitled*' *(Perfect Lovers)*. Gonzalez-Torres was reported to have said in an interview: 'When people ask me, "Who is your public?" I say honestly, without skipping a beat, "Ross." The public was Ross. The rest of the people just come to the work' (Storr, 1995). Looking back to the clocks, they no longer seem to be just mechanical objects or thought experiments, and the mind is riddled with anthropomorphisms and the body with affects. Pathetic as substitutes for heartbeats, and taunting as tokens of both togetherness *and* separation, the clocks mark the patience of desire. The second hand marches forward, unaware of what it leaves behind, flowing blindly into the future. Now the synchrony seems tragic, perhaps even callous. Gonzalez-Torres, the creator of this simple timekeeping memorial to his lover, also died of AIDS-related complications five years later, in 1996. Again, this fact transfigures the clocks. Although the artist supplied photographic editions where the clocks are fixed in perfect symmetry, standing in front of the clocks and watching time pass is different. In their jerky movement, the clocks seem to be animated, not so much in their discrete, clipped switches from second to second, but in their coherence. Yet, even this is shortlived. One clock begins to lag behind the other, as the artist left instructions for the synchrony to fail.

These various rational and intuitive inferences from the visual evidence in conjunction with contextual information helps to secure a cognitive-emotional complex and various conceptual blends, one of the most important of which is to do with how we socially and culturally tell the time as a functional process and how the status of the artwork diverts us from this purpose. Rather than telling the time and using the clocks as concrete concepts or tools, the artwork invites us to step outside of the ordinary and think about the clocks using abstract concepts to do with bereavement, cohesion, the endurance of desire and memory. It is as if the clocks do not simply tell the time but tell us of so many other things. However, the fact that they remain functional timepieces is not irrelevant and continues to remind us of the *duration* of this kind of reification. Each clock was a *momento mori*[1] for the artist and can be seen in the same way in the present by the viewer. A *momento mori* is a strange leveler, for it asks us

---

[1] *Momento mori* is the Latin phrase 'remember death' or 'remember you will die'. It is a term that denotes a system of relational knowledge in art, which brings together many diverse works intended to remind people of their mortality. Timepieces were part of this category. Public clocks were embossed traditionally with mottos such as *ultima forsan* 'perhaps the last' [hour] or *vulnerant omnes, ultima necat* 'they all wound, and the last kills', or *tempus fugit*, 'time flies'. Related semantic networks are artworks which deal with *ars moriendi* 'the art of dying' and *vanitas* artworks.

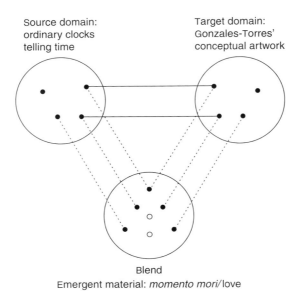

Figure 34. Conceptual blend involving ordinary clocks mapped onto Gonzales-Torres' conceptual artwork.

to imagine a time when we will no longer exist, where clocks will continue to mark time without us.

The diagram greatly simplifies how we 'transfigure' the clocks into meaningful experience. The blend is often a fantastical and impossible one, yet it helps us to bring together disparate parts, to make conceptual sense out of many situations. The significance of this kind of conceptual mapping is the emphasis it places on component parts of concepts, the ways in which these parts can accrue meaning in the frame of other concepts. It also opens our minds to the kind of integration of concepts we sometimes take for granted and which remain largely nonconscious. In an experiential sense, the blended mental space emerges unexpectedly because we are not conscious of the routes we take to this blend; it is itself doubly invisible because we do not see it blend, and we do not understand it in a literal sense. In other words, we understand it conceptually. This diagram is only an approximation of this conceptual thinking coming together, it is not prescriptive or absolute, and there are many routes. Such a basic schema can help us to build on a number of inferences as to how we build on generic mental spaces and integrate seemingly incongruous ones (as we often do in art, poetry and meta-phor) in conjunction with the affordances of the artwork.

Fauconnier and Turner's conceptual blending works primarily with concepts and tends not to specify how particular dynamic situations in the environment can affect or enhance conceptual blending. What is needed in art in the environment is a more careful mapping of its percep-tual cues in helping to order the relations between concepts within sys-tems or between systems. This is made more difficult when some of the aspects to be mapped are *non-perceptible* qualities.

4.6　'Invisible' blends

Figure 35 (Left). Marcel Duchamp, *L. H. O. O. Q.*, *Mona Lisa with Moustache*, 1930 (colour litho). Private Collection/Cameraphoto Arte Venezia/The Bridgeman Art Library. © Succession Marcel Duchamp/ ADAGP, Paris and DACS, London 2012.

Figure 36 (Right). Marcel Duchamp, *L. H. O. O. Q.*, *Shaved*, 1965 (colour litho). The Israel Museum, Jerusalem, Israel/Vera & Arturo Schwarz Collection of Dada and Surrealist Art/The Bridgeman Art Library. © Succession Marcel Duchamp/ADAGP, Paris and DACS, London 2012.

Look at these two copies of the 'Mona Lisa'. On the left, the artist Marcel Duchamp took a postcard of Leonardo's Mona Lisa in 1919 and, like a graffiti artist or naughty schoolboy, he painted a moustache and goatee on it. He called this act of vandalism, *L. H. O. O. Q.*, letters which, when vocalised with a French accent sound like the French equivalent of 'she has a hot ass' (*'Elle a chaud au cul'*), which, obviously, we do not see but which perhaps the artist would like us to form a mental image of in an attempt to scandalise us. On the right is a page on which is pasted a postcard of the Mona Lisa, labelled *L. H. O. O. Q. Shaved*, 1965. In *L. H. O. O. Q. Shaved*, the moustache and goatee have been 'removed' (or rather, the artist refrained from altering the picture). The work plays with notions of absence and presence, visibility and invisibility. It encourages us to suppress our perceptual responses and common sense that note the obvious: it is a print of the Mona Lisa. Yet we cannot help but imagine it as Duchamp had defaced it years before; we 'see' the absence of the moustache, we 'see' the 'shaved' (the postcard is also 'clean' of Duchamp's graffiti).[1] There are also many other levels of meaning involved here. Duchamp not only turns an icon of femininity and beauty into a man, he references Leonardo's homosexuality and the mythos in popular culture that Leonardo had painted some of his characteristics into the image. He also contrasts notions of traditional manual skill and authorship with the 'withholding' of these. Figure 37 is a schema of the conceptual blend we may achieve in our minds while looking at *L. H. O. O. Q. Shaved*, 1965 (target domain) while remembering *L. H. O. O. Q.*, 1919 (source domain).

The 'now you see it, now you don't' effect is achieved by importing units from both source and target domains. If we look at the *L. H. O. O. Q. Shaved*, we see a blend that consists of a mapping of the 'original' *L. H. O. O. Q.* upon *L. H. O. O. Q. Shaved*. The Mona Lisa in *L. H. O. O. Q. Shaved* could be a man without a goatee, or the Mona Lisa who has shaved. Duchamp is aiming here to alter our lifelong familiarity with a cultural icon by questioning our habitual perceptual reflexes, not only to do with facial recognition systems, cleverly destabilised into a kind of conflict between conceptual and perceptual levels, but also to do with our definitions of art in a retinal sense. More importantly, perhaps, than just being iconoclastic and witty, we know there is nothing missing; the moustache has not been erased, yet we fill in the gap, we imagine the moustache and beard beyond this facticity. It is a kind of 'factual counterfactual', which questions what is original, what is being 'restored', and whether we can actually go back to the

[1] Much has been written on the enigmatic beauty of the Mona Lisa's smile and more recently from a neurobiological point of view (Livingstone, 2002, p. 73). Yet, with *L. H. O. O. Q. Shaved*, this response, although still available to us, is decidedly problematic as we turn our attention to Duchamp's act of defamiliarising a well-known face and a questioning of habitual ways of experiencing beauty.

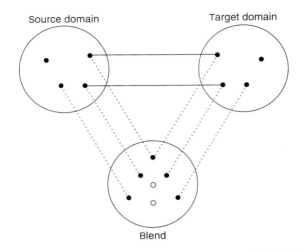

Figure 37. Conceptual blend involving a memory of *L. H. O. O. Q.* while looking at *L. H. O. O. Q. Shaved*.

original state at all to achieve a *tabula rasa*. The after-image of the moustache persists, questioning the Mona Lisa's sexuality, which is also a reference to that of Leonardo. The paradoxes supported by the blend here are mainly to do with Duchamp's favourite subject, creating perceptual situations that are unstable with conceptual understanding and playing with the visible, questioning its facticity. The blend also provides the viewer with the interplay of imagining the Mona Lisa with a moustache, imagining Duchamp's original intention of drawing the moustache on an image of the Mona Lisa (as if we were reliving Duchamp's original thought or intention, as if imagining her with a moustache is similar to drawing a moustache on the image) and this somehow seems conspiratorial, as in a secret joke. It is interesting that the conceptual blend can work by mapping a remembered perceptual detail (a moustache) onto the absence of it (in *L. H. O. O. Q. Shaved*); it is also interesting that this amply demonstrates, as 'emergent material' from the blend, Duchamp's dualism of non-retinal/retinal experiences of art and how this reinforces implicit or 'in the closet' (non-retinal) and explicit or 'out of the closet' (retinal). Androgyny for Duchamp was yet another form of ambiguity that was consistent with his interest in double entendres. Meanwhile, *L. H. O. O. Q.* may also be pronounced as 'look' in English, whereas in the French, 'she has a hot ass', cannot be 'looked' at.[2]

Although Fauconnier and Turner suggest that constituent parts of the source concept are identified in the target concept, the table of Duchamp's works (Figure 37) shows that this identification is not simply a matter of perceptual resemblance, as there are differences and abstractions involved. Figure 37 shows that various *different kinds of relation* are used to match details from source to target domains, such as a perceptual detail mapped onto another perceptual detail. That we are also dealing with a relation between the source and target domain here is inferential, based on counterfactuals. We may map a memory from an internal resource (Duchamp's *L. H. O. O. Q.*) onto a material anchor (Duchamp's *L. H. O. O. Q. Shaved*). It is reasonable to assume that some mapping relations will be subpersonal (we see resemblances without having to exercise conscious control) while other mapping will require inference with more deliberate thought based on idiographic factors and experience. It is important to note that without ever having seen the 'original' *L. H. O. O. Q.*, we could not achieve the blend and we would

[2] This perhaps is a good example of how Fauconnier and Turner's model seems flawed: the 'elemental' units mapped from one domain to another in their schema are, in fact, blends already: another version of the frame problem.

only see a reproduction, like any other, of the Mona Lisa. The artwork (through its gaps and lack of perceptual cues) can thus be seen to provide a situation that helps cognition to arrive at meanings that fill in these gaps.

A useful blend for many of Duchamp's works is signified by what I call an (in)visible device, which comes about in two ways: (1) something is made visible, which suggests an object or person not present *outside of the artwork* (a crown suggesting a king, a person looks at another outside of the frame, or this could be the viewer herself); or (2) something is shown not to be visible *within the artwork*, as with Martin Creed's *The Light's Going On and Off*, the blanket covering the object in Man Ray's *Enigma of Isidore Ducasse*, or in Sol LeWitt's *Variations of Incomplete Open Cubes*, 1974, where the artist constructed a set of cubes with sides missing, which the viewer mentally completes through *a priori* knowledge. As with Magritte, Duchamp was keen to encourage these kinds of ambiguity in order to undermine naïve expectations regarding the natural world, its perfect intelligibility and art's assumed duty of fidelity to such narrow perceptual definitions of reality. For Duchamp, this (in)visible aspect, the linguistic equivalent of which was a double entendre or pun, was continually signalled by the use of glass in his artworks, something that is both visible to the naked eye yet transparent and invisible when we look through it, a material token for the blend of perceptual and conceptual processes that was a lifelong pursuit in his art. It could also be noted here that there is a kind of transformative quality or an instability with Duchamp's readymades, where one perceptually views the *Fountain* as an ordinary object such as a urinal and then, with the title in mind, transforms it into something extraordinary or mischievous (a fountain suggests waterworks for public display or urinating), and one therefore 'sees' the object differently. Psychologically, the urinal acts as a kind of diagram or lexical symbol for something that is not present, but when the nonpresent is brought to mind, the urinal seems temporarily to become invisible.

Duchamp pursued the concept of 'non-retinal art' throughout his oeuvre and it has proven to be one of contemporary art's major wellsprings.[3] It became a means by which Duchamp and later conceptual and contemporary artists could thematically explore perceptual vision and its cooperation with abstract conceptual thought. In addition to the examples of *L. H. O. O. Q.* and *L. H. O. O. Q. Shaved*, Duchamp's *Bride Stripped*

---

[3] The non-retinal emphasis in art continued into the 1960s where Sol LeWitt wrote that he wanted his works to 'engage the mind of the viewer rather than his eye or emotions' (LeWitt, 1969) and with the 'dematerialization of the object' in conceptual art (Lippard, 1973). I look at other contemporary artworks that deal with non-retinal concepts in later pages.

Bare by Her Bachelors, Even (known as the 'Large Glass'), 1915–1924, Figure 38, also deals with themes of visibility and invisibility in a rigorous manner. This elegant and enigmatic work is made of twisted metal wire and flattened metal plates, cut into suggestive shapes mimicking machine forms, pressed between two sheets of glass held up by a metal frame. It is thus free-standing, so one can walk around the work, see through it and look upon it. According to the artist's notes, it is divided into a female area, above, suggesting an anagogic, heavenly presence, versus the gravitational pull of machine parts, chocolate grinder, filters and scissors, below. It has been interpreted as a metaphor for sex, but the piston mechanism, which is supposed to connect the section above with that below, fails to make contact and instead suggests unfulfilled desire. It is clear already that the work not only sets up formal binaries but traps us in the mechanical circuit of disconnected meanings, a failure to conceive, which the failed coupling denotes.

A richer involvement with *Large Glass* is achieved by using at least two ways of seeing: the processing of perceptible qualities using feature detectors or sensorimotor mechanisms, in addition to areas of the brain responsible for semantic processing, and rational induction. The *Large Glass* is more than a neurological stimulation of sensorimotor movements, despite its exacting (yet ironic) system of illusionism based on geometries in perspective. It also involves a distancing from the optical 'point of view' when we begin to create concepts using a series of poetic associations linked to notions of transparency and light 'shining through' the sensible properties of the work.

The transparency of the glass engages different ways of seeing. We can think about the flatness of the work and the formal features of the machine parts, while the glass invites us to see beyond them, thereby suspending our awareness of the perceptible elements of the work, as we would with the shapes of letters on a page while trying to understand their meaning. While the machine parts tell us a story of a reproductive cycle that misfires, seen from the point of view of the transparent glass, one is reminded of St Thomas Aquinas' description of the Immaculate Conception as a ray of light that passes through a glass leaving the glass (and the Virgin's body) intact. The light shines through the glass as we gaze through it; we 'read through' objects (and our sense perceptions of them).

While it is possible to interpret Duchamp's machinism in a visceral sense as a representation of sensorimotor movements in the sex act, it can also be viewed within a tradition depicting technology as a model for processes of thought. Hobbes and Leibniz used mechanics in this way. Freud used thermodynamics as a way to articulate psychological pressures, and cognitive science sometimes uses the computer as a model for

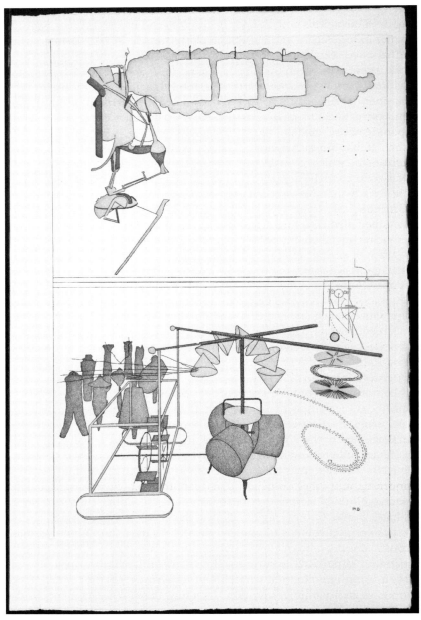

Figure 38. Design for *The Large Glass* from *The Large Glass and Related Works, Vol II*, by Arturo Schwarz, published 1967 (litho)/Private Collection/The Stapleton Collection/The Bridgeman Art Library. © Succession Marcel Duchamp/ADAGP, Paris and DACS, London 2012.

the brain (Manovich, 2006, p. 211). Seen from the perspective of this tradition, Duchamp's intricate system of machine parts in *Large Glass* may only literally reference sex. It can also be seen as a body, the top part is the mind, the chocolate grinder below, the sexual organs. Furthermore, it invites a kind of rotation of visual systems that depend not on isolating individual elements but in considering the relations of these systems to each other. The work invites a continual shift of different systems: the careful perspective in which the bachelors have been placed below, and the parody of the window; the suggestion of psychological sex drives; the mechanics of industrial machine forms; the absence of freedom suggested by automata and the methodical procedures of sadomasochism; the automatism of biological reproduction; the theological implications of the light and the glass and predeterminism; and perhaps, above all, a life-affirming and endlessly complex relation of concepts. Each conceptual system is an interpretative framework that can be engaged at any moment while we are visually inspecting the work with perceptual processes that need not be employed thematically.

Duchamp's *Green Box* (1934) is an album containing notes, diagrams and documents that index the *Large Glass*, guiding our understanding of its 'workings'. Duchamp explained: 'I wanted that album [the notes to the "Large Glass"] to go with the "Glass," and to be consulted when seeing the "Glass" because, as I see it, it must not be "looked at" in the aesthetic sense of the word. One must consult the book, and see the two together. The conjunction of the two things entirely removes the retinal aspect that I don't like' (Cabanne, 1979, p. 42). This brings to mind the notion of invisible, or at least non-perceptible, concepts and phenomena that many scientific diagrams nevertheless try to schematise using diagrams. Barbara Tversky writes: 'abstract or invisible concepts like forces, traits, counterfactuals, and negations are not easily conveyed unambiguously in depictions. Even so, conventions for conveying these kinds of concepts have evolved as needed, in road signs, mathematics, science, architecture, engineering, and other domains, a gradual process of symbolisation akin to language' (2010, p. 5).

What I would like to suggest, concerning Duchamp's *Large Glass*, is that it can be regarded as a kind of scientific diagram meant to integrate concepts about systematic processes that cannot be experienced phenomenally, such as Darwin's theory of natural selection (Gooding, 2004, p. 22). The diagram is not a mimetic illustration of the system so much as an invitation to think about types of relation. In this regard, it shares similarities with maps that may also reference non-visual referents: spheres of influence or historical events, for example. We infer the potential of objects to move in relation to others in terms of

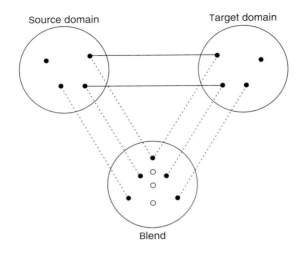

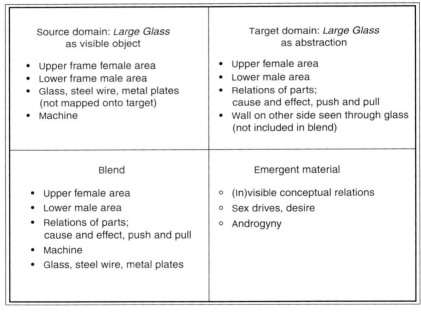

Source domain: *Large Glass* as visible object	Target domain: *Large Glass* as abstraction
• Upper frame female area • Lower frame male area • Glass, steel wire, metal plates (not mapped onto target) • Machine	• Upper female area • Lower male area • Relations of parts; cause and effect, push and pull • Wall on other side seen through glass (not included in blend)
Blend	Emergent material
• Upper female area • Lower male area • Relations of parts; cause and effect, push and pull • Machine • Glass, steel wire, metal plates	○ (In)visible conceptual relations ○ Sex drives, desire ○ Androgyny

Figure 39. Conceptual blend involved in understanding *The Large Glass.*

cause and effect, quantities of force, particle and wave paradoxes, analogy and resemblance to cogs and wheels from machines and tools with which we are familiar. Because the *Large Glass* can be seen through as well as looked upon, it is a veritable thought experiment producing

Figure 40. Marcel Duchamp, *La Boîte-en-valise*, 1935–1941. National Gallery of Scotland, GMA 3472. © Succession Marcel Duchamp/ ADAGP, Paris and DACS, London 2012.

metacognitive thought about different affordances and ways of seeing. The system of force relations and mechanisms its perceptual cues suggest lead us to a theory of mind. Apart from this, the *Large Glass* does have a visual allure, accompanied by feelings of pleasure and delight, but it manages to sustain these responses even while the object of our thought is the conceptual complexity it is able to suggest. Spatial cognition is a highly specialised area dealing with a broad interdisciplinary range of visual representations from scientific diagrams (Gooding, 2004), overviews of conventional signs and graphs (Tversky, 2010), cartography (Berendt et al., 1998) and reasoning with mental models and diagrams (Johnson-Laird, 1983).

Duchamp's *Large Glass* remains one of the most widely discussed works of art. It has a visual allure encouraging both conceptual complexity and self-reflection. However, it is placed into an even more fascinating conceptual context in the form of *La Boîte-en-valise* ('box in a suitcase'), 1935–1941, a suitcase in which there is a box of hand-tinted prints and miniature artefacts that catalogue Duchamp's oeuvre. The artist worked on over 300 editions of this valise from 1935 to 1941. In many of them, the *Fountain* was reproduced in miniature form, as if to re-admit it into another 'gallery' context in the valise, often called a portable museum. Each artwork similarly gains new significance by being recontextualised and juxtaposed next to other works.

The valise is a visual mnemonic system as well as a form of conceptual exploration. The valise is an excellent example of how some artworks allow for kinds of situated cognition. It is a model for an exhibition of several component artworks. In the valise, each artwork, the *Large Glass* prominent among them, is a token of a distinct concept or concepts, which can be seen in any order from right to left, or vice versa, or from top to bottom. We can combine the objects in Duchamp's box, put them in different sequences, and use them as touchstones for concepts in relation to others. It uses localised perceptual processes and the processes of memory and conceptual planning ahead. This experience thus engages dynamically with many brain areas and other parts of the body requiring multiple levels of explanation.

Reinforcing the themes of visibility and invisibility, in the valise is an image of *L. H. O. O. Q.*, a miniature model of Duchamp's *Fountain*, 1917, a urinal turned on its side in order to challenge the 'retinal' (perceptual) categories of art; and *50 cc Air de Paris*, 1919, Figure 41 (an empty glass ampoule usually used by pharmacies to contain medicine), which, as a joke, contains 'Parisian air', taken with him when he migrated to America). A conceptual blend for this artwork would begin by recognising it as an ordinary object, a glass ampoule with a label on it (source domain of ordinary objects). With expert knowledge of Duchamp or readymades (target domain of art object), some of the attributes of the ampoule, transparency, glass, would be mapped onto the target domain, perhaps leaving out the object's ordinary status and adding the abstract concept of readymade. The blend would include readymade, semantic memory, Paris, precious substance or medicine, museum exhibit (inferences), transparent object, invisible air, 'dematerialization of the art object' (Lippard, 1973) (abstract concepts).

In the valise there is also the *Traveler's Folding Item*, 1916, Figure 42, a reduced version of an Underwood typewriter cover suggesting a typewriter underneath, a tool which can be used to write a letter or poem. The blend here would include imaginative associations between the typewriter as a symbol of creativity that has been 'put away', unseen, and the fact that

Figure 41. Marcel Duchamp, *50 cc Air de Paris*, 1919/1964 (glass). The Israel Museum, Jerusalem, Israel/Vera & Arturo Schwarz Collection of Dada and Surrealist Art/The Bridgeman Art Library. © Succession Marcel Duchamp/ADAGP, Paris and DACS, London 2012.

Figure 42. Marcel Duchamp, *Traveler's Folding Item*, 1916/1964 (mixed media). The Israel Museum, Jerusalem, Israel/Vera & Arturo Schwarz Collection of Dada and Surrealist Art/The Bridgeman Art Library. © Succession Marcel Duchamp/ADAGP, Paris and DACS, London, 2012.

the conceptual work continues beyond the visual, manual or mechanical manipulation of perception.

Included as well is the fluttering love-heart print, a famous diagram used in perceptual experiments, which Duchamp has used to alert us to the theme of the retinal and non-retinal in art. There is also the image of his famous *Nude Descending a Staircase*, 1915, a conceptual depiction of motion in a fixed medium: do we see the figure or the motion? As a whole, the valise helps to activate an intensity of conceptual production through a continuous parody of visual codes. We are able to see each individual object not in the customary perceptual way, using feature detectors or sensorimotor capabilities, but as part of a jigsaw puzzle, which uses other processes of memory, rational induction, linguistic analysis and the imagination in order to produce a conceptual way of seeing, but one which is structured as a network of relations characteristic of many kinds of art experience.

It is quite surprising how thinking about Duchamp's valise can utilise a series of interrelated conceptual systems (each one betokened by the artworks I have discussed here), rapidly deployed and compared while sensations of colour, motion and form are stimulated, together adding a richness, depth and intensity to the experience. The density of the conceptual network is impressive, and it is difficult to keep even small sections of it in mind at any one time when attending to it thematically. One has to keep referring back to the artworks. The valise and its contents help us to think, and the valise helps us to re-access and adjust our ongoing and dynamic conceptual production as well as our reflection on this process.

There are several consistent superordinate categories or themes that emerge from these artworks as new material from each conceptual blend: androgyny, the body, fetish and the invisible. Many of the works function as some kind of container comparable to bodies full of air, shot through with light or containing darkness (in the case of the typewriter cover). Such properties reference embodied experience, sensorimotor sensibilities and phenomenal concepts to do with touch, shape, the suggestion of movement and visibility.[4] In addition, many of the works reference glass, the visible and yet transparent properties of which blend into an interesting paradox: the presence of the visible and invisible, retinal or non-retinal properties of art, respectively. The 'now you see it, now you don't' concept is consistently found as a theme in many of Duchamp's works in the

---

[4] Luchjenbroers (2004) suggests that one mental space (lexical) can be mapped onto another (gestural, visual or sensorimotor) space to create rich conceptual blends. This can be seen in the way that Duchamp combined word games with 'visual' puns, 'under wood'; '*L. H. O. O. Q.*', etc.

valise, and is reinforced by the use of sexual innuendo and visual and lexical puns. Some of the objects are meant to suggest sexual encounters and thus their ordinariness is transformed into a fetish of sorts. What Duchamp succeeds in doing in the valise is to bring together a number of works that function on several amalgamated levels of signification, where each level of one artwork may correspond with other levels in other artworks, creating a system of relations. However, these relations are not the same kind of relations; some are lexical, others sensorimotor and perceptual, still others analogical and counterfactual.

This complex picture of how artworks are related to each other will come as no surprise to art historians, curators and students of art who are familiar with Duchamp's valise and the enormous influence its themes have exerted on contemporary art, which continues to develop and extend these kinds of relations between readymades. This should be significant for neuroscientists and psychologists who, so far, have failed to grasp the complexity of relational knowledge routinely activated in the viewing of art in groups, in exhibitions, and when considering movements or styles or, indeed, an artist's oeuvre.

I am not suggesting that the superordinate categories I have identified here are the only correct ones. Any interpretation of the valise will probably rely on a similar systematicity of comparison and contrast, perhaps picking out other superordinate categories (displacement, bourgeois detachment, dandyism, for example). This systematicity relies on linguistic processing areas of the brain, rational induction and categorisation, as well as a number of sensorimotor processes that follow the curve and shape of the art objects and other perceptible properties. This is a process that is suspended somewhat when we dig deeper into the semantic system of relations indicated by the objects as a collection of artworks. Such systematicity and compositionality also depend on the ability to go beyond physical and perceptual similarities between art objects to symbolic connections and art historical relational knowledge. Clearly, Duchamp wanted us to look at each artwork individually, both for perceptual cues and for symbolism suggested by some of the properties of each artwork that could be applied abstractly across instances. The valise encourages us to use higher-order cognition to piece together a system of relations with crosslinks. All of these processes involve a continual shifting of our 'retinal' or 'non-retinal' responses.

It is also notable that the valise is conceivable as a single artwork, or as a collection or gallery of artworks. The *50 cc Air de Paris* is a container of medicine meant for injection, suggesting the transfer and internalisation of fluids. The object is conceivably either dry or wet, a precious souvenir, worthless or invaluable (as air is for breathing). It is both mass-produced and stylishly sculptural, its slender neck hooking round into a question

mark. In the *Large Glass*, one of Duchamp's most famous works, reproduced in the valise as a hand-tinted print, there is both a male and female
area, both parts of an interlocking machine that is both static and in motion
(or intentional). I have mentioned that the *Large Glass* is also a body of sorts,
containing the machine (in *glass*). We can look at this as a machine or as a
metaphor for coitus, with the coffee grinder and liquid below, and the cloud
form or vapour above. The typewriter cover suggests a woman's skirt as well
as a man's briefcase (according to Duchamp's own suggestion), and it is
also a container: a (black) body whose shiny exterior suggests both wet and
dry possibilities. As a body, it is a container and a cover for 'conceptual
work', as well as the notion of fumbling for typewriter keys under a skirt.[5]

Additionally prominent in the valise is *Belle Haleine eau de Violette*, 1921
(a pun suggesting sweet breath), which is a *glass* bottle of perfume. It is a
complex schema of an elegant gift, intimacy as it is worn on the skin for
allure, and feminine pleasure and eroticism, relying on the olfactory
modality, touch and sensorimotor action, holding, tilting, anointing. It
also refers to Duchamp's cross-dressing alter-ego, which he took pains to
cultivate, Rose Sélavy (Eros/'*c'est la vie*' and the French verb, *arroser* also
means to moisten). The perfume bottle doubles as a body of glass, full of
liquid, both wet and dry. Thus, there are a number of linguistic concepts
or puzzles evident here, relying on semantic processing.

The gender confusion and visual equivocation of *L. H. O. O. Q.* and *L.
H. O. O. Q. Shaved* have already been discussed, and these aspects are
shared by Duchamp's *Fountain*. This is a male container put on its side to
resemble female genitalia, a hollow belly or a body designed to receive the
male fluid. The 'fountain' remains invisible to the naked eye and is only
suggested, as is the object's ambiguous state of wet/dry, and it is static or
dynamic depending on whether one 'sees' it as a urinal or fountain. This
series of binaries and yin-yang paradoxes culminates in the concept that
the *Fountain* is a dual object, with a dual status, a vulgar, mass-produced
object and an artwork. Although using sensorimotor concepts in terms of
its fluent shape and form, it also invites linguistic semantic puzzles.
Duchamp's title reverses the function of the urinal: instead of a stream
entering into it, a fountain suggests a jet of water streaming from it. Yet the

---

[5] The conceptual blends and analogical processes seen in the cross-referencing of features in
the valise enjoy a wide art historical currency. See, for example: 'Hidden under the "skirts"
of the cover' is not just any ordinary object, but a writing machine (*machine à écrier*). While
not particularly worthy of being looked at, the absent typewriter alludes to the mental and
verbal processes involved in the production of readymades (Judovitz, 1998). For the
gender implications of this cover as a kind of skirt and its potential reference to the bride
and the *Large Glass*, see Schwarz (1969, p. 196), and Archer (2002) who makes the analogy
between Manzoni's *Artist's Breath* and Duchamp's *50 cc Air de Paris*.

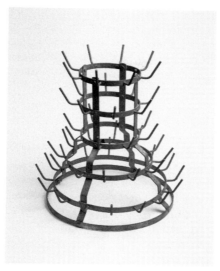

Figure 43. Marcel Duchamp, *Bottle Rack* (replica of 1914 original), 1961 (galvanized iron). Philadelphia Museum of Art, Pennsylvania, PA, USA / Gift of Jacqueline, Paul, and Peter Matisse in memory of their mother, Alexina Duchamp, 1998 / The Bridgeman Art Library © Succession Marcel Duchamp/ADAGP, Paris and DACS, London 2012.

work plays on the notion of how context (gallery) changes the meaning of a semantic unit (urinal), and how the unit suggests the context is a toilet.

The famous *Bottle Rack*, 1914, Figure 43, is a complex object that suggests bottles that are not visible. It is also a male or female body, which we blend from association: it is both a container and something one hangs containers (*glass* bottles) on, it resembles a hoop petticoat frame worn under dresses, or a skeleton with phallic parts that insert into bottle-necks, suggesting coitus. The blend here contains glass, as well as wet/dry, which we piece together imaginatively from the perceptual cues that it is a bottle dryer and is used for hanging wet bottles on. In the mapping for this work, we have the ordinary metal frame with prongs (before identification, many viewers most often do not know what it is and see it as an unusual sculpture). The bottle dryer is also transparent, we can see through it. This transparency plays on the imaginary transparency of the bottles. As with other objects in the valise, the hybrid nature of the bottle dryer, through the associative couplings of male and female, dry and wet (moist?), visible and invisible, protruding or invaginating (the prongs), ensconced (by the bottles), reinforces the art/mass-produced object

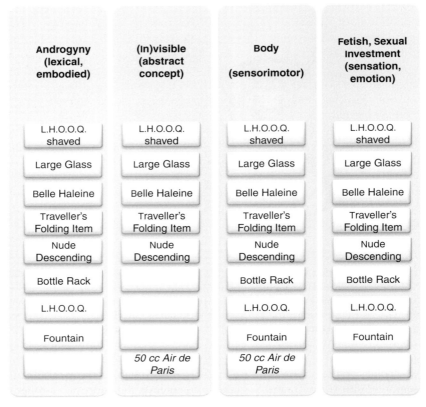

Androgyny (lexical, embodied)	(In)visible (abstract concept)	Body (sensorimotor)	Fetish, Sexual Investment (sensation, emotion)
L.H.O.O.Q. shaved	L.H.O.O.Q. shaved	L.H.O.O.Q. shaved	L.H.O.O.Q. shaved
Large Glass	Large Glass	Large Glass	Large Glass
Belle Haleine	Belle Haleine	Belle Haleine	Belle Haleine
Traveller's Folding Item	Traveller's Folding Item	Traveller's Folding Item	Traveller's Folding Item
Nude Descending	Nude Descending	Nude Descending	Nude Descending
Bottle Rack		Bottle Rack	Bottle Rack
L.H.O.O.Q.		L.H.O.O.Q.	L.H.O.O.Q.
Fountain		Fountain	Fountain
	50 cc Air de Paris	50 cc Air de Paris	

Figure 44. How objects in *La Boîte-en-valise* help to constrain, and are constrained by, four kinds of processes (these may flow into each other).

relation by which Duchamp intended to challenge traditional categories of art and non-art.

In the hand-tinted print of Duchamp's famous *Nude Descending the Staircase*, 1912, we have a body (neither overtly male nor female, organic nor metallic) contained in a staircase, ambiguously both still and in motion, visible and invisible. The picture is not only a fusion of Futurist and Cubist techniques with a knowledge of early photographic history and Muybridge's motion studies of figures walking, it also suggests a breaking of the frame by the body, seen here (or one should say understood here) as a blur. The painting is also, arguably, a depiction of abstract movement and the flow of time itself, rather than an object in its concrete aspect, frozen in time. Duchamp ingeniously sets up a static object/abstract motion binary, which we blend into the concept of a moving object descending, but one which momentarily 'materialises' as it pauses on each step to gather up its material stasis, so to speak, moving on to a metaphysical flux. The painting is a hide-and-seek game, a spot-the-figure, a 'now you see it, now you don't'. The work is itself worthy of a concept map analysing all these relations in order to appreciate its conceptual elegance.

This table above, Figure 44, is a summary of some of the superordinate categories that I have suggested it is possible to construct from some of the objects of the valise; note that these categories of understanding the objects in the valise also involve distinct physical responses in the viewer (in brackets under the category headings) which, however, are not sequential but may overlap. *This overlapping can occur when one object in the valise appears in two or more categories.* The interpretation of each item indicated here could involve a 'conceptual' blend (which may also be a sensation blended with a concept), as I have demonstrated for some of the objects in previous pages. It may be seen that some artworks fall into all four categories. This suggests that it is possible for the four categories to come together as a system of relational knowledge using a particular kind of relation: propositional, inferential, linguistic, analogical, metaphorical, perceptual (identifying shapes and properties that share similarities). The system of relational knowledge that the valise suggests may be difficult to keep in mind at any one time; the table allows for re-access to the conceptual system and helps us to realise how individual categories and characteristics carry, mutate and signify across the system, the body and Duchamp's artistic oeuvre and thought. Even as a crude visual caricature of possible semantic and biological associations, I believe it reveals, in a visual and spatial sense, some of the systematicity and compositionality of the artist's thought and the viewer's possible involvements with it. It also provides a basis for further creative thought, as there are many other works not mentioned here, and it can be extended to a whole network of inferences to other possible artworks in art history, which have the potential to further enhance our experience of this work of art. Again, I would insist that this is more typical of our experience of art than has been recognised. To those who would argue that this table merely reconstitutes a mentalistic model of engagement with the world, it is important to emphasise how the artwork's perceptual cues, in conjunction with the diagram itself, play a pivotal part in supporting, enhancing and organising the resources of working memory, offline mental imagery, rational processing and sensorimotor engagement, along with semantic memory and visceral effects, so that the character of this massive integration of resources is modulated and enhanced, yet is also constrained by the perceptual and conceptual experience that the valise affords.

Obviously, Duchamp did not necessarily organise his conceptualisation of the valise in exactly the same manner as suggested by this table. Consistent themes, the crosslinks between them and the contrasts that they suggest (the 'disconnects') do, however, show his intricate lines of thought. This thought is structured as a system of conceptual correspondences that enrich fundamental themes found in the valise. The table is built upon various forms of evidence, the features and qualities of the objects themselves, and how these are comparable. It explores what it is possible to infer from these comparisons and perceptual cues. It is also based on what we know of Duchamp's thought as documented in the *Green Box* and other sources, and is guided by the discourse analysis of art historical works, all of which indicate a network of relations of concepts visualised here (Bonk and Duchamp, 1989; Judovitz, 1998). Bringing together many of Duchamp's lifelong obsessions and themes, and the variety by which they were explored and actualised, it can be seen more clearly as a nonlinear map where the darting eye rapidly connects conceptual areas into systems. Alternatively, with a kind of bird's eye view, we are free to meditate on the general organisation of the network of concepts and their interrelations indicated here, and to discern the overall structure of conceptual processing that it is possible to unfold from the valise. Part of our involvement with the valise also concerns the monitoring and evaluation of our own states.

It is important to keep in mind that the diagram is not the conceptual system in its full accretion exhausting the valise, yet it helps us to hold a large part of a conceptual system in mind and to become aware of some of its relations rather than leaving it as a vague, background hum in the art experience. As I have mentioned, organising concepts and their relations with the aid of visual material helps us to re-access or find out more about works of art in a qualitatively different manner than we do reading about them, as texts are usually ordered in a linear fashion and inherent in this structure are built-in temporal and hierarchical assumptions and values concerning cause and effect. The diagram has a certain systematicity that we impose on our looking at the valise, but we can look at the valise again, try different sequences of looking and tinker with the diagram.

I suggested that the art experience can be understood – and visualised – as a complex mapping of conceptual relations. The valise is body oriented because, as a suitcase, it invites us to imagine manual manipulation, the packing and unpacking of objects that we might carry out planning a trip or organising a stay. The valise encourages a supplemented kind of mental rotation: the ability to group or combine different objects in a different order so as to obtain new meanings.[6] Bottom-up processes of perception and top-down processes of conceptual thought are mutually reinforcing. The suitcase engages with many brain areas and body movements in the context of a trip, different environments and contexts, make-believe or otherwise. Importantly, then, the valise cuts across crude internalist and externalist binaries by suggesting a cooperation between brain processes, embodied action and situated cognition.

---

[6] Although describing perceptions, the term 'mental rotation' is taken from the well-known paper by Shepard and Metzler (1971). Concerning Venn diagrams, tables and models, Pylyshyn writes: 'Having the diagram in front of you not only lessens the burden on memory, but also encourages certain assumptions and ways of thinking about the problem.' (2006, p. 454).

4.7   Extending relational knowledge

> The aim of science is not things themselves, as the dogmatists in their
> simplicity imagine, but the relations among things; outside these rela-
> tions there is no reality knowable.   (Poincaré, 1905, p. xxiv)

Although Duchamp's glass ampoule of Parisian air might be thought to be a
visual metaphor of a breathing body, or a swan, the object itself does not
force such a reading. Conceived of as a problem, we can entertain a number
of solutions to its identity. Whether we call these 'statistical attractors'
(Simmons and Barsalou, 2003) or 'weakly intended' metaphorical associations (Sperber and Wilson, 2008), the artwork is able to suggest a number of
associations, simulations and hybrid situations that we have learnt to value in
contemporary art. Even more so, we have come to value this 'within-system'
(Goldstone and Rogosky, 2002) of associations for one artwork, when
extended to a wider relational system *between* artworks ('between-systems'
relations). Even though it is labelled '50 cc of Parisian air', the implication is
that the glass ampoule is a kind of tincture meant to be applied to a body but
also that it is a blown glass, its shape the result of a human breathing into it
when liquid. Piero Manzoni's *Artist's Breath*, 1959–1960, is often associated
with Duchamp's glass ampoule and strengthens the metaphorical association with a glass 'body' of air in its title (the direct translation of *Corpo d'Aria*
is '*body* of air'). Manzoni's work is a conventionalisation of the metaphor.
As the art historian David Hopkins writes, *Corpo d'Aria*: 'involved the artist
blowing up balloons, in an allusion to the classical notion of the "divine
pneuma" whereby the artist "breathes life" into the work of art. The brief
lives of Manzoni's balloons were subsequently memorialised with their
wrinkled remains being affixed to plaques. There is a direct Duchampian
allusion here, namely to his ampoule of *Paris Air* of 1919, but it is clear that
Manzoni has expanded the idea to encompass the "life" of the art work,
which is keyed to his physical expenditure' (Hopkins, 2006, p. 149).[1]

---

[1] Hopkins also mentions Jasper John's *Metered Bulb* of 1963 'which bears direct comparison
with Manzoni' (2006, p. 150), although it must be mentioned that Yves Klein's *Void*, 1958,
the exhibition of an empty display case, prefigures all of the other examples given here.

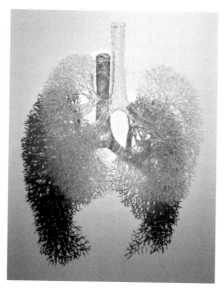

Figure 45. Annie Cattrell, *Capacity*, 2008 (glass and acrylic). 3/3 edition of 3. Courtesy of the artist.

However, there are many other examples in contemporary art that create a type of relational knowledge premised on extended metaphor and art historical references. If the diagram of the valise I have provided were truly an accurate representation of how we might experience the valise, we would have much more noise and detail from our existing knowledge structure, which would intervene sporadically during visual scanning. There are many artists who have referenced Duchamp's examples seen in the valise. Any of the following works, which are associated with principles established in the valise, could be brought to mind while inspecting the valise. Hans Haacke's *Condensation Cube*, 1963–1965, is a glass container filled with condensation that brings to mind breath on cold glass, while Alan Sonfist's *Crystal Enclosure*, 1965, a series of white crystals growing in a sealed glass container and, like Haacke's cube, is a work that is contingent upon the ambient temperature of viewers' bodies and breath, which have a direct effect on the exhibit. There is also Robert Barry's *Inert Gas, Helium*, 1969, a canister of gas released in a desert, as elusive and transparent as Duchamp's *50 cc Air de Paris*. In addition, in contemporary art, there is Martin Creed's, *Work no.360, Half the Air in a Given Space*, 2004, silvered balloons full of air filling half a gallery space.

There is also a fascinating piece by Annie Cattrell, *Capacity*, 2008, which is blown glass, as is the *50 cc Air de Paris*, but is a much more intricate work where the artist has breathed into the 'lungs' of the sculpture to create a complex bronchial network that speaks of presence and absence. Her work reminds us of our own embodiment, while bringing to mind the invisibility of the air and of breath. While it is scientific, the work encourages us to maintain a focus on a non-visible object (breath) or the lungs, which is a meditative practice. There is a precious fragility here that seems to reference breath.

A different treatment of this may be seen in Giuseppe Penone's Study for *Breath of Clay*, 1978. Penone's works in the 1970s explored the nature of skin as a container creating a boundary with the environment. They are terracotta pots bearing the imprints of the artist's body such as his open mouth at the 'lip' of the pot: 'They bring together the two ingredients from which man is made in the Biblical myth of creation: clay and (divine) breath, and represent the immaterial in solid, three-dimensional form. An exhaled breath is equivalent to the air the potter introduces into his vortex, and it is equivalent to the word. The word is charged with connotations and is capable of giving rise to an image, apparently creating something from nothing' (Celant, 1989, p. 91).

Along similar themes is New Zealand artist Dane Mitchell's *Spoken Heredity Talisman (Robert Johnstone)*, 2011, from a series of blown glass objects formed by the artist's utterance of the name of a particular ancestor into the liquid glass. Each object in the series differs in size and shape, depending on the word used, and these objects suggest capturing or making visible the word, thought and breath carrying the name of the artist's ancestor, which the artist mouths, channels, visualises and externalises. In a sense, the name is a source of inspiration for the artwork and, because these are glass objects, the light shines through them suggesting animation in glass. Yet they also bring to mind the mental exercise in traditional meditation where one imagines the light in one's breath.[2] The work brings together air, fire, earth and water (at least in its transparency and the bubble-like appearance of the form), all fastened to the word. On the one hand, it appears natural and elemental (a sac filled with air); on the other hand, it resembles a Brancusi sculpture, solid and heavy. It also plays with many of the visible and invisible equivocations of Duchamp's ampoule. Another lineage, besides the artist's ancestors, is traced back to Manzoni's *Corpo d'Aria*. In other works, the artist assembled a glass cube (reminding one of both Haacke's

---

[2] In Tony Ourseler's work *Blue Husk*, a film image of a woman's face is projected through a glass vessel and is another play on capturing life in glass.

Figure 46. Dane Mitchell, *Spoken Heredity Talisman (Robert Johnstone)*, 2011 (glass, breath). 220 mm × 70 mm (approx). Image by Dane Mitchell. Courtesy the artist and Starkwhite, Auckland.

and Sonfist's glass cubes) and a circular opening is cut out of one of its sides in order for viewers to smell the scent inside. This further elaborates the notion of the invisible air and breath to include olfactory experience, touch and presence. Other artists who have dealt with the air and breath as metaphors for artistic creation and making the invisible visible include Lygia Clark, whose *Air and Stone*, 1966, is a plastic bag filled with air upon which a stone sits and which she squeezes with her hands. This work depends on a tactile and phenomenal grounding for what otherwise might have been conceptual or Minimalist work, for she attempts to hold the invisible in her hands and to feel it.

All of the artists that I have brought together here under the category of air and glass, visibility and invisibility are part of a particular kind of art historical system of relational knowledge that seems to point back to an origin in Duchamp's readymades. However, it is important to emphasise that each artist's work is a very different expression of breath. Along with Amelia Jones (1994), Hopkins (2006) is keen to re-evaluate the aura of Duchamp as an intellectual mastermind, or 'patriarch' in Jones' case, where she seeks to 'embody' him, showing the sexual investment in his works. Hopkins, meanwhile, pleads for an end to the continual homages to Duchamp in art history.[3] It is important to note that relational knowledge of this sort does not aim to make everything the same in a category but should be used more productively to discuss differences in approach and visual display as well as context. As always, the art historical method, par excellence, of contrasting and comparing works is not only one followed by artists but is adopted frequently by curators when organising exhibitions, and allows art historians to bring together different artworks in order to write about their underlying discursivity. As with the nature of myth and the notion of the divine pneuma or artist's breath, each artist activates a part of a continual cascade of a tradition shown differently in each case. It is important to note that not every similarity between works denotes a deliberate referencing of previous works by artists, as they often pursue independent lines of inquiry. Yet, in terms of interpretation and art history, it is often important to seek out difference and an underlying 'discursivity'[4] through comparisons *and* contrasts.

The relational knowledge system, along with art theory activated here in words, is highly abstracted and carried along with lightening speed during the inspection of a work of art. One need not jump to the conclusion that the usual or, indeed, the natural way of experiencing these artworks is to privilege phenomenal and embodied experience as themes, or to dwell on perceptual details in order to stress traditional aesthetic responses. The underlying discursivity between these works, the paradigm upon which the relational system of knowledge is built, represents a systematicity well beyond the abilities of the senses to organise. Yet it is also important not to overemphasise Duchamp's famous championing of 'non-retinal' art; many of his works and those we can compare with them in systems of relational knowledge are also visually attractive, encouraging distinct

---

[3] Joseph Beuys stated that 'the silence of Duchamp is overrated'; an equivocal statement that both detracts from yet reaffirms Duchamp's eminence.

[4] A term indebted to the French philosopher, Foucault. Similar to his ideas, I intend it to mean a historic epoch's system of discourses, values, arguments and conflicts, which may occur in particular disciplines, between them, and in the context of particular formations of power, but is a systematicity that may be subpersonal and emerge from the way a system is aligned through balances and counterbalances.

perceptual and embodied, visceral or empathetic responses theorised by traditional aesthetics.[5]

A relational knowledge system of this kind, also active when interpreting Tracey Emin's *My Bed*, is theoretical (a feminist intervention against traditional phenomenology, for example, or a goading of the sensationalist press and its patriarchal allegiance to decorum and the rules of public display concerning the feminine ideal or nude). There is no need for a sensorimotor simulation of getting into Emin's bed, especially if we are constructing a relational knowledge system with regard to how her bed activates connections with other beds in art. Thus, for example, the following analysis of Emin's *My Bed* by Deborah Cherry involves constructing a complex relational system rather than dwelling on sensorimotor perceptions: 'the bed, the mortuary slab and operating table slide into one another in the work of several contemporary artists. Rachel Whiteread's numerous bed pieces placed on the floor, inviting yet denying rest, cots by Permindar Kaur or Mona Hatoum, Richard Hamilton's brutal *Treatment Room* of 1984...or Bill Viola's *Science of the Heart* of 1983...play on, prey on, the oscillations between life and death, the body's presence and absence' (Cherry, 2002). The bed is found as a symbol, theme and construct in many other artworks; see, for example, Rauschenberg's *Bed*, 1955; Kienholz's *State Hospital*, 1966; and in the work of Louise Bourgeois and Sarah Lucas, to name only a few.

Each artist's name acts as a category heading, a container for stylistic concepts and features we have come to learn about each: Whiteread is a sculptor who works with synthetic materials, so her beds are rubbery; Mona Hatoum put metal teeth on her beds to suggest torture; Viola is a video artist whose recurrent themes are to do with life, death and rebirth. At the same time, the concept 'bed' undergoes an elaborate transformation of meaning when found in each different situation (note that each 'situation' is actually itself a category). These different examples of beds in art form a conceptual system or 'theory' as a situation or context. I have already explained the usefulness of defining 'theory' as a 'system of relationships between concepts' (Kemp et al., 2010, p. 167). A 'theory' can be built up in a variety of ways: we may examine Emin's *My Bed* as a single artwork, or we may process its perceptual cues to piece together a mental state, recognising the fact that it references her depression after

---

[5] I would like to thank Professor Emeritus John Onians for suggesting this balance in understanding Duchamp, which I have been at pains to stress is part of more general art experience throughout this book. His book on neuroarthistory (2008) aims to follow how various artists and theorists have attempted to trace perceptual response to neural underpinnings.

having an abortion, and how she isolated herself from the world, not venturing beyond her bedroom for many weeks (in which case, the unmade bed seems to indicate the doldrums, a wreck, or even a hospital bed). We may also build up a system of art references that helps to locate the bed within a broader dialogical and cultural context. Neither kind of 'theory' depends on sensorimotor interpretations and simulations, although some of these processes may be called upon for extra perspectives. This is less to do with the naïve notion of a situation as a sensorimotor experience containing an ego having that experience. The problem or opportunity that arises here is that there are multiple situations and scripts that are simulated from the singular encounter with *My Bed*, and multiple encounters with other artworks retrieved from memory. Each, potentially, may stimulate a number of other scripts. An artwork may help to stimulate 'statistical attractors' (background situation types and pattern completion inferences) but it can also provide constraints upon these sometimes competing inferences.

Barsalou and Wiemer-Hastings state: 'People don't normally process either concrete or abstract concepts in isolation' (2005, p. 155), and they suggest that concepts are constrained by the ongoing situation. However, with artworks we are frequently presented with a situation that is extremely difficult to conceptualise, causing various, often incoherent concepts and schemata to arise, as we have seen with hybrid objects. Cognitive extension here is not the sort proposed by theorists of situated cognition; if cognition is to be enhanced by these artworks, it is often in spite of the situation rather than because of it. The situation that an artwork can present is often a *problem* and should perhaps be understood better by applying some of the lessons we have learnt from the psychology of problem solving rather than traditional 'gestalt' psychology (Arnheim, 1969; Gombrich, 1966), which is based on the assumption that we seamlessly organise the visual world into stable forms. Given that many artworks function as puzzles, and often without any satisfactory solution, it seems important that the relevant psychology of problem solving should be made available for analyses of aesthetic experience, because our problem solving is pleasurable and cognitively interesting, and these are important characteristics of our engagement with art. David Kirsh (2009) believes that the issue of problem solving and situated cognition is rather more complex than theorists of situated cognition suggest, often involving idiosyncratic or variable behaviour depending on the knowledge base of the subject and the kind of problem being solved, thus making such problem solving psychologically difficult to generalise. As Kirsh notes: '[I]t is not enough that we recognise the central insight of situated cognition – that the environment provides organisation for cognitive activity, that the world enables and supports such activities – we must go further. We must explain how internal control processes work with these supports' (2009, p. 302).

This is precisely what should be advocated for any empirical research into aesthetic experience. Kirsh lists a number of internal activities that subjects are involved in when solving the 'situations' that problems present. An important question is how much internal control is exercised over a 'problem space', an internal representation of the problem's structure, a working model that the subject has to begin with and keeps in working memory as a target to test against hypotheses. In other words, the literature on problem solving could be directed fruitfully to the 'problems' that artworks are able to present. We might surmise that a 'problem space' operates when artworks are viewed as puzzles and as highly coded bundles of information with variously complex affordances and variations that help to situate a system of relational knowledge. The problem for situated cognition is finding the right balance between how people solve problems and interpret the particular puzzle of an artwork using local, situated resources at hand, and the more general picture of how general types of 'problem' or problem solving occurs using abstract rules or procedures (Kirsh, 2009, p. 273). The degree of relational knowledge a person is able to depend on will not only present a different kind of problem, and different ways to deal with it, but it will also determine the situation to a large extent.

Relational knowledge can be vast. A situation, an artwork, a specific event, a place, a group of artworks can constrain relational knowledge but with the risk of bringing many more related situational models to bear upon it, extending the system of relational knowledge. Artworks can thus be extremely efficient statistical attractors, some of which may consist of possible solutions to solving the 'problem spaces' that various artworks present, with possible links being made to other artworks in order to engage with the artwork. As these probabilistic scenarios are 'tried on' and referred back to the artwork to see if they fit, these possible solutions and schemata are not necessarily random and may involve a certain systematicity and compositionality required of knowledge.

4.8   The archive as relational knowledge

Elaborating on the example of Duchamp's valise, which assembled together works of art in order to visualise systematicity, many contemporary artists bring together collections of works, a strategy often referred to in contemporary art theory as 'the archive'. Psychologically, this tendency can be theorised as a way of creating a 'cognitive niche', problem space or situation. Many of these installation works are collections of things. Song Dong's *Waste Not*, 2005, is a collection of his mother's possessions that she refused to throw away over her lifetime – old radios, TVs, clothes, bottles, furniture, all meticulously put into proper groups and categories in order to provide a profile of a woman's life, yet also a way of parodying the system of presentation, patronage, distribution and commodification of art, and the meticulous cataloguing and organisation of knowledge that lies behind the institutionalisation of knowledge. At the Venice Biennale, 2011, Song Dong collected hundreds of wardrobe doors constructing them into a winding passage. These works are not dissimilar to those of Thomas Hirschorn's, also at the Venice Biennale, that I mentioned in earlier pages. Many of these artworks suggest the duration of time (the time it takes to explore these collections, the composite parts of which represent many lapsed moments of past time) but links this with notions of consumption, accumulation and detritus. Damien Hirst's *Pharmacy*, 1992, was a dizzying archive of pharmaceutical products that neatly fitted into the artist's obsession with death. Christian Boltanski is famous for displaying groups of faded photographs and clothes that suggest the possessions left over from concentration camps; a museum of the dead. This is similarly the case with Gerhard Richter's *Atlas* (various dates from 1962), an archive of photographs used for artistic source material, collected and displayed. Other artists construct single installations, which appear as several rooms, organised as a journey or a memory palace (Mike Nelson's *Imposter* at the Venice Biennale, 2011, comes to mind). New Zealand artists Christine Hellyar who brings together a number of trays of stone axes and tools to mimic an ethnological museum display, and Fiona Pardington whose photographs of life-casts raises a number of questions

314

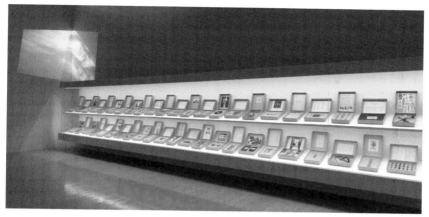

Figure 47. Susan Hiller, *From the Freud Museum*, 1991–1997 (vitrines installation, dimensions variable). Tate Photography. © the artist, courtesy of Timothy Taylor Gallery, London and the artist.

concerning representation (or lack of it) in museum displays. Many of these works parody the psychology behind exhibitions and critique how knowledge is organised by museum displays as a way to forward a particular historical narrative, drawing upon Foucault's ideas in the *Archaeology of Knowledge*. In recent times, the role of the curator and the artist seem to blend.

In Susan Hiller's installation work *From the Freud Museum*, 1991–1997, for example, the artist collected a number of objects in archaeological sorting boxes (boxes designed to contain rigorous categorising methods for grouping objects), resembling Duchamp's valise, with photographs, notes and memorabilia that create the atmosphere of a museum dedicated to Freud (and was, in fact, lodged inside the Freud Museum). The objects are linked together using various Freudian theories on psychoanalysis. Hiller writes about her installation work in a way that is very telling for the approach to understanding art followed in this book: 'The "meaning" of the entire bounded unit, of each box, would need to be investigated by seeing the relationship between word, picture and the objects, as well as by the placement of an individual box in an extensive series of boxes. Now in the Freud Museum we already have a complex situation...to situate another collection here is bound to make it available to be read in the context of the primary collection' (Hiller, 1994/2006, p. 42). It is interesting that Hiller's installation functions on the premise of a within-system series of objects placed within another collection (the Freud Museum) that creates between-system complications of relationships between images, words and objects, using the archive as an extended metaphor for how the mind creates superordinate categories within which there are subcategories and groups that can be related to each other to form meanings.

Other artists are interested in constructing the archive in order to explore categorisation and models of the mind. This may be seen with Keith Tyson's work, *Large Field Array*, 2007, a massive collection of games, objects and compendia that the artist likens to a 'rhizome', referring to the philosopher Deleuze and Guattari's notion of non-hierarchical collections of concepts and ideas. Matthew Barney's immense *Cremaster Cycle*, 1994–2002, at the Guggenheim, brought together a large collection of items for display that seemed to be costumes, crests and ceremonial objects from Masonic rituals keyed into mythological narratives concerning hierarchies of knowledge. In all these cases, we not only see artists coming to terms with methods of categorisation and theories to do with the politics of display, we also see them engaged in theories of mind and relational knowledge that exists between groups of objects signifying categories.

Thomas Hirschorn's *Cavemanman*, 2002, was a series of rooms modelled on the four lobes of the human brain. The work was re-presented in the Hayward Gallery exhibition *Walking in My Mind* in 2009, where many other artists constructed installations that brought together a number of objects that acted as mental images, memories or categories of knowledge (in other words, playing on the term 'representation' to mean mental representation). Many of the artists' works here were conceptualised as journeys through the mind, as imaginative spaces or as dreams, with Hirschorn representing neural firings as firecrackers connected to books and pictures. None of these archival works (there are far too many others to mention here, which form a superordinate category of archives, systems of artworks) have been studied by cognitive psychology or neuroaesthetics, both of which seem intent on looking at single works from formalist perspectives. Needless to say, formalist concerns here are less important than the relations between things, rooms and groups of objects. These installations are physical ways of organising ideas and categories and they show us how we can journey through them to connect them.

Related to this but more consistently concerned with the real-time processes of component parts in systems as a way to help us reflect on the systematicity of conceptual thought (often with political undertones against totalitarian systematising systems) are many of Hans Haacke's 'system art' projects from the 1960s and 1970s. Many of these were explorations of components in many different kinds of systems, as the artist stated: 'Systems can be physical, biological or social; they can be man-made or naturally existing, or a combination of any of the above systems' (Skrebowski, 2008, p. 67). Haacke's *Condensation Cube* was an artwork that made viewers aware of the ambient space of the gallery. A similar attempt to make us aware of the institution as a system of display was his *Ice Stick*, 1962–1964, a freezing copper coil that drew moisture out of the gallery environment and froze it, and his *Recording the Climate in Art Exhibition*, 1970, displayed the museum's precision instruments to measure temperature and moisture in the air, which usually remain hidden. The systematicity here is about exposing the gallery system, and to get us to think about the reality within which exhibits, artworks and artefacts are staged. The works function on the psychological premise of metacognition and theory of mind: we not only become aware of where we are as visitors in the controlled environment of the gallery space, but we are also encouraged to think about the underlying logic of display and categorisation. Rather than the gallery being assumed to be a neutral or invisible stage (which, in fact, creates a schism between art and life), it is part of a system that is both economic, cultural, scientific and psychological: the artist attacked what he called the strategies and techniques of 'the consciousness industry'. The gallery could not exist as it does without these systems of power and knowledge, and the gallery system itself here becomes the observed object. In 1974, Haacke revealed some embarrassing facts and figures about some of the members of the Guggenheim Museum of Board Trustees. That year, Haacke submitted a proposal for an exhibition at the Wallraf-Richartz Museum, Cologne, in which he documented the history of the ownership of a painting by Manet, *Bunch of Asparagus*, 1880, in the museum collection, exposing connections between its donor and the Third Reich. The proposal was rejected. Following this, in 1975, Haacke exposed the history of ownership of Seurat's *Les Poseuses*, 1888, in the John Weber Gallery, New York.

Another artist working along similar lines, Marcel Broodthaers, devised a project titled *Musée d'Art Modern*. Starting in 1969, the artist displayed, in various cities around the world, various objects from different 'departments' of his virtual museum, including a documentary section and a nineteenth century section (various packaging crates with instructions stamped on them and postcards of traditional artworks). In 1992, Fred Wilson, in *Mining the Museum*, arranged objects from the Maryland Historical Society that either suggested a history of exclusion of African–American history (plinths with names but no busts) or stereotypes. Meanwhile, Joseph Kosuth's *Play of the Unmentionable*, 1990, involved curating many objects from the Brooklyn Museum that were controversial in their time for explicit sexual content, political non-correctness or irreligiousness. This was seen as a veiled attack on the various United States senators who had vilified artists such as Andres Serrano and Robert Mapplethorpe for being immoral and obscene. In sum, it was an exhibition showing historically distinct periods of censorship.

Many of these artworks tacitly or explicitly deal with systematicity as a theme in art beyond the naïve model of vision as an optical experience of a single artwork and its facture. These artworks are evidence of important tendencies in contemporary art, which emphasise relations between objects rather than the valuing of the formal properties of the objects themselves: the artwork becomes 'the collection'. Ultimately, such collections attempt to provide images of thought, but not any kind of thought: the kind involved in creating relations and systems. It is interesting that, in all these examples, we are being asked to visualise systems of political, cultural and economic influence as they help to produce art collections, either by parodying collections or by connecting objects together into relational systems that speak of a narrative or syntax of vested interests underlying aesthetic presentation. These works, and many others, present an important dilemma: in creating a visually powerful critique of positivist assumptions behind the public display of knowledge, power, wealth, beauty and pleasure, these works are also rational, purposeful and held together by relational knowledge. Their conceptual content and overall intentions might be different from those of the art gallery system but there is also an intelligible structure to their critiques. In other words, even our satirical attacks on systems of control, and any nihilism, postmodern, eclectic multiplicity or irony, which might ensue from these, cannot stand outside of systematicity. We cannot pretend that we do not know, and what we know is organised systematically. Even avoiding systematicity requires systematicity.

4.9 Performing relational knowledge

Beyond these conceptual and installation works that bring together aspects of relational knowledge, either as a critique or as an extension of such knowledge, several works of performance art may be said to create a relational system, or 'theory', recalling the definition of theory as a system of relationships between concepts. A major difference, however, is that these works use the body of the artist as a medium to express systematicity in relational knowledge. How is this remarkable idea made possible?

Marina Abramović's *Seven Easy Pieces* is the re-enactment of older and 'iconic' performance works, performed over seven days in the great spiralling architecture of the Guggenheim in New York in 2005. The work is a relational system made more complex by the final work, *Entering the Other Side*, where the performer places herself on a high platform with outstretched arms at the centre of the spiral. This bears some relation to Matthew Barney's hierarchical levels of initiation, in his *Cremaster Cycle*, where he linked the semiotics of the body with architecture by scaling the levels of the same spiralling form of the Guggenheim Museum years before. Abramović disciplines the docile body into the diagram of the mandala, nested into the architectural spiral of the Guggenheim. Consistent with the underlying logic of the mandala, she becomes a symbol not of fixity but of the transformation of self to a 'higher plane'. As Barney imaginatively transformed the spiral form into a hierarchy of levels of initiation, from novice below to adept above, the building is turned into a cult sanctuary by attendance of the circling visitors below. Seven pieces, seven hours, seven days, the seven levels of the Guggenheim Museum are implicated in the tradition of the artist–creator coming full circle and emerging, as an epiphany, from a series of seven tests: *Entering the Other Side*, the last act, suggests the threshold that joins an end to a new beginning, a rite of passage.

It is interesting that in 2010, Tino Sehgal extended the mythical tradition associated with the spiral as a kind of 'interpretation' of Barney's and Abramović's examples. The idea of using the ascending levels of the spiral of the Guggenheim's architecture, a spatial and visual facticity, to make concrete and to situate the structure of relational knowledge that we call myth, not only as something that returns, but which has many levels of progressively more expert knowledge, was also used in Sehgal's 2010 show, *This Progress*, again at the Guggenheim Museum. A child meets visitors at the base of the spiral and asks them the meaning of progress. Visitors ascend the spiral, discussing progress with the child and, at a higher level, a high-school student continues the conversation. At the next level, the conversation progresses with a teenager, until they meet an adult and then, eventually, they meet a much older adult in her later years at the upper-most level of the spiral. The slow ascent in a spiral by the walking visitors is both actual and ritualistic. Thus, relational knowledge is not only indicated within one composite work (*Seven Easy Pieces*) and across works, such knowledge can also be embodied by various individuals and their actions and re-enactions anchored by the spiral architecture, which forms a concrete reference point or diagram situating the continuity and difference that relational knowledge involves.

Another example of performing relational knowledge systematically is Francis Alÿs' *Seven Walks*, an archive of film clips (2005), exhibited most recently in the UK in 2011. The set of walks may be seen as a good example of how relational knowledge can be embodied, situated and performed. The official catalogue describes the collection of work in the following way:

Over a span of five years, Alÿs walked the streets of London, evolving *Seven Walks* for Artangel, a project which delved into the everyday rituals and habits of the metropolis. The walks were enacted in different parts of the city – Hyde Park, the City of London, the National Portrait Gallery, the streets close to Regents Park.

Guards follows sixty-four individual Coldstream Guards as they move through the Square Mile of London.

Shady/Sunny consists of a walk in South East London on the sunny side of the street always and a walk in South East London on the shady side of the street always.

In *The Commuters* a painting is hung on a wall of the entrance hall in a house situated in Portman Square, No. 21. At 7:00 PM, a chosen carrier takes the painting off the wall. He brings the painting back to his home by walking or taking whatever means of transport he would normally use.

Railings explores the rhythmic possibilities afforded by a characteristic feature of Regency London.

In *Ice4Milk* slide images of a large block of ice being pushed through the streets of Mexico City are juxtaposed with the morning delivery of milk bottles to London doorsteps.

The *Nightwatch* uses surveillance cameras to observe a fox exploring the Tudor and Georgian rooms of the National Portrait Gallery at night.

Pebble Walk is Alÿs's postcard homage to Richard Long, based on a walk Alÿs took through Hyde Park in 1999.[1]

I will analyse some of these works now, informed by relational knowledge 'theory' outlined here, which emphasises different kinds of connections between brain–body–world in order to contrast and compare different works by the same artist (what might be called a 'within-system') and provide links to other, similar performance artworks in art history (a 'between-systems' approach). Although this is a standard comparative method adopted by most historians, it represents the way in which semantic memory is itself structured and utilised by artists and viewers in the production and reception of art. This is consistent with Alÿs' own explanation to the conceptual exploration involved in walking, which suggests a relational knowledge approach: 'You can function at multiple levels simultaneously. It's like my method of working on lots of different scenarios in parallel, I always bounce from one project to another, it's the only way I can progress.'

Firstly, it must be said that *Seven Walks* needs to be contextualised within previous works by Alÿs that centre on the activity of walking. For his first performance, *The Collector*, 1991, Alÿs wheeled, through Mexico City, a small magnetic toy dog that attracted debris; a commentary perhaps on 'a rolling stone gathers no moss' or the notion of accumulation and automatic attraction. In *Fairy Tales*, 1995, the artist took a walk after unravelling a woolly sweater, leaving a thread in his wake, bringing to mind the thread used by Theseus to slay the minotaur in the labyrinth; the walk suggests aimlessness but also a 'guiding thread'. In São Paulo in 1995, Alÿs performed *The Leak* in which he walked from a gallery, around the city, returning to the gallery, all the while trailing a line of blue paint from a tin can. This referenced not only Klee's famous phrase 'taking the line for a walk' and the existentialism of action painting, but also the notion of leaving a trace behind one to be followed, and creating a loop back to the gallery. Adding political commentary to this type of action, in 2004 Alÿs walked along the armistice border in Jerusalem, known as 'the green line', with a tin can leaking green paint. Another work, *Paradox of Praxis 1 (Sometimes Making Something Lead to Nothing)*, documents a Sisyphean performance in 1997 where Alÿs pushed a block of ice through the streets of Mexico City for nine hours until it melted away. In all these works, Alÿs uses materials that dissipate or dissolve, leaving only the idea or a film of the performance. The work is comparable to another artist's

---

[1] www.artangel.org.uk/projects/2005/seven_walks/about_the_project/about_the_project The following quotes from the artist are taken from this interview on this website.

work, Song Dong's *A Pot of Boiling Water*, 1995, a series of photographs of the artist walking with a hot kettle, pouring boiling water down the centre of a back alley in a Chinese town, with the steam lifting off the ground and quickly dissipating; the performance was destined to leave no trace, except for the photographs. In using extremely simple and bare essentials, such performances remind us of what they share with the beauty of Minimalism. In both Song Dong's and Alÿs' work, the indexical trace of the performance disappears, leaving behind only a whisper of the notion of place, time or cultural identity.

The accent in all of Alÿs' urban interventions is on purposelessness and control, movement and bodily involvement situated within the urban context, and the conceptual constraints of the conceptual work. The streets, the body, action and thought become the medium for each artwork, their material anchors; yet, piecing these artworks together, one gets an overall view of the artist's conceptual system based on a series of relations between each artwork (and others' artworks) to create a 'theory', which we might term 'psychogeography'. This is a term that is associated with the Situationist International and the ideas of Guy Debord in the 1960s and 1970s, which valorised an aimless wandering, letting oneself float or drift (*dériver* is the French word used) as a way of unraveling the allure of the 'society of the spectacle'. This society of the spectacle is structured by consumer images and ways of organising desire that severely reduce the freedom to act 'unproductively': to browse and wander and to experience chance happenings rather than have every action through the city – from home to the high street shop – circumscribed in order to support purposeful consumer habits and behaviours. Instead, with psychogeography, the individual was encouraged to discover his or her own ambient, eccentric or personal ways of 'parsing' the city, personalising it into a sense of discovery through an alienation from capitalist productivity, the spectacle of the high street. Sharing a synergy with this is Alÿs' series of exploratory and aimless walks that appear to amount to nothing (seeming to confirm Oscar Wilde's quip that 'all art is quite useless'). Alÿs claims that a 'journey implies a destination, so many miles to be consumed, while a walk is its own measure, complete at every point along the way.' It is important that, in psychogeography, the *dérive* encourages drift and the arbitrary, because its ethos is against the Enlightenment telos of rational organisation, progress and control. Wandering the streets and byways is also a way of exploring a semantic drift, to suspend the desire to structure all meaning rationally. In the various expressions of this ethos in performance art, the psychology is concerned with opening the mind to one's surroundings, and walking allows an attentiveness to a prereflexive state of rhythmically being in the world and being within the work of art, defined as a set of parameters within which such absorption may take place. There is also a connection here with mind wandering as a kind of inattentive engagement and openness to chance encounters.

Sticking to the rules of the game, the conceptual structure that underlies the walk becomes the object of desire. Thus, in Alÿs' *Railings*, part of his *Seven Walks*, the artist rhythmically strikes the railings surrounding the park in Fitzroy Square, London, with a drumstick while walking around in a circle following the railings. The paradox is that a purposeless, rhythmical and trance-like walking is guided by the topographical facticity of the railings. The walker is free to wander within a circumscribed patterning, and freedom and predestination seem locked in a carousel. The artist transforms the urban space and architecture into music and into a series of mental spaces. The repeat rhythm of the tapping is in harmony with the circular architectural space, the railings, traversed with steps. Tapping, railings, steps bring together brain, body and the world, becoming the distributed system for the conceptual performance piece. In themselves, these elements form the artwork and describe the rules of the conceptual game, Minimalist as it is, yet also dynamic, evocative and, in terms of classical definitions of art, strangely immaterial and intangible. It is indeed an achievement that *Railings* is structurally quite simple and brings to mind, as Alÿs says, a kind of

kid's game, you know, picking up a stick and running it along the railings. A lot of the walks have had that kind of echo, like kicking a bottle along the pavements, or dragging a magnet through the streets at the end of a string...I tried something similar in Mexico City but not on railings but on the metal shutters of shops in the centre of the city. But the shutters in Mexico require more of a vertical movement of the stick, so it doesn't combine so well with the horizontal motion of the walker.[2]

Railings appears on the surface to be a naïve and simple child's game, where a child creates a boundary, a mental space, suggesting the refrain of a song that brings rhythm and a sense of surety to a place. Here, walking and a sense of dance allow the body to be recruited in measurements of time and self-control, while architecture, the railings themselves, also seems to buttress these rhythmic assurances with their own circular form, helping to create an exteriority that seems to express perfectly an interior world of rhythmic repeat and cyclical return. The child 'territorialises' or channels desire, mapping the emotional landscape upon the railings in the park. Alÿs suggests this childhood regression (another circular movement) in his performance work, but there are many other concepts in the form of other artworks that are referenced here and

[2] www.artangel.org.uk/projects/2005/seven_walks/

become part of the system of relations. Alÿs acknowledges that aspects of his *Seven Walks* are a homage to British sculptor Richard Long, famous for *A Line Made by Walking*, 1967, where he walked back and forth creating a line in the grass, which he photographed. The work was regarded as an important innovation in contemporary art, bringing together the fleeting and intangible aspect of performance (walking) and sculpture (the mark on the material substrate of the land), stimulating concepts associated with questioning presence, permanence and place, and engaging with the phenomenology of Minimalism. This conceptual artwork and many other sculpture/performance walks in rural England were important in many different ways for other artists such as Andy Goldsworthy and Ana Mendieta. The effect on Alÿs, however, is less to do with nature and more to do with the psychological and physical unity suggested by walking. Long explained:

I started making work outside using natural materials like grass and water, and this led to the idea of making a sculpture by walking. This was a straight line in a grass field, which was also my own path, going 'nowhere'. In the subsequent early map works, recording very simple but precise walks on Exmoor and Dartmoor, my intention was to make a new art which was also a new way of walking: walking as art. Each walk followed my own unique, formal route, for an original reason, which was different from other categories of walking, like traveling...Thus walking – as art – provided a simple way for me to explore relationships between time, distance, geography and measurement. These walks are recorded in my work in the most appropriate way for each different idea: a photograph, a map, or a text work. All these forms feed the imagination.[3]

Most art historians of contemporary art would be quick to make analogies between *Seven Walks* and two other extremely well-known performance pieces pre-dating Alÿs work: Vito Acconci's *Following Piece*, 1969, and Sophie Calle's *Suite Venitienne*, 1979. In the first of these, the artist's rules of the game were set along these lines: he had to select any person from the stream of passers-by walking in the street and was to follow that person until he or she disappeared into a private place where Acconci could not follow. This piece could be over and done relatively quickly if the person vanished behind closed doors, or in several hours if he or she went to a library or a hospital. Acconci carried out this performance every day for a month. It has become a key part of performance art to adopt a method and commit to it as a matter of principle or integrity even if it leads to absurd conclusions; Alÿs' work also bears this stamp. The play here is between commitment to these conceptual constraints, a general freedom provided by the ability to arbitrarily pick someone to follow, and being free to follow

[3] www.tate.org.uk/britain/exhibitions/richardlong/explore.shtm

the rules of the game, which are, paradoxically, very limiting in terms of one's own personal freedom. Acconci cannot walk in any direction he pleases, he is 'free to follow' a rule that restricts him to structure the work, and this point is pertinent to critiques of the society of the spectacle where one is 'free' to obey the rules of capitalist societies, to settle down, to get a job, to become a consumer. Walking here is 'enacted' as a mechanised motion of imprisonment, of mice on a treadmill, with a predetermined destination (unknown to the artist, taken on a wild goose chase). It is also, perversely, anti-productive (as art should be, according to Wilde). The artist is free to give up his freedom.

Similary, and resorting to more disturbing lengths, Sophie Calle in her project, *Suite Venitienne*, followed a man she met at a party in Paris to Venice, where she disguised herself and followed him around the city, photographing him. Calle's surveillance of the man, who she identifies only as Henri B., includes black-and-white photographs accompanied by diary entries. The preposterous extension of Acconci's *Following Piece* sets the rules of the game at the level of imitating, at least outwardly, the actions of obsessive desire: a woman intervening in psychogeography as the hunter, not the hunted. Not only is she physically tied to the actions of the unsuspecting Henri B., committed to tracking his every move, Calle is also herself psychically ensnared in the make-believe of obsession. At one point, she writes, 'I'll do it this way every day…I must not forget that I don't have any amorous feelings toward Henri B.', suggesting that the commitment to the conceptual rules of the artwork, a game obsessively performed for a long period every day, could possibly be confused with the obsession of desire she feigns. Calle walks a thin line between obsessive commitment to the project required of performance art, on which her integrity as an artist rests, and method acting the obsessive behaviour of stalking an individual. The mapping of one mental space, the artist's, on the stalker's is uncomfortably direct. Getting into the mind of a stalker and into the heart of desire are physically enacted by Calle, but do these actions begin to lay the basis for an emotional attachment to the mission? Again, as with Acconci's *Following Piece* and Alÿs' elegant circular psychogeography in *Railings*, these works bring to a head the issues of agency and control, discipline over the body and wandering free. Such conceptual features are also found in Alÿs' *Guards* where he follows a group of sixty-four Coldstream Guards as they move through the Square Mile of London and converge from different directions to form one large group. Not only are the guards following a conceptual structure, a method and commitment to a traditional practice, dissolving their individuality in their roles, which require them to move as a group, they are also followed by Alÿs who enacts the role of an automaton himself. However, Alÿs films them from the point of view of CCTV cameras to suggest surveillance, controlling movement through the gaze and through the gaze of authority that one internalises.

Acconci's, Calle's and Alÿs' psychogeographical (or anti-psychogeographical) works use walking in several ways. What ostensibly appears as physical action in perception is, in fact, a medium for the artist's larger conceptual goals. These walking performance pieces suggest that the body is caught up in a conceptual system that structures not only the artwork-as-walking but also the history of artworks that consist of walking performances. Both conceptual transformations of art and art history have a direct bearing on the intentions behind the walking performed in these works.

As for Alÿs' other works in *Seven Walks*, there is ample room to discuss how walking is filtered through various conceptual experiments that also reference other artworks in a system of relational knowledge. Alÿs explains:

The prototype of the idea for the piece in the City of London [*Guards*] came from a project I made in Venice called *Duett*. I entered the city by the train station and a friend of mine, the artist Honoré d'O arrived through Marco Polo Airport. We arrived the same day, carrying the two different parts of the Tuba, trying to find each other in the labyrinth of Venice. There was a basic dramatic construction to the piece, with the two protagonists needing to find each other. Eventually, there was a happy end, maybe even a moral, to the story with the meeting and the physical reunion of the two halves, and the resulting production of a sound...The Venice piece was inspired by the speech of Aristophanes in Plato's Symposium, which in short is that it is in our nature to be incomplete, to be bisexual. There is always a missing half, a confusion, a split identity. So in London, I was looking for another version, a different way of staging the drama of being alone and then being joined with someone else.[4]

This could be a reference to Calle's work, also staged in Venice. In terms of the history of performance art, one would have to mention here an iconic performance work of Abramović and Ulay. In 1988, after several years of tense relations, Abramović and Ulay decided to make a spiritual journey that would end their relationship. Each of them walked the Great Wall of China, starting from the two opposite ends, and they met somewhere in the middle. As Abramović described it: 'That walk became a complete personal drama. Ulay started from the Gobi desert and I from the Yellow Sea. After each of us walked 2500 km, we met in the middle and said good-bye'.

Such a context engages with the reasoning behind Alÿs' *Guards*. Both performance works provide 'concrete' simulations of the abstract concept

---

[4] www.tate.org.uk/britain/exhibitions/richardlong/explore.shtm

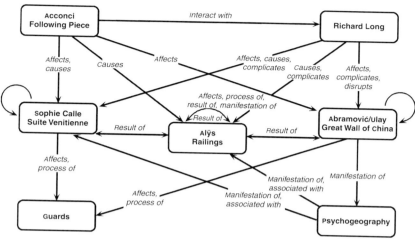

Figure 48. Relational knowledge sustained by different psychogeographic works of art.

DUTY. They are also mutually enforcing (of each other) in the mind of the interpreter, steeped in a knowledge of conceptual and performance art, who automatically maps the features of one artwork onto another, not only to see how they may come together but also to see those aspects that are different. Alÿs seems to suggest a coming together of desires to create a whole (while blending himself into that whole in terms of surveillance and personal involvement), while Abramović and Ulay come together to pay respect to something that no longer exists, as a perfunctory yet exhausting enactment of duty to the conceptual rules of the artwork, going their separate ways after the artwork has been performed. Both *Guards* and Abramović and Ulay's walk on the Great Wall of China are about coming together from different directions in order to disperse, to separate, to fall out – and this is the conceptual blend. Ten years later, the Chinese artist Fen Ma Liuming commemorated this walk with his own. Known for his feminine long hair and make-up, the artist walked on the Great Wall naked. Abramović and Ulay were always billed as a fusion of male and female, and many of their performances explored this idea. Fen Ma Liuming's performance takes this fact and Abramović and Ulay's last walk in his stride. Alÿs speaks of the walking as a coming together of two halves, as do many of these other works, linking walking with desire, togetherness and separation, purpose and purposelessness, embodied symbolism and psychogeography.

Figure 48 allows us to grasp, in a simplified manner, the kind of relational knowledge that extends Alÿs' work and allows it to become more meaningful and absorbing for those interested in contemporary art and performance. Note that the diagram shows a system of relations based on the cognitive psychology of Kemp et al. (2010), and captures some of the dynamic and manipulable connections between categorical concepts, each one of which is a work of art or a complex abstract concept. Although manipulable suggests moving something with the body and precise actions, it is also about the flow of action or, more precisely, *pace* Gibson, the 'optic flow' of spatial, environmental, attentional, rhythmic and sometimes arbitrary complementary processes involved in 'reading' a map, which is also about being organised by a particular reading of the map (depending on where one wants to go, a map can be read in many different directions and routes, noting different features along the way). Like the horizon, a map expresses the reciprocity of self and environment, which is 'neither subjective nor objective' (Gibson, 1979, p. 164). The map uses the names of artists or performance works, not to explore the relationships between fixed perceptual cues but between different acts or routes of walking – not only walking as a physical action, but also as a series of performances, semantic connections that breach or connect particular psychological states.[5] In this sense, the map is a map of the relations between artworks as well as the *relations* between mental states enacted by these performances. This relational knowledge is about relations *between* sensorimotor performances, but this knowledge cannot be confused with or reduced to sensorimotor action engaged in a performance. This would be tantamount to saying that an artwork's meaning *is* its perceptible content.

Remarkably, each set of mental states, as embodied and explored in each performance piece, is never a discrete set. Each performance piece is a porous 'container' and, therefore, not really a container at all. It may interact and share common features with others, and it can play the role of cause or effect when we think of the knowledge map involved that brings together a series of different works in a collection. This shows that art is a

---

[5] This eventually should lead to reconceptualising what a performance 'event' actually consists of, whether, for example, it is prefigured by previous events and is rechannelled into subsequent ones and co-extensive with our relational knowledge of such relations, which continue outside of the 'container' or discrete moment of the event. This is in harmony with how artists and art theorists in contemporary art, informed by Deleuze *pace* Bergson's productively different theories of what an event is, as well as by Badiou's, which have fed into the reconceptualisation in contemporary art practice of the art event as something beyond artificially defined beginning and end points. On these different views, the event is recast as a continuum of influences and reinvestments of themes or creative oppositions prefiguring or prolonging the event as a superordinate category or system of relational knowledge.

system of relational knowledge based not only on the shared features of discrete concepts but also on their relational roles in the system. The model thus shows us that, in contemporary art, it is possible for a complex artwork to derive its meaning from its relationship with other artworks, whether these are complementary or antagonistic. Thus, while the structural features of an artwork can be complex and composite, representing a series of internal relationships, this 'within-system' will have a series of relations to other artworks to create 'between-system' semantics.

The map is an attempt to represent the approach taken by the work of Goldstone and Rogosky, using relations within conceptual systems to translate across conceptual systems (2002). Goldstone et al. (2005) have this to say about the kind of relational knowledge envisaged by this map: 'It is not viciously circular to claim that concepts gain their meaning by their relations to other concepts that, in turn, gain the meaning in the same fashion. Remarkably, a concept's connections to other concepts in the same system can suffice to give it a meaning that can transcend the system, at least in the sense of establishing proper connections to concepts outside of the system' (p. 309).

It is the very distinction between within-system relations and between-system relations that takes the notion of internal and external cooperation of resources to a higher level of cognition. In other words, such cooperation occurs on a number of levels of complexity. It is important to note that the authors acknowledge the pivotal role of the lowest level, that is, external cues, 'an externally grounded component' or 'affordance-revealing cues' (Kirsh, 2009, p. 293); in this case, the documentation, videos, photographs and reports that each performance artist has left, by which the system of relational knowledge is constrained and stabilised across individual minds and across-system relations. Systematicity and compositionality, which this relational knowledge map of walking clearly indicates, would require a massive connectivity between brain areas as well as situational knowledge. Each artwork is itself a system of perceptual cues that anchor conceptual blends and analogical structure mappings, and each artwork functions across system relations. With the continual referencing of external cues, psychological theories of extended cognition would help us to understand more clearly that this relational knowledge is not held in the mind all at the same time, but that working memory is aided by these kinds of maps that help support further mental manipulations of the concepts indicated spatially.[6] These

---

[6] Working memory is 'the workspace where relational representations are constructed and it is influenced by knowledge stored in semantic memory. Therefore, it plays an important role in the interaction of analytic and nonanalytic processes in higher cognition' (Halford et al., 2010, p. 499).

maps are visual ways to make explicit what is in the writing of art historical relational knowledge. The map helps to represent the combination of semantic and syntactic cognition that is involved in relational knowledge, which has: 'unique properties, including structure-consistent mapping and the ability to construct new representations in working memory. These confer the ability to break free from previous experience and are the basis of much human inference' (Halford et al., 2010, p. 503). It must be noted that human inference, analogical thinking and relational structures are processes that help to enrich our experience of art by producing a mental and physical absorption in meaning creation that may be glimpsed in the map, indicating how different walking-as-art performances are related. It is this building up of relations that generates meaning. Thus, walking as an activity in art is one way to bring together many different art practices providing variations on theme, and a way of thinking in groups and across works that is typical of artists, curators and art historians. The interesting, generative thing about creating networks of this kind is that they are always being augmented by later works that extend the group of works as a kind of living tradition, which can also become intertwined with other relational systems of artworks.

Another elaboration on the theme of the art of walking is a video piece by David Pérez Karmadavis, *Estructura Completa*, 2010, which simply shows a man walking down the streets in Guatamala City carrying in his arms a woman who has no limbs. She is his eyes, for he cannot see ahead as carrying her in front of him blocks his view entirely, and she has to 'wave' people out of their way. The film is strangely tender and stoic, and we marvel at the strength of the relationship between these people who share a brazen determination to be mobile and visible in the street, in public, in art. As with Marc Quinn's *Alison Lapper* sculpture or Matthew Barney's casting of Aimee Mullins in his baroque and often sublime *Cremaster Cycle*, the visibility of differently abled bodies can be beautiful, meaningful and moving, against universal notions of normative aesthetics.

Rather than watching artists walk 'offline', it is possible to be engaged in walking directed by an artist, stepping into her shoes. Another part of this knowledge system is Janet Cardiff's work. *The Missing Voice (Case Study B)* was a 1999 project commissioned by Artangel, the same organisation responsible for commissioning Alÿs' walks. It consists of an audio tour guiding the walker from the Whitechapel Library, through London's East End, relaying fictional narratives with descriptions concerning actual stops and points on the journey. Another walk was designed for Central Park, New York (2005), where Cardiff reads texts about historical figures associated with the park and also from poems and stories. The work is punctuated by observations about the park's appearance, along with sound effects. The walker feels as if she is in the artist's, or that the artist is in the listener's body or mind. The visual descriptions sometimes overlay the listener's actual experience, or are discordant, producing arbitrary spatial effects. Thus, while the recording is always the same, it is continually experienced differently because each walker's observations and rhythms adopted during the journey will vary. The work also deals with notions of following instructions, surveillance, freedom and inter-subjectivity, as well as negotiating urban space while relinquishing control as a kind of thought experiment. In Cardiff's work, the listener and walker seems to get 'into' the performance, and is channelling Cardiff's perform-ativity. Such an artwork requires physical and embodied movement, semantic reasoning, social cognition, spatial awareness, relational know-ledge and emotional exploration, and it is also inherently social and participative and, consequently, wholly absorbing.

If we were to use sensorimotor explanations of the meaning of these artworks, without references to the broader picture of how they are related to each other in a system of relational knowledge, we would be guilty, *pace* Derrida, of a kind of violence to the artwork that consists of forcing a single explanation upon it, disguised as a claim to discovering its literal truth. Cardiff's work constrains the retrieval of previously stored episodes in the artist's memory, helping to combine them with new, ongoing insights, evaluations and emotional nuances that the listener provides. This is just another example of how art plays an important role in linking personal memory with 'publically' shared cultural memory; this is where art is not only intersubjective, but the memories that it is able to activate also become negotiated and intersubjective.

4.10 From relational aesthetics to relational knowledge

I have mentioned Bourriaud's *Relational Aesthetics*, an influential text that drew attention to the long-standing tradition in contemporary art, which holds that art presents an encounter and extends a series of social relations. According to Bourriaud, although contemporary artists such as Braco Dimitrijevic, Rikrit Tiravanija, Douglas Gordon and Franz West, for example, adopted a great range of artistic strategies and materials, and were very different in their approaches: 'Their works bring into play modes of social exchange, interaction with the viewer inside the aesthetic experience he or she is offered, and processes of communication in their concrete dimensions as tools that can be used to bring together individual and human groups. They therefore all work within what we might call the relational sphere' (1998, p. 107). As Bourriaud implies, inherent in this view of art is a move away from the perceptual aspect of art's materials and facture, the art object, and a move towards the situational aspects of art, as we witness with performance art and artworks that require viewers to become participants, similarly explored by Norma Jean's work and by Jacob Dahlgren. In Norma Jean's work, the bright red blocks of modelling clay in the gallery are soon dispersed and layered in the space and extended across time. Individuals model or build upon the remnants of previous work, and their work will become the medium for their successors, with the work continually being remade along the lines of social interaction across time and space. Dahlgren's *Signs of Abstraction*, 2005, was set in a Stockholm shopping mall where a large number of participants were invited to dress in brightly striped shirts and jumpers. An ordinary day usually devoted to buying clothes, spending money and making corporate profit was transformed into 'a living abstraction, a kinetic painting that constantly changed its shape and dimension'.[1] The work enabled a cooperative and irreverent creative interaction between individuals, outside the structures and purposes of consumer spaces (and the

---

[1] Artist's website, www.jacobdahlgren.com/texts/timo_valjakka.htm

fashionable imperatives one needs to follow in such spaces), and offered the possibility for reflection, for a stepping outside of the ordinary. There are a great many new contemporary artworks that consist of urban interventions involving social participation or the disruption of normative routes, uses and spaces situated in the city. If psychology and neuroaesthetics are at all to be relevant in understanding this kind of art, they need to change many of their approaches to the visual and, instead, seek to understand the ethical, social, cooperative, spatial and conceptual practices of these artworks, which cannot be adequately explained by appealing to sensorimotor experiences, or visual experience alone, even though these are very much part of these urban interventions.

Immersion in the social exchange in and around the artwork becomes the theme of the artwork. The 'artwork' still has a structure; the premise, place or social situation involved in Norma Jean's and Jacob Dahlgren's work must be designed and facilitated, and the *interpretation* of the conceptual design can be the same as participation in it. The artwork is constituted by the very act of viewing, doing and interpreting, and this in a sense is another form of absorption. However, importantly, this is an absorption not bound by the model of introspection; rather, it is sustained by the fluidity of the social world where the conceptual constituents of introspection are distributed and exchanged among individuals.

This slightly different emphasis on art as social and interactive, which we have seen with Dada, Fluxus and performance artworks, and which has continued with the contemporary artworks treated here, presents a particular challenge to the psychology of art. In order to understand the complexity of relational aesthetics and the exchange of relational knowledge that I believe is the thing actually being exchanged in these encounters, there needs to be some understanding not only of 'the world out there' with its social relations and public actions, but also of the cooperative 'world in here' that is affected by it. Immersion has both social *and* introspective aspects. Social cognition, situated cognition, situated aesthetics and cognitive psychology have important and cooperative roles to play in helping us to understand this kind of phenomenon in contemporary art. On the one hand, the systematicity of relational knowledge and situated cognition should reveal the underlying structures and engagements of relational aesthetics and collaborative art, which might otherwise seem amorphous and open to any definition of sociality. On the other hand, relational aesthetics and participative art practices provide situated cognition with new challenges beyond the ordinary bounds of social psychology.

What is remarkable about relational aesthetics from a psychological point of view is that it is inherently social *and* metacognitive, promising an 'emancipation' of seeing and doing in aesthetic exploration with others (Rancière, 2009). What I have tried to show in this book is that this kind of emancipation can be studied from psychological perspectives as an important form of creative thinking and doing, which art invites us to initiate socially and in the world. This kind of social interaction through relational aesthetics offers an alternative to the entropy and isolation of relational knowledge that results from our interest in the glossy surface appearance of newness: technological innovations, the latest tunes, cutting-edge fashion, news events and entertainment, which often blind us to the underlying repetitive formats, formulae, scripts and value systems that organise these presentations. Organising entities, grouping new objects and details, constructing a purpose within which to situate these innovations are processes that resist passive spectatorship where all of the organising is done for us. The relations and connections in our accumulation of facts and details are readymade for us in many examples of mass entertainment, work and social situations, effortlessly slipping into the flow of the unremarkable. Sometimes, we need to stop and think how we relate concepts to each other, and do so purposefully, in order to avoid slipping back into passive spectatorship.

In contrast, chances to experiment with different kinds of connections between concepts must be sought out. Thus, active and creative spectatorship is, in many ways, psychologically distinct from ordinary consumerist habits, values of commodity exchange and normative expectations, which rarely require effort to change our relational knowledge. Many of the artworks I have analysed in this book are interesting because they require that, psychologically, we become more aware of the formats and formulae of the everyday that do not require that we make creative connections between concepts. Furthermore, they do not require that we do this increasingly more aggressively. Those who imply that participative practices were and are engaged in the pursuit of an ideal goal, to 'bring art closer to everyday life' (Bishop, 2006, p. 10), surely do not mean *this* kind of everyday life. Perhaps the idea is that having art more often in our midst can change the everyday, making it slightly more unrecognisable. Either way, all of this has interesting psychological properties and assumptions. It is worth spending some time explaining why participative practices and disagreements about its efficacy are so important for understanding the nature and psychology of contemporary art.

On the surface, Rirkrit Tiravanija's work seems simple: in *Untitled (Free)*, 1992, at the 303 Gallery, New York, the artist transferred the contents, furniture and technology of the gallery's back office into the main display area. I have mentioned how Hans Haacke's system art also attempted, in various ways, to make us aware of the gallery as a social, political and economic reality, which the artist wanted us to think about thematically, rather than veiling it off from our thoughts. Tiravanija then occupied part of the gallery space and, with a stove and cooking utensils, transformed the space into a makeshift kitchen and provided food for visitors. The artwork here is both an installation piece and a performance, it is participative involving the viewer and the artist. It is a kind of trans-figuration of the commonplace, and has been interpreted in various ways by critics as a work that deals with an institutional critique, anthropolog-ical notions of the gift, or a critique of commodification, anti-form and dematerialisation (Kraynak, 2010). It seems that the only thing that makes it art is theory, or critique.

In recent years, there has been something of a backlash against the ideals of this kind of participative art. Clare Bishop (2010), for example, argues that inherent in participative art is the assumption of a kind of utopian view of social organisation, that social interaction and discussion are naturally the best way of securing democratic ideals or innovative art practices that critique traditional power structures. Instead, Bishop reminds us that it is *antagonism* between groups that exercises the com-munication of views, differences and social change. She cites the antag-onistic and disruptive work of Santiago Sierra, whose participative work uses subjects and exploits them in order to show how money and power corrupt. In *Persons Paid to Have Their Hair Dyed Blonde*, a work for the Venice Biennale, 2001, illegal street vendors, immigrants from China, Senegal and Bangladesh were paid to have their hair bleached. He then invited them to sell their goods in the gallery space. In *160 cm Line Tattood on Four People*, 2000, he paid four people to have a line tattooed on their backs. Others works include *A Person Paid for 360 Continuous Working Hours*, 2000, and *Ten People Paid to Masturbate*, 2000. Although shocking, contextual knowledge reveals that the performance pieces merely repeat many of the things people are paid to do in the real world. They also refer back to performance artworks in the 1960s, such as Yves Klein dragging women smeared with paint across canvases on the floor, and Piero Manzoni signing his nudes with his signature as works of art. Of course, they also refer to women being paid to pose for the artist in more tradi-tional scenarios. Bishop states: 'While Tiravanija celebrates the gift, Sierra knows that there is no such thing as a free meal: everything and everyone has a price. His work can be seen as a grim meditation on the social and political conditions that permit disparities in people's prices to emerge' (2010, p. 266).

Bishop's comments thus drive a wedge between cooperative participa-tion, which in Tiravanija's work is seen as utopian and ineffectual, and antagonistic practices exemplified by artists such as Santiago Sierra and

Thomas Hirschorn. The value judgement here is that Sierra and Hirschorn produce better art because they are supposedly more effective in resisting power structures and systems of knowledge in which art and the gallery system play a part, because they disrupt them and make them objects of thought. The notion is that Sierra's work is more shocking and, therefore, more able to jolt us out of our easy commingling with art. Yet, surely, this depends on the knowledge base of the viewer. There are plenty of people (in fact, I would say, the majority) with traditional views on art who would hold Tiravanija's work in contempt and would feel antagonistic towards it. Some of these people, presumably, may have changed their minds about art through contact with others when exposed to the reasoning behind it, and perhaps his work could have altered their stereotypes and changed their systems of relational knowledge regarding art and the social. Many art historical and theoretical works have dealt with the issues involved here, and even Bishop's criticism shows that her own thought has been affected conceptually by Tiravanija's work, in the sense that his work is now on the map and has changed what we think is possible with participative art. We do not need to repeat the experiment, but we can build on it. Bishop supposes Sierra's work to be the opposite of the 'cosy situation' (2010, p. 274) of Tiravanija's participative art, a situation that is nevertheless uncannily displaced in a gallery space rather than naïvely reproduced, as Bishop supposes. Sierra's work, or Bishop's characterisation of it, is thus to some extent dependent on Tiravanija's for a system of dualisms. Tiravanija's work may be accused of lapsing into the very system of power relations it seeks to critique, but this may also be true of Sierra's work and of Bishop's comments. It is a kind of aporia that consists of judging artworks by how they *might*, probabilistically, produce a certain 'quality of the audience relations' (p. 273), which is almost impossible to gauge given that audiences are made up of individuals, some of whom may be antagonistic towards a great number of things, including each other. In Tiravanija's works, viewers might have changed their categories of what an art object is, and it may have primed them to expect different things about art. Alternatively, such work might be interpreted as superficial and inconsequential in terms of providing critical thought. The problem is that antagonism in itself is not a quality that would remedy this situation; it is a relational concept. One can be antagonistic towards teddy bears but, again, antagonism in itself is not a gauge of value. Similarly, with participation and social harmony, one can participate in the overthrow of fascism or in ushering in a dictatorship. I could also easily participate in a group antagonising another group.

Certainly, both antagonism and cooperative dialogue can be ways of exchanging aspects of relational knowledge between individuals. Much of this depends on the individuals involved, as well as the situation provided by the artwork. The underlying exchange between individuals, whether in terms of antagonism or participation, is really what is important. Tiravanija's work seems participative and social and offers the possibility of recoding expectations and knowledge systems from within, creating an ephemeral moment that may or may not affect the viewer's categories and values or her relations with others in the gallery space. Tiravanija asks us to imagine social relations as art, which can fail or be successful, depending on the use to which they are put. If they fail, it may be because of a lack of imagination or experience. There is no imperative that the artwork *must* create an outcome, at least if it is to retain its open-endedness. Tiravanija's spaces are also problem spaces because we are asked to engage in certain kinds of social activity in an unfamiliar frame; we are asked to assess our agency in switching artificiality on or off. Sierra's work is anti-social; it offers us no imagination, although his are also problem spaces. One is an art of making problems out of human relations through a kind of stealth, the other is an art of creating problems by documenting violence towards others. Both approaches to art can make people think differently and change pre-existent schemata and knowledge structures, yet this depends on the state of one's system of knowledge in the first place, and one's desire to rechannel what one has learnt into other creative activities.

Neither antagonism nor cooperative participation, each in itself, guarantees corrective action or enlightenment. Neither approach has succeeded in bringing about change in the economic system of relations it sets out to make visible. One could, however, argue that Sierra's antagonistic art and Tiravanija's participative art both offer opportunities for an exchange of relational knowledge between individuals. If the mark of success is that one rechannels lessons learnt from such art encounters into constructing different kinds of relations with others, or taking action in the world in terms of deeds, speech, writing and creative endeavours, all of which undoubtedly require a *change* in one's system of knowledge, a premise for many other kinds of change, then both works are successful to some extent.

This change in psychological processes – in fact, relational knowledge – occurs before, during and after the execution of the actions one takes. Actions are part of relational knowledge, and so is resolve. This change in relational knowledge may happen gradually or suddenly: there can be a gathering of concepts previously estranged; passive resistance to social pressures, self-reflection, transvaluation, anger, physical violence, and countless external expressions and actions that intervene in the flow of the everyday. These can be overlapping and co-present in an individual's responses to either Tiravanija's or Sierra's work. Each of these responses makes a change or prepares us for change. Change through participation or antagonism depends on idiosyncratic differences in relational knowledge, what it is possible to change from or change into, and what we think is possible to do with such knowledge when it does not cohere with the world around us. It is a gross characterisation that Tiravanija's work is a portrait of kindness or Sierra's a simple act of exploitation. I believe that Tiravanija's work complements Sierra's. Both artists create problems, but in different ways and for different people. They have the same enemy: the still popular and dominant belief that the aim of art is to provide optical pleasure and beauty, regardless of exploitation, and that it should guarantee familiarity, instead of too much thought.

Another critic of participative art, Janet Kraynak, suggests that with such art the 'danger is to idealise this communicative dimension, for communication, the relaying of knowledge, [which] is rife with symbolic power relations' (2010, p. 177). This suggests that adopting non-communicative behaviour and not relaying knowledge can be beneficial. Such a statement also has its problems. Kraynak's comment should, of course, alert us to the fact that the psychological aspects of an exchange of relational knowledge systems between the viewer and the work of art, and between individuals with regard to the artworks I have examined in the book, should not be seen as a utopian, voluntary exercise of freedoms between equals. Economic, political and cultural systems of relations exert power over the assembly, exchange and use of our systems of relational knowledge that, in the first place, may have been encoded under the conditions of privilege suggested by years of access to art galleries, educational institutions and democratic freedoms. I have acknowledged how this aspect of relational knowledge acts as an important tacit and subpersonal kind of situated cognition. The way in which this may become explicit in one's self-awareness is a key question that social psychology as well as the psychology of art should try to answer.

At times, this book has functioned as a meta-analysis of recent psychological and neurocognitive studies that are directly relevant to art, in particular, using contemporary art as a way to test these theories and approaches in the hope of shedding light on implicit structures of knowledge employed in aesthetic experience. Understanding contemporary art requires the integration of various approaches in visual perception and cognition that I have organised into three main sections: brain, body and world. These different approaches in themselves are quite specific, either addressing the neural processes of perceptions and sensory experience, focusing on the experience of action, or intent on providing explanations for cognitive processes such as categorisation and relational knowledge.

While all of these approaches are valuable in their own way, so far there has been no attempt to join up these areas of expertise in order to understand how we experience artworks that depend on all of these processes, even in one sitting and with regard to a single artwork.

What has emerged is the importance of relational knowledge: how we blend and combine concepts, sensations, perceptions, movements and emotions in order to create richly absorbing experiences of art. Using various well-known contemporary artworks as test cases, I have attempted to show how artworks help to integrate embodied, emotional, conceptual and social aspects of experience. I believe this justifies integrating the broad range of theories and empirical studies I have analysed in previous pages, which might not ordinarily come together. These unconventional juxtapositions offer new areas of research in the psychology of art and visual cognition.

It could be argued that creative, social and situated relational knowledge can be exchanged between individuals at an international conference on financial investment; there is nothing about relational knowledge that is special to art. I have insisted that the principles by which the psychological complexity of relational knowledge is constructed are neutral to the contents of the concepts themselves, otherwise there would be no idiographic differences in the way we experience the same artwork, even though I believe that an artwork often constrains the infinite variety of concepts that are possible. In art historical relational knowledge, however, the meanings of the concepts, the things to which they refer and the ways in which like-minded concepts are aggregated will be sufficiently distinct from other organisations of relational knowledge, due to their contents. One could argue that all forms of relational knowledge must, by definition, have systematicity and compositionality. However, the ways by which concepts are connected to each other using references to artworks, the themes that artworks have dealt with in the past, the feelings and experiences that artworks typically engage with, how resemblances and differences create relationships between artworks, even arguments about what defines art are all ways of combining art's concepts. Art's heterogeneity and the framework that it enables for communication between individuals, groups, institutions and generations is unique to art because they reference traditions of thinking about art. I have shown that this relational knowledge is intimately connected with sensations, emotions and perceptions in ways that are distinct to art. What makes art's relational knowledge interesting to psychology are the phenomenal, ethical, sensuous, ideal and irrational qualities of absorption that may be brought together in the experience of one artwork, and rapidly elaborated and sustained in an exhibition of artworks.

It might be objected that this integrative approach, which raises the profile of conceptual combination in a research area normally dominated by embodied and perceptual empirical studies, places too much emphasis on intelligible rational processes, downplaying arbitrary connections and nonsensical, humorous and nonconscious experiences of art. Even Dada, automatism, Surrealism and seemingly irrational Fluxus and perform-ance artworks, as well as contemporary artworks that similarly engage with such experiences are structured by systems of relational knowledge, grouping, cross-referencing and the contrasting of individual artworks in order to create categories, inviting us to move beyond the idea that each artwork can or should be viewed in isolation. If an artwork appears as an irrational anomaly, it cannot be divested of context and there may be an underlying method in the madness. There is something of this in Sol LeWitt's parody of rationalism: 'Irrational thoughts should be followed absolutely and logically.'

Even in the attempt to resist conceptual content in art – the stripped down simplicity of Minimalism (or Malevich), the perceptual emphasis of Op Art, the nonsense art of Dada, the subconscious stirrings of Surrealism, Anti-Form, Process art, *Arte Povera*, or Land art – the very pattern of resistance to conceptual production consistently betrays a systematicity worth examining. Thus, even attempts to produce mean-inglessness tend to be grouped together by their commonalities or by the things towards which they are meant to be antagonistic. There is thus a structure of 'antonyms' of rational or conceptual content, or these art-works are organised into complex conceptual relationships themselves, while denying coherence. Relational knowledge is structured by a system of analogies and resemblances *as well as* a series of disconnects and counterfactuals. This has not been studied by psychology. This system-aticity most often remains tacit even with quite high levels of cognition and metacognition. I have tried to make this systematicity explicit, using psychological models that take into account idiographic differences. We do not all connect the same concepts together while looking at artworks, but we all manipulate our differing systems of relational knowledge. We contrast and compare its components in conjunction with the perceptual cues of the artwork, we are creative viewers. This is put rather more forcefully by the philosopher Jacques Rancière, whose work in recent years has been extremely influential for contemporary artists.[2] For

---

[2] The artist, Thomas Hirschorn among others, for example, has endorsed his book *The Emancipated Spectator*. This central idea in the thesis is not new and is related to Barthes' theory of the death of the author and the birth of the reader, and other approaches to literary theory to do with the concept of 'refiguration' and reception theory. Ricoeur also

Rancière, the spectator 'also acts, like the pupil or the scholar. She observes, selects, compares, interprets. She links what she sees to a host of other things that she has seen' (2009, p. 13), and more analytically he asserts: 'It is in this power of associating and dissociating that the emancipation of the viewer consists...Being a spectator is not some passive condition...We also learn and teach, act and know, as spectators who all the time link what we see to what we have seen and said, done and dreamed' (p. 170).

However, this does not mean that we retreat into our own private mental lives. Often the artwork is able to produce commonalities that we discuss with each other, further enriching our systems of relational knowledge. Art is social, whether participative or antagonistic, and so is relational knowledge. Moreover, if art is social, it also teaches us to be silent in order to let the other speak. Krauss' notion of adopting an attitude of openness and humility before the artwork (1981, p. 283), in order not to pre-judge it and force meaning upon it, is important in providing a counterbalance to the idea that the viewer is also the co-creator of the work. I have been arguing that this balance is maintained by negotiating systems of relational knowledge in an encounter with the artwork, and that the balance is an 'immersive' experience in which we might lose ourselves or find ourselves.

These comments should provide at least some assurance to those who might worry that the approach taken in this book is too cerebral and rational, and that it is purely about propositional logic or logical positivism with an underlying sympathy for computational approaches enclosed in a brain detached from the body or world. Embodied, sensory and emotional involvement in art is a fundamental aspect of experience, and cannot be explained solely in terms of logical connections and structures. However, emotions and sensations have a certain systematicity, producing, among other things, creative thought, resistance to political structures, the irrational imaginary and irreverent eclecticism. This is especially so when meshed with various kinds of concepts premised on involvement with the perceptual cues and social dynamics presented by the artwork that help to constrain and direct action and meaning. The balance I have mentioned is maintained by a dynamic systematicity that the psychology of art can and should observe, and I have given many examples of how this is possible.

This dynamic complexity might occur in giving a speech, discussing politics, playing a game of chess, cooking, solving a puzzle or working out

writes: 'The emplotment...is a conjoint work of the text and its reader' (1991, p. 151). On this view, the reader shares in the creative act, reactivating and fusing the structures of text with numerous personal memories and the imagination, ethical judgements and beliefs.

a mathematical equation. All of these *strictly* non-art situations will provide us with frustration, pleasure or fascination, so what is it that makes art different? I will leave this problem to those interested in the philosophy of art. On the one hand, there is a case for including some of these non-art examples in an expanded definition of art. On the other hand, it could be argued along with Danto that the difference between art and non-art experience is theory (Danto, 1964). However, this cannot mean any old theory. The quality of theory will depend on the quality of the things theorised, in this case, the art. In addition, what I have tried to show is that the theory itself often presupposes a theory of mind, an awareness of the likely content of other people's minds, processes of inference and attribution tacitly presumed in thinking about and making art. In other words, art theory, art practice and theory of mind increasingly engage with each other in contemporary art, and we should perhaps think about the advantages and disadvantages of keeping these subterranean connections tacit.

We may simply acknowledge or *suppose* that we are looking at an artwork, and bracket out ontological arguments over whether it is art or not, for the sake of focusing on the qualities of the experience of an artwork and the theory arising from it that we are able to generate among ourselves. This may eventually feed back into ontological considerations. This requires an acculturated open-mindedness, which would be interesting to examine psychologically. It might be that such flexibility is the result of a kind of problem-solving strategy that entertains a large number of possibilities, and that a reward system is engaged with the delay this entails. Some artworks evidently engage with this mechanism. What is undeniable is that the lightning complexity of thought, when accompanied by some awareness of it, is somehow an event that takes us out of our habitual and automatic experience of ordinary objects in the world, and this 'going outside' can sometimes be problematic, pleasurable or meaningful in ways we are wont to attribute to the category of art. Feldman Barratt reminds us that 'Once conceptual knowledge is brought to bear to categorize something as one kind of thing and not another, the thing becomes meaningful. It then becomes possible to make reasonable inferences about that thing, predict about how best to act on it, and communicate our experience of the thing to others' (Feldman Barrett, 2006, p. 27).

For art, where imaginary objects abound, many of these 'natural' processes are put into question as part of an anxious aesthetics. In many cases in art, the thing depicted is difficult to discern and takes time to categorise. This goes against the principle of most psychological experiments where the fastest and most efficient object identification and categorisation processes are assumed to be the most evolutionarily fundamental and normative. However, art is not 'normal'; it often requires that we go the long way round, and that we are 'inefficient' with object identification, particularly because this encourages innovative thought, imaginative categorisation, self-reflection, visionary scenarios of human destiny that require unusual conceptual combinations, and leaps of faith.

The exercise of relational knowledge is invariably accompanied by a phenomenal experience of immersion in art. I have tried to demystify, to some extent, this 'immersion' in art without destroying its charm. Immersion can be likened to a kind of enchantment we might experience when mesmerised by an art object, ceremonial mask, architectural threshold or musical passage. Yet, this immersion is not to be explained as the result of some metaphysical aura emanating from an art object, but rather in the viewer's ability to stimulate conceptual, emotional and sensory complexity in reference to the artwork's details that constrain their proliferation. Lest this might sound too rational and intellectual, the artwork also sensitises us, triggers emotions, memories and sensations, which seem to arise of their own accord in random order but which we learn to fold into a self, narrative or moment. These complications promise order and disorder, pleasure and anxiety.

There are also different kinds of pleasure and anxiety. There is the pleasure of recognition, of not having to process or think much about an object because we know it so well, and the simple pleasures of sensuous enjoyment that might require little voluntary thought. With Rothko or Barnett Newman's abstract paintings, we are probably required not to 'overthink' them, but to experience these kinds of paintings at the level of sensations, along with an emptying out of the mind. Yet even these experiences need not be inexplicable; they are structured, they have qualities, and we tend to structure our conversations about these artworks in groups of concepts in relation to sensations and with references to perceptual cues.

It is in the examination of these kinds of combinations of physical resources involved in viewing and interpreting an artwork, and which are influenced by the artwork, that one is able to be more precise about the particular configurations of immersion in and distancing from the artwork.[3] There are different kinds of immersion (and a state of immersion where they seem to converge), such as immersion in emotional states, perceptual and sensory responses, and conceptual intricacy. Importantly, immersion in relational knowledge is inherently social. Different kinds of art will help to produce distinct kinds of immersion. Importantly,

---

[3] For a history of how art has been defined in terms of distancing and its opposite, one of the best summaries is by Cupchik (2002).

the dominance of one kind of immersion over the other may involve a distancing effect that will inhibit other kinds of immersion that are available, thus distancing and immersion may alternate in intensity. Phenomenological accounts of art have yet to deal with this very real and dynamic range of differences involved in the experience of an artwork and artworks in an exhibition.

Future empirical research into aesthetic experience could benefit from reframing art in a number of different ways that I have tried to indicate in this book. Many contemporary artworks require expert knowledge systems; they are also metacognitive, stimulating not only the monitoring of internal states but also a theory of mind concerning how these internal states function with regard to each other. We become aware of how our schemata, scripts and situational knowledge, habitual perceptions and object recognition are put into doubt by many contemporary artworks, thus they are often to be seen as thought experiments or counterfactuals. They often puzzle us and present problems that encourage us to be creative about 'solving' them. Interestingly, people read, write and talk about art, and so art should also engage those interested in social cognition. Many contemporary artworks create problems: they allow us to recognise stereotypes that we are familiar with regarding gender, sexuality and race, and invite us to disabuse ourselves of our unthinking allegiance to them. Yet these artworks' positive effects, providing alternatives to the mainstream saturation of normative images of a homogenised lifestyle as promoted by advertising, have not been studied in cognitive psychology in any comprehensive way beyond the basic documentation. There are no studies that shed light on the psychology behind this kind of *positive* problem making in art.

Kirsh writes that when experts solve knowledge-rich problems, that they engage with the environments in very complex ways, and that they: 'spend more time than novices in the early phases of problem solving, such as determining an appropriate representation of a problem...they interactively probe the world to help define and frame their problems. This suggests that deeper ethnographic studies of everyday problem solving may show a different style of activity than found in formal accounts of problem solving' (2009, p. 290). Thus, more idiographic empirical research is needed. If psychology were to reframe artworks as problems, this would allow new paradigms and areas of expertise to emerge.

In addition to looking at art from the perspective of social cognition, problem solving, analogical modification, metaphor, conceptual combination, spatial cognition, mind wandering and relational knowledge, areas of psychology that are usually not addressed when trying to understand how we respond to contemporary art, all of these psychological processes and subfields richly inform and mediate our knowledge of art, and art provides important examples of how these processes are engaged in configural ways. Science and philosophy both involve many cognitive, rational and procedural thought processes. Art does the same, but with an added sensitivity to embodied and emotional experience. In many ways, art is the most complex of our psychological engagements. One encounter with an artwork can bring together an unparalleled, variable range and diversity of resources commonly associated with scientific or philosophical endeavours, but with the addition of aesthetic experience, emotions and sensations. Usually we attribute the cause of these responses to individuals we admire and love. How artworks come close to this remains an area of study usually ignored in favour of the psychological effects usually involved with television, advertising, design principles, or interpersonal relationships represented by figures and faces. Artworks constitute a special class of objects that do not conform to the study of the effects of other objects on our lives. Contemporary art provides a delimited domain of research into cognitive processes that allows us to refer back to the artworks that are the causes of these processes.

Ultimately, it might be said that much of contemporary art is essentially recalcitrant. This is not surprising given that the world wavers between the polar opposites of suburban comfort and war, and contemporary art matches it at every step but it is also often one step ahead. It is in the nature of art to disown cliché. Sometimes it seems like an unruly id, and sometimes like the only sane place there is to find. Art is a constellation of concepts that cohere and separate, a galaxy of regular and intelligible orbits and eclipses, yet it is also unpredictable, with irruptions and clashes. It reminds one of a kind of life form. I have been arguing that the only comprehensive way to do justice to this dynamic complexity is to integrate not only different disciplines but also different theories within these disciplines, such as situated and extended cognition, analogy, embodied approaches, conceptual blending and relational knowledge. I believe that these are not simply psychological approaches that explain artistic practice, art history and theory, but that they have the potential to change both art and theory, creating new possibilities. This is particularly so because science speaks of meta-cognition, whereas art talks of new cognition. Both are important for change. It is simply not enough to know about how things work, we also need to know what to do with this knowledge. Many contemporary artworks exercise the imaginary and visionary and, in this, they help us to exercise a fluid freedom of thought and an improvisation of relational knowledge that can be likened to jazz, which also requires systematicity and compositionality. Philosophers might argue that this exercise of freedom also has ethical dimensions.

Artworks do not *necessarily* educate us, and they are not bound to make us change our behaviour for the better. Nevertheless, often they require the exercise of psychological operations distinct from everyday cognition, particularly because art's 'effects and meanings are not anticipated' (Rancière, 2009, p. 103). With this view, and by definition, contemporary artworks create the extraordinary. Against the customary cynicism with which contemporary art is often met, even within its ranks, it still offers the opportunity to exercise an emancipated imagination consisting of aesthetic *and* ethical possibilities. Such an imagination may be antagonistic yet also participative, consisting of social involvements where agency is both assured and shared. It is here that unpredictable connections between concepts open up to new and creative knowledge systems. All of these complications are of crucial importance to psychological research, as they are to art, philosophy and politics.

References

Adams, F. and Aizawa, K. (2009). 'Why the mind is still in the head.' In P. Robbins and M. Aydede (eds.), *The Cambridge Handbook of Situated Cognition*. Cambridge: Cambridge University Press, pp. 78–95.

Anderson, J. R. (1990). *The Adaptive Character of Thought*. Hillsdale, NJ: Erlbaum.

Andreasen, N. C., O'Leary, D. S., Cizadlo, T., et al. (1995). 'Remembering the past: two facets of episodic memory explored with positron emission tomography.' *American Journal of Psychiatry*, **152**, 1576–1585.

Archer, M. (2002). *Art Since 1960*. London: Thames and Hudson.

Arnheim, R. (1969). *Visual Thinking*. Berkeley, CA: University of California Press.

Augustin, M. D., Leder, H., Hutzler, F. and Carbon, C. C. (2007). 'Style follows content: on the microgenesis of art perception.' *Acta Psychologica*, **128**, 127–138.

Baddeley, A. D. (1993). 'Working memory and conscious awareness.' In A. F. Colins, S. E. Gathercole, M. A. Conway and P. E. Morris (eds.), *Theories of Memory*. Hove: Erlbaum, pp. 11–28.

   (1996). 'Exploring the central executive.' *Quarterly Journal of Experimental Psychology*, **49**(A), 5–28.

Badiou, A. (2004). Fifteen Theses on Contemporary Art. *Lacanian link*, Vol. **23**, www.lacan.com/frameXXIII7.htm

Bakhtin, M. M. (1984). *Problems of Dostoevsky's Poetics*. C. Emerson (ed. and trans.). Minneapolis, MN: University of Minnesota Press.

Bar, M. (2004). 'Visual objects in context.' *Nature Reviews Neuroscience*, **5**, 617–629.

   (2009). 'A cognitive neuroscience hypothesis of mood and depression.' *Trends in Cognitive Sciences*, **13**(11), 456–463.

Barrett, L. F. (2006). 'Solving the emotion paradox: categorization and the experience of emotion.' *Personality and Social Psychology Review*, **10**, 20–46.

   (2009). 'Variety is the spice of life: a psychological construction approach to understanding variability in emotion.' *Cognitive Emotion*, **23**(7), 1284–1306.

Barrett, L. F., Lindquist, K. A. and Gendron, M. (2007). 'Language as context for the perception of emotion.' *Trends in Cognitive Sciences*, **11**(8), 327–332.

Barsalou, L. W. (1999). 'Perceptual symbol systems.' *Behavioral and Brain Sciences*, **22**, 577–660.

   (2003). 'Abstraction in perceptual symbol systems.' *Philosophical Transactions of the Royal Society of London: Biological Sciences*, **358**, 1177–1187.

   (2009). 'Simulation, situated conceptualization, and prediction.' *Philosophical Transactions of the Royal Society of London: Biological Sciences*, **364**, 1281–1289.

Barsalou, L. W. and Wiemer-Hastings, K. (2005). 'Situating abstract concepts.' In D. Pecher and R. Zwaan (eds.), *Grounding Cognition: The Role of Perception*

348   References

and Action in Memory, Language, and Thought. New York, NY: Cambridge University Press, pp. 129–163.

Bartels, A. (2009). 'Visual perception: converging mechanisms of attention, binding, and segmentation?' *Current Biology,* **19**(7), 300–302.

Bartels, A. and Zeki, S. (2004). 'Functional brain mapping during free viewing of natural scenes.' *Human Brain Mapping,* **21**, 75–85.

Bartlett, F. C. (1932). *Remembering: A Study in Experimental and Social Psychology.* Cambridge: Cambridge University Press.

Baxandall, M. (1988). *Painting and Experience Fifteenth Century Italy: A Primer in the Social History of Pictorial Style.* Oxford: Oxford University Press.

Bell, C. (1914). *Art.* London: Chatto and Windus.

Berendt, B., Barkowsky, T., Freksa, C. and Kelter, S. (1998). 'Spatial representation with aspect maps.' In C. Freksa, C. Habel and K. F. Wender (eds.), *Spatial Cognition: An Interdisciplinary Approach to Representing and Processing Spatial Knowledge.* Dordrecht: Springer, pp. 616–617.

Bhabha, H. K. (1994). *The Location of Culture.* London: Routledge.

Binder, J. R., Frost, J. A., Hammeke, P. S., et al. (1999). 'Conceptual processing during the conscious resting state: a functional MRI study.' *Journal of Cognitive Neurosciences,* **11**, 80–93.

Bird, J. (1999). 'Minding the Body'. In M. Newman and J. Bird (eds.). *Rewriting Conceptual Art.* London: Reaktion, pp. 88–106.

Bishop, C. (2006). *Participation.* London: Whitechapel; Cambridge, MA: MIT Press.

  (2010). 'Antagonism and relational aesthetics.' In A. Dezeuze (ed.), *The 'Do-It-Yourself' Artwork: Participation from Fluxus to New Media.* Manchester: Manchester University Press; New York: Palgrave Macmillan, pp. 257–280.

Boetzkes, A. (2009). 'Phenomenology and interpretation beyond the flesh.' *Art History,* **32**(4), 690–711.

Bonk, E. and Duchamp, M. (1989). *The Box in a Valise.* D. Britt (trans.). Paris: Rizzoli.

Bonnardel, N. (2000). 'Towards understanding and supporting creativity in design: analogies in a constrained cognitive environment.' *Knowledge-Based Systems,* **13**, 505–513.

Bosanquet. B. (1915/1963). *Three Lectures on Aesthetics.* Indianapolis, IN: Bobbs.

Bourriaud, N. (1998). *Relational Aesthetics.* Paris: Presses du réel.

Bowden, E. M. and Jung-Beeman, M. (2003). 'Aha! Insight experience correlates with solution activation in the right hemisphere.' *Psychonomic Bulletin and Review,* **10**(3), 730–737.

Brandt, P. A. (2006). 'Form and meaning in art.' In M. Turner (ed.), *The Artful Mind: Cognitive Science and the Riddle of Human Creativity.* New York, NY: Oxford University Press, pp. 171–188.

Brooks, R. A. (1991). 'Intelligence without representation.' *Artificial Intelligence,* **47**, 139–159.

Brown, S. and Dissanayake, E. (2009). 'The arts are more than aesthetics: neuroaesthetics as narrow aesthetics.' In M. Skov and O. Vartanian (eds.), *Neuroaesthetics.* Amityville, NY: Baywood, pp. 43–57.

Burger, P. (1984). *Theory of the Avant-Garde*. M. Shaw (trans.). Manchester: Manchester University Press.

Burgin, V. (2009). *Situational Aesthetics: Selected Writings by Victor Burgin*. A. Streitberger (ed.). Leuven: Leuven University Press.

Butler, J. (1989). *Gender Trouble, Feminism and the Subversion of Identity*. London: Routledge.

(2002). *Postmodernism: A Very Short Introduction*. Oxford: Oxford University Press.

Cabanne, P. (1979). *Dialogues with Marcel Duchamp*. R. Padgett (trans.). London: A Da Capo.

Camille, M. (1992). *Image on the Edge: Margins of Medieval Art*. London: Reaktion Books.

Cantwell-Smith, B. (1999). 'Situatedness/embeddedness.' In R. A. Wilson and F. C. Keil (eds.), *The MIT Encyclopedia of the Cognitive Sciences*. Cambridge, MA: MIT Press, pp. 769–770.

Caramazza, A. and Shelton, J. R. (1998). 'Domain specific knowledge systems in the brain: the animate–inanimate distinction'. *Journal of Cognitive Neuroscience* **11**, 1–34.

Carroll, J. M. and Russell, J. A. (1997). 'Facial expressions in Hollywood's portrayal of emotion.' *Journal of Personality and Social Psychology*, **72**, 164–176.

Carroll, N. (2006). 'Aesthetic experience: a question of content.' In M. Kieran (ed.), *Contemporary Debates in Aesthetics*. Oxford: Blackwell Publishers, pp. 69–97.

Carston, R. (2002). *Thoughts and Utterances: The Pragmatics of Explicit Communication*. Oxford: Blackwell.

Cavell, S. (1994). *A Pitch of Philosophy: Autobiographical Exercises*. Cambridge, MA: Harvard University Press.

Cela-Conde, C. J., Agnati, L., Huston, J. P., Mora, F. and Nadal, M. (2011). 'The neural foundations of aesthetic appreciation.' *Progress in Neurobiology*, **94**, 39–48.

Celant, G. (1989). *Giuseppe Penone*, exhibition catalogue. Bristol: Arnolfini Gallery.

Changeux, J. P. (1994). 'Art and neuroscience.' *Leonardo* **27**(3), 189–201.

Chase, W. G. and Simon, H. A. (1973). 'Perception in chess'. *Cognitive Psychology*, **4**, 55–81.

Chatard-Pannetier, A., Brauer, M., Chambres, P. and Niedenthal, P. (2002). 'Représentation, catégorisation et évaluation: différences entre experts et novices dans le domaine des meubles d'antiquité.' *L'Année psychologique*, **102**, 423–448.

Chatterjee, A. (2003). 'Prospects for a cognitive neuroscience of visual aesthetics.' *Bulletin of Psychology and the Arts*, 4(2), 55–60.

(2010a). 'Neuroaesthetics: a coming of age story.' *Journal of Cognitive Neuroscience*, **23**(1), 53–62.

(2010b). 'Disembodying cognition.' *Language and Cognition* 2(1), 79–116.

Cherry, D. (2002). 'Tracey Emin's *My Bed*', www.egs.edu/faculty/tracey-emin/articles/tracey-emins-my-bed/ Accessed 20/02/2012.

Chrisley, R. and Ziemke, T. (2003). 'Embodiment.' In L. Nadel (ed.), *Encyclopedia of Cognitive Science*. London: Macmillan Publishers, pp. 1102–1108.

Christoff, K., Gordon, A. M., Smallwood, J., Smith, R. and Schooler, J. W. (2009a). 'Experience sampling during fMRI reveals default network and executive system contributions to mind wandering.' *Proceedings of the National Academy of Sciences, USA*, **106**(21), 8719–8724.

Christoff, K., Keramatian, K., Gordon, A. M., Smith, R. and Mädler, B. (2009b). 'Prefrontal organization of cognitive control according to levels of abstraction.' *Brain Research*, **1286**(25), 94–105.

Christoff, K., Ream, J. M. and Gabrieli, J. D. E. (2004). 'The cognitive and neural basis of spontaneous thought processes.' *Cortex*, **40**, 623–630.

Christoff, K., Ream, J. M., Geddes, L. P. T. and Gabrieli, J. D. E. (2003). 'Evaluating self-generated information: anterior prefrontal contributions to human cognition.' *Behavioural Neuroscience*, **117**(6), 1161–1168.

Church, J. (2000). '"Seeing as" and the double-bind of consciousness.' *Journal of Consciousness Studies*, 7(8/9), 99–112.

Clark, A. (1998). *Being There. Putting Brain, Body, and World Together Again.* Cambridge, MA: MIT Press.

(2001). 'Visual experience and motor action: are the bonds too tight?' *Philosophical Review*, **110**(4), 495–519.

(2005). 'Intrinsic content, active memory and the extended mind.' *Analysis*, **65**(1), 1–11.

(2008). *Supersizing the Mind.* Oxford: Oxford University Press.

(2011). 'Finding the mind.' *Philosophical Studies*, **152**, 447–461.

Clunas, C. (1997). *Art in China.* Oxford: Oxford University Press.

Colman, A. M. (ed.). (2009). *A Dictionary of Psychology.* Oxford: Oxford University Press. Oxford Reference Online, Oxford University Press. Accessed from Auckland University, 19 January 2011, www.oxfordreference.com

Collins, A. M. and Quillian, M. R. (1969). 'Retrieval time from semantic memory.' *Journal of Verbal Learning and Verbal Behavior*, **8**, 240–248.

Crary, J. (1990). *Techniques of the Observer: On Vision and Modernity in the Nineteenth Century.* Cambridge, MA: MIT Press.

Crutch, S. J. and Warrington, E. K. (2005). 'Abstract and concrete concepts have structurally different representational frameworks.' *Brain*, **128**, 615–627.

Cupchik, G. C. (2002). 'The evolution of psychical distance as an aesthetic concept.' *Culture and Psychology*, **8**(2), 155–227.

Cupchik, G. C., Vartanian, O., Crawley, A. and Mikulis, D. J. (2009). 'Viewing artworks: contributions of cognitive control and perceptual facilitation to aesthetic experience.' *Brain and Cognition*, **70**, 84–91.

Currie, G. (2003). 'Aesthetics and cognitive science.' In J. Levinson (ed.), *The Oxford Handbook of Aesthetics*. Oxford: Oxford University Press, pp. 706–721.

(2006). 'Anne Brontë and the uses of imagination.' In M. Kieran (ed.), *Contemporary Debates in Aesthetics*. Oxford: Blackwell Publishers, pp. 209–221.

Dahl, D. W. and Moreau, P. (2002). 'The influence and value of analogical thinking during new product ideation.' *Journal of Marketing Research*, **39**, 47–60.

Damasio, R. (1989). 'The brain binds entities and events by multiregional activation from convergence zones.' *Neural Computation*, **1**(1), 123–132.

(1995). 'Toward a neurobiology of emotion and feeling: operational concepts and hypotheses.' *Neuroscience*, **1**, 19–25.

Danto, A. C. (1964). 'The artworld.' *Journal of Philosophy*, **61**(19), 571–584.

(1981). *The Transfiguration of the Commonplace*. Cambridge, MA: Harvard University Press.

(1997). *After the End of Art*. Princeton, NJ: Princeton University Press.

Davies, S. (1991). *Definitions of Art*. Ithaca, NY: Cornell University Press.

Davies, S. (2004). 'The cluster theory of art.' *British Journal of Aesthetics*, **44**, 297–300.

(2006). *The Philosophy of Art*. Malden: Blackwell Publishing.

de Araujo, I. E., Rolls, E. T., Velazco, M. I., Margot, C. and Cayeux, I. (2005). 'Cognitive modulation of olfactory processing.' *Neuron*, **46**(4), 671–679.

de Beauvoir, S. (1949). *Le deuxième sexe*. Paris: Gallimard.

de Beni, R. and Moè, A. (2003). 'Imagery and rehearsal as study strategies for written or orally presented passages.' *Psychonomic Bulletin and Review*, **10**, 975–980.

de Bruin, L. C. and Kästner, L. (2011). 'Dynamic embodied cognition.' *Phenomenology and the Cognitive Sciences*, 1–23. Online: www.dx.doi.org/10.1007/s11097-011-9223-1

de Groot, A. D. (1978). *Thought and Choice in Chess*. Oxford: Mouton.

de Preester, H. and Tsakiris, M. (2009). 'Body-extension versus body-incorporation: is there a need for a body-model?' *Phenomenology and the Cognitive Sciences*, **8**(3), 307–319.

Deleuze, G. and Guattari, F. (1994). *What is Philosophy?* H. Tomlinson and G. Burchill (trans.). London: Verso.

Donald, M. (2006). 'Art and cognitive evolution.' In M. Turner (ed.), *The Artful Mind, Cognitive Science and the Riddle of Human Creativity*. Oxford: Oxford University Press, pp. 3–20.

Doumas, A. A., Hummel, J. E. and Sandhofer, C. M. (2008). 'A theory of the discovery and predication of relational concepts.' *Psychological Review*, **115**(1), 1–43.

Dickie, G. (1984/1997). *The Art Circle: A Theory of Art*. Evanston, IL: Chicago Spectrum Press.

Dove, G. (2009). 'Beyond perceptual symbols: a call for representational pluralism.' *Cognition*, **110**(3), 412–431.

Egan, F. and Matthews, R. J. (2006). 'Doing cognitive neuroscience: a third way.' *Synthese*, **153**, 377–391.

Ellamil, M., Dobson, C., Beeman, M. and Christoff, K. (2012). 'Evaluative and generative modes of thought during the creative process.' *NeuroImage*, **59**, 1783–1794.

Ellis, R. D. (1999). 'The dance form of the eyes. What cognitive science can learn from art.' *Journal of Consciousness Studies*, **6**(6–7), 161–175.

Everhart, D. E., Shucard, J. L., Quatrin, T. and Shucard, D. W. (2001. 'Sex-related differences in event-related potentials, face recognition, and facial affect processing in prepubertal children.' *Neuropsychology*, **15**(3), 329–341.

Fairhall, S. L. and Ishai, A. (2008). 'Neural correlates of object indeterminacy in art compositions.' *Consciousness and Cognition*, **17**(3), 923–932.

Fauconnier, G. and Turner, M. (2002). *The Way We Think*. New York, NY: Basic Books.

(2008). 'Rethinking metaphor.' In R. W. Gibbs (ed.), *The Cambridge Handbook of Metaphor and Thought*. Cambridge: Cambridge University Press, pp. 53–66.

Figdor, C. (2010). 'Neuroscience and the multiple realization of cognitive functions.' *Philosophy of Science*, 77, 419–456.

Firth, J. R. (1957). *Papers in Linguistics 1934–1951*. London: Oxford University Press.

Fodor, J. (1975). *The Language of Thought*. New York, NY: Thomas Crowell.

(1998). *Concepts: Where Cognitive Science Went Wrong*. New York, NY: Oxford University Press.

Foster, H. (1996). *The Return of the Real*. Cambridge, MA: MIT Press.

Fredrickson, B. L. and Harrison, K. (2005). 'Throwing like a girl: self-objectification predicts adolescent girls' motor performance.' *Journal of Sport and Social Issues*, 29(1), 79–101.

Fredrickson, B. L. and Roberts, T. A. (1997). 'Objectification theory: toward understanding women's lived experiences and mental health risks.' *Psychology of Women Quarterly* 21(2), 173–206.

Freedberg, D. (2006). 'Composition and emotion.' In M. Turner (ed.), *The Artful Mind, Cognitive Science and the Riddle of Human Creativity*, Oxford: Oxford University Press, pp. 73–89.

(2009). 'Movement, embodiment, emotion.' In T. Dufrenne and A.-C. Taylor (eds.), *Cannibalismes Disciplinaires. Quand l histoire de l art et l anthropologie se rencontrent*. Paris INHA/Musee du Quai Branly, pp. 37–61.

(2011) 'Memory in art: history and the neuroscience of response.' In S. Nalbantian, P. M. Matthews and J. L. McClelland (eds.), *The Memory Process: Neuroscientific and Humanistic Perspectives*. Cambridge, MA: MIT Press, pp. 337–358.

Freedberg, D. and Gallese, V. (2007). 'Motion, emotion and empathy in aesthetic experience.' *Trends in Cognitive Science*, 11(5), 197–203.

Freksa, C., Barkowsky, T. and Klippel, A. (1999). 'Spatial symbol systems and spatial cognition: a computer science perspective on perception-based symbol processing.' Commentary on Barsalou's 'Perceptual symbol systems.' *Behavioral and Brain Sciences*, 22(4), 616.

Fried, M. (1967). 'Art and objecthood.' *Artforum* 5, 12–23.

Friston, K. (2002). 'Beyond phrenology: what can neuroimaging tell us about distributed circuitry?' *Annual Review of Neuroscience*, 25, 221–250.

Fry, R. (1924). *Art and Psychoanalysis*. London: Hogarth Press.

Fuster, J. (2003). *Cortex and Mind: Unifying Cognition*. Oxford: Oxford University Press.

Gabora, L. (1999). 'Grounded in perceptions yet transformed into amodal symbols.' Commentary on Barsalou's 'Perceptual symbol systems.' *Behavioral and Brain Sciences*, 22(4), 617.

Gadamer, H. G. (1997). *Truth and Method*. New York, NY: Continuum.

Gallagher, S. and Cole, J. (1995). 'Body schema and body image in a deafferented subject.' *Journal of Mind and Behavior*, 16, 369–390.

Gallagher, S. and Crisafi, A. (2009). 'Mental institutions.' *Topoi*, 28, 45–51.

Gallese, V. (2007). The 'conscious' dorsal stream: embodied simulation and its role in space and action conscious awareness.' *Psyche*, **13**(1), 1–12. Archived electronic journal: www.psyche.cs.monash.edu.au/

Garis, L. (1975). 'The Margaret Mead of Madison Avenue.' *Ms.* (March), pp. 7–40.

Gaut, B. (2006). 'Art and cognition.' In M. Kieran (ed.), *Contemporary Debates in Aesthetics*. Oxford: Blackwell Publishers, pp. 115–126.

Gauthier, I. Skudlarski, P., Gore, J. C. Anderson, A. W. (2000). 'Expertise for cars and birds recruits brain areas involved in face recognition.' *Nature and Neuroscience*, **3**(2), 191–197.

Gauthier, I. and Tarr, M. J. (1997). 'Becoming a "Greeble" expert: exploring mechanisms for face recognition.' *Vision Research*, **37**(12), 1673–1682.

Gentner, D. (1983). 'Structure-mapping: a theoretical framework for analogy.' *Cognitive Science*, 7, 155–170.

(1989). 'Metaphor as structure mapping: the relational shift.' *Child Development*, **59**, 47–59.

Gentner, D. and Bowdle, B. (2008). 'Metaphor as structure-mapping.' In R. W. Gibbs (ed.), *The Cambridge Handbook of Metaphor and Thought*. Cambridge: Cambridge University Press, pp. 109–128.

Gentner, D. and Kurtz, K. J. (2006). 'Relations, objects, and the composition of analogies.' *Cognitive Science*, **30**, 609–642.

Gibbs, R. W. (ed.). (2008). *The Cambridge Handbook of Metaphor and Thought*. Cambridge: Cambridge University Press.

Gibson, J. J. (1977). 'The theory of affordances.' In R. Shaw and J. Bransford (eds.), *Perceiving, Acting and Knowing: Toward an Ecological Psychology*. Hillsdale, NJ: Lawrence Erlbaum, pp. 67–82.

(1979). *The Ecological Approach to Visual Perception*. Boston, MA: Houghton Mifflin.

Glaser, R. (1994). 'Expertise.' In M. W. Eysenck, et al. (eds.), *The Blackwell Dictionary of Cognitive Psychology*. Cambridge: Blackwell Publishing, pp. 139–142.

Glenberg A. M. and Kaschak M. P. (2002). 'Grounding language in action.' *Psychonomic Bulletin Review*, **9**, 558–565.

Glucksberg, S. (2008). 'How metaphors create categories quickly.' In R. W. Gibbs (ed.), *The Cambridge Handbook of Metaphor and Thought*. Cambridge: Cambridge University Press, pp. 67–83.

Godfrey, T. (1993). 'Richard Serra: London and Düsseldorf.' *The Burlington Magazine*, **135**(1079), 160–161.

Goel, V. (1995). *Sketches of Thought*. Cambridge, MA: MIT Press.

Goldie, P. (2003). *The Emotions: A Philosophical Exploration*. New York, NY: Oxford University Press.

Goldie, P. and Schellekens E. (eds.) (2007). *Philosophy and Conceptual Art*. Oxford: Clarendon.

(2010). *Who's Afraid of Conceptual Art?* London: Routledge.

Goldstone, R. L., Feng, Y., Rogosky, B. J., Pecher, D. and Zwaan, R. A. (2005). 'Connecting concepts to each other and the world.' In D. Pecher and R. A. Zwaan (eds.), *Grounding Cognition: The Role Of Perception and Action in*

Memory, Language, and Thinking. Cambridge: Cambridge University Press, pp. 282–314.

Goldstone, R. L. and Rogosky, B. J. (2002). 'Using relations within conceptual systems to translate across conceptual systems.' *Cognition*, **84**, 295–320.

Gombrich, E. H. (1966). *Norm and Form: Studies in the Art of the Renaissance*. London: Phaidon Press.

Gooding, D. C. (2004). 'Cognition, construction and culture: visual theories in the sciences.' *Journal of Cognition and Culture*, **4**, 551–593.

Gorno-Tempini, M. L. and Price, C. J. (2001). 'Identification of famous faces and buildings: a functional neuroimaging study of semantically unique items.' *Brain*, **124**(10), 2087–2097.

Greeno, J. G., Smith, D. R. and Moore, J. L. (1993). 'Transfer of situated learning'. In D. K. Detterman and R. J. Sternberg (eds.), *Transfer on Trial: Intelligence, Cognition and Instruction*. Norwood, NJ: Ablex, pp. 99–167.

Griffiths, P. E. and Scarantino, A. (2009). 'Emotions in the wild: the situated perspective on emotion.' In P. Robbins and M. Aydede (eds.), *The Cambridge Handbook of Situated Cognition*. Cambridge: Cambridge University Press, pp. 437–453.

Grush, R. and Mandik, P. (2002). 'Representational parts.' *Phenomenology and the Cognitive Sciences*, **1**(4), 389–394.

Halford, G. S., Wilson, W. H. and Phillips, S. (2010). 'Relational knowledge: the foundation of higher cognition.' *Trends in Cognitive Sciences*, **14**(11), 497–505.

Harnad, S. (1990). 'The symbol grounding problem.' *Physica D*, **42**, 335–346.

Harth, E. (2004). 'Art and reductionism.' *Journal of Consciousness Studies*, **11**(3–4), 111–116.

Hasenkamp, W., Wilson-Mendenhall, C. D., Duncan, E. and Barsalou, L. W. (2012). 'Mind wandering and attention during focused meditation: a fine-grained temporal analysis of fluctuating cognitive states.' *NeuroImage*, **59**, 750–760.

Haser, V. (2005). *Metaphor, Metonymy and Experientialist Philosophy*. Berlin: Mouton de Gruyter.

Hauser, M. and Spelke, E. (2004). 'Evolutionary and developmental foundations of human knowledge: a case study of mathematics.' In M. Gazzaniga (ed.), *The Cognitive Neurosciences*. Cambridge: MIT Press, Vol. 3, pp. 853–864.

Hayhoe, M. and Ballard, D. (2005). 'Eye movements in natural behaviour.' *Trends in Cognitive Sciences*, **9**(4), 188–194.

Hekkert, P. and van Wieringen, P. C. W. (1996). 'Aesthetic preference for paintings as a function of expertise level and various stimulus properties.' *Acta Psychologica*, **94**, 117–131.

Held, J. S. and Posner, D. (n.d.). *Seventeenth and Eighteenth Century Art, Baroque Painting, Sculpture and Architecture*. New York, NY: Prentice Hall/Abrams.

Henderson, J. M. (1997). 'Transsaccadic memory and integration during real-world object perception.' *Psychological Science*, **8**, 51–55.

Hermans, H., Rijks, T. and Kempen, H. (1993). 'Imaginal dialogues in the self: theory and method.' *Journal of Personality*, **61**, 207–235.

Hiller, S. (1994/2006). 'Working through objects.' In C. Merewether (ed.), *The Archive*. London: Whitechapel and Cambridge, MA: MIT Press, pp. 41–48.

Hohwy, J. (2007). 'The sense of self in the phenomenology of agency and perception.' *Psyche*, **13**(1), 1–20. Archived electronic journal: www.psyche.cs.monash.edu.au/

Holyoak, K. J. and Thagard, P. (1995). *Mental Leaps: Analogy in Creative Thought*. Cambridge, MA: MIT Press.

Hopkins, D. (2006). 'Re-thinking the Duchamp effect'. In A. Jones (ed.), *A Companion to Contemporary Art Since 1945*. Malden, MA: Blackwell, pp. 215–245.

Hubbard, E. M. (2003). 'A discussion and review of Uttal (2001), "The New Phrenology".' *Cognitive Science Online*, **1**, 22–33.

Huppert, F. A. and Piercy, M. (1976). 'Recognition memory in amnesic patients: effect of temporal context and familiarity of material.' *Cortex*, **12**, 3–20.

Husserl, E. (1983). *Ideas Pertaining to a Pure Phenomenology and to a Phenomenological Philosophy*. F. Kersten (trans.). The Hague: Martinus Nijhoff.

Hutchins, E. (2005). 'Material anchors for conceptual blends.' *Journal of Pragmatics*, **37**(10), 1555–1577.

   (2011). 'Enculturating the supersized mind.' *Philosophical Studies*, **152**, 437–446.

Hyman, J. (2008). 'Art and neuroscience.' *Interdisciplines*. www.interdisciplines.org/artcognition/papers/15

Ione, A. (2000). 'Connecting the cerebral cortex with the artist's eyes, mind and culture.' *Journal of Consciousness Studies*, 7(8–9), 21–27.

   (2003) 'Examining Semir Zeki's neural concept formation and art: Dante, Michelangelo, Wagner.' *Journal of Consciousness Studies*, 10(2), 58–66.

Irigaray, L. (1993). *An Ethics of Sexual Difference*. Ithaca, NY: Cornell University Press.

Ishizu, T. and Zeki, S. (2011). 'Toward a brain-based theory of beauty.' *PLoS One*, **6**(7), e21852.

Itkonen, E. (2003). *What is Language? A Study in the Philosophy of Linguistics*. Turku: Turku University Press.

Jackendoff, R. (1987). *Consciousness and the Computational Mind*. Cambridge, MA: MIT Press.

Jacob, P. and Jeannerod, M. (2005). 'The motor theory of social cognition: a critique.' *Trends in Cognitive Science*, **9**, 21–25.

James, W. (1890). *The Principles of Psychology*. Oxford: Holt.

Jeannerod, M. and Jacob, P. (2005). 'Visual cognition: a new look at the two-visual systems.' *Neuropsychologia*, **43**, 301–312.

Johnson, M. (2008a). *The Meaning of the Body: Aesthetics of Human Understanding*. Chicago, IL: University of Chicago Press.

   (2008b). 'Philosophy's debt to metaphor.' In R. W. Gibbs (ed.), *The Cambridge Handbook of Metaphor and Thought*. Cambridge: Cambridge University Press, pp. 39–52.

Johnson-Laird, P. N. (1983). *Mental Models: Towards a Cognitive Science of Language, Inference, and Consciousness*. Cambridge: Cambridge University Press.

Johnson-Laird, P. N. and Miller, G. A. (1976). *Language and Perception*. Cambridge, MA: Belknap Press.

Jones, A. (1994). *Postmodernism and the En-Gendering of Marcel Duchamp*. New York, NY: Cambridge University Press.

(1998). *Body Art/Performing the Subject*. Minneapolis, MN: Minnesota University Press.

(2010). 'Space, body and the self in the work of Bruce Nauman.' In A. Dezeuze (ed.), *The 'Do-It-Yourself' Artwork: Participation From Fluxus To New Media*. Manchester: Manchester University Press and New York, NY: Palgrave Macmillan, pp. 145–164.

Joselit, D. (2003). *American Art Since 1945*. London: Thames and Hudson.

Judovitz, D. (1998). *Unpacking Duchamp: Art in Transit*. Berkeley, CA: University of California Press.

Jung, C. G. (1921/1971). *Psychological Types, Collected Works*, Vol. 6. Princeton, NJ: Princeton University Press.

Kästner, S. (2004). 'Attentional response modulation in the human visual system.' In M. I. Posner (ed.), *Cognitive Neuroscience of Attention*. New York, NY: Guilford Press, pp. 144–156.

Kawabata, H. and Zeki, S. (2004). 'The neural correlates of beauty.' *Journal of Neurophysiology*, **91**, 1699–1705.

Kemmerer, D. J., Castillo, G., Talavage, T., Patterson, S. and Wiley, C. (2008). 'Neuroanatomical distribution of five semantic components of verbs: evidence from fMRI.' *Brain and Language*, **107**(1), 16–43.

Kemp, C., Tenenbaum, J. B., Niyogi, S. and Griffiths, T. L. (2010). 'A probabilistic model of theory formation.' *Cognition*, **114**, 165–196.

Kennedy, J. M. (2008). 'Metaphor and art.' In R. W. Gibbs (ed.), *The Cambridge Handbook of Metaphor and Thought*. Cambridge: Cambridge University Press, pp. 447–461.

Kieran, M. (2004). *Revealing Art: Why Art Matters*. Abingdon: Routledge.

Kirchhoff, M. (2012). 'Extended cognition and fixed properties: steps to a third-wave version of extended cognition.' *Phenomenology and the Cognitive Sciences*, **11**(2), 287–308.

Kirk, U., Skov, S. Hulme, O., Christensen, M. S., and Zeki, S. (2009). 'Modulation of aesthetic value by semantic context: an fMRI study.' *NeuroImage*, **44**, 1125–1132.

Kirsh, D. (2009). 'Problem solving and situated cognition.' In P. Robbins and M. Aydede (eds.), *The Cambridge Handbook of Situated Cognition*. Cambridge: Cambridge University Press, pp. 264–306.

Kirsh, D. and Maglio, P. (1994). 'On distinguishing epistemic from pragmatic actions.' *Cognitive Science*, **18**, 513–549.

Kober, H., Feldman Barrett, L., Joseph, J., et al. (2008). 'Functional grouping and cortical–subcortical interactions in emotion: a meta-analysis of neuroimaging studies.' *NeuroImage*, **42**(2), 998–1031.

Korsmeyer, C. (2006). 'Terrible beauties.' In M. Kieran (ed.), *Contemporary Debates in Aesthetics*. Oxford: Blackwell Publishers, pp. 51–64.

Kosslyn, S. M. (1999). 'If neuroimaging is the answer, what is the question?' *Philosophical Transactions of the Royal Society B*, **354**(1387), 1283–1294.

Kosslyn, S. M., Thompson, W. L. and Ganis, G. (2006). *The Case for Mental Imagery*. Oxford: Oxford University Press.

Kounios, J., Frymiare, J. L., Bowden, E. M., et al. (2006). 'The prepared mind: neural activity prior to problem presentation predicts subsequent solution by sudden insight.' *Psychological Science*, **17**(10), 882–890.

Kowatari, Y., Lee, S. H, Yamamura, H., et al. (2009). 'Neural networks involved in artistic creativity.' *Human Brain Mapping*, **30**, 1678–1690.

Krauss, R. (1977). 'Notes on the index: seventies art in America.' **3**, 68–81.

(1981). *Passages in Modern Sculpture*. Cambridge, MA: MIT Press.

Kraynak, J. (2010). 'Rirkrit Tiravanija's liability.' In A. Dezeuze (ed.), *The 'Do-It-Yourself' Artwork: Participation From Fluxus To New Media*. Manchester: Manchester University Press and New York, NY: Palgrave Macmillan, pp. 165–184.

Kringelbach, M. L. (2005). 'The human orbitofrontal cortex: linking reward to hedonic experience.' *National Review of Neuroscience*, **6**(9), 691–702.

Lacey, S., Hagtvedt, H., Patrick, V. M. et al. (2011). 'Art for reward's sake: visual art recruits the ventral striatum.' *NeuroImage*, **55**(1), 420–433.

Lakoff, G. (2006). 'The neuroscience of art.' In M. Turner (ed.), *The Artful Mind: Cognitive Science and the Riddle of Human Creativity*. Oxford: Oxford University Press, pp. 153–170.

Lakoff, G. and Johnson, M. (1980). *Metaphors We Live By*. Chicago, IL: University of Chicago Press.

(1999). *Philosophy in the Flesh: The Embodied Mind and its Challenge to Western Thought*. New York, NY: Basic Books.

Lamarque, P. (2006). 'Cognitive values in the arts: marking boundaries.' In M. Kieran (ed.), *Contemporary Debates in Aesthetics*. Oxford: Blackwell Publishers, pp. 127–140.

Lambon-Ralph, M., Lowe, C. and Rogers T. T. (2007). 'Neural basis of category-specific semantic deficits for living things: evidence from semantic dementia, HSVE and a neural network model.' *Brain*, **130**, 1127–1137.

Lambon-Ralph, M. A., Sage, K., Jones R. W. and Mayberry, E. J. (2010). 'Coherent concepts are computed in the anterior temporal lobes.' *Proceedings of the National Academy of Sciences, USA*, **107**(6), 2717–2722.

Lamm, C., Batson, C. D. and Decety, J. (2007). 'The neural basis of human empathy, effects of perspective-taking and cognitive appraisal: an event-related functional MRI study.' *Journal of Cognitive Neuroscience*, **19**, 42–58.

Langacker, R. W. (1999). 'A view from cognitive linguistics.' Commentary on Barsalou's 'Perceptual symbol systems'. *Behavioral and Brain Sciences*, **22**(4), 625.

Leder, H., Belke, B., Oeberst, A. and Augustin, D. (2004). 'A model of aesthetic appreciation and aesthetic judgments.' *British Journal of Psychology*, **95**, 489–508.

Leder, H., Carbon, C. C. and Ripsas, A. L. (2006). 'Entitling art: influence of title information on understanding and appreciation of paintings.' *Acta Psychologica*, **121**, 176–198.

Levinson, J. (1996). *The Pleasures of Aesthetics: Philosophical Essays*. Ithaca, NY: Cornell University Press.

LeWitt, S. (1969). 'Sentences on conceptual art.' *0–9*, **5** (New York).

Limb, C. J. and Braun, A. R. (2008). 'Neural substrates of spontaneous musical performance: an fMRI study of jazz improvisation.' *PLoS One*, **3**, e1679.

Lippard, L. (1973). *The Dematerialization of the Art Object from 1966 to 1972*. New York, NY: Praeger.

Livingstone, M. (2002). *Vision and Art: The Biology of Seeing*. New York, NY: Harry N. Abrams.

Locher, P. J., Smith, J. K. and Smith, L. F. (2001). 'The influence of presentation format and viewer training in the visual arts on the perception of pictorial and aesthetic qualities of paintings.' *Perception*, **30**, 449–465.

Low, G. (2008). 'Metaphor in literature.' In R. W. Gibbs (ed.), *The Cambridge Handbook of Metaphor and Thought*. Cambridge: Cambridge University Press, pp. 212–231.

Luchjenbroers, J. (2004). 'Verbal and visual cues for navigating mental space.' In G. Malcolm (ed.), *Multidisciplinary Studies of Visual Representations and Interpretations*, Vol. 2. Amsterdam: Elsevier Science, pp. 147–164.

Machery, E. (2007). 'Concept empiricism: a methodological critique.' *Cognition*, **104**, 19–46.

Mack, J. (2003). *The Museum of the Mind: Art and Memory in World Cultures*. London: British Museum.

Magnani, L. (2003). 'Constraining questions about the organisation and representation of conceptual knowledge.' *Cognitive Neuropsychology*, **20**, 433–450.

(2007). 'Creating chances through cognitive niche construction.' *Knowledge-Based Intelligent Information and Engineering Systems Lecture Notes in Computer Science*, **4693**, 917–925.

Mahon, B. Z. and Caramazza, A. (2008). 'A critical look at the embodied cognition hypothesis and a new proposal for grounding conceptual content.' *Journal of Physiology*, **102**, 59–70.

Mandler, J. (2010). 'The spatial foundations of the conceptual system.' *Language and Cognition*, **2**(1), 21–44.

Manovich, L. (2006). 'Visual technologies as cognitive prostheses: a short history of the externalization of the mind.' In M. Smith and J. Morra (eds.), *The Prosthetic Impulse*. Cambridge, MA: MIT Press.

Mar, R., Djikic, M. and Oatley, K. (2008). 'Effects of reading on knowledge, social abilities, and selfhood.' In S. Zyngier, M. Bortolussi, A. Chesnokova and J. Auracher (eds.), *Directions in Empirical Literary Studies: In Honor of Willie van Peer*. Amsterdam: Benjamins, pp. 127–137.

Marr, D. (1982). *Vision*. New York, NY: Freeman.

Martin, A. (2007). 'The representation of object concepts in the brain.' *Annual Review of Psychology*, **58**, 25–45.

Martindale, C. (1984). 'The pleasures of thought: a theory of cognitive hedonics.' *Journal of Mind and Behavior*, **5**, 49–80.

(1988). 'Aesthetics, psychobiology and cognition.' In F. H. Farley and R. W. Neperud (eds.), *The Foundations of Aesthetics, Art, and Art Education*. New York, NY: Praeger, pp. 7–42.

Massey, I. (2009). *The Neural Imagination: Aesthetic and Neuroscientific Approaches to the Arts*. Austin, TX: University of Texas.

Mazzone, M. and Lalumera, E. (2010). 'Concepts: stored or created?' *Minds and Machines*, **20**, 1–19.

Mesquita, B. (1993). *Cultural Variations in Emotions: A Comparative Study of Dutch, Surinamese, and Turkish People in the Netherlands*. Unpublished PhD thesis. Amsterdam: University of Amsterdam.

Mesquita, B., Feldman Barrett, L. and Smith, E. R. (eds.). (2010). *The Mind in Context*. New York, NY: Guilford.

Meteyard, L., Cuadrado, S. R., Bahrami, B. and Vigliocco, G. (2012). 'Coming of age: a review of embodiment and the neuroscience of semantics.' *Cortex*, **48**(7), 788–804.

Michelson, A. (1969–1970). *Robert Morris*. Washington, DC: Corcoran Gallery of Art and Detroit: Detroit Institute of Art.

Miller, E. K., Freedman, D. J. and Wallis, J. D. (2002). 'The prefrontal cortex: categories, concepts and cognition.' *Philosophical Transactions of the Royal Society*, **357**(1424), 1123–1136.

Milner, D. and Goodale, M. (1995). *The Visual Brain in Action*. Oxford: Oxford University Press.

Minsky, M. (1975). 'A framework for representing knowledge.' In P. Winston (ed.), *The Psychology of Computer Vision*. New York, NY: McGraw-Hill, pp. 211–277.

Muelder Eaton, M. (2006). 'Beauty and ugliness in and out of context.' In M. Kieran (ed.), *Contemporary Debates in Aesthetics*. Oxford: Blackwell Publishers, pp. 37–50.

Mulvey, L. (1989). *Visual and Other Pleasures*. Bloomington, IN: Indiana University Press.

Munroe, A. (2000). *YES Yoko Ono*. New York, NY: Harry N. Abrams.

Murphy, G. and Medin, D. (1985). 'The role of theories in conceptual coherence.' *Psychological Review*, **92**, 289–316.

Muzur, A., Pace-Schott, E. F. and Hobson, J. A. (2002). 'The prefrontal cortex in sleep.' *Trends in Cognitive Science*, **6**(11), 475–481.

Myin, E. and Veldman, J. (2011). 'Externalism, mind, and art.' In R. Manzotti (ed.), *Situated Aesthetics: Art Beyond the Skin*. Exeter: Imprint Academic.

Nakayama, K. and Shimojo, S. (1992). 'Experiencing and perceiving visual surfaces.' *Science*, **257**, 1357–1363.

Neisser, U. (1967). *Cognitive Psychology*. New York, NY: Appleton-Century-Crofts.

Newell, A. (1980). 'Physical symbol systems.' *Cognitive Science*, **4**, 135–183.

Newell, A. and Simon, H. A. (1976). 'Computer science as empirical inquiry: symbols and search.' *Communications of the ACM*, **19**(3), 113–126.

Niedenthal, P. M. (1990). 'Implicit perception of affective information.' *Journal of Experimental Social Psychology*, **26**, 505–527.

(2006). 'Emotion.' In L. Nadel (ed.), *Encyclopedia of Cognitive Science*. www.onlinelibrary.wiley.com Accessed 03/09/2012.

Noë, A. (2000). 'Experience and experiment in art.' *Journal of Consciousness Studies*, **8–9**, 123–135.

(2005). *Action in Perception*. Cambridge, MA: MIT Press.

(2006) 'Précis of Action in Perception.' *Psyche*, **12**(1): 1–34. Archived electronic journal: www.psyche.cs.monash.edu.au/

Noë, A. and Thompson, E. (2004) 'Are there neural correlates of consciousness?' *Journal of Consciousness Studies*, **11**(1), 3–28.

Northoff, G., Heinzel, A., de Greck, M., et al. (2006). 'Self-referential processing in our brain: a meta-analysis of imaging studies on the self.' *NeuroImage*, **31**, 440–457.

O'Shea, M. (2005). *The Brain: A Very Short Introduction*. Oxford: Oxford University Press.

Ohlsson, S. (1999). 'Selecting is not abstracting.' Commentary on Barsalou's 'Perceptual symbol systems'. *Behavioral and Brain Sciences*, **22**(4), 631.

Okada, T., Yokochi, S., Ishibashi, K., Namba, K. and Ueda, K. (2009). 'Analogical modification in the creation of contemporary art.' *Cognitive Systems Research*, **10**(3), 189–203.

Onians, J. (2008). *Neuroarthistory: From Aristotle and Pliny to Baxandall and Zeki*. New Haven, CT: Yale University Press.

Paivio, A. (1986). *Mental Representations: A Dual Coding Approach*. Oxford: Oxford University Press.

Pardo, J. V., Pardo, P. J., Janer, K. V. and Raichle, M. E. (1990). 'The anterior cingulate cortex mediates processing selection in the Stroop attentional conflict paradigm.' *Proceedings of the National Academy of Sciences USA*, **87**, 256–259.

Pepperell, R. (2011). 'Art and extensionism.' In R. Manzotti (ed.), *Situated Aesthetics: Art Beyond the Skin*. Exeter: Imprint Academic.

Pessoa, L. (2010a). 'Emergent processes in cognitive-emotional interactions.' *Dialogues in Clinical Neuroscience*, **12**(4), 433–448.

(2010b). 'Emotion and cognition and the amygdala: from "what is it?" to "what's to be done?"' *Neuropsychologia*, **48**, 3416–3429.

Pessoa, L. and Adolphs, R. (2010). 'Emotion processing and the amygdala: from a "low road" to "many roads" of evaluating biological significance.' *National Review of Neuroscience*, **11**(11), 773–783.

Piazza, M. and Dehaene, S. (2004). 'From number neurons to mental arithmetic: the cognitive neuroscience of number sense.' In M. Gazzaniga (ed.), *The Cognitive Neurosciences*, Vol 3. Cambridge, MA: MIT Press, pp. 865–875.

Pinker, S. (1997). *How the Mind Works*. New York, NY: Norton.

Pizzichini, L. (1998). 'Art: another pile of bricks at the Tate.' *The Independent*, Sunday, 8 February.

Plassmann, H., O'Doherty, J., Shiv, B. and Rangel, A. (2008). 'Marketing actions can modulate neural representations of experienced pleasantness.' *Proceedings of the National Academy of SciencesUSA*, **105**(3), 1050–1054.

Pobric, G., Jefferies, E. and Lambon-Ralph, M. A. (2007). 'Anterior temporal lobes mediate semantic representation: mimicking semantic dementia by using rTMS in normal participants.' *Proceedings of the National Academy of Sciences, USA*, **104**, 20137–20141.

Poincaré, H. (1905). *Science and Hypothesis*. London: Walter Scott Publishing.

Potts, A. (2000). *The Sculptural Imagination: Figurative, Modernist, Minimalist*. New Haven, CT: Yale University Press.

Prinz, J. (2006). 'Putting the brakes on enactive perception.' *Psyche*, **12**(1), 1–19. Archived electronic journal: www.psyche.cs.monash.edu.au/
 (2009). 'Is consciousness embedded?' In P. Robbins and M. Aydede (eds.), *The Cambridge Handbook of Situated Cognition*. Cambridge: Cambridge University Press, pp. 419–436.
Pylyshyn, Z. W. (2006). *Seeing and Visualizing. It's Not What You Think*. Cambridge, MA: MIT Press.
Pylyshyn, Z. W. and Storm, R. W. (1998). 'Tracking multiple independent targets: evidence for a parallel tracking mechanism.' *Spatial Vision*, **3**(3), 179–197.
Radua, J. and Mataix-Cols, D. (2009). 'Voxel-wise meta-analysis of grey matter changes in obsessive-compulsive disorder.' *British Journal of Psychiatry*, **195**, 393–402.
Ramachandran, V. S. and Hirstein, W. (1999). 'The science of art: a neurological theory of aesthetic experience.' *Journal of Consciousness Studies*, **6**(6–7), 15–51.
Ramnani, N. and Owen, A. M. (2004). 'Anterior prefrontal cortex: insights into function from anatomy and neuroimaging.' *National Review of Neuroscience*, **5**(3), 184–194.
Rancière, J. (2009). *The Emancipated Spectator*. London: Verso.
Rensink, R. A. (2000). 'The dynamic representation of scenes.' *Visual Cognition*, **7**(1–3), 17–42.
Ricoeur, P. (1991). *A Ricoeur Reader: Reflection and Imagination*. M. J. Valdes (ed.). Toronto: University of Toronto Press.
Rizzolatti, G. and Craighero, L. (2004). 'The mirror-neuron system.' *Annual Review of Neuroscience*, **27**, 169–192.
Rosch, E. (1973). 'On the internal structure of perceptual and semantic categories.' In T. Moore (ed.), *Cognitive Development and the Acquisition of Language*. New York, NY: Academic Press.
Rosch, E. (1999). 'Principles of categorization'. In E. Margolis and S. Laurence (eds.), *Concepts: Core Readings*. Cambridge, MA: MIT Press, pp. 189–206.
Rowlands, M. (1999). *The Body in Mind: Understanding Cognitive Processes*. Cambridge: Cambridge University Press.
Rüschemeyer, S. A., Brass, M. and Friederici, A. D. (2007). 'Comprehending prehending: neural correlates of processing verbs with motor stems.' *Journal of Cognitive Neuroscience*, **19**, 855–865.
Ryle, G. (1954). 'The world of science and the everyday world.' In G. Ryle (ed.), *Dilemmas: The Tanner Lectures 1953*. Cambridge: Cambridge University Press, pp. 68–81.
Schwarz, A. (1969). *The Complete Works of Marcel Duchamp*. New York, NY: Harry N. Abrams.
Scott, G. M., Lonergan, D. C. and Mumford, M. D. (2005). 'Conceptual combination: alternative knowledge, structures, alternative heuristics.' *Creativity Research Journal*, **17**, 79–98.
Searle, A. (2011). 'Tracey Emin: excess all areas.' *The Guardian*, Monday, 16 May.
Setti, A. and Caramelli, N. (2005). 'Different domains in abstract concepts.' In B. Bara, L. Barsalou and M. Bucciarelli (eds.), *Proceedings of the XXVII Annual Conference of the Cognitive Science Society*. Mahwah, NJ: Erlbaum, pp. 1997–2002.

Shepard, R. N. and Metzler, J. (1971). 'Mental rotation of three-dimensional objects.' *Science*, **171**, 701–703.

Simmons, W. K. and Barsalou, L. W. (2003). 'The similarity in topography principle: reconciling theories of conceptual deficits.' *Cognitive Neuropsychology*, **20**, 451–486.

Skrebowski, L. (2008). 'All systems go: recovering Hans Haacke's systems art.' *Grey Room*, **30**, 54–83.

Smallwood, J., Fishman, D. and Schooler, J. (2007). 'Counting the cost of an absent mind: mind wandering as an under-recognized influence on educational performance.' *Psychonomic Bulletin and Review*, **14**(2), 230–236.

Smith, E. R. and Conrey, F. R. (2009). 'The social context of cognition.' In P. Robbins and M. Aydede (eds.), *The Cambridge Handbook of Situated Cognition*. Cambridge: Cambridge University Press, pp. 454–466.

Solso, R. (2003). *The Psychology of Art and the Evolution of the Conscious Brain*. Cambridge, MA: MIT Press.

Sontag, S. (1995). 'Against interpretation.' In E. Fernie (ed.), *Art History and its Methods*. London: Phaidon.

Sowden, P. T. and Schyns, P. G. (2006). 'Channel surfing in the visual brain.' *Trends in the Cognitive Sciences*, **10**, 538–545.

Sperber, D. and Wilson, D. (2008). 'A deflationary account of metaphors.' In R. W. Gibbs (ed.), *The Cambridge Handbook of Metaphor and Thought*. Cambridge: Cambridge University Press, pp. 84–108.

Sporns, O. (2010). 'Brain networks and embodiment.' In B. Mesquita, L. Feldman Barrett and E. R. Smith (eds.), *The Mind in Context*. New York, NY: Guilford, pp. 43–64.

Stafford, B. M. (2007). *Echo Objects: The Cognitive Work of Images*. Chicago, IL: Chicago University Press.

Storr, R. (1995). 'Félix González-Torres: être un espion.' *ArtPress*, January, pp. 24–32.

Stuss, D. T., Gallup, G. G. and Alexander, M. P. (2001). 'The frontal lobes are necessary for "theory of mind".' *Brain*, **124**, 279–286.

Sutton, J. (2009). 'Remembering.' In P. Robbins and M. Aydede (eds.), *The Cambridge Handbook of Situated Cognition*. Cambridge: Cambridge University Press, pp. 217–235.

Tallis, R. (1996). *Times Literary Supplement*, April 19, pp. 5–6.

Talmy, L. (1996). 'Fictive motion in language and "ception".' In P. Bloom, M. Peterson, L. Nadel and M. Garrett (eds.), *Language and Space*. Cambridge, MA: MIT Press, pp. 211–276.

Teasdale, J. D., Dritschell, B. H., Taylor, M. J., et al. (1995). 'Stimulus-independent-thought depends upon central executive resources.' *Memory and Cognition*, **28**, 551–559.

Thomas, N. J. T. (1997). 'Mental Imagery', plato.stanford.edu/entries/mental-imagery/

Tong, F., Meng, M. and Blake, R. (2006). 'Neural bases of binocular rivalry.' *Trends in Cognitive Science*, **10**, 502–511.

Tranel, D., Damasio, H. and Damasio, A. R. (1997). 'A neural basis for the retrieval of conceptual knowledge.' *Neuropsychologia*, **35**(10), 1319–1327.

Tribble, E. B. (2005). 'Distributed cognition in the Globe.' *Shakespeare Quarterly*, **56**(2), 135–155.

Tulving, E. (1983). 'Ecphoric processes in episodic memory.' *Philosophical Transactions of the Royal Society of London*, **302**(1110), 361–370.

Turner, M. (2003). 'The Origin of Selkies.' *Journal of Consciousness Studies*, **11**(5–6), 90–115.

(2006). 'The Art of Compression.' In M. Turner (ed.), *The Artful Mind: Cognitive Science and the Riddle of Human Creativity*. New York, NY: Oxford University Press, pp. 93–114.

Turvey, M. T. and Carello, C. (1995). 'Some dynamical themes in perception and action.' In R. Port and T. van Gelder (eds.), *Mind as Motion*. Cambridge, MA: MIT Press, pp. 373–402.

Tversky, B. (2010). 'Visualizing thought.' *Topics in Cognitive Science*, **2**, 1–37.

Uttal, W. R. (2001). *The New Phrenology: The Limits of Localizing Cognitive Processes in the Brain*. Cambridge, MA: MIT Press.

Vartanian, O. and Goel, V. (2004). 'Emotion pathways in the brain mediate aesthetic preference.' *Bulletin of Psychology and the Arts*, **5**(1), 37–42.

Versace, R., Labeyea, E., Badarda, G. and Rosea, M. (2009). 'The contents of long-term memory and the emergence of knowledge.' *European Journal of Cognitive Psychology*, **21**(4), 522–560.

Vickery, J. (2003). 'Art and the ethical: modernism and the problem of Minimalism.' In D. Arnold and M. D. Iverson (eds.), *Art and Thought*. Oxford: Blackwell, pp. 111–128.

Vigliocco, G., Meteyard, L., Andrews, M. and Kousta, S. (2009). 'Toward a theory of semantic representation.' *Language and Cognition*, **1–2**, 219–247.

Visser, M., Jefferies, E. and Lambon-Ralph, M. A. (2010). 'Semantic processing in the anterior temporal lobes: a meta-analysis of the functional neuroimaging literature.' *Journal of Cognitive Neuroscience*, **22**(6), 1083–1094.

Wallendorf, M. and Arnould, E. J. (1988). '"My Favorite Things": a cross-cultural inquiry into object attachment, possessiveness and social linkage.' *Journal of Consumer Research*, **14**, 531–547.

Wang, J., Conder, J. A., Blitzer, D. and Shinkareva, S. V. (2010). 'Neural representation of abstract and concrete concepts: a meta-analysis of neuroimaging studies.' *Human Brain Mapping*, **31**, 1459–1468.

Weisberg, R. W. (1995). 'Case studies of creative thinking: reproduction versus restructuring in the real world.' In S. M. Smith, T. B. Ward and R. A. Finke (eds.), *The Creative Cognition Approach*. Cambridge, MA: MIT Press, pp. 53–72.

Werth, P. (1999). *Text Worlds: Representing Conceptual Space in Discourse*. London: Longman.

Wheeler, M. (2010). 'In defense of extended functionalism.' In R. Menary (ed.), *The Extended Mind*. Cambridge, MA: MIT Press, pp. 245–270.

Wiemer-Hastings, K. and Graesser, A. C. (2000). 'Contextually representing abstract concepts with abstract structures.' In *Proceedings of the 22nd Annual Conference of the Cognitive Science Society*. Hillsdale, NJ: Lawrence Erlbaum Associates, pp. 983–988.

Wiemer-Hastings, K., Krug, J. and Xu, X. (2001). 'Imagery, context availability, contextual constraints and abstractness.' In *Proceedings of the 23rd Annual*

Meeting of the Cognitive Science Society. Hillsdale, NJ: Lawrence Erlbaum Associates, pp. 1106–1111.

Wiemer-Hastings, K. and Xu, X. (2005). 'Content differences for abstract and concrete concepts.' *Cognitive Science*, 29(5), 719–736.

Williams, R. F. (2008). 'Gesture as a conceptual mapping tool.' In A. Cienki and C. Müller (eds.), *Metaphor and Gesture [Gesture Studies 3]*. Amsterdam: John Benjamins, pp. 55–92.

Wilson-Mendenhall, C. D., Barrett, L. F., Simmons, W. K. and Barsalou, L. W. (2011). 'Grounding emotion in situated conceptualization.' *Neuropsychologia*, 49, 1105–1127.

Wittgenstein, L. (1953). *Philosophical Investigations*. G. E. M. Anscombe (trans.). New York, NY: Macmillan.

Xu, F. (2005). 'Categories, kinds, and object individuation in infancy.' In L. Gershkoff-Stowe and D. Rakison (eds.), *Building Object Categories in Developmental Time: Papers from the 32nd Carnegie Symposium on Cognition*. Hillsdale, NJ: Lawrence Erlbaum, pp. 63–89.

Young, I. (1980). 'Throwing like a girl: a phenomenology of feminine body comportment motility and spatiality.' *Human Studies*, 3(1), 137–156.

Zaidel, D. W. (2010). 'Art and brain: insights from neuropsychology, biology and evolution.' *Journal of Anatomy*, 216, 177–183.

Zeki, S. (1999). 'Neural concept formation and art: Dante, Michelangelo, Wagner.' *Journal of Consciousness Studies*, 9(3), 53–76.

　(2002). *Inner Vision: An Exploration of Art and the Brain*. Oxford: Oxford University Press.

　(2009). *Splendours and Miseries of the Brain: Love, Creativity, and the Quest for Human Happiness*. London: Blackwell.

Zlatev, J. (2010). 'Phenomenology and cognitive linguistics.' In S. Gallagher and D. Schmicking (eds.), *Handbook of Phenomenology and Cognitive Science*. Dordrecht: Springer, pp. 415–446.

Index

'ception', 14, 15, 121
abject, 28, 168, 215
Abramović, Marina, xxvii, xxviii, 83, 107,
    136, 257–260, 319–320, 326–327
absorption, xiii, xvi, 30, 69, 104, 129, 173,
    204, 236, 237, 241, 242, 323, 330, 333,
    339 See also immersion
abstraction, 35, 36, 38, 49, 117, 128, 147,
    171, 332
Acconci, Vito, xxvii, 230, 255, 324–326
across-system relations, 127, 139 See also
    between-system relations; within-
    system relations
ad hoc processes, xiii, 10–11, 38, 47, 56, 61,
    192, 262 See creativity; improvisation
aesthetics, xvi, 62, 88, 100, 134, 140, 154,
    197, 215, 219, 221, 239, 253, 311, 333
affect, xix, 16, 26, 33, 79, 100, 106, 107,
    108, 117, 125, 220, 245, 246
affordances, 113, 114, 151, 188, 264, 285,
    295, 313
agency, 10, 27, 68, 115, 133, 136, 137, 173,
    225, 226, 228, 229, 230, 233, 236, 270,
    274, 275, 325
agnosia, visual, 74
amodal symbols, 13, 18, 19, 48, 260
analogy
    analogical mapping, 12, 32, 146, 148,
        150, 159, 252, 329
    analogical modification, 53, 127, 134,
        140, 146, 148, 150, 156, 192, 248, 344
Andre, Carl, 150, 154, 155, 156, 182, 183,
    265
antagonism, and art, 329, 335, 337, 341
anthropomorphism, xix, 178, 188, 223, 283
anti-aestheticism, 46
anti-art, xvii
anti-formalism, 43, 181, 340
Antoni, Janine, 170, 172
anxiety, xix, 29, 209, 210, 342
    anxious objects, 58

Apollonian, 16
apraxia, 74, 87
Arnheim, Rudolf, 45, 312
art market, 26
Arte Povera, xxxi, 340
attention, 3, 15, 19, 22, 23, 24, 26, 34, 36,
    46, 50, 54, 56, 62, 64, 69, 70, 71, 72,
    76, 78, 80, 81, 94, 95, 98, 100, 106,
    107, 122, 132, 140, 176, 193, 220,
    225, 236

Bacon, Francis, 16, 17, 79, 241
Bakhtin, Mikhail M., xxix, 208, 228, 229
Banksy, xxvii
Barney, Matthew, xxviii, 176, 316, 319, 330
Baroque, 43, 118, 176, 330
Barry, Robert, xxvii, 255, 307
Barsalou, Lawrence W., 13, 18, 28, 47,
    48–49, 51, 52, 53, 55, 56, 116, 118,
    125, 128, 175, 228, 260, 306
Baudrillard, Jean, xxx, 209
Baxandall, Michael, 146
beauty, 31, 77, 78, 79, 80–83, 94, 102, 132,
    133, 134, 136, 154, 180, 200, 203, 219,
    220, 221, 246
belief, 8, 9, 66, 68, 73, 78, 85, 91, 126, 207,
    212, 213, 214, 338
between-system relations, 127, 128, 139,
    306, 316, 321, 329 See across-system
    relations; within-system relations
Beuys, Joseph, xxvii, 310
bicycles, 48, 51–55, 57
binding problem, 28, 62
binocular rivalry, 54, 58, 76, 93, 281
Bishop, Claire, xxvii, 138, 334, 335–336
Boadwee, Keith, 206
body
    blood, 28, 178, 214, 215, 216, 217, 219,
        220, 221
    body image, 178, 200, 201, 203, 204, 208,
        209, 210, 212, 230, 258

365